Total Relationship Marketing

Achieving Proper Customer Relevance

Jeen Su Lim   John Heinrichs

COPYRIGHT

Copyright © 2021 by Jeen Su Lim and John H. Heinrichs

All rights reserved.

Jeen Su Lim, Ph.D.
Professor of Marketing and e-Commerce
Department of Marketing and IB
John B. and Lillian E. Neff College of Business and Innovation
The University of Toledo, jlim@totalcrm.net

John H. Heinrichs, Ph.D.
Associate Professor of Information Systems
Department of Management and Information Systems
School of Business Administration
Wayne State University

Identifiers: ISBN 978-1-7345382-2-9 (Ebook)
                ISBN 978-1-7345382-3-6 (Paperback)

PREFACE

In the 21st century, firms are pressed more than ever to be responsive to the changing environment. The environmental changes experienced by firms in the past several decades have been drastic and unpredictable. Firms are pursuing ways to be responsive to the changing environment and to empower their customers. Complicating the situation is the advancement of e-commerce and digital technology and its impact on the way that firms do business. Firms are developing a new marketing paradigm driven by the customer relationship management (CRM) perspective to remain competitive and profitable in the global market and marketspace.

This book is about creating total CRM-based relationship marketing programs in a digital age. One trend on the technology front is the rise of CRM, marketing automation, artificial intelligence, and marketing analytics software that goes beyond data analysis to help guide marketing actions. While many companies have adopted these tools in recent years, they have experienced great difficulties in making full use of their investment. The software tools can provide excellent means for making responsive analytics-based strategic decisions, however, managers are not accustomed to using them. While managers are trained to use the marketing analytics and CRM tools, most of the training focuses on the technical and mechanical aspects of the software tools. The intent of this book is to provide meaning, context, and a framework for better utilization of these tools for the development and implementation of relationship marketing programs. The basic or core requirements for becoming customer-focused is capturing, analyzing, and utilizing customer and market data. We attempt to provide marketing managers the means by which to apply the insight that they obtain from total CRM and marketing analytics to drive relationship marketing decisions. For many firms, the road to growth, brand loyalty, customer equity, and competitive advantage is a road of ever more demanding excellence. Only a small number of firms have been able to sustain that excellence through years of changing technology and leadership.

We think one fundamental prerequisite for sustaining that excellence in the digital age is the capability to manage customer data and relationships effectively. We think a systematic approach to planning, developing, and controlling customer relationship activities can minimize the risk of extinction in a drastically changing turbulent environment. We present a new framework of total CRM-based relationship marketing. This framework provides marketing managers the guidelines and processes to plan, manage, and control relationship marketing activities to build, grow, and manage customer relationships effectively.

The theme of this book is highlighted in three important concepts: exploring marketing's role in the expanding digital era, understanding the total CRM-based relationship marketing approach, and practicing with the evolving marketing decisions that are driven by enhanced customer relationships.

Part I of this book deals with marketing's role in the digital age. Effective decision-making begins with a clear understanding of the nature of the environment. Over the course of the past decade, the business environment has gone through dramatic changes. The nature of the environmental changes and the need for adopting the total CRM based relationship marketing approach in a digital age are discussed in detail. In addition, this section deals with understanding the customer relationship management approach therefore a customer relationship management process model and framework are presented. The CRM process model and framework are the basis for relationship marketing strategy and programs. To cope with the risky competitive environment, firms require a new way of thinking. Given the pressures of the market environment, it is increasingly necessary for a firm to establish a system and set of processes whereby marketing managers can make decisions that serve the customer and build customer relationships. To help all marketing managers, a framework and architecture of total CRM is developed and described. With this framework, the marketing managers in a firm have a pattern to follow as they generate insights and develop solutions to managerial problems or questions.

Part II of this book covers issues related to establishing strategic directions for the total CRM based relationship marketing. Currently, the advancement of technology in CRM and relationship marketing is driving the profitability and growth of firms. Increased global competition, fast product development cycles and product life cycles, the internet, social media, and e-commerce are contributing factors to business volatility and risk. In managing this risk, analytics-based strategic decision-making capabilities and total CRM based relationship marketing are the only sustainable core competence of firms in a digital age. Strategic marketing concepts such as customer portfolio management, customer life time value approach, and customer experience management are introduced. These concepts are used for generating customer insights and customizing the marketing offerings for effective relationship marketing.

Part III of this book focuses on applying the developed total CRM based relationship marketing framework and processes for use in marketing strategies and programs. Various relationship marketing components are described: customer solution driven product management, customer-focused service with supply chain, and traditional, eCRM, social CRM touchpoint management strategies for customer relationship. In each of these contexts, marketing tactics and techniques to build strong customer relationships are described in detail.

In conclusion, this book is about how to create powerful and effective marketing programs that set the standard for relationship marketing in the digital era. To illustrate the total CRM based relationship marketing processes, each chapter includes relationship marketing templates that can be used to apply the total CRM based relationship marketing concepts and practices for customer focused marketing decisions. This book can build an important bridge between the understanding of total CRM perspective and effective implementation of relationship marketing programs.

ACKNOWLEDGEMENT

First and foremost, we give praise and thanks to God without whom this endeavor would not have been possible. Also, we thank our families for their love and support.

This book is dedicated to my wife Kee Sook and to my son Eugene.

– Jeen Su Lim

This book is dedicated to my wife Karen, to my son John, and to my daughter Sarah.

– John H. Heinrichs

Table of Contents

PART I. NEW MARKETING PERSPECTIVE IN THE DIGITAL ERA

"You have to set goals that are almost out of reach. If you set a goal that is attainable without much work or thought, you are stuck with something below your true talent and potential."
Steve Garvey

In the first part of this book, the role of marketing and customer relationships in the new digital era are examined. In the age of digital commerce, this section highlights the importance of customer relationship focus in marketing decision-making as well as the role of the total CRM perspective and marketing analytics in strategic marketing.

Chapter 1 examines the impact of the turbulent and competitive environment in the digital age on marketing management. As the business environment has gone through dramatic changes in the past decade or so, effective decision-making begins with a clear understanding of the nature of this environment. The chapter concludes with discussion of the concept of total CRM and the critical importance of achieving relevance in relationship marketing.

Chapter 2 discusses the concept of customer relationship management and explores customer relationship management perspectives. A CRM process model and framework are presented as the basis for relationship marketing strategy and programs. To help marketing managers, a framework and architecture of customer relationship management is developed. With this framework, marketing managers in a firm will have a pattern to follow as they generate insights and develop solutions to managerial problems or questions. The chapter concludes with the importance of business and marketing analytics in relationship marketing.

Chapter 1: New Strategic Marketing Decision Environment

Section 1. Assessing the Strategic Marketing Environment

"Wherever there is danger, there lurks opportunity; whenever there is opportunity, there lurks danger. The two are inseparable. They go together."
Earl Nightingale

Strategic marketing is based on an understanding of organizational capabilities and behavior, an evaluation of the competitive environment, and the notion that strategic marketing is an on-going process of strategic learning rather than a periodic task. Strategic marketing aims to create an action plan that is capable of being changed as the external competitive environment and the internal organizational conditions change. Strategic marketing analysis attempts to make sense of the environmental data and available information. Also, strategic marketing analysis evaluates the progress, relevance, and adaptability of existing strategies through the filter of new environmental information. Included in strategic marketing analysis is an assessment of the organization's overall marketing strengths and weaknesses as well as the major strategic industry trends, threats, and opportunities. Strategic marketing decision-making involves selecting the appropriate strategic responses to external and internal environmental changes with respect to the firm's strategic position.

The term "strategic marketing analysis" is then composed of and based on the various concepts involving strategy, marketing, and analysis. The "strategy" portion of the term is based on traditional concepts and approaches to strategy formulation and strategy implementation. Traditionally, strategy was approached as a top-down function where senior management integrated the functional areas of the firm into an overall organizational direction. The "marketing" portion of the term is based on the concepts and traditional approaches to marketing as one of the organization's key functions. Traditionally, marketing has been externally oriented toward the firm's customers, distributors, and competitors. Thus, marketing was primarily responsible for continuously looking at the environment and keeping the organization in synch with the environment with the goal of achieving profitability. The "analysis" portion of the term is based on the necessary functions of information acquisition and sense-making about the environment. Traditionally, a major information generation and analysis activity is the marketing research and analysis function. Marketing research specifies and supplies accurate information about consumers and the marketplace. This information is used to reduce uncertainty in decision-making and to aid in the development and implementation of marketing plans and strategies.[1]

Analysis in both the strategy and marketing disciplines has traditionally assumed a relatively stable and slowly-changing environment. Likewise, traditional strategic marketing assumes a stable environment. The assumption of strategic marketing analysis is that the various elements in the environment can be identified and related to other environmental elements. These elements are used to detect marketing threats and opportunities for the organization. With the threats and opportunities detected, further analysis identifies favorable business unit positions for competitive advantage. However, what if the basic assumption of a stable environment is altered? What if the environmental elements are changing very rapidly? With these questions in mind, the discussion proceeds to investigate the current globally competitive environment.

10

Key Driving Forces

Firms are facing radical transitions. These radical transitions are characteristics of the emerging paradigm shift to the information age or digital era. Marketing theorists have been discussing this transition for over a decade.[2] Surviving in the turbulent and hyper-competitive environment represents a daunting challenge for many firms. The four key drivers that seem omnipresent in this information age or digital era are:

1. Rapid and accelerating rates of change,
2. Extreme complexity,
3. Huge volumes of information, and
4. Hyper-competition.

Rapid and Accelerating Rates of Change

Anticipating market changes and responding quickly to strategic opportunities and threats has always been a success criterion for businesses. There are many examples of corporate struggles or failures because the firm failed to detect and respond to fundamental changes in their environments. One example involves Western Union Corporation. Advances in the telecommunications technology severely threatened Western Union's competitive advantage in telex services. The failure to recognize and respond to this threat by re-defining its business and re-positioning itself caused Western Union to struggle.

Digital technology changes and their rate of change present serious challenges for businesses. Businesses must stay abreast of the relevant changes occurring in their markets. Yet, these markets are changing themselves. As society becomes more information and knowledge intensive, the sensitivity to change will occur through the very changes in information and knowledge. Stated differently, the more society changes, the more information is generated about the changes. This self-generating process of change feeds upon information and knowledge which in turns produces more change that results in more information and knowledge.

Deciding upon what changes and information are important is in itself a difficult task. On one hand, firms might think that all of its competitors are in similar boats in the sea of information. However, the possibility exists that some competitors may be better at navigating this sea. Thus, management's challenge is making sure that their business is better than their competitors' businesses at navigating through the sea of information and change. As businesses formulate and implement strategy, they face "moving targets" in the environment. These "moving targets" manifest themselves in the form of changing customers' requirements, changing competitors, and changing relevant technologies. In this competitive environment, these moving targets are moving much faster. The digital age has accelerated change from the more stable times of previous eras.

Extreme Complexity

The traditional concept of strategy suggests a set of decisions and resource commitments regarding particular courses of action for a firm. The concept of "the firm" originally implied a clear distinction between what was inside the organization and under the control of management and what was in "the environment" and consisting of uncontrollable factors. The traditional concept of strategy assumed a reasonably static environment. As such, this static environment was analyzable and consisted of mostly tangible resources that could be rationalized.

In the digital age, a firm's source of sustainable competitive advantage is mostly intangible. The competitive advantage exists in the form of knowledge, routines, capabilities, and core competencies. These elements enable the advantageous use of tangible resources. In the firm, knowledge is embedded in a variety of forms. It is in products and services, administrative and productive processes, in organizational culture, in the machinery, and in the skills and abilities of its people. As the number of different kinds of knowledge and skills increase, the more complex the firm's internal environment becomes.

The major factors of a firm's external environment and their interrelationships are also changing rapidly. The uncertainties and ambiguities inherent in these changes make it difficult for decision-makers to discern what is going on in the environment. It requires more time and effort for decision-makers to develop a clear picture of what is happening with regard to customers, competitors, technology, sales, and products. These elements are changing so rapidly and in such interrelated ways that it is increasingly difficult for managers to detect and/or interpret changes. It becomes a challenging task for managers to discern problems or opportunities, specify possible courses of action, and foresee the likely consequences from each course of action.

As technology and knowledge continues to grow and intensify, all actors within the firm will have to engage in continuous learning. Such learning is required to detect and respond to potentially threatening or opportunistic circumstances. Addressing the external knowledge and technological activities occurring in the environment represents an expansion of the internal knowledge of the firm. This growth in internal knowledge leads to more complexity, as this knowledge must also be managed.

Huge Volumes of Information

Information technologies have resulted in a global information and communications network. The possibilities exist for transmitting information in a variety of forms anywhere on the globe. It is now technologically possible for people in remote parts of the globe to instantly become exposed to the lifestyles of various cultures. Technology is not the barrier to communication; illiteracy is. With the widespread availability of information, competitive advantage lies in the ability of the firm to sift through, make sense of, and act appropriately to that information. This task is essentially a human-centric function. Humans must guide the selection of and use of technological tools for managing information. Humans must make sense of and make decisions regarding this information.

Given the mountains of information available in the form of big data, the traditional approach of senior managers devising strategy must change. This huge volume of information necessitates moving the strategy formulation function down the organizational ladder. It should no longer remain the purview of a select few senior managers and marketing. Senior managers simply do not have the information, time, skill, and relevant expertise necessary to make detailed decisions, to formulate the plans and to implement plans, and to monitor the execution of such plans.[3]

Hyper-Competition

The threat of global competitors, the virtualization of markets, the shifting consumer wants and needs, and the technological innovations have combined to create hyper-competitive markets for most firms. The source of competitive advantage is not in possessing the tangible and intangible resources but, rather, in the know-how of bundling and the skill at managing these tangible and intangible resources. Similar tangible resources and knowledge can be purchased, but the savvy for mixing these resources to meet the requirements of the market is not easily imitated.

Implications of the Four Key Drivers

As a result of the four drivers, firms are compelled to constantly scan and monitor the environment for timely, relevant and accurate information about threats and opportunities to their competitive advantage and to their target markets. In addition, these four drivers are forcing firms to change their traditional approaches and ways of doing business. Because of rapid rates of change, firms must shift the time intervals for receiving, processing and acting upon information from years, quarters, and months to days, minutes, and seconds. Because of the extreme complexity, it is difficult to manage and sift through the environment to find the right information at the right time. Further, the huge volumes of information make it nearly impossible for the environmental scanning and sense-making function to remain the responsibility of just a few senior managers. Finally, the hyper-competition is compelling firms to stay abreast of competitor actions in real time and provide a timely and appropriate response. These four key drivers, and the requirements they impose on corporations, have profound implications for firms utilizing traditional approaches to strategic planning and marketing.

Digital Technology

At the core of these four drivers is digital technology. Digital technology is dramatically transforming our way of life and of doing business. With internet-based electronic commerce, the capability exists for large companies to behave like small companies. They can personalize their product offerings and customer services. Small companies can also behave like large companies. They are no longer constrained by the time, distance, and distribution chain barriers that used to exist in offering products and services to customers worldwide.

There are many other ways digital technology is altering the way firms conduct business. The following list captures several of the most profound impacts.

- The internet, electronic commerce, and social media are enabling global communication and commerce.
- Voice and image recognition technology is enabling people to utilize information technologies more easily.
- Telecommunications is eliminating location as a barrier to commerce and communications.

- Big data and business analytics technologies are facilitating the storage, retrieval, mining and analyzing tremendous volumes of data with relative ease.
- Artificial intelligence is extending the human information and knowledge management capabilities.
- Microprocessor speeds and capacities are enabling the design of simpler and more functional "smart" and Internet of Things (IoT) devices.
- Storage capacities are increasing the amount of information to analyze.

The impact of digital technology on our way of life is so profound that civilization as we know it is in transition to a "brave new world". Yet, no one agrees on what this new world will look like. Some assert that the boundaries that separate business from the external environment are being blurred by digital technology's impact.

Sources of Environmental Turbulence in the Digital Age

There are six major categories of environmental forces. These forces are categorized as demographic, social, economic, technological, political and legal, and competitive. Demographic forces refer to information about the population such as age, race, gender, birth rates, death rates, location, and household income. Social forces are the influences in society that may change the behaviors, values, and relationships among and between people such as husbands and wives, friend and associates, work peers and superiors, and community residents. Often, these social dynamics manifest themselves as changing consumer wants and buying patterns. Economic forces pertain to the macroeconomic factors such as capital markets, inflation, recession, deflation, interest rates, consumer price and purchasing power indices, and currency exchange rates. Technological forces refer to any technological changes that may influence either positively or negatively the firm's ability to sustain competitive advantage. Political and legal forces deal with any change in the regulations and laws that change the rules or change the boundaries and conditions of the market. Competitive forces look at the market in the aggregate and marketing strategy of the firm's competitors. On the aggregate level, the firm examines the market structures in terms of their competitiveness. For individual competitors, the firm assesses, tries to understand, and anticipates their competitive movements. Information technology has influenced, intensified, and accelerated the dynamics of all of these environmental forces.

These environmental forces are important considerations at any time in the firm's life. The digital age, however, has yielded seven specific characteristics of these environmental forces that are the sources of turbulence. Some researchers refer to these characteristics as "permanent whitewater" [4]

1. Globalization of markets and competitive pressures.
2. Rapid technological innovation and diffusion.
3. Shorter product life cycles.
4. Changing customer wants and expectations.
5. Changing business relationships.
6. Changing governmental laws and regulations.
7. Interdependent economies.

Globalization of Markets and Competitive Pressures

The removal of access barriers, the expansion of free trade zones, available energy sources, worldwide telecommunications and computer technology, and the fluid movement of financial capital has created a global market and competitive playing field. Global entities and regional trade agreements will enhance trade and global capital movement. Many companies like Samsung and Apple are manufacturing mostly outside of their country of origin.[5] Some American companies like Coca-Cola and McDonald's earn more revenue outside of the United States than they earn domestically. Over 100,000 American firms are invested in global ventures. Strategic and virtual alliances are an increasing trend.

The computer, transportation, and telecommunications technologies enable businesses to overcome the limitations of space, time, format, and medium to manage tightly coordinated but globally dispersed supply chains. These firms may have supply chains that are vertically integrated, virtually integrated, or some combination of the two. Likewise, with the transportation industry, the internet, and social media, the world can truly function as a "global village and marketplace". Various products like Coca-Cola, Disney, McDonald's Big Mac, Nike sports wear, and Calvin Klein jeans have struck a responsive chord in people around the globe. These product brands have given the world's people a set of global symbols that evoke a common identity. Thus, people around the world have the capability of sharing common experiences with English, spoken by over 1 billion people, as the common language. For example, global icons like Michael Jordan, the late Princess Diana, and John Lennon are recognized and admired on every continent.

Accompanying the global opportunities of additional revenue sources and market share are the threats of new foreign competitors. Companies must not only struggle to compete with domestic firms but now must contend with foreign firms as well. Aggressive foreign competitors can set new standards and seriously weaken established domestic markets. One only needs to look at the U.S. consumer electronics and automotive markets for early examples of this. Additionally, depending upon the product or service, competitors do not necessarily have to be large, well-capitalized enterprises. Levered with information technology, smaller-sized, more nimble competitors, paradoxically, may be able to outperform their larger counterparts. Recently, smaller Chilean companies backed by large reserves of natural resources have flourished in exporting to international markets by cutting distribution costs, utilizing vertical integration, and implementing successful promotional strategies.[6]

Rapid Technological Innovations and Diffusion

We are experiencing a rapid technological innovation and diffusion. Significant changes and the convergence of technologies are occurring in biotechnology, genetic engineering, nano-technology, ceramics, advanced composites, and superconductivity. These technologies will radically change life as we know it but we just do not know exactly how.

The information technologies are enabling the above mentioned technologies to accelerate and sometimes combine to create whole new industries and radically alter existing industries. These technologies seem to defy the laws of entropy in that the more data they consume, the more data and information they yield, and the more information producers they birth.

The evolution and convergence of technological innovations in hardware, software, networking, workstations, robotics, and microprocessors have earmarked the technology revolution. Now, this convergence has yielded us global information systems. Technology and technological innovations will continue to undergo sustained growth because of the digital technology revolution and the convergence of aforementioned technological domains. This process is self-generating in that as our knowledge of technology grows, developments accelerate, which results in an explosive growth of ideas, inventions, products and processes, which in turn lead to more knowledge of technology.

Shorter Product Life Cycles

Because of changing customer tastes and expectations, partially due to globalism and other environmental factors, products are not going through complete life cycles. The life cycle of a product can be described in terms of three major stages: uncoordinated, segmented, and systemic.[7] The uncoordinated stage is early in the life cycle of the product where market growth, expansion, and redefinition result in frequent competitive product improvements and great varieties. The segmented stage emerges as competitive turbulence results in certain product versions becoming more popular in the market and their higher volumes result in more efficient production systems. At some point a few stable products evolve in such a way that significant product standardization emerges. In the systemic stage, industry maturity sets in and the most economies of scale are achievable due to high standardized volumes. Cost minimization becomes a strategic lever.

With the rapid growth and convergence of technological innovations, the evolution may never get beyond the segmented stage as frequent innovations and modifications are characteristic of the digital age. At best, many products are being frequently modified via continuous improvement and innovation efforts. At worst, products are becoming obsolete during early stages of their life cycles. Additionally, the intense global competition results in greater product innovations. Such product innovations have provided a greater variety of product offerings to customers than were available in more stable times. Thus, in the midst of such competitiveness, existing products are no longer evolving through the traditionally defined life cycle-stages completely before they are modified. When product life cycles go through the full stages, they are often compressed to a shorter life. Firms are competing to put products first in this type of market to avoid missing a short-lived window of opportunities.

Changing Customer Wants and Expectations

As the global electronic village spreads, new customers are being found in various pockets of the world. People around the world are being exposed to the conveniences and lifestyles of Western civilization through its movies, media, global icons, and products.

Consequently, people are changing their wants and expectations. This translates into changes in the products and services they demand. Customers are demanding higher quality products, product variety, product customization to their needs, convenience, and price competitiveness. With advanced information and manufacturing technology, companies are able to offer a broader range of products, in smaller lot sizes, with shorter life cycles, in more customized ways to customers who increasingly know and want more. Furthermore, customers will continue to demand more as they become more aware and knowledgeable and as competition gives them better and more innovative products and services.

Changing Business Relationships

At a heightened rate and level of intensity, firms are forming strategic alliances, partnerships, joint ventures, collaborative agreements, and virtual alliances and virtual enterprises. Emphasis is now on value chain management in order to establish more trusting and closer supplier relationships, which may include technology sharing and co-development. Even competitors are now engaging in "coopetition"[8] and to some extent, are coming together out of mutual interdependence.

Changing Governmental Laws and Regulations

Changes in the rules of any game can modify strategies as well as the nature, speed and intensity of competition. Regulatory and governmental environments in less stable countries are likely to change more frequently. Thus, the potential "rippling effect" of these regulatory and government changes on economic forces of the global economy is another source of turbulence.

Interdependent Economies

Global economies are enabled by electronic, telecommunications, financial, transportation, and computer systems. The risks of one economy are measurable risks on other economies. The Asian economic crisis of 1998 had negative effects on the Russian economy, the Latin American continent's economies, and threatened the U.S. economy. Similarly, the economic crisis during the summer of 2011 affected the entire world's economies. Such is the nature of the interdependency among national economies due to the fluid flow of capital and the significant percentages of domestic corporate revenues stemming from foreign markets.

Interrelationship of These Forces Leads to More Turbulence

The interrelationship of these environmental forces leads to more turbulence and more rapid changes in the environment (Figure 1.1). For example, changes in societal turbulence can lead to changes in customer wants. To see this, one only need to examine the case of the booming security products and services industry as a response to consumer demands for safety that can be associated with a rise in crime in society. Another example is the increasing social consciousness about environmental fragility. This has resulted in the introduction of a variety of environmentally friendly products and services.

Competitive Environment Dimensions

Figure 1.1: Competitive Environment Dimensions

For the most part, these environmental changes are uncontrollable. There is a need for firms to respond quickly in a proactive manner to the dynamic market conditions, changing customer wants, and competitive moves. In other words, the firm's management must become more responsive. Surviving the competitive environment of the digital age requires fast analysis of business conditions and the ability to consider various response scenarios quickly.

Section 2. Impact of Digital Age on Strategy and Marketing

> "Today knowledge has power. It controls access to opportunity and advancement."
>   Peter Drucker

The traditional definition and approaches to strategic planning, marketing, and analysis must be questioned, re-considered, and perhaps even changed, in light of the digital age's impact. The following discussion briefly reviews several of the ideas associated with the impact of the digital age on strategy and marketing.

Impact on Strategy

The traditional views of strategy suggest a linear or sequential model involving the assumption of strategy formulation follow by strategy implementation.[9] Strategy formulation additionally assumes that planners, senior managers, and marketing analysts perform the "thinking" functions (situational analysis and goal setting). Likewise, strategy implementation or the "doing" functions are assumed to be performed by people other than the thinkers.

There are many traditional definitions of strategy, which emphasize both the planning and action orientations. Strategy can be defined as the pattern of objectives, purposes, or goals and the major policies for achieving these goals, which define what business the company is in or is to be in and the kind of company it is or is to be.[10]

Although traditional definitions of strategy are many, they tend to share a common thread. This thread deals with the decision-making rules regarding the scope, growth, competitive advantage, and synergy for a company's products and markets. Traditional definitions tend to have four major components. Those components are:

- An environmental analysis.
- A statement of the company's missions, goals and objectives.
- A situational analysis of the company's resources.
- A resource allocation plan for achieving the corporate mission, goals and objectives.

Some scholars have suggested the strategy-in-action by practitioners does not mirror the traditional strategy-in-theory stated by scholars. Mintzberg is one such scholar who emphasizes the action-perspective in his definition of strategy. He defines strategy as a pattern in the stream of actions over time: strategy is a combination of intended or deliberate strategies and emergent strategies (i.e., patterns emerging without intentions). Emergent strategies occur in the "heat of battle" when decisions are made and actions are taken that make strategic sense, given the circumstances.

The digital age has brought us the rapid rates of change, extreme complexity, huge volumes of information, hyper-competition, and virtualization of markets, processes, and customers. These factors imply a radical influence on the strategy formulation and implementation and on the degree to which strategy is more deliberate or emergent.

Virtualization of Markets, Processes and Customer Interfaces

The convergence of information, communications, imaging, artificial intelligence, and related technologies have enabled small businesses to compete more effectively with big businesses, especially in knowledge-intensive industries. These competitive dynamics have resulted in the "virtualization" of markets and distribution channels.

Virtualization means the replacement of the physical function or thing with a digital version. For example, Amazon.com provides customers on the internet with a virtual marketplace for clothes, books, movies, electronics, music, and anything else that can be shipped. Amazon.com provides web-based product offerings of millions of book titles and music albums. Customers, however, do not have to leave the comfort of their homes and/or offices in order to shop and sample from Amazon.com's vast collections. In fact, with the advent of Amazon Prime customers can now instantly stream nearly unlimited amounts of movies, television shows, books, and music. Customers do not know or even care how Amazon.com processes its order, warehouses its book titles, or even whether or not it has a warehouse of books.

Much of Amazon.com's processing is virtual in that many steps in processing the order are performed via computer software. Customers have the simple option of browsing, sampling, and ordering their choices via the internet with the assurance that the product will be delivered to their doorstep within a few days. Imagine the advantages Amazon.com had over its competitors who were late adopters of an internet-based commerce.

To some extent, even "customers" are becoming virtual. As intelligent software "agents" become more sophisticated, surfing the World-Wide Web for products and negotiating price bargains will become commonplace. Certainly, the virtual interfaces with customers present a challenge to businesses to re-think and, perhaps, redefine "salesperson" and "the selling process". Already, Amazon.com employs intelligent software agents to monitor customer book preference categories and make suggestions to them.

Linkages of suppliers, manufacturers, distributors, wholesalers, retailers, and customers become more integrated via computer and communication technologies. These linkages are yielding significant changes in the economics of marketing channels, patterns of physical distribution, and the structure of distribution.[11] Some of the physical links in the value or supply chain are being replaced by virtual links. The nature of other physical links in the value chain is being significant modified by:

- Lowering the coordination costs for some producers and retailers.
- Lowering physical distribution costs.
- Eliminating some retailers and wholesalers entirely, as customers directly access manufacturers.

Researchers define the industry value chain as "the collection of companies involved in producing, distributing, and selling a related set of products from raw material to the consumer" describe several ways how the information superhighway impacts members of the industry-level value chain.[12]

o *Producers of Knowledge*
Software, books, movies, music, etc. can be maintained in digital form and transmitted over the information superhighway on demand with little or no physical inventory movement.

o *Producers of Physical Goods*

Physical goods sold through e-store fronts can be sold over the information superhighway. In addition, computer technology can simplify product complexity.

o *Physical Distribution Networks*

These can be simplified to move from the manufacturer to the customer directly, or coordinated by electronic retailer or market-maker transactions. Customers can buy the product over the information superhighway and either receive the product via Federal Express, USPS, or United Parcel Service delivery or pick the product up at a conveniently located depot the same day.

o *Electronic Retailers*

Both specialty retailers like Teavana and multiple product retailers like Walmart and Macy's can link directly to customers.

o *Electronic Markets*

These can be expanded to include the travel and financial industries, and specialty niches such as shirts, computer software, or baseball cards.

o *Electronic Channels*

The cable, telephone, cellular, and electric utility industries that can all provide access to the home and provide alternative direct ways of advertising and selling directly to consumers.

o *Customers*

It is still too early to tell how customers will modify their buying habits and levels given to potential changes possible and given the electronic transaction capabilities currently available. Substantial changes are likely but what forms these changes take are difficult to predict.

The virtualization of markets forces strategic decision-makers to ask several questions:[13]

1. How will virtualization change the products and services the company sells?
2. What new ways might the company locate, engage, and serve its current and potential customers?
3. How might the relationship with customers be enhanced, changed, or threatened by virtualization?
4. How can the company embrace new channels of distribution without damaging existing channels?
5. How can the company obtain and use the volumes of extant customer and competitor data to gain and sustain customer delight and customer relationships?
6. How must the company align its business structures and processes with the emerging realities of the World-Wide Web and electronic commerce?

Impact on Marketing

We have seen how the impact of the digital age is changing the traditional concepts and approaches to strategy. The digital age has had a marked influence on the concepts and approaches to marketing, too. Until very recently, few marketing scholars had formally examined the effects of digital technology on marketing theory and practice

First, with the rapid growth of the internet, electronic commerce, corporate intranets, and social media, markets are no longer considered merely physical.[14] The traditional concept of "marketplace" is becoming the "marketspace". The traditional marketplace consisted of a physical buyer interacting with a physical seller. With the marketspace of electronic commerce and the internet, the customer is not physically present in front of a physical buyer, a physical store, or even a physical product. The transaction medium and infrastructure is electronic and information-based.

Thus, the customer knowledge of the product and price, the place where the transaction occurs, and the promotion which induces the purchase are blended into one electronic interface with the customer. Hence, internet and electronic commerce blurs traditional marketing mix of four Ps into one bundled electronic presentation. Thus, successful management of the marketspace requires managing a virtual value chain. The traditional intermediaries between customer and sellers, retailers, distributors, and wholesalers are becoming virtually eliminated.[15]

With the marketspace in electronic commerce, the content, context, and enabling infrastructure of the transaction are different.[16] In contrast with a physical buyer and seller at a physical location, within the marketspace, the transaction content is information-based, the transaction context is electronic, and the enabling infrastructure is significantly virtual.

Marketing is understood to be a set of activities involved in the facilitation of exchange of goods and services along the value chain.[17] As these exchanges occur from supplier to firm to distributor to consumer, information is being created and exchanged. Information technology is enabling the integration and virtualization of the value while it expands channel capacity to store, process, and transmit information. There is subsequently an increase in the transmission speed and the amount of information being processed and stored.

Hence, another impact of the digital age on marketing is the challenges presented by best utilizing the additional information about processes, customers, and suppliers made available by integrated customer relationship marketing technology. Some authors are discussing the idea of "real-time" marketing. By harnessing new and emerging technologies, firms can start real-time dialogues with their customers, provide interactive services, involve broader numbers of customers in new product development, and speed up the time it takes to get the market to accept a new product.[18]

Strategy's Future: A Marriage with Business Analytics and Competitive Intelligence

In the digital age, strategic adjustments in direction, goals, objectives, and action plans have to be made more frequently utilizing big data and business analytics. To stay abreast of the changes in the digital age, firms may have to implement ongoing business analytics and competitive intelligence gathering processes. Competitive intelligence processes involve gathering environmental information in various forms from various media and transforming it into strategic insights. Firms in the digital age will need to build and update daily a knowledge base about customers, competitors, suppliers, opportunities, threats, and any information relevant to its market position.[19]

Business analytics and competitive intelligence processes require utilizing this knowledge base for ongoing analytics and model creation. What makes business analytics and competitive intelligence processes different from strategic formulation and implementation processes? One main difference is the time-frames within which each traditionally takes place. Strategy formulation and implementation usually requires weeks and months to complete. Additionally, strategy formulation typically involves careful thinking, planning, decision-making based upon analytical methods, consultants' expertise, and primary and secondary research.

Alternatively, business analytics and competitive intelligence processes usually involve only hours and days before knowledge is obtained, a decision is made, and an action taken. Then, depending on the form of knowledge obtained via business analytics using big data, the insights may or may not be scientifically based or well-grounded in rigorous methods of derivation. For example, a rumor about a potential competitor move may not be accurate or complete but it still might be acted upon. Also, a discovered correlation between two or more attributes in the market and product sales may or may not be significant or meaningful but, again, may be acted upon. Thus, this "intelligence" might be flawed or incomplete, although perceived to be valuable and useful.

Perhaps a marriage of some sort between the business analytics and strategic planning activities will enable strategic thinking and planning to be timelier while providing for more current market and competitor intelligence during the decision-making processes.

Section 3. Market Orientation and Customer Relationship Focus

"For ease and confidence in doing, you must develop abilities and then develop excellence in the use of these abilities."
Rhoda Lachar

The impact of rapid and accelerating change, extreme complexity, huge volumes of information, and hyper-competition of the digital age has resulted in a more dynamic approach to strategy and marketing. In marketing, this new approach is called the "market orientation", "capabilities", or "market-driven". Market-orientation, defined as "superior skills in understanding and satisfying customers", in its current evolution is both internally and externally focused.[20] Its external focus represents an orientation on current and potential customers, markets, competitors, and the environment. Its internal focus represents an orientation on improving the firm's people, processes, and technology so that customer value is delivered and competitive advantage maintained. Both the internal and external foci of market orientation require continuous learning. In turbulent environments, firms must learn and adjust at least at the rate of their competitors and of the environmental changes, if they want to maintain competitive advantages.[21]

Market Orientation Components

In developing marketing strategy and plan, firms would adopt an appropriate market orientation considering their task environment. The concept of market orientation is critical in marketing strategy and has a significant impact on business performance and marketing activities.[22] Researchers identified three key dimensions of market orientation - customer orientation, competitor orientation, and inter-functional coordination.[23] Customer orientation refers to having sufficient understanding of target markets to better create superior value. Competitor orientation means assessing both short term and long term capabilities and strengths of current as well as potential competitors. Finally, inter-functional coordination involves utilizing company resources in creating superior value for target customers.

The Three-Stage Model of Market Orientation

Each of the three components of market orientation allows firms move forward in a certain strategic direction. The market orientation is guided by the firm's overall strategic orientation.

The three stage model of market orientation shows three transitional states of the market orientation components over time (Figure 1.2).

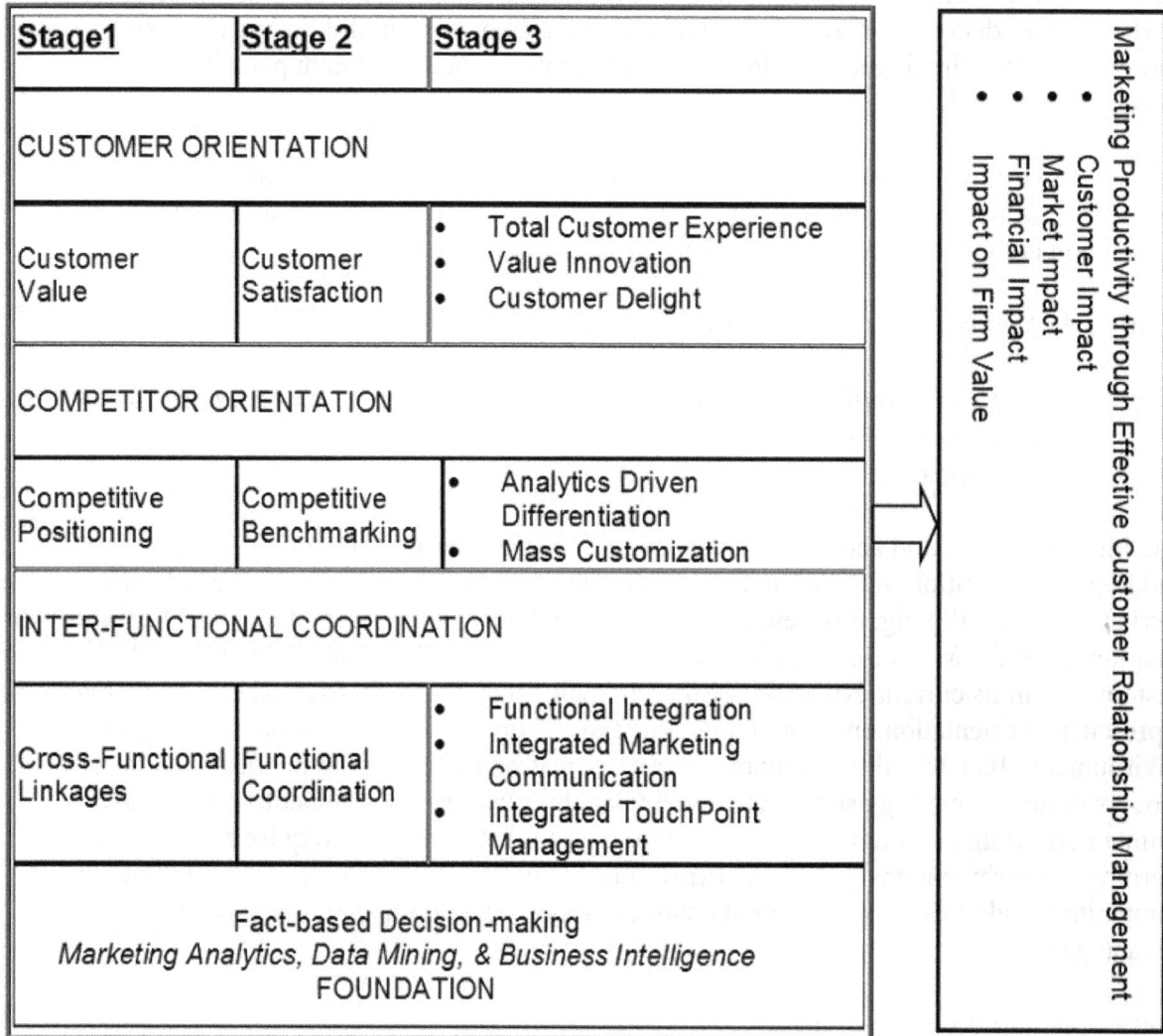

Stage1	Stage 2	Stage 3
CUSTOMER ORIENTATION		
Customer Value	Customer Satisfaction	• Total Customer Experience • Value Innovation • Customer Delight
COMPETITOR ORIENTATION		
Competitive Positioning	Competitive Benchmarking	• Analytics Driven Differentiation • Mass Customization
INTER-FUNCTIONAL COORDINATION		
Cross-Functional Linkages	Functional Coordination	• Functional Integration • Integrated Marketing Communication • Integrated TouchPoint Management
Fact-based Decision-making *Marketing Analytics, Data Mining, & Business Intelligence* FOUNDATION		

Marketing Productivity through Effective Customer Relationship Management
• Customer Impact
• Market Impact
• Financial Impact
• Impact on Firm Value

Figure 1.2: The Three-Stage Model of Market Orientation

A strong customer orientation allows firms to be close to their customers. Marketing strategies in these firms are developed based on customer needs and customer satisfaction. Firms focus on listening to their customers through marketing surveys, focus group studies, customer satisfaction survey, social media postings, and other sources of customer input. With the input of the customers, firms initially develop marketing strategies to achieve superior customer value leading to customer satisfaction. With the development of integrated customer data base, firms are now refocusing their customer orientation to achieve exceptional total customer experience through value innovation and customer delight creation.

Another important component of market orientation is competitor orientation. Firms need to develop the ability to understand key competitors and new or emerging competitive forces. Competitor orientation provides firms the ability to respond to competition by tracking relative competitiveness in such areas. Firms can also predict the competitive actions and reactions.

Competitor orientation can be achieved initially by developing the right competitive position in the market place. With the development of competitive positioning map, firms can benchmark key competitors by matching or surpassing the determinant attributes used by their target markets. In the third stage, firms develop competitive orientation by utilizing analytics driven marketing mix differentiation and mass customization. Firms are utilizing business analytics and big data tools and methodology extensively to understand markets and offer competitive product and service offerings.

Firms with a strong market orientation also achieve cross-functional coordination. They begin with understanding cross-functional linkages and move forward achieving functional coordination. To achieve market orientation, firms should achieve functional integration to manage customer relationships effectively. Various functions of a firm need to work well as a team to leverage cross-functional skills and business activities that affect customer response, satisfaction, and experience. With functional integration, firms can develop and implement integrated marketing communication and integrated touchpoint management plan. The real benefit of a strong market orientation is achieving effective relationship marketing. This is well highlighted by the recent definition of marketing by American Marketing Association. The new definition emphasizes the importance of relationship marketing resulting superior customer satisfaction, delightful customer experience, customer retention, and profitability.

One important point noted in this figure is the foundation of the market orientation. Traditional marketing management would have utilized managers' intuition and experience along with limited market information. Analytics and intelligence driven strategic marketing would utilize fact-based decision-making in implementing market orientation practices. Fact-based decision-making requires real time big data and marketing analytics tools to analyze and report important trends and patterns hidden in the database. Marketing analytics tools are used to generate business intelligence and marketing analytic insights. The generated business intelligence and marketing analytic insights are disseminated throughout the firm including marketing and sales so that marketing managers can make fact-based marketing decisions.

Marketing Productivity Impact

Firms adopting market orientation should reap the benefit of market orientation in the form of effective customer relationship creation and management as well as increased marketing productivity. Marketing actions will influence a chain of marketing productivity. Customer impact should consider important measures of mind set that are affected by marketing expenditures. These factors include customer awareness of the firm (customers' recall and recognition of the firm, products, and services), customer association (the strength, favorability, and uniqueness of perceived attributes and benefits for the firm and brand), customer attitudes (customers' overall evaluations of the firm and the brand, customer attachment, customer loyalty toward the firm and the brand), and customer experience (the extent to which customers seek out information about and use the brand as well as talk about and share the positive and negative experience with the firm's products, brands, and all touchpoints of the firm). Market impact can be measured by the firm's market share, sales, and competitive position. These measures are influenced by customer impact. For example, superior brands or products offering superior value lead to higher levels of customer satisfaction, loyalty, and retention. Firms having better differentiated brands can enjoy lower price elasticity, more loyal customers, and less impact from competitive actions. They can command price premiums, increase market share, and develop more efficient marketing programs because loyal customers are more responsive to advertising and promotion and positively react to brand extension efforts. Loyal and satisfied customers allow firms to establish competitive market advantage because they are willing to pay a price premium, provide referrals, and use more of the product. As a result, firms can lower the sales and service cost, increase customer retention and longevity, increase market share, and attain greater profitability. Financial impact from marketing actions can be assessed in many different ways. The most common and traditional approach is calculating return on investment (ROI). As marketing expenditures are often associated long-term effects in the market place, short-term ROI can misrepresent the true impact of marketing. If ROI is used in the marketing context, future cash flows need to be considered. Other financial measures include the internal rate of return, the net present value, and the economic value-added (the net operating profit minus the cost of capital). Impact of marketing on the value of the firm requires linking marketing actions through customer value to changes in market value. As the market value of the firms focuses largely on growth prospects and sustainability of profits, assessment of firm value impact requires tracking metrics such as brand or customer equity in addition to balance sheet metrics and focusing on both current and expected performance derived from marketing actions.

Marketing productivity impact can be also evaluated using the balanced scorecard components. The balanced scorecard is a presentation and reporting tool to help the firm broaden its strategic focus from traditional financial only measurements and analytics to other areas such as customer and supplier relationships, product and services quality, and marketing manager skills and capabilities. As such, these analytics can help the firm move from being focused in the past to being future oriented. The balanced scorecard provides the marketing managers with a report card on firm's progress in achieving its vision. Coupled with the strategy map, the balanced scorecard links the firm's strategy to its initiatives. It provides the key measure thus enabling the firm to focus its resources toward achieving its targets and initiatives.

The balanced scorecard includes the traditional financial measures such as sales, profit, and cost, as well as a greater and more diverse set of analytics that can include supplier, competitor, and customer information, information resources, business processes performance, and employee skill and capability growth. These diverse analytics are designed to help the managers gain a better understanding into the true performance of the organization. The intent of these measures is also to reflect on the required balance between the organization's short term and long term objectives, between financial and non-financial analytics, and between internal and external performance factors. When Kaplan and Norton developed the balanced scorecard concept, they focused on providing four views or perspectives of the organization: financial, customer, process, and learning and growth perspectives.[24] Since its inception, organizations have added and altered these views. However, the initial views represent a good starting point for all organizations. These views should be used to ensure the alignment between the organizations goals and the analytics its uses to assess performance. The features of the views are the listing of the objectives for the view, the definition of the analytic, the target value and date, and a measurement cycle.

Financial Perspective

The financial analytics used by the for-profit organization can include the traditional measures such as ROI, revenue growth, asset utilization, and profitability as well as analytics that can relate to the defined strategic objectives of the organization. The financial analytics used by the non-profit organization can include budget summaries, ratios of services provided for dollar expenditure and impact to the consumer. This perspective can (and probably should) be relabeled for non-profit organizations because their "financial" focus is on providing value for the budget provided. These "financial" outcomes can include analytics such as budget per employee or expenditures per category. Each organization can develop its own meaningful analytics.

Customer Perspective

The customer (consumer, client, or patron) analytics are related to the value being delivered to the customer. Many organizations have recognized that the customer is the purpose and reason for their existence and are striving to become more customer-centric. Whether the organization is for-profit or non-profit, the organization must understand its satisfaction levels, the market it serves and the share of that market they "own", and the organization's ability to attract new customers and retain existing customers.

Process Perspective

The internal organizational process analytics focus on the operational processes of the organization. The focus of these analytics is on how efficient and how effective the organization is in using the resources to provide value to the customer. Focusing on processes helps in determining those that are out-of-date or missing. The focus of process management investigation can include analytics to highlight the time required to provide the product or service, the cost to deliver the product or service, and the quality of the product or service. The result can require improvement or reengineering in processes.

Learning and Growth Perspective

The learning and growth analytics focus on the employee skills and capabilities of the knowledge embodied in the organization. The employee skill and capabilities will enable the organization to improve and adapt to the changing environment. The organization can include analytics reporting on employee motivation, tools required for collaboration, training budgets, and retention rates.

These four perspectives form the basic structure for the balanced scorecard application as depicted in Figure 1.3. As the firm progresses in its development and use of the balanced scorecard, it may add additional analytics or modify the views it is using. These views and the use of the balanced scorecard shift the organization's focus from the past performance to its future vision.

Financial
- Profitability
- ROE
- Cash Flow
- Sales

Customers
- Satisfaction
- Market Share
- Retention
- Complaints

Innovation
- %new products
- Employee Skills
- R&D Conversion
- Training/worker

Process
- Cycle Time
- Quality Index
- Rework
- Productivity

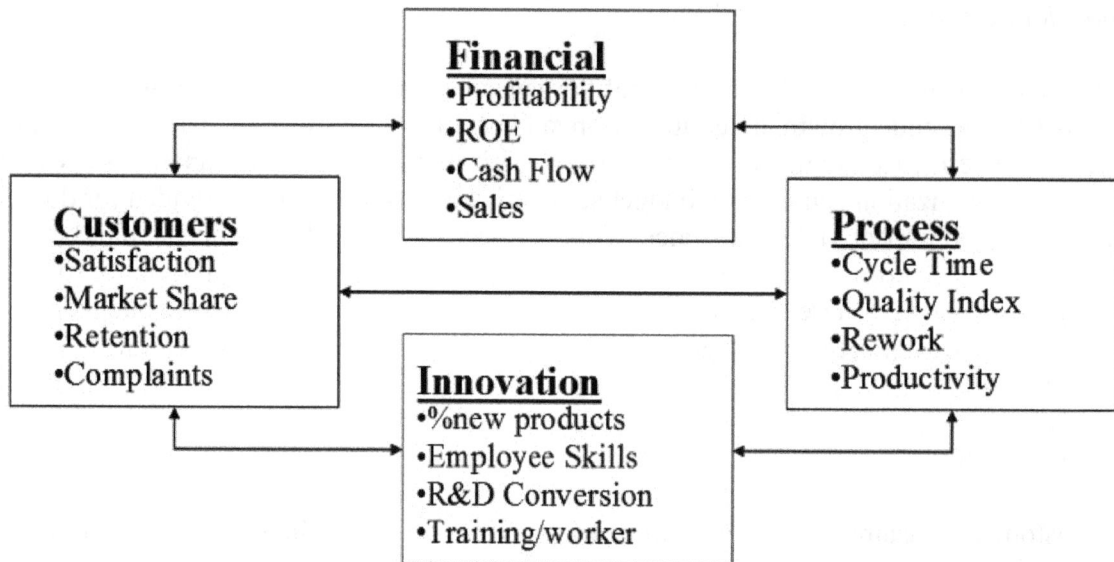

Figure 1.3: Balanced Scorecard Application Example

Strategy Map

A strategy map is a visual representation of the firm's strategy providing the marketing managers with a view of how the firm's objectives integrate and combine. The strategy map illustrates the interrelationships among the various organizational processes enabling it to create a sustainable competitive advantage.

Distinctive Capabilities

The market-oriented (or "capabilities-based") approach extends the resource-based approach to strategy, which prescribes that the firm leverages its mix of material, financial, and human resources to gain competitive advantage. The market-oriented approach emphasizes identifying and managing the processes that enable the value-creation, learning, responsiveness, innovativeness, and adaptability capabilities firms need to compete effectively in turbulent environments.[25]

The market-oriented approach to strategy requires a different mind-set from the traditional approach to strategy. In this regard, the market-oriented approach emphasizes several important characteristics:[26]

- Importance of developing a shared vision about the market and how it is expected to change in the future.
- Importance of selecting avenues for delivering superior value to customers.
- Importance of positioning the organization and its brands in the marketplace using distinctive competencies.
- Importance of recognizing the potential value of collaborative relationships with customers, suppliers, distribution channel members, internal functions, and even competitors.

- Importance of reinventing organizational designs to implement and manage future strategies.

This shift re-orients strategic marketing from assuming a somewhat stable environment to acknowledging dynamic internal and external environments for firms. Under the old assumption of a stable environment, strategic marketing focused on obtaining a fixed, competitively advantageous marketplace "position" and "resource endowments". Given the uncertainties brought about by rapid changes and extreme complexity, advantageous positions, if identifiable, can be short-lived. In addition to the advantageous position emphasis, the "capabilities" approach encourages firms to also focus on identifying and building upon the capabilities. Capabilities are complex bundle of skills that enable firms to obtain such positions and resource endowments. With these capabilities and competencies understood, firms can use them to build new capabilities and competencies for competitive advantages, if future environmental changes eliminate existing advantages.

Capabilities enable businesses to carry out the activities required to move their products or services through the value chain in order to satisfy customer wants and expectations. Competitiveness of businesses is in the relative strengths of these activities. Those businesses with superior performance in carrying out some of these activities will have a competitive edge over those competitors who do not perform these activities as well. The bundle of activities that a business provides represents the distinctive capabilities of that business. These distinctive capabilities offer competitive advantage because they are valuable and difficult to match. These distinctive capabilities must be identified and properly managed. Corporate management must set stretch goals for improvement and then support achieving these goals by committing resources, assigning dedicated people, and promoting continuous learning. Distinctive capabilities have three key attributes:[27]

- Significant contribution to providing superior perceived customer value.
- Difficult to imitate.
- Enable versatility and adaptability to environmental change.

Thus, strategic marketing still stresses a firm obtaining defensible competitive positions. The key is for firms to obtain such positions through their deployment of distinct, difficult-to-imitate capabilities that they have developed. Decision-makers must have a shared understanding of the industry structure, the needs of the target customer segments, the positional advantages being sought, and the trends in the environment.

Prescriptions for Strategic Marketing in the Digital Age

These "capabilities" or market orientation perspectives offer prescriptions for strategic marketing vis-à-vis the complex environment. These prescriptions[28] that are relevant for strategic marketing include shifting focus:

- From content to process explanatory variables.
- From industry structures to cognitive processes.
- From strategic commitment to strategic flexibility.
- From "decide and control" strategic management to self-managing systems.
- From marketing as a function to cross-functional processes.

- From product/service management to customer relationship management and recognition of the new economics of information.
- From traditional to "fact-based" marketing decision-making.
- From traditional measurements to new concepts of strategic performance measurements and dashboards.

Shift Focus from Content to Process Explanatory Variables

Given the rapidly changing environmental terrain, strategic marketing of the firm must shift its focus from identifying the firm's specific resource mix at a given point in time to understanding the dynamic processes by which the firm identifies and develops its strategic resources. The process orientation allows firms to better respond to the dynamic and complex nature of the environmental changes.

Shift Focus from Industry Structures to Cognitive Processes

The traditional view of strategic management sees industry structures as static and determined by external forces. Industry structure, however, results from decisions about resource deployments and asset accumulations made out of the mental models of managers in various competing firms. Thus, industry structure is to some extent a function of the mental models of individual managerial decision-makers. Insightful exploitation of new technologies, innovative processes and products, and other managerial cognitions can sometimes impact industry structures. For example, Dell Computer's CEO Michael Dell decided, rather insightfully, to utilize information technology to produce and deliver his computer products to customers via "virtual integration"[29] Through information technology, Dell is able to manage a network of suppliers as a tightly integrated value chain as if they were inside the company. At the same time, as independent businesses, these suppliers have the loose coupling and specialization to respond quickly to the ever-changing demands of their sub-industries. Hence, Dell gets the benefits of a vertically integrated firm without the associated investments and risks. Such savings enables Dell to provide a high quality product at a lower price than more vertically integrated competitors.

Shift Focus from Strategic Commitment to Strategic Flexibility

Traditionally, strategic marketing is done with respect to predetermined commitment to specific strategic goals and course of action, which is a definition of strategic planning.[30] However, as Mintzberg and others have pointed out, in the midst of executing intended strategies, the environment can change such that an in-process adjustment is necessary. The strategy realized, therefore, is a combination of emergent strategies with deliberate strategies. In a dynamic and complex environment, the strategic flexibility to change a course of action as changing circumstances warrant is more important than directing attention of assumed fixed targets.

Shift Focus from "Decide and Control" Strategic Management to Self-Managing Systems

The traditional view of strategic management emphasizes top-down decision-making and strategy formulation, and the implementation of top-heavy controls to assure plan execution. Given the rapid changes, dynamic complexity, huge volumes of information, and the importance of local competitive intelligence, the cognitive limits of top managers prevent them from maintaining this traditional approach. Specifically, top managers do not have enough information, expertise, or time to make timely strategic decisions, to develop implementation plans, and to monitor all the relevant implementation details.

Instead, senior managers should design as designers of adaptive organizational systems in which decision-making is widely distributed so that it can be brought into alignment with the information, expertise, and other resources needed to make good decisions at various levels of complexity in the decision-making process. In essence, to reduce complexity in decision-making and to avoid cognitive overload, competence theory suggests that the content of traditionally strategic level decision-making must be devolved to other levels and entities in an organization where more fully informed decisions can be made.

Shift Focus from Marketing as a Function to Cross-functional Processes

Marketing and customer-value orientation must become a shared responsibility throughout the business enterprise in the information age or digital era. Multifunctional teams at varying layers of the organization must assume a shared responsibility for generating superior customer-value. This idea is best portrayed by Kotler. Marketing was considered an equal function to production, human resources, and finance. Then, the marketing function continued to undergo more evolution in its increasing importance to the business enterprise. Kotler described the need for marketing to be integrated and coordinated with all functional departments as a cross-functional process of serving customers.[31] Thus, no longer is marketing assumed to be a separate function, "turf", and specialty of the marketing department (Figure 1.4).

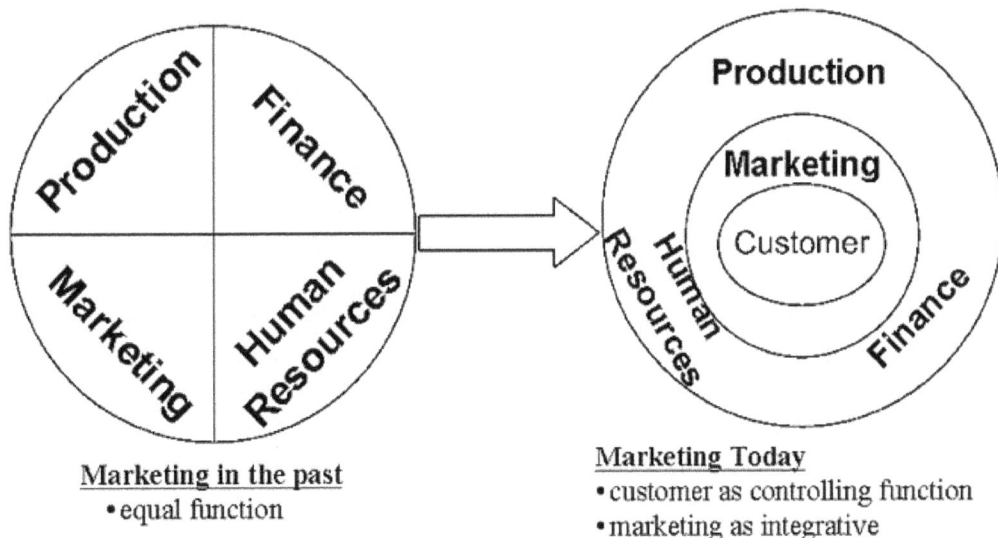

Marketing in the past
• equal function

Marketing Today
• customer as controlling function
• marketing as integrative

Figure 1.4: Integrated Marketing

Several interrelated factors are influencing major changes in which marketing is becoming a process instead of a function, including the following:

- Enterprise integration of traditional business functions including marketing.
- Flattening of organizational structures and increase emphasis on business processes.

- Linking of organizational distinctive capabilities to business processes.
- Virtualization of external markets, internal processes and customer interfaces.

Shift Focus from Product / Service Management to Customer

With the recognition of the importance of managing customers effectively, firms are shifting their focus from product or service-oriented marketing to a customer-centric marketing approach. In customer-centric marketing, firms develop a 360-degree view of customers and develop marketing strategy to improve customer retention, acquisition, and customer loyalty. The focus is on developing, improving, and maintaining long-term customer relationship.

Shift Focus from Intuition-Driven Marketing Decision-Making to "Fact-based" or "Deep Intelligence-based" Marketing Decision-Making.

With the advancement in data storage, processing, and retrieval capability, firms are developing huge amount of marketing and customer data. Instead of using inaccurate, often biased, intuition and judgment of marketing managers, firms are more relying on marketing data, customer database, marketing insights, and business intelligence generated from big data and marketing analytics.

Shift Focus to Recognition of the New Economics of Information

Two characteristics of the economics of information suggest a possible impact on strategy. Those characteristics are a reduction in the ability of entities and individuals to monopolize and control information, and the opportunities to leverage information access to compress the time necessary for strategy implementation. Strategy ought to be enhanced because the expanded access to information facilitates cooperation between functions, reduces the power associated with possessing information, and enables a more complete analysis within a short time span.

Shift Focus to New Concepts of Strategic Performance Measurement

Because of the importance of focusing on customer-value, processes, continuous innovation, and learning, many firms have adopted the "balance scorecard" approach to performance measurement. The balanced scorecard approach incorporates performance measures of customer, business process and innovation, and learning in addition to the traditional financial measures. Hence, a balanced scorecard may include customer related performance measures.

Shift Focus to Customer Relationship Management

Customer relationship focus is deeply embedded on a firm's culture. This customer relationship focus affects the firm's choice of outcomes and the means to accomplish those outcomes. This focus guides the firm's efforts to adopt and implement customer relationship management and its related processes. Customer relationship focus will establish the organizational mindset that customer relationship is an asset and capability required to remain competitive in a global market. In addition, firms with this focus will establish organizational structures and incentives that motivate the behaviors consistent with the customer relationship focus.

Section 4. Total CRM and Relationship Marketing

"The aim of marketing is to know and understand the customer so well that the product or service fits him (her) and sells itself. All that should be needed then is to make the product or service available ...".
Peter Drucker

Traditional Outbound Marketing and CRM

Traditional or outbound marketing deals with building awareness of the organization's brands, products and services using tools and techniques such as telemarketing, direct sales, or television advertising. Traditional marketing tactics include the use of direct mail, radio, television, telemarketing, magazines, and newspapers to describe the organization's brands, products, and services. The tactics are typically one-way communication from the organization to the prospect or customer. In the past, traditional marketing techniques included creating websites that contained only static information. Perhaps these static websites had a series of PDF files that were available to the website visitor as downloadable or viewable documents. These documents may have been old printed brochures the organization used that were subsequently digitized and put on the static website. Another traditional marketing technique to gain insight and understanding for what prospects and customers wanted was for marketers to use traditional marketing research techniques such as focus groups. "Focus groups are a thing of the past; today, you have to draw people out in their own environment."[32]

Traditional marketing concepts have and continue to evolve. Newer marketing concepts incorporate ideas such as relationship marketing and permission-based marketing. Relationship marketing was first defined as a form of marketing developed from traditional direct response marketing campaigns. These campaigns "emphasize customer retention and satisfaction, rather than a dominant focus on sales transactions. As a practice, relationship marketing differs from other forms of marketing in that it recognizes the long-term value of customer relationships and extends communication beyond intrusive advertising and sales promotional messages. With the growth of the internet and mobile platforms, relationship marketing has continued to evolve and move forward as technology opens more collaborative and social communication channels. This includes tools for managing relationships with customers that go beyond simple demographic and customer service data. Relationship marketing extends to include interactive marketing efforts (a combination of search optimization and strategic content), public relations, social media and application development."[33]

"It is all about building and developing relationships. Hence, business-to-business (B2B) marketing is adopting social media application tools at a greater rate than business-to-consumer (B2C) marketing." With the explosive growth of social networking tools to facilitate communication and information-sharing, the firm's brand is not what the firm says it is, but rather, what others are saying it is. The developed relationships provide objective opinions for the firm. Therefore, social media sites are tools that are providing objective opinions whereas the firm's website typically provides objective technical specifications.[34]

Permission marketing is being used in marketing in general and in e-marketing specifically. In permission marketing, marketers obtain permission before advancing to the next step in the four step (awareness, information acquisition, consideration, decision) buyer journey process. For example, marketing managers will ask permission to send email newsletters to prospective customers. It is mostly used by online or inbound marketers, notably by email marketers and search marketers, as well as certain direct marketers who send a catalog in response to an information request. This form of marketing requires that the prospective customer has given either explicit permission for the marketer to send their promotional message (e.g., an email or catalog request) or implicit permission (e.g., querying a search engine). This can be either via an online email opt-in form or by using search engines, which implies a request for information, which can include that of a commercial nature. The undesirable opposite of permission marketing is interruption marketing. Marketers feel that it is a more efficient use of their resources if the offers are only sent to people that are actually interested in the product.[35] The use of the traditional marketing and CRM is decreasing. Hence, firms are shifting their marketing budget funding to digital CRM and inbound marketing techniques.

Digital Marketing and CRM

Firm-defined processes drive the traditional marketing communication model where the marketing messages are transmitted through defined channels. In this communication model, the inside-out approach, where the message is created and defined internally and then pushed out to prospects and customers, is used to achieve marketing and organization goals. In this case, the focus of the process is on the identified transaction. In contrast, the web and social media applications open a new avenue of communication. User-defined processes drive this new communication model where customer-generated content is exchanged through customer-driven dynamic channels. This new model adopts the outside-in approach, where the message is defined by the customer and then pulled into the firm, and focuses on the interaction between the customer or prospect and the firm. Consistent to this new communication mode, the network co-production model is proposed in the academic literature. Figure 1.5 shows this network co-production communication model.[36] This model can capture the interaction better and is more applicable to online communities.

The network co-production model places increased importance on the role of consumer networks, groups, and communities. In this model, customers are regarded as active co-producers of value and meaning. The user-generated content can be idiosyncratic, creative, and even resistant. The unique aspect of this model is the acknowledgement of the fact that marketing messages and meanings do not flow uni-directionally but rather are exchanged among members of the customer network. In interacting with other members of the network, users can use the four social media communication strategies that include evaluation, embracing, endorsement, and explanation. The customer is an active participant in the new communication model. It is important to note that the linkages among customers indicate that ideas and knowledge are shared.

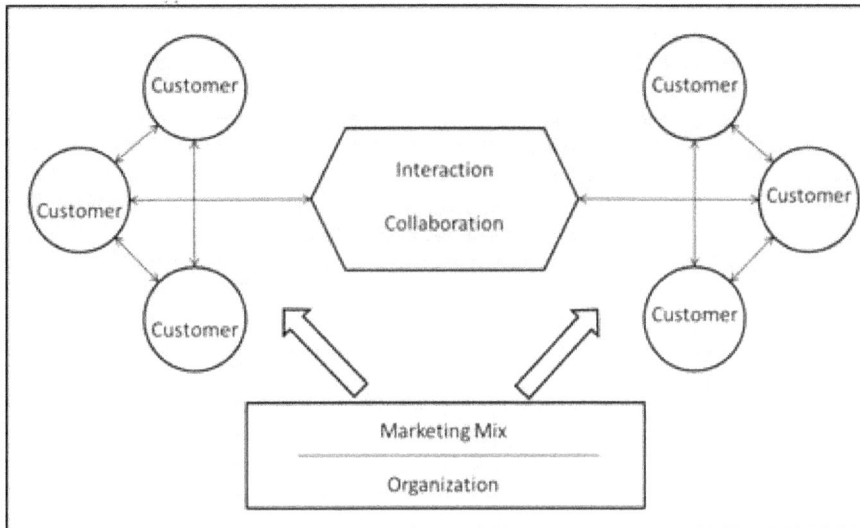

Figure 1.5: Network Co-Production Model

Firms are hard pressed to develop the necessary response to the changing role and empowerment of their customers. Customers are transforming from passive spectators as newspaper readers, television watchers, and browsers of information to active participants as bloggers, product raters, and producers of social media content. Customers are no longer purchasers of brands but have become co-owners of brands. As a result of the adoption of this new communication model, firms are required to take different approaches and tactics to influence the customers and virtual community leaders. For the better understanding of the network-based marketing communication, firms are exploring various ways to take advantage of these new emerging touchpoints in their relationship marketing efforts.

Digital (internet or inbound) marketing encompasses the use of web and social media tools and applications, online video, search engine optimization, mobile marketing, paid placements, email campaigns, and displayed ads. "Instead of concentrating on getting new customers, (the firm) should aim for more referrals, more transactions with existing customers, and larger transactions."[37] Customer-driven marketing is a method of promotion that relies on customers helping to market an idea, brand, product, or service by choosing to share something with their friends. It assumes people are active participants in the promotion process.

Customer-driven marketing assumes content must not only be share-able, but also highly share-worthy. This implies that the content is relevant to the customer. "It requires a deep understanding of how and why people share things and a willingness to put those motivations front and center."[38] Customer-driven marketing relies on people sharing ideas and information about the firm's brand, product, and service with their friends. This requires the firm to understand and use the share capability of web and social media applications.

Examples of customer-driven marketing include previous marketing campaigns from Cisco, Mountain Dew, Burger King, Ford, Pepsi, and especially Shoes of Prey. "Cisco's largest ad campaign to date asked regular folks as well as celebrities like Stephen Colbert and Usher to submit videos of their everyday and unique moments shot on flip cameras for use in upcoming TV ads."[39] Mountain Dew kicked off the first dewmocracy campaign by letting fans design new dew flavors and packaging. With dewmocracy 2, the consumer-driven marketing effort had fans submitting, voting on, and ultimately selecting and creating Mountain Dew's new TV ads.

Burger King's whopper sacrifice campaign invited fans to delete Facebook friends in exchange for free whoppers. Within 10 days of the campaign's debut, the whopper sacrifice app was installed 60,000 times. Two weeks later, some 85,000 people had deleted over 230,000 friends, prompting Facebook to shut the app down, and garnering Burger King a whopper-size portion of free media coverage. Ford kicked off The Fiesta Movement, a social media campaign in which they literally handed 100 young influencers the keys to a Ford Fiesta, asking them only to engage in monthly "missions" and to document and share these missions via social media. After generating 31,000 pieces of original content, tens of millions of media impressions, and a slew of high-profile media coverage, The Fiesta Movement achieved what was once unthinkable: making 60% of the public aware of a car that had not yet even debuted in the United States all without spending a dime on traditional media.

Table 1.1 shows nine potential areas of change in the digital age. These potential areas of change will affect how firms will communicate and interact with their customers.

	Today - Was	Tomorrow – Will Be
1. Analytics	Simple	Encompassing video, mobile, user feedback
2. Authority	Links	Interaction
3. Information Delivery	Publish Content	Interaction
4. Information Locator	Search / Decision Engine	Social Media Tools
5. Information Representation	Static including text and images	Dynamic including video, pictures, simulations, and gaming
6. Information Source	Websites	Mobile, Social Media Pages
7. Marketing	Traditional or Outbound Marketing	Interactive or Inbound Marketing
8. Message Ownership	Creator Controls the Message	Shared Ownership of the message – Reputation Management is required
9. Tool Access		SmartPhone

Table 1.1: Trends Projected For the Digital Age

With the rapid projected growth in Smartphone usage and the rapid increase in the use of video, the future of analytic applications will require tools to provide more information on and encompass video and mobile. Smartphones will also increasingly be the tool used to access information as well as the firm's websites on the internet. This information will increasingly be dynamic and constantly changing. The information will be presented in various formats such as gaming, video, pictures, and simulations more so than the traditional text format of "older" organizational websites. The authority of a web page will be derived more from social interaction of various users and friends and less from links from other websites or blogs.

Knowing the power that real-time information can provide the firm only increases the sense of urgency for the firm to ensure it is focused and that it provides relevant, timely information. This knowledge and sense of urgency requires that the firm's strategy and tactics are clear and focused. The firm's "strategy is the method for focusing the firm's energies and resources on a course of action which can lead to increased sales and dominance of a targeted market space." Consider that "90% of individuals who can, skip through television commercials, and for those who do not, only 14% of those individuals trust advertisements. However, 78% of individuals trust the recommendations of other consumers."[40] The apparent shift is that individuals are trying to find and understand the recommendations of other consumers because they trust their opinions.

New marketing tactics include the use of social media, mobile media, blogs, and grassroots promotions. One of the goals for blogs is to educate individuals and get information about the organization and its brands, products, and services out to as many people as possible. The ability to share information is much easier today. Sharing information and being found on the internet does not require the use of public relations firms as organizations have the ability to blog and email information.

Achieving Relevance with Total CRM for the Relationship Marketing

The logic for the firm to focus on being relevant (i.e., current, pertinent, significant, applicable, lending support) is to attract and keep customers and users returning. Being relevant has been the focus of relationship marketing and CRM efforts by firms. As shown in Figure 1.6, customers are involved in brick and mortar commerce and e-commerce as well as social commerce. In response to these changes, organizations are developing and implementing their CRM plans. Total CRM is defined as a firm's integrative development, implementation, and continued improvement of traditional CRM, e-CRM, and social CRM activities and programs. The goal of total CRM is to achieve relevance for the right target customers in managing relationships with them. Relevance can be achieved by creating relevant interactions and collaborations with the right customers. The interaction with customers must be managed such that all their interactions are at the right time, through the right channels or touchpoints, and in the right context.

In the purchase and usage processes of products and services, customers are demanding relevance of the relationship marketing and CRM efforts. To become relevant, firms need to engage with customers through relevant interactions and collaborations in the perspective of customers. Customers want to have proper interactions and collaborations at the time they want through their preferred channels or touchpoints in the right decision or purchase context. In order to meet the relevance demand of customers, firms should be flexible and agile in their strategic deployment of resources and capabilities. By becoming relevant, a firm can create a win-win strategy of achieving higher value for both customers and the firm.

Customers		
Brick and Mortar Commerce	E-commerce	Social commerce

⇩

Relationship Marketing	Relevant Interactions and Collaborations: • At the Right time • Through the Right channels • In the Right context

⇧

Traditional CRM	E-CRM	Social CRM
Total CRM		

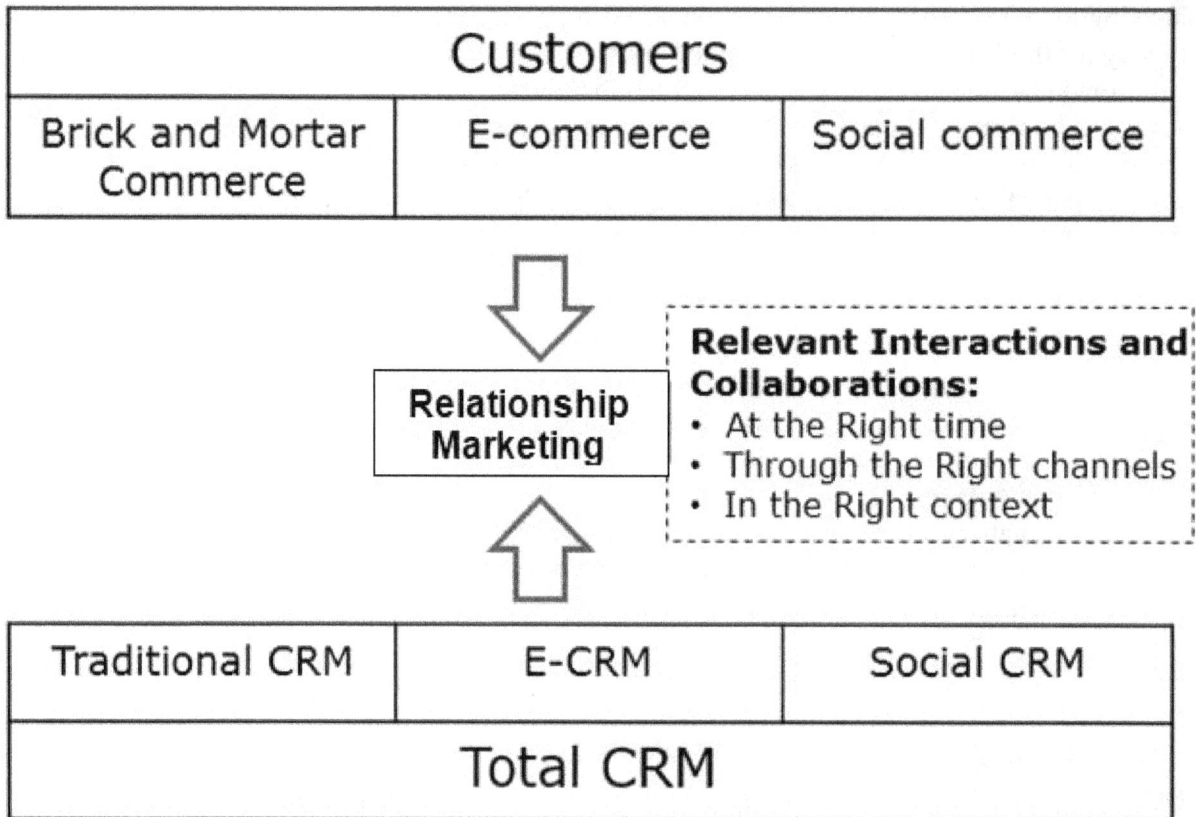

Figure 1.6: Achieving Relevance with Total CRM

It is important that the firm's digital presence, both the website and social media site pages, be relevant for the user searching for information and interacting with the brands, products, services, and/or organization. In this interactive context, being relevant can be achieved in many different ways. One example of the organization remaining relevant is by ensuring that the keywords the user chooses to enter into the search engine query matches the specific keywords the organization has chosen to focus. Being relevant is very important in the interactive inbound marketing process. What makes Facebook so powerful is that unlike Google, which currently works on search history and a proprietary algorithm, Facebook operates on real-time data, real names, real email addresses, real shared thoughts, tastes, and news. Facebook has a shot at mastering targeted contextual advertising, which would become an irresistible opportunity for marketers because of the richness of the profile data that you can leverage. Facebook has evolved from a being simply a social networking tool to a communication platform and is now becoming a social operating system. Key components of being relevant on the internet and social media environment include performing keyword research, ensuring website landing pages are accurate and focused, and targeting digital advertising campaigns to the right target visitors. It is important for the firm to ensure that their right message is targeted to just the right market.

Keywords match the interests of the user to various web pages and social media contents, and are specific to the firm search strategy. More and more customers are finding businesses online through search engines. They find these businesses through keywords. Fortunately, the firm can optimize their website around keywords that are relevant to their business. This will increase their chances of getting found by people searching with those keywords, which will drive more and better quality leads for the business." With the efforts of total CRM, firms can keep track of their customers, understand how to interact with them, and gain insights regarding the nature of their relationships.

In addition to the traditional CRM and e-CRM efforts, firms are increasingly adopting social CRM initiatives. Social CRM started with the discovery and utilization of collaborative approaches. It then moved to the monitoring customer conversations and user-generated content. Social CRM focuses on first listening to the customers, analyzing the relevant conversation and user-generated content to come up with insights, and developing customer engagement strategies using these insights. These capabilities can help an organization better track, assess, and improve customer engagement and make their interactions and engagement more relevant. This relevance can provide competitive advantage to organization with greater total CRM capabilities.

Relationship Marketing

It is important to understand the nature of relationship marketing and how it relates to CRM. Many academics and practitioners provide a wide variety of definitions and goals of relationship marketing. Relationship marketing is considered a facet of customer relationship management that focuses on customer loyalty and long-term customer engagement rather than short-term goals such as customer acquisition and individual sales.[41] Relationship marketing can be a form of marketing that highlights customer retention and satisfaction rather than sales transactions and recognizes the long-term value of customer relationships.[42] Relationship marketing must be considered as a long-term strategy that focuses on building customer relationships, customer loyalty, and brand value through relationship marketing strategies and activities.[43]

While various definitions of relationship marketing exist, the components or features that are commonly included are described next. First, relationship marketing recognizes the value of customer loyalty and long term customer engagement. Long-term customers are less likely to switch products and less price-sensitive leading to more stable unit sales volume and increased sales dollar amount. Customer acquisition is more expensive than customer retention. Relationship marketing enhances customer retention over the long term and builds up customer loyalty. Loyal customers are valuable assets to firms and allow them to make more profit in the long run with higher customer retention rates. They are also less likely to switch brands and remain as long-term and loyal buyers.

Second, relationship marketing values a strong, emotional connection to brand. In building meaningful customer relationships, relationship marketing cultivates greater engagement and emotional connections with brands. The strong emotional brand connections can bring more consistent sales and a greater customer lifetime value. The relationship can be strengthened by offering new features and brand offerings that can satisfy the unmet needs of the customers.

Third, relationship marketing utilizes customer life time value approach to identify and target profitable customer and maximizes customer equity. Life time value approach calculates the value of sustained customers to a firm. Life time value represents a prediction of the net profit from relationship of a customer with the firm. Relationship marketing creates loyal customers leading to repeat purchases and a higher customer life time value. If firms extend the life time value to all customers, customer equity can be calculated. Customer equity shows the total value of all customers of a firm over the expected life of each customer. Relationship marketing concentrates on increasing customer equity with relevant marketing strategies and programs. Customer equity can be increased with loyal customers who can recommend products and services to others.

Fourth, relationship marketing puts an emphasis on effective customer experience management. Relationship marketing is built on the concept of customer experience. Managing customer experience effectively helps firms improve customer interactions through a better understanding of customers' pain points in every stage of customer interaction process. Effective customer experience management can foster stronger brand loyalty. Relationship marketing recognizes the importance of the customer experience for every current customer. Relationship marketing can help firms provide relevant and exceptional experience at every stage of the customer experience journey. This relevant and exceptional experience will make customers show their trust, loyalty, repeated purchase leading to a higher life time value. If firms understand their customers and can solve their pain points in their experience journey, customers will be more likely to remain loyal and become advocates of brands and products.

Finally, relationship marketing relies on customer data management to achieve tailored access to targeted information. As relationship marketing involves two-way communications between customers and the firms, thus firms can be in a better position to track customer activities and provide tailored information to customers based on marketing analytics. With better marketing analytics and richer big data, firms can design and offer relevant customer experience and provide customized and one-to-one customer care. With customer insights generated from big data, firms can implement relationship marketing to demonstrate how much they care about customers.

Total CRM Based Relationship Marketing Template

Template 1.1: Relationship Marketing Program Organizational Readiness Diagnostics

Template 1.1 measures a firm's organizational readiness to implement relationship marketing programs.

Diagnostics Items[44]	Response[a]
Business Alignment	
Every relationship marketing investment is justified by a reasonable case with measurable projected benefits.	1　2　3　4　5
Every relationship marketing investment has a sponsor who is adequately involved in project scoping and oversight.	1　2　3　4　5
Program Coordination	
Our firm forms a central cross-functional group to coordinate relationship marketing efforts to identify opportunities for process and technology reuse.	1　2　3　4　5
Performance criteria and incentives for marketing managers steering relationship marketing program deployment focus on specific customer goals.	1　2　3　4　5
Our firm maintains a multiyear relationship marketing work plan,	1　2　3　4　5
Our firm charters a relationship marketing competency center to support relationship marketing programs and serve as a conduit for external sources for relationship marketing expertise.	1　2　3　4　5
Marketing Personnel Readiness	
Our firm redefines roles and responsibilities for marketing, sales and service staff to include the capture, analysis and use of information on individual customers.	1　2　3　4　5
All sales and service staff are regularly trained and scripted to use each customer interaction to solicit information that deepens the firm's understanding of the customer.	1　2　3　4　5
All sales and service staff are incented to document accurately information that deepens the firm's understanding of the customer.	1　2　3　4　5
All marketing, sales and service staff are trained to use analysis of customer profitability and preferences.	1　2　3　4　5
Total Response Score[b]	

[a]Please circle a number that best indicates your perception of your firm using the following scale; (1 = Strongly Disagree; 2 = Slightly Disagree; 3 = Neutral; 4 = Slightly Agree; 5 = Strongly Agree).

[b]Please add all the circled numbers. The total score of 40 or higher shows the firm's full readiness for relationship marketing program implementation. The score between 30 and 39 indicates that your firm needs some organizational adjustment before implementation.

Template 1.2: Qualitative Assessment of Current Relationship Marketing Practices

Template 1.2 assesses the status of the firm's current relationship marketing practices and programs.

Qualitative Assessment Questions
1. Identify reasons (2 – 3) to move your firm toward relationship marketing.
2. Name the leading direct competitors to your firm that are implementing relationship marketing practices. List the practices you know of and their impact on your business.
3. What are the biggest obstacles to relationship marketing your firm is likely to encounter based on what you know so far? Identify the leader in your firm who will help you overcome these obstacles.
4. What are the biggest sources of customer dissatisfaction or complaints about your firm and your industry? Put an asterisk next to those you think can benefit from relationship marketing.
5. When your customers speak positively about your firm, what do they most often cite? Which of these items reflects relationship marketing practice as you know it?
6. Which area or function at your firm is weakest where customer relationships are concerned? What could your firm do most easily to strengthen this area?

Real World Application Cases

Case 1-1: Scientific and Chemical Supplies Ltd.[45]

Scientific and Chemical Supplies Ltd. is the leading supplier of scientific equipment in the education field as well as a major supplier to laboratories and industries including aerospace, automotive, pharmaceuticals, and food manufacturing. Despite being an international supplier to over sixty countries and being in business for over fifty years the company has maintained its focus on excellent customer service. In recent years the company has expanded its product line and won exclusive distribution agreements for innovative products. In addition, the international branch experienced rapid growth thanks to the acquisition of several large contracts. According to Operations Director, Philip Palser this was "all good news in business terms, of course, but it meant we had a lot to manage."

In order to maintain quality customer service with the growing customer base, Scientific and Chemical Supplies Ltd. found a solution in the UK software company SAGE and its product SAGE CRM. The user friendly SAGE CRM linked users in different functions into a single system. By doing so all transaction and communication history throughout the company could be pooled together allowing for a complete shared view of each customer. As a result customers can contact any branch of the company and any customer service coordinator can provide and share any needed information as well as handle any requests, quotations, or complaints that arise. In addition, SAGE CRM also allows purchasing representatives to obtain product and tracking information without ever having to make a phone call.

Not only does the CRM software allow for improved customer service but, it also allows managers to have at-a-glance information for their division on performance indicators, shipping orders, and budget data. SAGE CRM also allows for vital customer information to be sent to sales teams as they meet with clients. Since implementing its CRM strategy, Scientific and Chemical Supplies Ltd. has experienced an increased efficiency and effectiveness of its employees which has in turn increased consumer confidence in the company as a major supplier which has led to rapid growth.

Case Questions

1. What metrics do you recommend that Scientific and Chemical Supplies ltd. use to ensure their customer relationship process works effectively?

2. How did the purchase of CRM products make Scientific and Chemical Supplies ltd. improve its customer focus and gain competitive advantage?

3. If you worked for Scientific and Chemical Supplies ltd., what additional CRM initiatives would you implement to enhance relevance to customers?

Case 1-2: Calia Salotti[46]

Creating a visual representation of the organization's strategic intent helps the marketing managers understand how the various organizational resources can be used to create value. These visual representations can take the form of either a strategy map or a value creation map. Each visualization technique can be used to complement the other.

Strategy maps are tools to chart how intangible assets are converted into tangible outcomes. Strategy maps provide the marketing managers with a clear line into how their jobs are linked to the overall objectives of the organization. The strategy map provides a visual representation of the objectives and relationships among them that drives performance. Strategy maps show how an organization will convert its initiatives and resources into tangible outcomes.

Organizations perform well and create value for their stakeholders when they implement strategies that respond to market opportunities by exploiting their internal resources and capabilities. Traditionally, organizational resources or assets were viewed as being physical in nature. Recently, however, intellectual capital or organizational knowledge was identified as an important resource affecting organizational performance. By using the strategy map, the marketing manager can visually highlight how the various organizational causal relationships work. The strategy map has various outcome measures linked to identify performance drivers in a cause-and-effect manner. However, the marketing manager needs to understand how these various organizational processes and resources interact to inhibit or create value.

The organization can be viewed as a bundle of resources or tangible and intangible assets in which the various assets depend upon each other to create value. The contribution of one organizational asset, such as technology, can rarely be expressed independently from other organizational assets, such as skills or culture. The value that is generated or inhibited is a function of the manner in which the organizational resources are managed and deployed.

The organization possesses knowledge-based or information-based assets. These assets are invisible assets in the organization. These invisible assets include technology, consumer trust, brand image, corporate culture, and employee skills as well as management skills. These invisible knowledge-based assets can be thought of as those assets whose essence is an idea or concept and whose nature can be defined and recorded in some way. These invisible or intangible assets are used to drive sustainable competitive advantage and can be defined as the sum of everything everybody in the organization knows. These intellectual assets, then, provide the competitive edge for the organization in the marketplace.

Calia Salotti, SPA is an upholstered furniture manufacturer located Matera, Italy. It designs, manufacturers, and markets residential upholstered furniture that is primarily sold in Europe and North America. Calia Salotti has over 600 employees and manufacturers approximately 250 different models of upholstered furniture. The management team at Calia Salotti has determined that new product development (NPD) is one of its key core competencies and believes that the craftsmanship of its workers provides it with a competitive advantage in the highly competitive furniture marketplace.

The various products manufactured by Calia Salotti have a brief, limited life cycle. The life cycle is brief since the products are highly stylistic. For this reason, continued success in the marketplace requires the NPD process at Calia Salotti to be clearly focused on the customer requirements and requires a strong focus on time-to-market as a key measurement objective.

The NPD process at Calia Salotti is characterized as a non-formalized process. Those in charge of the NPD combine different tangible and intangible assets to develop new products. It is dependent on the tacit knowledge and creative intuition of key individuals. The management team wanted to focus on improving this process. To develop a value creation map, they chose time-to-market as the performance improvement variable. The components of this variable included the number of iterations between design and production and the time to develop a prototype of a new model. It was determined that the conformity of the prototype product to the product design was the key dimension in the process requiring improvement. The five drivers of performance were identified and their relationship to the overall identified performance variable determined. By examining each of the drivers, various problems were identified that needed to be addressed.

These initiatives were implemented at Calia enabling NPD to be measured and improved. As a result, the time to prototype a new model and number of iterations performance indicators were significantly improved.

Case Questions

1. How does mapping the value creation process improve the understanding of the strategy map and ultimately, the overall strategic direction of the firm?

2. What are other examples of how knowledge influences an organization's competitive advantage?

3. What performance measures should be used when shifting from product focus to customer relationship focus?

Chapter 2. Foundations for Relationship Marketing

Relationship marketing is built upon two fundamental foundations. These two foundations are the customer relationship management philosophy and analytics driven marketing decision-making. This chapter discusses the concept and framework of customer relationship management and issues related to customer and marketing analytics generation, utilization, and dissemination. Customer relationship management also relies heavily on this analytics approach that is built upon big data, business analytics, and customer relationship management analytics tools and technology.

Section 1. Customer Relationship Management Perspectives and Components

"Change before you have to."
Jack Welch

Three CRM Perspectives

The term Customer Relationship Management, otherwise known as CRM, came into usage in the mid-1990's, and refers to the information technology component of customer relationships. This can include all kinds of different information sources, including direct mail, loyalty card schemes, data bases, help desks, and contact centers. However, there are multiple perspectives on the true scope and depth of the concept.[1] To begin our discussion of CRM, we will consider three most common perspectives, and determine one that best exemplifies the idea.[2]

Perspective 1

CRM can be defined narrowly as the implementation of CRM software or technological tools.[3] As an example, consider a firm setting up a sales force automation software package. This type of software allows salespeople to keep in contact with their employers, update information about customers, and track the status of orders over time, as well as helping managers better manage their salespeople. Due to the reduction of redundancy and time, there are significant benefits to be gained from implementing the software. Firms need to manage the relationship with each and every customer, and to make each relationship as profitable as possible. Those firms that are successful will find increased revenue at lower cost of sales and marketing, and decreased cost from lost customers and ineffective sales and marketing. The methodology or software that makes this possible is viewed as CRM. Thus, a firm that views CRM narrowly sees the predominant method of enhancing customer relationships through software applications.

As CRM is a process, technology is just one element of CRM[4]. While well-implemented CRM platform as technology solution is vital to operationalize information-based customer strategies, significant institutional obstacles remain that must be addressed jointly by corporate IT and the business through changes to process, governance and incentives. There are problems technology can help remedy. CRM applications can help remove six obstacles to capturing, integrating, analyzing and disseminating information on individual customers. Technology can be deployed in each channel to solicit and capture more customer information. Data consolidation is supported by integrating legacy data silos and by providing robust links between geographically dispersed staff and channel partners. Finally, user-friendly desktop analytical tools aid staff in analyzing customer needs and matching them to promotions or products, thus deriving value from customer data without waiting for assistance from an overworked central analysis team.

However, there are problems technology cannot remedy. Even the most technically successful CRM implementation is likely to produce little return if a series of organizational obstacles are not overcome. The firm may fail to capture adequate customer data if sales and services staff are not given the necessary training and incentives. While the technical obstacles to consolidating siloed data can be overcome with integration tools, the task remains problematic without efforts to standardize customer codes, data formats and rules - running the classic risk of "garbage in, garbage out." Moreover, business unit owners of the data may resist data consolidation until questions about customer ownership are clarified. Channel partners may show equal reluctance to share data until their fears of disintermediation are assuaged. Firms may fail to use customer data effectively until marketing and sales staff are trained to create and use customer analytics, and until their incentives and job descriptions change to reflect this new role. A further barrier can arise if users of existing customized analytics refuse to migrate to standard analytics reports. Finally, as data access is democratized, pioneers point to the importance of establishing mechanisms to coordinate customer touchpoints and privacy promises across all data users.

Perspective 2

Looking at the perspective 1, it is clear that there is merit to the argument of CRM software implementation. A single, well thought out software upgrade can help improve customer relationships dramatically. However, more tangible benefits can be gained by moving to CRM perspective 2. Under this perspective 2, CRM is viewed as a series of upgrades or capacity to benefit customers.[5] Here, care is taken to make a larger plan of the change, and roll out each successive step in a way that builds up the company smoothly. Customer relationship management provides the framework for analyzing customer profitability and improving marketing effectiveness. In order to stay competitive, firms develop strategies to become customer-focused, customer-driven, and customer-centric. All these terms define the firms' desire to build lasting customer relationships. CRM is viewed as a solution that makes these efforts valuable to the company and the customer alike, so that customers don't view these efforts as trivial or useless.

Perspective 3

The most strategically-oriented perspective on CRM is perspective 3. In this perspective, CRM is views as a strategy or philosophy.[6] As such, the effect of the change is viewed throughout the entire company, and the rollout is made part of the firm's strategic plan. Most importantly, the CRM initiative is not looked at as an IT strategy, but instead represents a strong level of understanding at a corporate level of what drives customer value.

Under this perspective 3, CRM is defined as encompassing all processes to capture, integrate, analyze and disseminate information on individual customers to boost the effectiveness of customer-facing functions and maximize the lifetime value of customer relationships. The processes are those needed to enable customer information based responses. When various firms implement diverse CRM initiatives, these initiatives are shaped by the specifics of a firm's customer base, product offerings, and nature of business. As a result, a tight definition of CRM becomes impractical. Many executive meetings on CRM have been sidetracked by debates over whether efforts such as sales force automation, database marketing and even e-business are subsets of CRM. These efforts need to be considered as merely a part of broader undertakings of CRM. Under this broader perspective of CRM, CRM can be inclusive of enterprise philosophy, management discipline, business model or strategy, methodology or software, and customer information based response.

When firms consider CRM as the enterprise philosophy or management discipline, its adoption means a new order of things for most firms and requires careful planning, an understanding of CRM critical success factors, and an ability to manage these success factors while continuing to facilitate change. This is why money and a mandate alone may not be enough for successful implementation of CRM. Through enterprise-wide CRM efforts, firms attempt to better coordinate customer contact points, so that the enterprise can more efficiently manage its marketing resources and establish more meaningful relationships with its customers. Effective customer relationship management requires an understanding of what this relationship entails, an ability to provide personalized services, a means for building mutual value and respect, and a commitment to the relationship itself. CRM allows firms to better discriminate and more efficiently allocate resources to their most-desirable customers. The caveat, however, is that as CRM matures, many firms will compete for the same set of attractive customers. Because most customers tend to have only a handful of meaningful relationships, some firms will lose their existing customers. Thus, the need and the capability to develop, maintain and continuously execute effective customer relationship programs are paramount.

As CRM is considered a strategic process, CRM cannot be viewed as a simple software solution that is used to acquire and grow a customer base. It requires a synthesis of strategic vision with customer management. It requires a corporate understanding of the nature of customer value in a multi-channel environment. It also requires the utilization of the marketing analytics and CRM application tools along with customized support for operation, fulfillment, and service. As this is the most long-term, broad definition of CRM, it is the chosen perspective that will be used in this text.

Customer relationship management can be defined as "a strategic process that uses cross functional integration and information technology to identify, gather information about, improve relationships with, and maximize value for key customer segments."[7] The full definition of CRM must include components focused on all of the requirements of a well-integrated customer relationship strategy. Thus, it must include each of the following components:

1) Identifying key customer segments,
2) Gathering useful information about these customers and segments,
3) Using IT to enhance interactions and relationships with these key groups,
4) Creating value for both the firm and customers,
5) Requiring cross-functional coordination within and outside of the marketing department, and
6) Focusing on creating shareholder value.

It is important to note the portion of the definition that refers to "key" customer segments. Remember the "80-20 Rule": 80% of the revenues are from 20% of the customers in many firms. Identifying and managing relationships with these valuable segments of customers is crucial for business success. CRM is a strategic process that focuses on creating increased shareholder value by developing and maintaining relevant relationships with key customers and customer segments. CRM allows firms to achieve full potential of relationship marketing strategies and effective information management by creating profitable and long-term relationships with customers and key stakeholders of the firm. CRM facilitates understanding of customers and co-creation of value with customers through a cross-functional integration of processes, people, operations, and marketing capabilities.[8]

Architecture of CRM

A typical CRM architecture offers integrated automation of business processes and encompasses all relevant customer touchpoints. This includes sales, contact management, campaign management, telemarketing, customer service, contact center, and field service. The architecture also accommodates various customer channels such as physical store, catalogue, and on-line stores. It is important to ensure that customers will receive identical delightful experience regardless of the channels used. The CRM architecture will also integrate the customer information flowing through various customer touch points and channels. Three distinct components of CRM have been widely accepted and used by marketing managers to understand CRM and to serve the customer better.[9] Figure 2.1 shows the three components of CRM architecture: operational CRM, analytical CRM, and collaborative CRM.[10]

Operational CRM

The Operational CRM component is concerned with the automation of integrated business processes related to various customer touchpoints. This involves the integration between the front-office and back-office applications and handles the customer contact and processing. It synchronizes customer interactions in marketing, sales, and service. This component offers multiple touchpoints or contact points for customer communication and brings efficiencies to customer interactions. Traditional applications in this component area include sales force automation (SFA) and customer service enhancement tools such as customer service and call center management. The operational CRM component improves day-to-day operations. This component requires manual interfaces with other operational systems such as order processing, billing, and inventory management. This component generates data showing what activities have occurred but it does not offer any explanations regarding their cause or impact. Unfortunately, many firms consider only this component as CRM initiatives and miss the real impact and benefits of CRM. While operational CRM does provide some business value by improving customer contact efficiencies, it does not improve the firm's understanding of its customers and cannot contribute to a firm's effort to strengthen its relationship with customers.

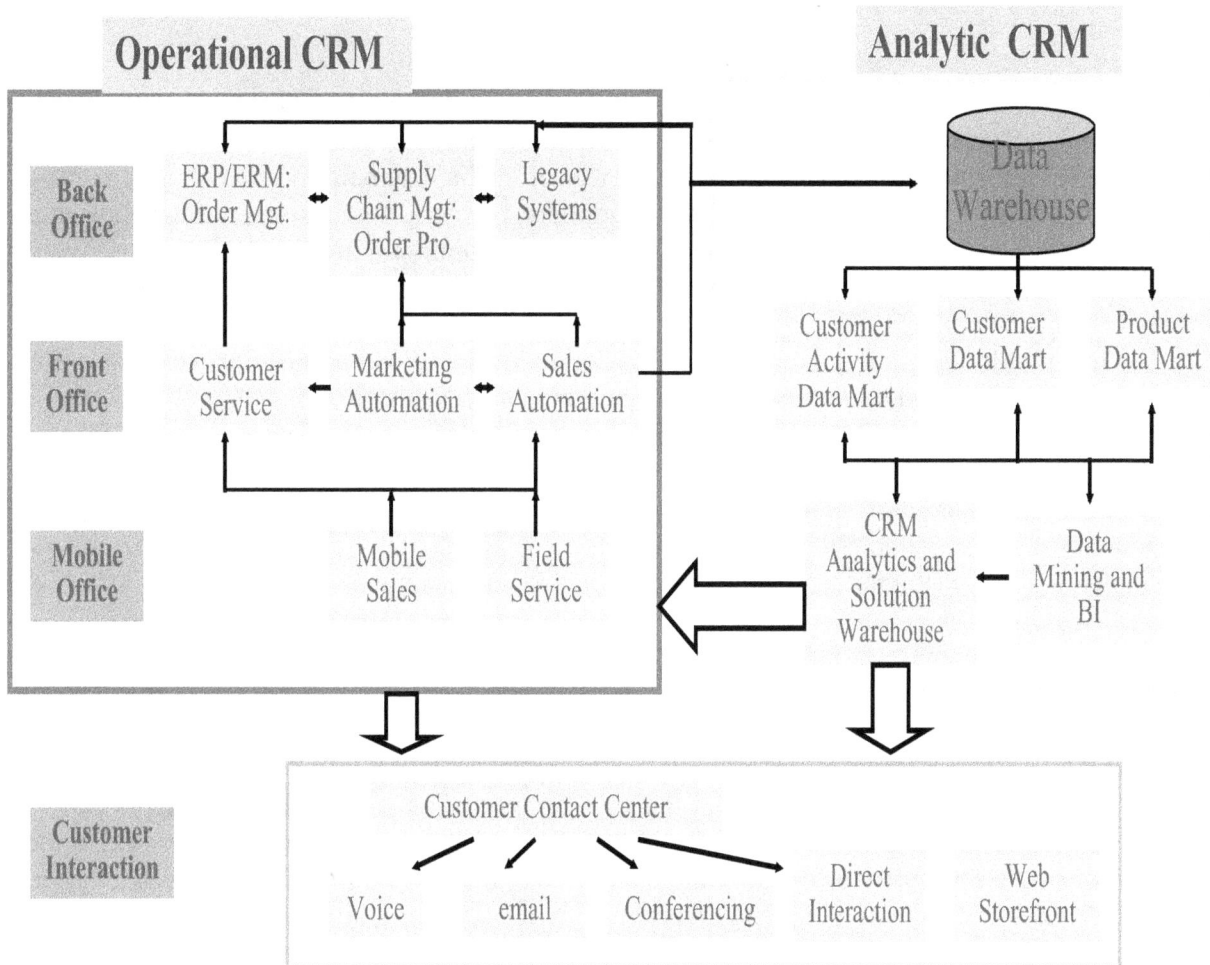

Figure 2.1: Typical CRM Architecture

Analytical CRM

The analytical CRM component deals with the analysis of big data for the purpose of achieving greater marketing and business performance. It is related to the analysis, modeling, and evaluation of big data stored in the firm's data warehouse or data marts, and the generation of customer insights useful for creating mutually beneficial relationships between the firm and its customers. The analytical CRM component allows firms to optimize information sources for a better understanding of customers and to enable the contacts with the customer to be highly personalized. Analytical CRM provides marketing analytics and is built upon data warehouses and data marts. The data warehouses hold cleansed customer data with the documentation of its source, transformation rules, calculations, and analytic models. Data marts are subset of the data warehouse. Analytic CRM is the most critical component to the successful implementation of CRM. The marketing analytics solutions and intelligence generated from this component enable the effective management of a customer relationship. With the generated marketing and customer analytics, firms can begin to understand customer behaviors, identify buying patterns and trends, discover causal relationships, and accurately model and predict future customer satisfaction and behavior. It lays a quantified foundation for fact-based strategic marketing decision-making.

Collaborative CRM

The collaborative CRM component focuses on the collaborative interfaces that facilitate a firm's interactions with its customers and other stakeholders. It improves the delivery and management of communications with customers through a variety of media channels and touchpoints. It also enables collaboration between the firm and its suppliers, partners, and customers for improving the value chain processes to better serve customers. Collaborative CRM services and infrastructure components allow firms to make efficient interactions between the firm and its channels. This component ties the internal and external customer facing arms of a firm together to make teamwork easier and more productive. Collaborative CRM solutions provide the means for strategic decisions to be implemented and integrated across customer facing activities.

Each CRM component is dependent on the others. In the past, firms focused on improving the operational and collaborative components of CRM. Firms, however, realized that the analytical component is necessary and critical to drive the strategic and tactical relationship marketing decisions regarding customer acquisition, retention, and enhancement.

Rethinking Customer Relationship Management

With many firms are implementing CRM, firms are facing the harsh reality of increased pressure on profitability. With CRM initiatives, firms now can measure influence on the profitability of each customer. This is possible because of the development of new technology and tools that provides a unique opportunity that many firms are rushing to exploit. These firms are seeking to move from single sales models to continuing selling relationships with their customers. They are seeking to understand how to build and maintain a loyal customer relationship, and to discover the most profitable way to build that relationship. Unfortunately, only a small portion of a customer's positive feelings and loyalty are generated by your products. The rest comes from the intangibles such as service, store experience, websites, and social media platforms. Firms need to know their customers' preferences for products as well as style, service, image, and communications. Firms are nowadays spending far more money than before to get a new customer than to retain an existing customer. It is also becoming far more expensive to win back a customer after they have left than it is to keep them satisfied in the first place. While some customers are vastly more profitable than other customers, some customers are unprofitable, and some customers are unprofitable and will never be profitable. CRM allows firms to better discriminate and to more efficiently allocate resources to their most-desirable customers. With the increased adoption of CRM by firms, many firms will end up competing for the same set of attractive customers. In recent years, a firm's profitability per customer or product has decreased. This puts tremendous pressure on customer profitability. Firms are trying to defend customer profitability in any way possible by adopting and implementing CRM creatively.[11]

Defending Customer Profitability

Firms are seeking to leverage information on individual customers to counter mounting pressure on customer profitability. The firms are pursuing information-based strategies that rely on a deep understanding of the profitability, preferences and transaction history of individual customers to increase product value and improve the effectiveness of marketing, sales and service. These information-based customer strategies are especially critical in addressing areas of pressure on customer profitability. Firms are experiencing rising customer acquisition costs and customer turnover. As the effectiveness of traditional marketing and sales tactics diminishes, firms are holding down customer acquisition costs by personalizing marketing and sales. Recognizing that additional sales to existing customers are estimated to be less than half of the cost of acquiring a new customer, firms are developing targeted cross-selling capabilities. Even with the significant focus on customer retention, customer turnovers are reported to be rising in many industries. To counter rising customer defections driven by heightened competition and improved price transparency, firms are investing in evaluating defection risk and deploying retention offers shaped by individual customer value and preferences. They are also providing information-based product support to embed themselves in customer work flows. With the increased acquisition costs and higher customer turnover, the cost to serve customers is also rising. As greater customer scale, increased price transparency and experiments with auction-based purchasing force greater price competitiveness, firms are compelled to find cost reduction opportunities. For example, firms can lead value-based customers to self-service and increase service staff productivity as a response to profitability pressure. Faced with the threat of product commoditization, firms are seeking to differentiate themselves by adding value through product customization and the provision of information-based services such as personalized support, usage data, analytical tools and consumption benchmarks. Further differentiation stems from product innovation based on a greater understanding of customer data to expedite the development cycle.

Common CRM Objectives

A set of core CRM objectives can be identified by their complexity and impact on life time customer profitability. Four common objectives of CRM initiatives are discussed next.[12] First, CRM can be used to reduce cost to serve customers. For example, CRM initiatives aimed at online self-service or customer demand signal capture can be used to achieve this objective. Online self-service can reduce the cost to serve while customer demand signal capture can cut inventory and stock outs. Using customer data proactively can help firms avoid costly ordering errors. Second, CRM can enhance productivity. Sales force, channel partner and new product development productivity can be gained with CRM implementation. Third, CRM can identify and build renewable revenue streams. Firms can leverage CRM capabilities to develop new revenue streams. Using granular knowledge about customer preference and consumption patterns, firms seek to support customer workflows, provide higher value through product integration, and mitigate revenue from product to services by selling solutions based on response sensing. CRM allows firms to implement one to one relationship marketing. CRM for one to one marketing, sales and service remains a long term goals of many B2C and B2B firms .These firms can benefit from CRM with the increased marketing and sales productivity through better targeting, and increased revenue from improved price realization, heightened retention and cross sales.

Critical Success Factors for CRM

The critical success factors for CRM are something firms must do exceedingly well to succeed in the short-run and thrive in the long-run. Many executives are familiar with the concept of critical success factors because project scope documents routinely prioritize these issues in terms of risk factors. These risk factors are often issues that may endanger the ability to perform a necessary task well. Typical CRM project risk factors include the inability to obtain sufficient resources for the duration of a project due to other competing projects, or the lack of experience in a particular new technology, such as CRM software expertise. Business executives also identify critical issues when setting corporate or product goals and objectives. These issues can endanger the organization's ability to achieve its objectives and typically qualify strategic goals as follows: the revenue goals for this product line are dependent on the organization's ability to be first to market with a new service, or the increase in corporate profit is dependent on a change in government regulations currently prohibiting expansion across geographic boundaries. Dealing with CRM requires both business executives and technologists to change their perspectives on what constitutes a critical success factor. When technologists build customer-oriented systems, they can no longer look only at traditional concerns such as resource constraints or technical skill sets. Similarly, when business executives implement CRM corporate strategies, they must broaden their view to include more than external factors or specific technology constraints. Five mostly commonly cited success factors for CRM are presented next.[13]

First, the most critical success factor in CRM implementation is the coordinated, customer-focused business strategy. The firm must have business strategies that promote CRM across functional boundaries. To succeed, these strategies must be understood and accepted throughout the firm. As illustrated, a firm can have an enterprise goal to become more customer-focused or to increase customer satisfaction. However, if no underlying strategies are in place that force a customer view across business functions, the firm is not likely to move far from the traditional product focus. The key here is to avoid getting caught up in semantics: "Is this a goal or a strategy?" Instead, firms should use the organization goals as a starting point in the assessment. Ask first, "Do we need cross-functional strategies or action plans to achieve these goals?" If the answer is yes, then begin looking for the supporting detail steps or strategies as well. If no formal action plans have been made, firms have some work to do before it can successfully implement CRM initiatives. Firms must have business strategies that promote CRM across functional boundaries. In this case, the goals of the firm need to be providing customized services, increasing customer satisfaction and loyalty, and retaining valuable customers. The customer relationship marketing strategies or action plans must include customizing product packaging and pricing, making multiple billing options available, providing consistent service levels across multiple channels, and supporting one-call or one-click services across all product lines.

Second, creating a CRM-friendly organization structure is the next important success factor. The overall organizational structure must promote cross-functional cooperation. It can be hard to achieve CRM objectives like increased customer loyalty if the organization doesn't support coordinated processes and quality across independent business lines. Organization structure can also have a strong impact on technology. A decentralized organization makes it difficult to provide coordinated customer service. If each business unit has its own procedures for handling collections, it will be difficult to ensure that business units always check for the VIP indicator prior to sending a nasty letter. It can also be difficult to implement new CRM-friendly procedures to fix such problems. The inability to coordinate across multiple areas can, in turn, impact the quality and consistency of service that a customer receives from one product to another. For example, to change the billing information, a customer may be forced to make a separate call for each product purchased. What can be worse for satisfaction and loyalty than actually penalizing your best customers for owning multiple products?

Consider the following example where the separation of the frequent flier service center from the reservations center costs a major airline a very profitable customer: A consultant we know, who flies about 20,000 miles a month, recently had an experience with a major airline that antagonized him so much that he now refuses to fly this airline. As the consultant was making a reservation, the customer service representative tried to confirm his phone number. As it turns out, the phone number on the airline's record was a number that was cancelled 10 years ago, and the consultant had been providing the corrected number every time he made a reservation. The consultant provided the correct number (again) and requested that the airline update his permanent record and stop asking him this question. The customer service representative replied that she could only put the number in this particular reservation, and in order to change the number permanently, he would have to call the Frequent Flyer desk and update the information there. Understandably annoyed, the consultant informed her of his frequent flier status, and once again requested that the airline take care of this small matter. When the consultant was again told to call the Frequent Flier desk, his response was, "Not only do I not have to call the Frequent Flier desk, I don't have to call your airline ever again." In this case, the airline had the opportunity to gain the loyalty of a very profitable customer, but because of non-integrated systems, and because the service representative could not or would not step outside the normal business process to assist the customer, the airline lost him as a customer. In the preceding example, several factors contributed to the problem experienced by the customer. First, the service representative did not have access to the appropriate systems to change the customer's profile. Second, the service center and the Frequent Flier desk were completely independent organizations with no coordination or cooperation facilitated. Third, no business processes were designed to deal with the situation when a customer might expect to cross between the two service organizations. The fact that the customer took all his business elsewhere can be the expected outcome if the organization's structure is one that actually inhibits cross-functional coordination.

The third critical success factor is a CRM-savvy organization culture. Changing an organizational culture is a difficult task. The organization tends to continue on its traditional course. Change does not occur until the firm brings in an effective change agent such as a CRM expert from the outside. The change agent had to identify key employees at all levels within the company and work with these individuals to effect the change to CRM. Chances are that the culture for adopting change in this firm must be one of bottom-up, or middle-up-and-down change, rather than top-down change. History is usually a good indicator of future success. Because CRM may require changes in organization structure, business strategy, and customer systems, the history of change in a firm is particularly pertinent when assessing CRM readiness. How is change effected within your organization? The communications company that opens this section is a good example of this question in action. This company affected change from the bottom-up, with key employees sold on the change and added to the change-planning process. The senior management brought an outside change agent into the organization and established the authority to mandate the change. An equally viable alternative is to identify key change agents within the company and solicit their support for CRM change. Thought leaders in the firm are typically good drivers for change. These thought leaders are found at all levels within the firm; they should be identified and included in the planning process. If the change agents within a firm are not CRM experts, CRM expertise should be actively recruited in the form of consultants or new employees.

The fourth critical success factor is implementing an integrated customer information environment. As CRM requires integrated customer information at the enterprise level, firms need to facilitate the integration of customer information. Without comprehensive customer information, CRM business processes cannot be enabled to meet the increased demand to share customer information across business units. For the following insurance company example, after conducting several informal initiatives to help the top-producing agents better understand their customers, this firm determines that the available customer information was inadequate and not well distributed. Agents had extensive information about their individual customers that, if shared with marketing, would dramatically improve the quality of marketing analyses, leading in turn to more effective marketing campaigns and more profitable customers. Marketing had analysis capabilities and customer segmentation models that could be applied to an agent's customer base to enable that agent to understand the characteristics of their profitable customers and apply these characteristics when looking for new prospects. Marketing and the agent base agreed that an enterprise customer file, shared between the two groups, would resolve the problem and provide significant additional benefits. Higher profitability, better cross sales, and improved rapport between the agents and the insurance company were among the identified benefits. Marketing obtained support from the agents, customer service, and product development; prepared a solid business case; and asked for funding at the quarterly meeting of the CEO and his executives. Despite the vocal and enthusiastic support from all the business units, the CEO determined that an infrastructure project did not warrant the expenditure and vetoed the project.

The Marketing Department of a large national bank maintained an extensive marketing database to support customer and household analysis. This marketing database had numerous deficiencies: little historical information, no ability for campaign tracking, and a time lag of six weeks between database updates. In addition, the structure and complexity of the database limited access to a few computer-savvy marketing analysts. Marketing determined that a customer-oriented data warehouse would yield great benefits and eliminate the information bottleneck caused by the current limited access. When approached with the proposal to build the data warehouse, the managing director, a strong CRM proponent, was in full agreement. Not only did he agree to fund the endeavor, but he also gently but clearly mandated that all business areas provide funding and resources for the project. This firm went on to build one of the early banking data warehouses and is a CRM leader today.

The final critical success factor is executive commitment and support. An executive mandate is one of the most important factors in CRM success. Executive support facilitates the sweeping change required to attain CRM reality. Without executive backing, it is almost impossible to implement cross-functional business strategies, adopt a CRM-friendly structure and culture, and fund the integrated customer systems that support CRM.

Section 2. Customer Relationship Management Process

"Most of what we call management consists of making it difficult for people to get their work done."
        Peter Drucker

Now that we have an operational definition of Customer Relationship Management, the next step is to identify the various processes that are required to successfully implement a CRM strategy for relationship marketing. In all, there are five overarching processes that make up the entire CRM initiative.[14] Figure 2.2 presents the customer relationship management process model. In order of implementations, the processes are CRM roadmap, customer value process, touchpoint integration and management, integrated customer information management, CRM performance and metrics assessment. While this seems to be a linear group of processes, it is in fact circular. The final process, CRM performance and metrics assessment, leads right back into the first process, CRM roadmap. Thus, the firm should always be striving to better meet customer needs. This framework identifies all critical aspects of strategic processes involving CRM and offers systematic and process-oriented steps of successful CRM implementation. Each of the CRM processes of the model will be discussed in detail.

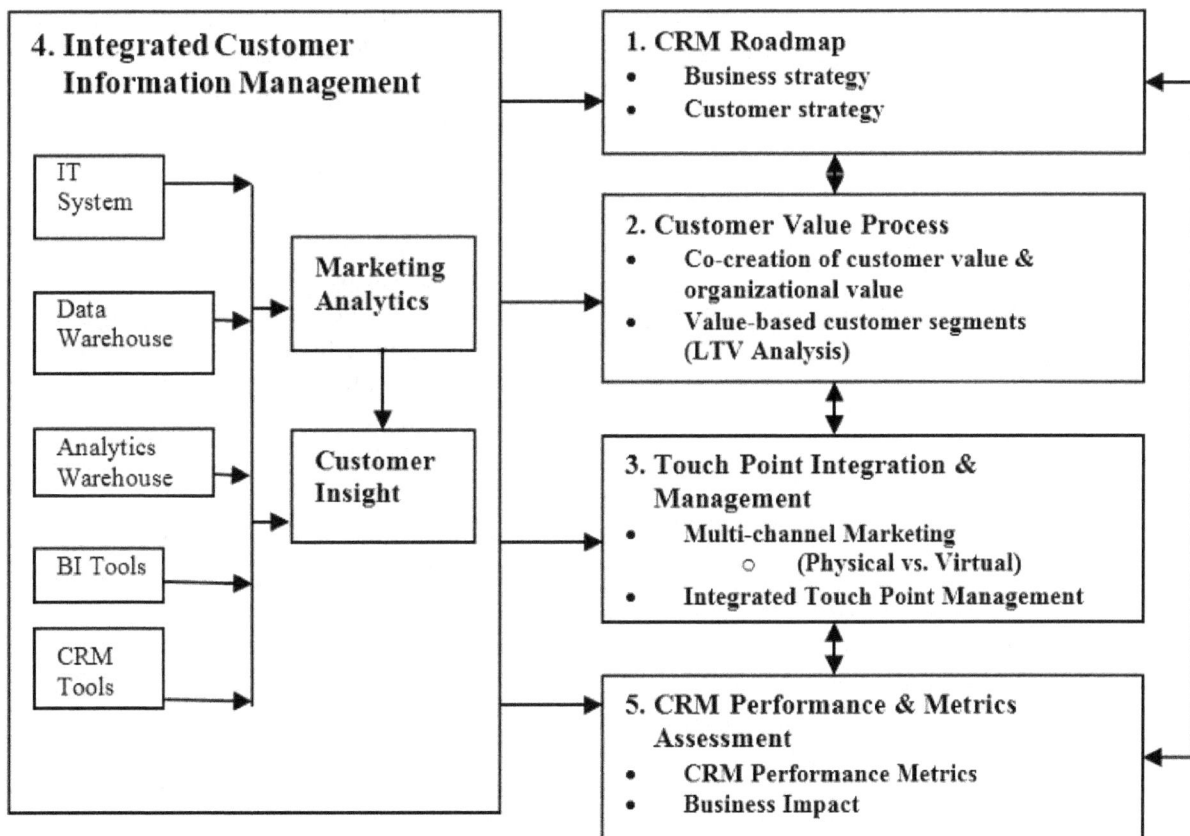

Figure 2.2: Customer Relationship Management Process Model

1. CRM Roadmap

The first step is for the firm to align two different strategies: its business strategy and its customer strategy. The business strategy is the firm's overarching strategy. When considering the business strategy, management should take into account the company's vision and mission, the competitive characteristics of the industry, and any other key external opportunities and threats to the company. The business strategy is normally determined by the board of directors and chief executives of the company.

The customer strategy, on the other hand, is more the responsibilities of the Marketing and, to a lesser extent, IT departments. This strategy is focused on trying to identify all potential customer groups, and determine what it will take for the company to reach these customers. Additionally, in this process, the firm should decide how targeted they want their customer segments to be. Should there only be a few global market segments, or should the company attempt to reach as close to one-on-one marketing as possible? This question is important for the firm to ponder.

To consider this more in depth, let us first look at the broadest possible segmentation type: the entire company targeting a single marketing segment. There are uses for analyzing customer interactions from this level. It is easy for managers to work with. Viewing the company from on high allows the company to get a good glimpse at the complete picture of the direction the company is heading and how to change if necessary. This method lends itself to benchmarking. As competitors have proprietary information regarding their individual segments, the firm can really only compare itself at a global level with any sense of certainty. Additionally, metrics such as the American Customer Satisfaction Index (ACSI) allow the firm to objectively compare their customer satisfaction figures to standards and rate themselves accordingly.

However, in most firms, the single segment model is not enough by itself. The firm-level model does not explain how individual customers and the relationships formed with them will be impacted by business decisions. For this analysis, segmentation is necessary. On the furthest end of the spectrum is one-on-one segmentation. This considers how business decisions could affect the profitability of every relationship in the firm and requires heavy information technology use. With today's advancements in technology, such a detailed one-on-one marketing is not impossible.

Still, care must be taken in determining whether this is a value-added activity for the firm. Currently, it is very difficult for companies to reach such a narrow, fine tuned level as one-on-one segmentation requires. Moreover, even if it is possible for the firm to reach such a micro view of its customer base, the costs of implementation may outweigh the benefits of undergoing such an effort. Thus, segment-based marketing is necessary in most situations. The difficult question lies in how far along the continuum of segmentation (from firm-level to individual customer-level) the company chooses to implement. For this reason, customer strategy and business strategy must be intertwined to create the most effective strategy for the firm.[15]

2. Customer Value Process

The next process is focused on the value exchange between customers and the firm. The value exchange is concerned with finding what customers value, how the firm can extract value from these customers, and how the firm can maximize the length and profitability of the relationship between the two parties.

In recent years, the view has been taken that customers should be looked at as co-creators and co-producers. The idea behind this is that customers place emphasis on certain attributes of a product. The firm must determine which attributes are key in the product, and thus which ones should be most worked on to please customers. In some products, this may simply mean making the product have high quality attributes. In others, the firm may have to allow for customization. When the customer is given the ability to customize, they are being made co-creators of the product, which will increase both the value they derive from it and the satisfaction they receive from it. To simplify the idea, the firm must develop a value proposition for its customers. This proposition will include the values of all products and services the firm offers, and how it will help co-create value for both the firm and the customer. In order to properly assign a value proposition, the firm must assess and compare the needs of different customer segments.

The next perspective to consider is how the firm gains value from customers. As stated in the strategy development step, it is important to understand where the profitable customer segments are for the firm, both current and potential customers. Next, the firm must consider the costs of customer retention and customer acquisition. Special attention must be kept regarding the costs and ability of the firm to make customers buy other products beyond their current catalog of purchases, as well as the ability of the firm to make customers buy more up-scale models.

The impact of retention rates (a by-product of creating customer value and maintaining customer relationships) has a greater impact on both firm and customer value than either the firm's overall discount rate or cost of capital. For this reason, it is important to treat customers as assets. Investments in customers need to be viewed as investments in assets rather than simply as expenses. Moreover, lowering costs to customers as a means of acquisition does not help increase firm value significantly. Thus, the company must determine which customers provide the most value to the firm and focus on these customers.[16]

An example of a firm that has well-aligned its needs with its customers' needs is BMW. As a leading manufacturer of luxury and sports cars, the firm has found a niche through creating value for customers. The firm sells models of its cars, but adds many different customizable features based on the wants of the customer. These features are installed on the car as it is manufactured: in short, the automobile is made-to-order. Because of the vast catalog of options available to car owners, as well as the superior service rendered to customers, BMW has been able to raise their profit margins on cars during a time when many car companies are slashing their margins in a fight for survival. Simply put, this kind of value co-creation strategy has forced a high-level executive of one of BMW's chief rivals, Lexus, to declare that BMW customers just do not leave BMW.[17]

3. Touchpoint Integration and Management

The multi-channel integration process is an important part of CRM strategy. Here, the firm combines what was learned in the strategy development process and in the value-creation process and puts them to strategic use for the firm. The goal of this step is to choose marketing channels that will capture the attention of the target market and prove to be the most convenient for them. In today's world, marketers have many different channels from which to choose. These include the following channels:

1. A traditional sales force,
2. Retail stores and other outlets,
3. Telephones, which includes telephone, fax, and call centers,
4. Direct marketing, including direct mail, radio, and TV,
5. E-commerce,
6. M-commerce, i.e., through mobile phones, and
7. Social commerce.

Most firms recently have chosen to use a multi-channel strategy to reach their customers. Thus, each of these divergent marketing channels must be managed at the same exacting standards compared to each other. The company must broadcast one unified face to the public, while at the same time attract the right customers to the right products. While this sounds straightforward, many problems can occur when trying to tie marketing communications together throughout the firm. For a moment, consider the example of a car company. Originally, car companies sold only through their dealerships. However, as computer technology developed, direct marketing became a new method of selling to customers exactly the right model cars with the right color and the right features.

This may have been a strong new channel for the firm, but it was seen as a threat by existing dealerships. This points to a common problem between traditional "brick-and-mortar" (retail stores) and e-commerce (website) sales: channel conflict due to the fear that retailers will lose their customer base. Although this is a legitimate concern, if handled carefully it can become an advantage to both the retail outlet and the firm. The firm must endeavor to create a solution that does not leave its retail outlet in the dark. Consumers usually want to test drive the cars they are purchasing, so retail outlets add significant value to customers. If the car company can give monetary advantage to dealerships to direct customers online (i.e. referral bonuses) and use dealerships primarily as testing and distribution locations, then the firm can better meet the needs of customers to get the right product the quickest with the least cost.

In all, there are four primary advantages that lead to the creation of synergy when integrating both traditional channels of distribution (i.e. retail stores) and new, more direct models (i.e. internet, m-commerce). First is the use of common infrastructure. By using such elements as a common warehousing system or IT systems, the company can achieve cost savings in their dealings with customers through avoidance of redundant systems. Second, common operations can provide a benefit to the company. An example of this is a common order processing system that allows for easy movement between channels for customers. A third source of synergy can come from the use of common marketing and sales programs. By using promotions for multiple sources through the same media, customers will be able to self-select the proper method for themselves. Finally, despite the fact that this tends to lead to the greatest number of brick-and-mortar versus e-commerce conflicts, the fact that the channels use common buyers can also be used as a synergy building advantage for the company. An example of both a negative interaction between channels and a positive alternative are given in the above example regarding car dealerships. Simply put, the firm needs to find a way to balance its customers' desires for both convenience (online) and immediacy (nearby stores).[18]

4. Integrated Customer Information Management

While listed fourth, this process is one that must be maintained throughout the entire CRM program. Data are key to understanding what customers want and how their values are being delivered. This process requires a large amount of coordination with the IT department.

The first necessity for CRM is that the company has IT systems, including all the necessary hardware, software, and middleware. Once, this has been fulfilled, the IT department needs to build a data repository to contain all the necessary information about customers. When large enough, this is called a data warehouse. In firms that have truly achieved cross-functional coordination, this data warehouse should serve the needs of all departments in the firm.

But how does the firm get the necessary data to put into the data warehouse? When first implementing a new CRM system, it may be necessary for the firm to upload data from antiquated files or legacy systems. Once this has been accomplished, the firm should institute some kind of system to facilitate acquisition of new data. Oftentimes, this includes Sales Force Automation software and call center management applications. Collectively known as "front office applications," these applications include all the necessary applications that are used during the communication with customers. Additionally, the firm should also have "back office applications." These are similar in concept to the front office applications, except that their goal is to collect internal data regarding human resources, logistics, procurement, and other business applications. The key question with these back office systems in regards to CRM is, "Does the back office application allow for an efficient workflow?" If the company's internal systems are chaotic, then customer service may be impacted negatively.

Collecting the data, however, is clearly not enough. The firm also needs analytical tools, such as data mining and business analytics software, to search the data warehouse and interpret its findings for managers. During the search, these software packages can help the firm uncover key trends that will be useful throughout the CRM program.[19] As an offbeat example, a supermarket was doing an analysis of its data warehouse to learn more about what type of customers were buying diapers. When they looked at the correlation between diapers and other products, they found a most peculiar one: most customers purchasing diapers on Friday were there for only that item and only one other, beer. As the researchers discovered, this was because young, married men coming home on Fridays would stop by the supermarket to pick up diapers for their newborn and pick up beer for weekend parties while they were there. The supermarket was able to cash in on this trend by placing the diapers closer to the beer. In short, business analytics can uncover some surprising trends. The marketer must be willing to go in with no expectations to find what customers truly need and value.

However, there are some common problems to be found with the data collection process. First, databases might not contain the correct information. This can mean either that human error played into the data entry method or, more significantly, the data entry method was not set up to gather the information needed. Before any data field is added to a database, the firm must know what the purpose of the data field is. The success or failure of a customer modeling process is about 80% due to the robustness of the data model used.

The database must gather basic information about the customer. Customers appreciate not having to give out their information multiple times, and will not form lasting relationships with the firm that does not store this data. Additionally, while it may be harder to gather attitudinal data rather than simple transactional data, the firm should make an effort to try to discover the customers' attitudes and desires. The customer must feel that their opinions and desires count. Thus, perceived empathy must be considered. More than anything else, however, an effort needs to be made to determine the firm's future needs of the data. The firm must determine what data they currently have available, what data are missing, and what data are needed to achieve its goals and objectives.

Another issue involves data quality control and data management. If the firm does not make an effort to create real company programs to manage the quality in the data, problems will go unfixed. To illustrate an example of a commonly missed quality issue, consider the customer that a firm is in danger of losing. When customers are considering leaving the firm, they may have fallen to a different customer segment. Without quality in the system (including updated information), this trend may not be noticed until it is too late. To sum up what is needed in terms of quality, every piece of information ideally should be filled, recent, unique (not in the system twice under different departments), and valid.

Next, the firm must have the right number of people to manage the system. Too often the firm trains only a few people in how to handle and analyze the data, and even these employees are not sufficiently empowered to use the information to directly impact the company's level of service. Tied into this issue is a general lack of managerial motivation with regards to CRM. Because it is hard to develop metrics that explain the impact of CRM initiatives with respect to data, managers see it as only a cost and not as a value adding activity.

Finally, while data is currently being used properly to handle one-to-one relationship marketing objectives, companies have been less effective in using it to determine macro trends that impact the company. While it is easy to determine that customer A bought product X, it is harder for the firm to use this information to determine their competitive advantages. Still, this is highly valuable information that must be determined. Internal data might need to be combined with external data in order to get a full view of the situation.

5. CRM Performance and Metrics Assessment

The final CRM process is the performance assessment process. Here, management must consider the overall success or failure of the process and determine what should be done the next time around. The success or failure of the process can be measured in terms of employee satisfaction, customer loyalty, company profitability, and shareholder value. Success in one area that hurts another may be more of a step backwards for the company than a step forward. Additionally, the firm should consider if everything was done to lower costs. Can customers be equally serviced by an automated phone system or a webbot? How much of the process can be automated? The company should also consider if online or e-commerce can be added to make the process run smoother.

In many cases CRM benefits have been found to not be worth their cost for implementation. Some research has found CRM success rates have varied between 30%-70% while as many as two-thirds of CRM projects fail.[20] Some of the main causes of these failures have been organizational change, company policies/inertia, little understanding of CRM, and poor CRM sales. However, there is a problem with current CRM performance evaluation. Currently, many companies do not use metrics that can really determine the success of the program. For example, more than half of the executive boards of companies do not evaluate their CRM programs on the basis of customer satisfaction or retention metrics. Without using or understanding the meaning of these metrics, it is easy to see only the short term, monetary situation rather than the company's long-term viability. Relationships often take a long time to obtain the full value. Thus, customer analytics must be more than mere historical data. Instead, they need to be future-oriented values that are forecasted by those with relevant knowledge. It is crucial that the company try to implement some kind of return-on-relationships metrics. If the company does not know what value they are deriving from their customers, then it is impossible for the board to decide if the relationships are worth investing in.

Once the success of the processes have been determined, the data should be fed back into the business strategic and value creation processes again to try to scale to even greater heights. While a positive metric may indicate that the company is moving in the right direction, the company cannot afford to stay still. Consider the example of Dell Computers. When the company unleashed its distinctive direct marketing model on the world, the company enjoyed a fairly sustained competitive advantage, and became one of the world's foremost computer companies.

Now, fast forward ten years. In this time, other computer companies began to emulate Dell's online and telephone direct marketing model, and began to gain competencies in this field. Dell, on the other hand, made few switches to their formula, except to cut costs wherever they could. As a result, Dell has lost some of the advantages associated with its customer value driven process. Thus, CRM should not be seen as a destination for a firm. Rather, it is a continuously cycling process that must be monitored and corrected to best align customer and firm value.

Section 3. Importance of Analytics in Customer Relationship Management

"Your most unhappy customers are your greatest source of learning."
Bill Gates

There are many different reasons why firms are adopting business analytics. Several key reasons firms are implementing business analytics processes include the ability to translate real-time insights into competitive advantage, the ability to provide various firm stakeholders with valuable information for improved problem-solving and decision-making, and the ability to process and evaluate the ever increasing, massive amounts of unfiltered and unstructured data being utilized by the firm's analysts and managers for insight generation.[21]

Business Analytics

The use of various business analytics by the firm is of paramount importance as business analytics is used to create knowledge and generate meaningful insights thus leading to more informed, fact-based conclusions.[22] Since the terms "business analytics", "business intelligence", and "big data" are used somewhat interchangeably, it is important to define, describe, and differentiate the term "business analytics" and its use by the firm. The term "business analytics" is created and defined as "the focus on the extensive use of data, statistical and quantitative analysis, explanatory and predictive models, and (a culture of) fact-based management to drive actions" for the firm.[23] Thus, business analytics can be viewed as "a broad category of applications, technologies, and processes for gathering, storing, accessing, and analyzing data to help analysts".[24] Business analytics can be used by the analysts to answer a variety of probing questions such as, "Why is this pattern occurring for this product line?", "What if specific performance trends continue?", "What is expected to happen in future time periods?", and "Given various options, what is the best possible outcome that can occur?". More recently, various "big data" terminology concepts have been incorporated into the business analytics definition by expanding the definition to include "a combination of skills, technologies, applications, and processes that enable firms to analyze an immense volume, variety, and velocity of data across a wide range of networks to support informed decision-making and action-taking."[25] By simplifying this discussion, business analytics can be further explicated by defining it as "a set of methods that transform data into action by generating insights used for decision-making by the firm".[26] Yet, its focus is more than just "decision-making". Business analytics is also concerned with evidence-based problem recognition and problem-solving within the context of business situations as not every situation requires decision-making. While the definition and use of the term, business analytics, is still evolving, business analytics has become the art and science of discovering insights by using artificial intelligence methods and machine learning as well as the sophisticated mathematical, statistical, and network science methodologies on the volumes of available structured and unstructured data as well as expert business domain knowledge to support decision-making.[27] Therefore, business analytics can be viewed as an enabler for decision-making and creative problem-solving.[28] As firms are increasingly being managed through the use of advanced information technology, it is more important than ever for managers to use available analytical methods and gain business analytical competence.

In defining, describing, and differentiating business analytics, marketing managers need to recognize the integration of business intelligence and big data concepts into business analytics along with the strong focus on data, models, analysis, and an evidenced-based culture. Big data adds massive amounts of data and data types from various sources which can be used to support a variety of actions over varying time-frames for the analyst. The strong focus on the creation of models by the analyst focuses primarily in the explanatory context for business orientation tasks. Further, an important, but often overlooked aspect of the definitions for business analytics involves the analytic culture of the firm. Firms need to ensure that the business analytics are generated for fact-based decision-making and problem-solving and the generated insights from the various explanatory, predictive, and prescriptive analytic models are actionable.[29] To become actionable, the generated insights need to be connected to all aspects of the process used to enhance problem-solving and decision-making in the firm.

Business Analytics as a Firm Strategy for Competitive Advantage

Previous research studies have established that firms can gain competitive advantages through improved problem-solving and decision-making performance. Increasing the competitive advantage for a firm can be achieved by effectively using the various skills and competencies of the firm's analysts performing the insight generation tasks. Firms can gain advantage by generating insights and intelligence that can answer a variety of important business questions. So, the vast quantity of data becomes both a monumental challenge and a tremendous opportunity for the firm's analysts tasked with providing useful, action-oriented support to the firm's management team.[30]

Firms can cultivate and maintain various types of competitive advantage supported by business analytics. Effective planning and decision-making require good, high quality information. Thus, valuable information can provide a firm with the ability to perform at a higher level, make better decisions, and participate effectively in the competitive marketplace. Five example focus areas for competitive advantage pursued by firms and how business analytics can help achieve competitive advantage include pricing, service, operational efficiencies, risk reduction, and performance monitoring strategies.[31]

In the first focus area, business analytics can support effective pricing strategies to increase customer profitability. Business analytics can provide detailed information on competitor products and allow firms to maintain price leadership. Firms can identify main competitors and then monitor, report, and accurately forecast competitive prices. This information can be used to keep the lowest cost profile while maintaining and measuring profit margins. This information can also be used to set prices to keep profit margins at a profit-maximizing level by balancing sales volume with lower prices and margins or increase prices to increase margins depending on competitor pricing.

In the second focus area, business analytics can support an effective service strategy. This strategy entails making customer transactions easier or more pleasant by improving the service characteristics of the firm such as decreasing service time and enhancing customer value. Business analytics provides information about customer opinions on problem service areas, possible solutions, and methods to improve the service operations.

In the third focus area, business analytics can help firms achieve operational efficiency and optimization. This strategy focuses on improving the internal business operations and activities over competitors and reducing cost. Business analytics can identify operational areas needing correction or modification and suggest optimal solutions to maximize business performance.

In the fourth area, business analytics can help firms achieve risk reduction and firm sustainability. This strategy focuses on identifying areas needing resource reallocations and reducing the risk of poor judgments. Business analytics can offer information about the probabilistically computed likelihood of certainty on sales, budgets, and the best optimal balance.

Finally, the fifth focus area examines how business analytics can provide information about business performance by continually tracking specific business performance parameters. A real time performance achievement index can be provided by business analytics so that managers can compare performance over time and set planning and performance goals to guide operations based on forecasts of expected performance.

Paradigm Shift: Business Analytics-Driven Decision-Making

Trends that facilitate or support the use of business analytics are emerging.[32] First, there exists the availability of large amounts of data. The sheer amount of information created in a day is huge and the pace of information creation is increasing. The current amount of data created every day exceeds 2.5 quintillion (2.5 million trillion) bytes of data.[33] A second trend is the increasing realization that data is a valuable resource and should be managed as an asset. A third trend is the well-established linkage of business strategy, data, and business performance. High level strategy is translated into a concrete set of performance metrics allowing the implementation of the firm's strategy based on metrics. Cultural change towards evidence-based management is becoming common in many firms as is the realization of the importance of fact-based decisions at every level of firm. Access to large databases and user-friendly tools provided analysts and managers with self-service analytics and sophisticated algorithms. Yet, there exists the need for better business decisions.

The application of analytics to business problems is the ultimate goal of business analytics.[34] Business analytics has been applied to enhance revenue, reduce costs, and mange risks resulting in competitive advantage for the firm. The term business analytics refers to a broad category of applications, technologies, and processes used for creating new insights and knowledge for better business decisions.[35] Business intelligence is used by the information technology community for similar applications, technologies and processes. Business analytics focuses on making business decisions based on large and complex datasets and providing solutions for analyzing big data with advanced statistical models, databases, and software tools. With the increased growth of structured and especially unstructured data, firms need to develop business analytics competence to remain competitive in global markets. Business analytics provides the ability to handle unstructured data such as voice, text, images, and video as well as structured data.

The rationale for utilizing and adopting business analytics includes many different reasons in addition to varying by firm.[36] Firms utilize business analytics to achieve a competitive advantage by supporting their strategic and tactical goals. Additionally, firms adopt business analytics for better organizational performance, better business outcomes, and a more informed decision process. Firms are pursuing superb knowledge production by obtaining value and generating insights from data. The ultimate goal of business analytics is generating value from big data in the sense of supporting knowledge acquisition, insight generation, problem finding, and problem solving to help decision-making.[37] Firms use data and related insights to drive fact-based planning, decisions, and execution, as well as the management, measurement, and learning for data-driven decision-making. With business analytics, evidence-based problem recognition and solving can happen within the context of business decision situations.

Types of Business Analytics

Various techniques are utilized to generate four distinct types of analytics: descriptive, diagnostic, predictive, and prescriptive.[38] Typically, data mining and business analytics procedures and techniques include many different statistical and analytic procedures such as data exploration, prediction, classification, clustering, and affinity analysis. These techniques and procedures require certain type of variables and data. The remaining parts in this section describes the different types of analytics that can be used by a firm's analysts and marketing managers.[39]

Descriptive Analytics

Descriptive analytics focuses on answering the questions, "What happened in the past?" and "What is happening now?" This analytics applies simple statistical techniques that explore data and describe what is contained in a dataset or database. For example, descriptive analytics can be used to identify possible trends in large datasets or databases to get a rough picture of what the data looks like. Descriptive analytics, based on historical and current data, is an important source of insights into what happened in the past and the correlations among various determinants identifying patterns using statistical measures such as mean, median, range, and standard deviation. Descriptive analytics using techniques like online analytical processing exploits knowledge from the past experience to provide answers to what's happening in the firm. Descriptive analytics identifies a problem by analyzing historical data. Descriptive analytics employs data visualization by using simple reports, dashboards, and scorecards as well as commonly provide information to marketing managers using business intelligence tools. Descriptive analytics can pinpoint and introduce problem areas and can lead to more advanced solutions with data exploration.

Data exploration focuses on data summaries, visualization, partitioning, and dimension reduction. Managers need to become familiar with the data and can explore the nature of data through summaries, tables, and graphs. Data summaries are presented with descriptive statistics such as average, standard deviation, minimum, maximum, median, counts, differences, and pairwise correlations. Data visualization can be quite useful in exploring data. Managers can explore graphs and tables as well as box plots and histograms to understand data distribution and relationships between numerical variables and detect patterns and outliers. Dimension reduction allows managers to reduce the number of categories or predictors. Principal components analysis and correspondence analysis are useful procedures for reducing the number of variables. Principal components analysis is used for continuous variables and the correspondence analysis is used for categorical variables. Common examples of descriptive analytics include data visualization, dashboards, reports, charts, and graphs presenting key performance metrics including, for example, sales, orders, customers, and other financial information. Descriptive analytics provides basic expository information in the form of canned reports such as canned sales reports or ad-hoc reports for specific issues.

Descriptive analytics focuses on analytics of the past and the present. Descriptive solutions are used to identify trends in large datasets or databases. The goal is to get an overall picture of what the data looks like and understand trends or future business behavior. Simple statistical techniques are applied to describe what is contained in a dataset or database. Descriptive statistics such as measures of central tendency (mean, median, and mode), measures of dispersion (standard deviation), and visualization tools (charts, graphs, frequency tables, and probability distributions) are typically used to derive descriptive analytic solutions.[40] Descriptive analytics provides managers with alerts (information regarding what actions are needed), query/drill down (information regarding what the problem exactly is), ad-hoc reports or scorecards (information regarding how many, how often, where problems or events are happening), and standard reports (information regarding what happened).

Often called performance analytics or effective analytics, descriptive analytics solutions are designed to provide analysts with a complete description and view of the firm's strategic and tactical activities, performances, customer history, and behavior patterns up to the present moment. These analytics can track the firm's as well as competitor's performance against the firm metrics set for managing strategy and tactical behavior. With these analytics solutions, firms can have a complete view of their customers; market comparison information; success and failure of tactical decisions; and customer and organizational performance. These solutions provide insights regarding how the firm reached its present situation and what behavior patterns it followed thus far. Pure descriptive analytics solutions cannot offer answers to future events and strategies. However, descriptive analytics are the foundation for predictive analytics.

Diagnostic Analytics

Diagnostic analytics provides answers to questions such as how and why did it happen in the past and why is it happening now. Diagnostic analytics based in historical data also provides insights about the root-cause of past outcomes. Diagnostic analytics searches for cause and effect to illustrate why something occurred and to compare past occurrences to determine causes. Diagnostic analytics helps managers by identifying outliers that need additional examination, isolating patterns that exist outside of the existing dataset and uncovering relationships by isolating unique relations.

Thus, firms can make better decisions by avoiding past errors and negative results. Diagnostic analytics tries to find why the problem occurs. Diagnostic analytics is typically generated after managers conduct descriptive analyses. To find the cause of a problem, data mining and drill-into analytics are needed to find patterns, trends, and relationships. Diagnostic analytics can provide context to a business problem using data models and more complex analysis. Diagnostic analytics requires managers' accurate interpretation of patterns to evaluate the cause of the problem in addition to accurate and complex analyses. Queries and drill-downs allow managers to generate more detailed reports.

Predictive Analytics

Predictive analytics can answer questions related to what possible trends or changes in markets and customers exist that can provide information about possible course of actions to be taken and likelihood of possible outcomes. Predictive analytics provides calculated predictions and is very complex. Predictive analytics is more likely to use advanced techniques such as data mining, machine learning, and predictive modeling to generate actionable insights and intelligence. These analytics can generate predictions from algorithms that can help managers to avoid mistakes and wrong decisions based on big data. Predictive analytics applies advanced statistical or operational research methods to identify predictive variables or build predictive models to identify trends and relationships. For example, predictive analytics can build a model that explains why a set of variables influence market performance in a given market.

Prediction techniques include multiple linear regression, regression trees, time series analysis, and neural networks. Classification techniques include logistic regression, Naïve Bayes, classification trees, neural networks, and discriminant analysis. Logistic regression extends linear regression to the categorical dependent variable case. Logistical regression can be used for classification (e.g., classifying customers into one of the two classes, loyal and non-loyal customers, based on the values of its predictors) and profiling (i.e., finding factors that differentiate among pre-defined groups). Neural networks can capture very complex relationships between predictors and a response providing high predictive performance. This technique combines the input information in a very flexible way in order to capture complicated relations among these input variables. This technique tries to find relationships from learning the patterns existing within the data. Discriminant analysis can also be used for classification and profiling. For example, this technique uses continuous variables to classify new items into one of the classes identified (e.g., classifying customers into non-users, light users, and heavy users). Clustering can be done using cluster analysis. Cluster analysis identifies groups or clusters of similar characteristics or records based on several measurements. The goal is to identify and characterize the clusters that can provide meaningful insights to managers. This technique is commonly used for market segmentation where customers are segmented based on predetermined variables such as demographics, behavioral measures, and transaction records. Affinity analysis utilizes association rules and is also called market basket analysis. This technique is looking for associations between items that are stored in the database.

Predictive analytics is about forecasting and providing an estimation for the probability of a future result as well as evaluating opportunities or risks in the future. Using various techniques including data mining, data modeling, and machine learning, the implementation of predictive analytics can be applied to various decision tasks of the firm. One of the most known applications of that type of analytics is the prediction of customer behavior, determining operations, marketing, and preventing risk. Using historical and other available data, predictive analytics are able to uncover patterns and identify relationships in data that can be used for forecasting. Predictive analytics in the digital era is a critical weapon for firms in the competitive race. Therefore, firms exploiting predictive analytics can identify future trends and patterns and present innovative products/services or innovations in their business models. Predictive analytics provides forecasts of the impact of future actions before they are taken, answering "what might happen" as outcome of the firm's actions. Therefore, the decision-making is improved by considering the prediction of future outcomes.

Predictive analytics offers metrics and models that are predictive of future events, outcomes, or occurrences. Predictive analytics provides predictive models designed to identify future trends. In developing predictive analytic solutions, advanced statistical techniques (e.g., multiple regression and ANOVA), information software (e.g., data mining and sorting), or operations research methods (e.g., forecasting methods) are used to develop predictive models with identified predictive variables. Predictive analytics provides managers predictive modeling/forecasting (information regarding what will happen next) and statistical modeling results (information regarding what is happening).[41] These analytics solutions get both interesting and challenging but, if successful, are most rewarding. Most of the strategic, customer-related, and tactical decisions are made with some form of predictions or estimations in mind. Traditionally, analysts rely more on their intuition, experience, or limited marketing research results to make these decisions. With the development of data-mining tools based on integrated multidimensional databases, more sophisticated analytical solutions can be easily developed and are accessible by marketing managers through web-based visualization and reporting tools. Additionally, the sophistication of these analytics models can reduce predictive errors significantly and render more rational decisions in the dynamic and fast changing decision environment.

Prescriptive Analytics

Prescriptive analytics provides answers to questions regarding how best to leverage what is known from the trends and forecasts as well as how firms can optimally allocate resources to maximize the business performance outcomes in the future. Prescriptive analytics applies decision science, management science, and operations research methodologies and techniques to provide the optimal solutions or alternatives for business problems. Prescriptive analytics generates prescriptive models and new rules based on historical and external information using machine learning techniques. This type of analytics requires extensive sophisticated analytical tools and analytical capability. For example, prescriptive analytics helps firms allocate resources optimally to take advantage of predicted trends or emerging opportunities. Prescriptive analytics offers value to firms through recommendations and specific suggestions built on the big data analysis.

Prescriptive analytics using high-level modeling tools can contribute to the performance enhancement and efficient operation of firms through smarter and faster decisions with lower costs and risk thus identifying optimal solutions for resource allocation. The advanced prescriptive analytics can play a crucial role in efficient strategic decision-making dealing with critical and important problems faced by firms such as the design and development of products/services and supply chain formation. Prescriptive analytics predicts outcomes based on numerous variables using machine learning with big data. Prescriptive analytics also uses artificial intelligence to generate probable answers to what-if questions and suggest courses of action.

Prescriptive analytics solutions focus on future directions and best solutions. The goal of prescriptive analytic solutions is to allocate the firm's limited resources optimally to enhance firm performance by utilizing predicted trends or future opportunities. Operational research methodologies (e.g., linear programming), decision science (e.g., decision analysis), and management science techniques (e.g., simulation and randomized testing) are typically used to generate prescriptive analytic solutions such as how to allocate the adverting budget to various advertising media or target customers. Prescriptive analytics provides managers optimization solutions (information regarding what is the best that can happen) and randomized test outcomes (information regarding what if we try this). Prescriptive analytics utilizes mathematically based methodologies, algorithms, and approaches to generate an optimal or best sub-optimal solution to complex problems. Using the prescriptive analytic solutions, firms can best plan future actions and directions based on the scientifically derived models and predictions. This is the final step in analytics-driven decision-making.

From problem identification to predictions and actionable alternative solutions, the four types of analytics provide value and competitive advantage for firms. These four types of analytics can help managers in different decision stages and contexts. These analytic types can provide solutions at the strategic, customer, and tactical decision areas of the firm.

Generating Business Analytic Reports and Gain Insights

The application of the selected analytic modules will generate analytics reports in the form of graphs, charts, tables, diagrams, formulas, and statistical outputs. These results are now stored in a separate document, added to the firm's customized report format, or reported in the firm's analytics dashboard. Some of the analytic modules and processes can be saved within the software tools as a customized solution. These solutions and related modules can be retrieved later for additional use. Newly created calculation can be stored in the data warehouse. New analytic solution modules can be stored in the analytics warehouse.

After generating analytic results and reports, marketing managers should generate insights. With the insights generated, marketing managers may need to reassess the problem and may want to generate additional analytical solutions to gain further insights and greater understanding. These insights would lead to valuable strategic and tactical directions for the organization.

The utilization of this information generates further insights and knowledge. Whereas "information" is understood as "purposeful and relevant data", "insight" and "knowledge" exist within people as a function of their values, framed experience, contextual information, and expert insight. Knowledge resides in the information user and not in the collection of knowledge. It is how the information user reacts to a collection of information that matters. Thus, "knowledge" can be seen as information that matters to people, given their values, frame of reference, experiences, context, and expertise.

When information is interpreted by a marketing manager, who assimilates it using his or her current knowledge, emotions, values and insights, new knowledge can be created. This is not to say that a firm's knowledge exists only in its people. There are at least six domains where organizational knowledge appears. These domains include employees, machinery, plant and/or equipment, organizational systems, organizational processes, organizational cultures, and finally, products. Furthermore, organizational knowledge can exist in the marketing managers in different forms ranging from "tacit" and difficult to control and communicate, to "explicit/codified" and easy to control and communicate. Explicit knowledge is formal and systematic while tacit knowledge is highly personal and rooted in action and in an individual's commitment to a specific context or skill. Tacit knowledge consists of mental models, beliefs, and perspectives so ingrained that it is taken for granted. Indeed, it is in the process of moving from tacit knowledge to explicit knowledge that conscious and articulated understanding of something is accomplished.

One important requirement of marketing managers in generating insights and creating knowledge is the ability to make sense out of the analytical solutions.[42] The decision problem is the starting point of the analytical process. Considering the available metrics and analytical tools, marketing managers select the appropriate analytic solutions that are consistent to their existing knowledge base. These analytic solutions are generated applying various modules of analytical tools to the problem at hand. The analytical solutions are typically in the form of charts, graphs, tables, and statistical values. They are interpreted to gain insights.

The ability to sense is related to the mental models of the marketing managers interpreting the information. The mental models of the marketing managers contain decision rules for filtering data and information and useful heuristics for deciding how to act on the information in light of anticipated outcomes. The marketing manager is to assign meaning to the data uncovered and to translate it from data through information and, ultimately, to knowledge that can be used by the organization for competitive advantage.

Section 4. Marketing Analytics for Relationship Marketing

> *"A good deal happens in a man's life that he isn't responsible for. Fortunate openings occur; but it is safe to remember that such 'breaks' are occurring all the time, and other things being equal, the advantage goes to the man who is ready."*
> Lawrence Downs

Relationship marketing is a process that seeks to create shared interests between the firm and its customers. By making both sides feel like they have incentives to maintain their relationship, a long and productive relationship will be the result. For this to happen, first communication needs to be open. Thus, the firm needs to provide information that will shape customer responses appropriately. Once the firm has proven their value and honesty, trust will begin to form. In this way, business relationships are not all that dissimilar from social ones.

Relationship marketing is quite dissimilar from transactional marketing. In transactional marketing, there is little value placed in the long-term viability of the relationship. Thus, the firm does not provide quite as much information to prospective customers. Unfortunately, in many companies, the cost of attracting sales from brand new customers is much higher than the cost of maintaining relationships with current customers. Thus, CRM becomes highly important for most firms. The core foundation of CRM and relationship marketing is marketing analytics. Firms must have the competence of creating and interpreting marketing analytics for relationship marketing decisions. A major component of the business analytics is marketing analytics that apply business analytics tools and procedures to marketing decision problems and generate marketing relevant analytics for marketing and customer insights.

Marketing Analytics Dimensions

The most important element in relationship marketing implementation is customer knowledge management. Firms need to acquire customer data, generate customer insights and knowledge, and use these insights and knowledge to create brand and customer value and customer experience. To maintain stronger relationships, five dimensions must be considered. These dimensions are information reciprocity, information capture, information integration, information access, and information use.[43] Below, each of these will be discussed.

Information Reciprocity

Before considering information reciprocity in a business sense, consider it in a normal, everyday sense. Assume you are talking with one of your friends in college. Over the course of the conversation, he or she mentions that they had trouble on a test in the previous class. Naturally, you may feel obliged to tell your friend how it went for you if you had similar difficulty. If you choose to share how the exam went for you, this is an example of information reciprocity.

Broadly defined, information reciprocity occurs when actions taken by one party in a relationship are matched by the other party. This is natural response in both a personal or business context, and is a cornerstone of the relationship marketing process. To take full advantage of this natural interaction, the firm should set up call centers, web communities, social media platforms, or other locations where information can be easily shared. Strong relationships are unlikely to form if communication is only one-way (from the business to the customer).

Information Capture

In today's business environment, companies tend to use many channels to successfully reach their customers. These include phone, e-mail, television, retail outlets, websites, and social media sites. Moreover, customers may choose to use more than one of these channels when gathering information or making purchases. For this reason, it is important that the information about these interactions be captured uniformly throughout the system. This information may need to be accessed later by other channel members.

Information Integration

Many different people in different departments of a firm will interact with customers. If the information maintained by the firm is not in order, then customers may be getting conflicting or improper information from each different source. Customer trust will be negatively impacted in this situation.

As an illustration, assume you are a student who is applying to a university. Having financial difficulties, you visited an advisor to ask about scholarship opportunities. You are told there are two scholarships that you can apply for, and so you go home happy and begin writing the necessary essays for the applications. However, the advisor did not have the correct information, and the deadline for the scholarships have passed. Clearly, this will not have a positive effect on the relationship between yourself and the college.

Information Access

Dissemination of information to customers is crucial for the success of relationship marketing. Thus, any employees who are likely to have contact with customers will need to have relevant information at their fingertips to give to customers. In most of the literature, the focus is only on continuously sending out information. While this can be useful to customers, it can also become a hassle if they receive too much in the way of information. Most people who have given their e-mail address to firms know of at least one firm that continues to inundate them with information. In many cases, this can create negative feelings among the firm's customers. This can be avoided by providing customers with the ability to unsubscribe to the e-mails or choose what type of information they receive.

Information access, however, is appreciated and is expected by customers. By allowing customers to be able to find the information they need in a timely manner, customer satisfaction and experience is likely to rise. Unlike mere distribution, as the previous example illustrated, this will help the firm form stronger relationships with its customers. Information access can be provided through multiple channels, including over the phone, online, and/or in-person if the firm has retail outlets.

Information Use

There are three ways that market information can be used: action-oriented use, knowledge-oriented use, and affective use. In relationship marketing, market information is first used for knowledge-gaining reasons. The company is interested in understanding its customers and what they desire. Once this has been done, the firm must take actions based on this knowledge. Often, these actions involve tailoring a new product or service to customer needs. However, a mismatch between customer information management and the capabilities of the CRM software may lead to significant problems in the program. If productivity goes down because of new CRM software, the gains may be drowned in the costs.

The availability of extensive customer data poses a challenge to many firms. They have to make sense of this immense amount of customer data that are potentially useful. The development and advancement of software and hardware brings a solution that utilizes customer data. Firms need to establish adequate processes to manage customer data. These tools allow firms to create a comprehensive and 360-degree view of customers. This total view of customers must be communicated to and shared with all customer-contacting employees across the organization. This shared customer knowledge is the backbone of relationship marketing. For specific strategic and tactical marketing decisions, customer insights generated from marketing analytics should be effectively utilized to bring forth the full benefits of relationship marketing efforts.

Marketing Analytics Stage Model

Marketing managers are required to use analytics for fact-based decision marketing. Analytics are becoming increasingly critical for market success in the highly competitive marketing environment. One important competence that marketing managers must have is the ability to effectively generate and utilize marketing analytics for marketing decision-making. The three-stage model (Figure 2.3) of the marketing analytics includes marketing analytics task definition; marketing analytics generation; and marketing analytics interpretation and application.[44]

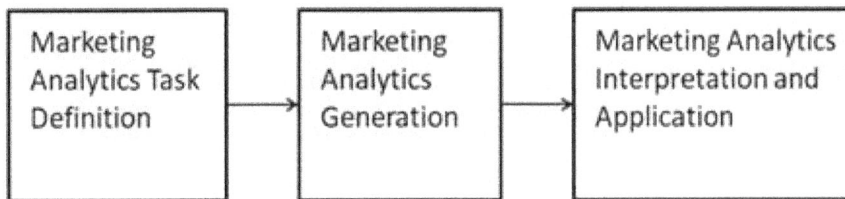

Figure 2.3: The Three-Stage Model of Marketing Analytics

Marketing Analytics Task Definition

The stage model starts with the first stage of defining the marketing analytics task. Managers need to understand what type of analytic task they are confronting in the marketing decision situation and what type of analytic solutions is desired. The analytics process begins with identifying the decision domain and related managerial need for new analytics solutions. Managers need to clearly understand what decision problems or issues are at hand that they want to resolve or tackle with the analytics process. A managerial problem can be an intuitive feel that something in the firm needs to be understood or addressed to a discrete, well-defined problem statement. Regardless, the question or problem must be converted into an analytical question. The analytic question contains the identified metrics or analytics that are to be used in determining the response or desired solution. Managerial problems can take many different forms and shapes. They can be best understood by the nature of the problems and the actions needed to be taken by managers to resolve the problem. The managerial problem can be evaluated by assessing what level of firm activities is associated with the managerial problem.[45] When marketing managers face a managerial problem to solve, it is important to assess what levels of activities and decision domains are associated with the problem. For the analytic problem, appropriate scope, unit of analysis and metrics need to be identified and assessed. This understanding offers the scope of the analytical solutions needed to solve the problem. It also defines the direction to take to generate analytical questions. Understanding the scope provides an important guideline in determining the type of metrics and unit of analysis required for analytical solutions.

The management problems exist within the context of the problem situation and decision domain. The situational analysis focuses on the metrics and decision maker that have produced the stated managerial problem. In defining the analytical problem, marketing managers need to assess available knowledge, anticipated actions, alternative scenarios, and actionable analytical solutions. The influencing factors that have led to the problem should be identified first. These factors include objectives, past information and forecasts, resource and constraints (such as metrics available in the data warehouse, metrics in digital form, and metrics in paper form as well as existing analytic solutions in the analytics warehouse), decision time, importance of the decision, marketing and technological skills (such as marketing implementation skills and data-mining tools and analytical sophistication), customer behavior, legal environment, and economic environment. Once managers know the decision problems, they need to determine the desired solution. Considering the firm's strategic position and current decision situation, marketing managers can identify the nature and type of solutions to be generated from the analytic process.[46] The solution must be realistic and practical for the firm. For the right solution, managers need to come up with right questions to ask. Marketing manager must convert the desired solution of the decision problem to appropriate analytic questions. These questions should provide explicit specification of objectives in performing the analytic task.

Marketing Analytics Generation

In the second stage, considering the defined task, marketing managers then need to generate the appropriated business analytics in the form of analytics output. This stage involves developing the detailed process of generating analytic deliverables that can answer the analytic questions generated in the first stage. Marketing managers need to select the right analytic tool from their analytics toolbox. They need to consider the tool's functionality, assumptions, and data requirement in selecting the analytic tool for use. Marketing managers need to understand whether the solution requires a simple display of metrics, a prediction of certain metrics, or some form of data-mining and/or statistical procedures. As each analytic tool requires a different data format, managers must identify the available data and evaluate whether the data is in the appropriated usable format and quality. If data is not readily usable, managers need to perform data pre-processing to make them usable for the selected analytics tool. In many cases, data pre-processing is needed as the available data in a firm's database or in a public domain is generally incomplete with missing values, or variables are inaccurate or inconsistent. Therefore, they must prepare the data by performing data selection and integration, and cleaning its correct missing values, noise, and inconsistencies.

Different from traditional data, big data contains data from many different sources. For example, online click-stream data, text, image, audio, video, or web and social media sites are unstructured data created recently but important data for business analytics. Marketing managers can run the selected analytical method or procedures. As various analytic tools require different set up and data input format, marketing managers must understand the basic functionality of analytic software used by their firm. Marketing managers evaluate the numerous analytic outputs generated from both the user-driven and AI-driven analytics run and select the relevant analytic tables and charts for interpretation and application

Marketing Analytics Interpretation and Application

In the final third stage, marketing managers should interpret the generated business analytics output, generate marketing insights, and apply those insights to marketing decisions they are facing and derive solutions or answers to complete the defined analytic task. After generating analytic results and reports, marketing managers should generate insights. With the insights generated, marketing managers may need to reassess the problem and may want to generate additional analytical solutions to gain further insights and greater understanding. These insights would lead to valuable strategic and tactical directions for the firm. The utilization of this information generates further insights and knowledge. In this stage, marketing managers are applying generated insights and intelligence to decision task. Managers should assess the generated insights and evaluate the nature of insights whether they are expected or unexpected. They also need to evaluate these insights that either confirm or contradict the managers' intuition and experience as well as current business practices and knowledge base. The generated new insights can be applied to decision task. New solutions or directions can be identified leading to new marketing strategy or modification of existing strategy.

Marketing Analytics Insight for Relationship Marketing

Customer insight generated from marketing analytics systems must be used to generate customer relationship marketing strategies. The importance of generating the right type of customer insight and its impact is well recognized.

Types of Customer Insight

Customer insight can come in many forms from many sources. It may relate to demographics of a customer and the customer's specific behavior before or after purchase. The information can be gathered in many different sources and methods such as online store Web site or face-to-face interaction. It may emerge from analysis of a database containing customer-buying history. In this section, various types of customer information that are typically captured by organizations are described. The following are types of customer insight with example elements:[47]

- *What and how often customers buy?*
  o Past buying history of the products and services;
  o Nature of purchase including the product configurations, additional features, service plans, or additional elements purchased;
  o Frequency of purchases of each product;
  o Products and substitute products purchased from competitors.
- *How customers decide what to buy?*
  o Customer's decision-making process;
  o Information used to make a purchase decision;
  o Interactions needed to make a purchase decision, and the length of the decision cycle.
- *Why customers buy?*
  o Key decision criteria such as price, convenience, and quality;
  o Psychological factors;
  o Past customer relations.
- *How customers buy?*
  o Channels and touchpoints used for purchase;
  o Nature of preferred or required interactions;
  o Special requirements such as delivery options.
- *What are the customer's internal/personal circumstances?*
  o Customer's financial circumstances;
  o Strategic priorities;
  o Product usage;

o Purchase preparation activities;
o Other factors affecting purchase decision or product use.
- *What relevant external factors are in play?*
o Competitive strengths and weaknesses of customer and competitors;
o Structural trends within the customer's industry such as outsourcing or commoditization;
o Key macro-economic and regulatory factors impacting customers;
o Other key factors affecting the customer's circumstances.
- *What post-sale interactions do customers require?*
o Type and frequency of required support after purchase;
o Information required after purchase;
o Preferred channel of interaction;
o Frequency of product returns or repair request;
o Required customized modification or repair.

Customer Insight from Holistic Customer View

Firms need to have the complete information base that delivers a holistic and integrated view of each customer. Creating a holistic customer view requires firms to cover all touch points and all information sources. A holistic view should include: all customer transactions, all interactions, all customer denials, all service history, new characteristics and profiles, interactive survey data, clickstream or browsing behavior from tracking systems, cross and direct references, external and internal demographics, psychographics and, in fact, all available and useful data surrounding each customer. Holistic customer view allows firms generate meaningful and actionable customer insights for relationship marketing. These various types of customer insights can help firms' relationship marketing efforts and improve marketing performance in many different ways. First, customer insight can increase marketing effectiveness. Use of customer characteristics and buying patterns for customer segmentation allows firms to develop tailored marketing approaches, sales, and service plans for each customer segment. Second, customer insight can help firms to deploy firm-wide resources more effectively. Use of customer-performance, segment value and needs data can be the driver of resource allocation and deployment. Third, customer insight can be used to improve product development process. Implicit information and customer feedback leads to refined product designs that can eliminate common service complaints or recurring defects. Fourth, customer insight can be used to tailor service levels to various customer segments. Use of segment characteristics and customer needs can be used to customize interactions and the types and levels of service delivered to customers. Fifth, customer insight increases pricing effectiveness. Pricing rules and discipline can be improved based on better insight into individual and segment performance. Finally, customer insight increases customer profitability. Customer and marketing analytics can provide customer value and cost-to-serve metrics for effective customer relationship management. These insights can be used for relationship marketing activities to help better manage under-performing customers leading to increased sales as well as optimize highly profitable customers or high potential customers.

Total CRM Based Relationship Marketing Template

Template 2.1: Customer Analytics Preparedness Index for Relationship Marketing

Template 2.1 measures a firm's preparedness to effectively use customer analytics for relationship marketing.

Preparedness Index Items[48]	Response[a]
Customer Data-Handling Protocols	
Our firm has appropriate governance mechanisms across channels and business units to determine customer ownership and coordinate customer touchpoints.	1 2 3 4 5
Our firm maintains a consistent customer privacy policy.	1 2 3 4 5
Adequate data handling processes are in place to ensure that the firm adheres to commitments made in the privacy policy.	1 2 3 4 5
Our firm invests in user-friendly tools and/or central team of analysts to assist marketing, sales and service staff in analyzing customer data.	1 2 3 4 5
Data Architecture Standardization	
Our firm standardizes customer and product identifier codes.	1 2 3 4 5
Our firm standardizes customer data formats and definitions.	1 2 3 4 5
Our firm charters a group to maintain customer data standards and audit compliances.	1 2 3 4 5
Institutionalized Customer Data and Resource Sharing	
Marketing manager incentives are aligned to encourage data sharing.	1 2 3 4 5
Our firm institutes effective incentives to encourage channel partners to share customer data.	1 2 3 4 5
Marketing regularly shares information or resources with other functional areas or business areas.	1 2 3 4 5
Total Index Score[b]	

[a]Please circle a number that best indicates your perception of your firm using the following scale (1 = Strongly Disagree; 2 = Slightly Disagree; 3 = Neutral; 4 = Slightly Agree; 5 = Strongly Agree).

[b]Please add all the circled numbers. The total score of 40 or higher shows the firm's full readiness for implementation. The score between30 to 39 indicates that your firm needs some organizational adjustment before implementation.

Template 2.2: Customer Identification Fact sheet

Template 2.2 lists the customer identifiers.

Identification Information	Information Source	Customer Types (✔)		Available Format (✔)			Applies To Your Business	Accuracy
		Existing	New	In digital form	In paper form	Not available	(1= no; 2 = Maybe; 3 = yes)	(1=Low; 2= Medium; 3=High)
	Internal Records							
	Marketing Communication							
	Customer Generated Data							
	External Source							

Template 2.3: An Example of Customer Identifier Information Source

Template 2.3 shows an example of information source for customer identifiers.

Identification Information	Information Source	Customer Types		Available Format			Applies to your business	Accuracy
		Existing	New	In digital form	In paper form	Not available	(1= no; 2 = Maybe; 3 = yes)	(1=Low; 2= Medium; 3=High)
	Internal Records							
	Billing and invoicing records							
	Warranty records							
	Repairs and service records							
	Existing company financial records							
	Other (List):							
	Marketing Communication							
	Sweepstakes and contest entry forms							
	Coupon redemption and rebate forms							
	Sales force records or other field personnel							
	Local or regional mailings and promotions							
	Loyalty user card/frequency program							
	Package inserts							
	Service and/or support calls							
	Trade show/seminars attendance records							
	Inquiries or call-ins							
	Free newsletter							
	Contest, promotion, or advertising							
	Telephone program for continual contact							
	E-mail program for continual contact							
	Business customers 'first name list'							
	Other (List):							
	Customer Generated Data							

	Customer comment and research data							
	User number groups, clubs, and affinity groups involving your company or product							
	Warranty card returns							
	Web site visits and registrations							
	Other (List):							
	External Source							
	Magazines or newsletters serving your industry							
	Cooperative ventures with retailers, resellers and distributors							
	Other alliances with companies close to the customer							
	"List swaps" with others in industry							
	Mailing list brokers and industry data providers							
	Other (List):							

Real world Application Cases

Case 2-1: Churchill Downs[49]

Churchill Downs Inc. owns horse racing venues all over the United States. The company was searching for technology to help improve their customer relationship management (CRM) initiatives. Churchill Down's criterion for such technology was ease of use, the ability to adapt to change, and the ability to effectively interpret data. With the previous requirements in mind, Churchill Downs adapted data mining technology from SPSS Incorporated in order to better satisfy their customers (both domestic and international). This technology is utilized by the company to obtain a better understanding of their customers and use this information to restructure their marketing operations. The ultimate goal through data mining is to create an environment for individual marketing communication to best fit each customer, and to maximize the return on every dollar spent.

The technology Churchill Downs acquired can use customer data to develop or draw upon existing marketing campaigns through predictive analysis. Changes in consumer behavior can also be analyzed to create a customer life cycle model that can then also be used to develop effective marketing strategies.

Through the adoption of CRM analytical technology, Churchill Downs is able to specialize their goods and services for each customer segment. This reduces costs while increasing effectiveness. Predictability and attendance patterns of consumers are analyzed. The importance of this data is to determine when to add races to best utilize the company's resources. The expected result of this is to increase customer's lifetime value and loyalty.

Case Questions

1. Name additional criteria that could be essential in CRM technology adoption.

2. How far should Churchill Downs go in terms of specialization, personalization, and individual marketing? Is it possible to have too much customization?

3. In addition to determining race times and promotions, what are some end solutions that can be reached from the information collected? How should Churchill Downs, a U.S. company, integrate information about international customers?

Case 2-2: cognitiveCX[50]

The firm cognitiveCX wants to find out what customers think about its products and services so it can improve the overall customer experience (CX). CognitiveCX mines data from social media, conducts focus groups and surveys, and collects feedback from customer service reps. It is expected that all this information can reveal what customers are thinking and feeling. However, these results are not sufficient for cognitiveCX to understand why customers feel the way they do. Their response may be another round of focus groups or surveys to gather even more data. In the meantime, firms continue to miss the mark with its customers because they still have not solved the reason why they feel that way.

At cognitiveCX, managers believe that the explanation exists in data that it already has. The firm has all the unstructured data collected from call center logs, focus groups and surveys, and comments made in emails, letters or on social media. The text data are untapped and contain the real customer insight. With the unstructured data, customers express their emotions and sentiment about a company, its products or services and its employees. Although the firm recognizes the importance and value of these data, the firm cannot generate the appropriate analytics from the unstructured data and can generate any meaningful insights in a timely manner. The firm does have the capacity to analyze the kinds of data volumes it accumulates from various sources and those volumes continue to grow.

Applying natural language processing and AI technology to the data has changed the decision task and offers a new direction for customer insights. The firm needs to understand the why behind their data at scale and provide information about customer sentiment, nuance and context. The firm can get amazing insights by applying AI to the clients' data. Marketing managers can look at everything – millions, maybe billions of documents, calls, posts, news articles available in big data. The firm does not need to sample 1,000 social media posts out of hundreds of thousands, or 100 people surveyed in focus groups. CognitiveCX can evaluate every relevant customer comment about a product.

The firm can analyze huge amount of data and generate relevant analytics. And the firm can focus entirely on actual customer responses and social sentiment to find out the reason for customers' response. For example, this firm conducted an analysis for a government body that was considering whether to expand bike lanes and paths in an urban area. The analysis on citizen feedback collected through surveys and other traditional shows high levels of anger and frustration concerning cycling. The analysis reveals that the negative sentiment is expressed by pedestrians who used the shared walking and cycling paths not by frustrated cyclists. The negativity is due to the cyclists' disregard for traffic rules and speed limits. Clearly, the problem wasn't a lack of bike paths. This insight cannot be obtained from typical analysis of the firm's big data. It is important to identify the root cause of the negativity and provide the relevant insight for resolving the decision task. Marketing managers need to extract key insights to deliver meaningful value from unstructured data stored in a firm's big data.

Case Questions

1. What metrics should cognitiveCX use to ensure that the right customer analytics are captured for customer relevance?

2. How can cognitiveCX use the knowledge of the customer's sentiment in improving its customer focus and gain competitive advantage?

3. If you worked for cognitiveCX, what additional marketing analytics initiatives would you implement?

PART II. ESTABLISHING STRATEGIC DIRECTIONS FOR RELATIONSHP MARKETING

"The thinking that created the problems we have today is insufficient to solve them."
Albert Einstein

In Part II, the critical task of establishing strategic directions for relationship marketing is presented. As marketing managers increasingly recognize the importance of developing and managing customer relationships, this part begins with a general discussion of the strategic planning process and total CRM based marketing planning. Building upon the literature of CRM, this section presents strategic choices for relationship marketing that can be used to develop relationship marketing strategy and programs. In addition, strategic marketing models and concepts including customer portfolio concept, customer life time value approach, and customer experience management are discussed in detail.

Chapter 3 addresses the need for managers and decision-makers to manage complexity and customer relationships. A strategic planning process is described first. Then, the importance and advancement of the relationship marketing strategy concepts are discussed. The chapter concludes with total CRM based marketing planning model. The detailed steps and required contents for the total CRM based marketing plans are also presented.

Chapter 4 discusses strategic marketing concepts relevant for relationship marketing. In this chapter, various traditional business portfolio analysis tools, such as the BCG model are described. The importance of customer equity was introduced. The customer life time value approach is discussed in detail. In addition, the customer portfolio management concept is introduced as a building block of relationship marketing.

Chapter 5 discusses the concept of customer experience and the importance of managing the customer experience journey in relationship marketing. Key topics include customer experience mapping and understanding key pain points of customers. The experiential targeting and positioning approach is discussed and how it can be developed and used for relationship marketing.

Chapter 3. Developing Total CRM Driven Strategic Marketing Plan

Section 1. Strategic Planning Process

> *"What strategy is all about; what distinguishes it from all other kinds of planning - is, in a word, competitive advantage. Without competitors there would be no need for strategy, for the sole purpose of strategic planning is to enable the company to gain, as effectively as possible, a sustainable edge over its competitors."*
>
> Keniche Ohnae

Marketing managers require an organized approach that will allow them to cope with the complexity of planning and to formulate a coordinated set of decisions. Strategic planning must be both externally and internally oriented. The external orientation must focus on creating and satisfying customers. The internal orientation must address the requirement to build and sustain capabilities that enable the firm to continuously respond and adapt to change. Strategic planning works best when treated as a constant work in progress rather than a fixed plan.

The strategic marketing planning process provides such an organized approach to decision-making in face of changing environments. The strategic marketing planning process deals with making a highly complex set of programming decisions in order to develop a marketing plan for a product or service. Marketing planning considers current decision alternatives compared with their probable consequences over time. Marketing planning represents the effective application of the available information to decisions that have to be made now to secure the future.[1]

Organization's "Response-Ability"

While the environmental forces are uncontrollable, the corporation's responses to the environment are controllable. The corporation can control its decisions about various product and market-related elements with which to respond to the environment. This is the role and function of strategic marketing planning. Strategic planning is defined as the managerial process of developing and maintaining a viable fit between the organization's objectives and resources, and its changing market opportunities. The aim of strategic planning is to shape and reshape the company's businesses and products so that they combine to produce satisfactory profits and growth.[2]

Marketing and other decision-makers in the enterprise have to be concerned about environmental changes. Changes in the environment may impact a company's marketing mix, customer-value delivery system, customer bases, and profitability. Such environmental changes may denote problems that threaten the firm's competitive position and advantage. Alternatively, environmental changes may denote opportunities for gaining a competitive foothold or advantage. In turbulent environments, adept analysis and on-going adjustments in business strategies are required for sustaining competitive advantage.

Strategic Planning Focus

Strategic planning is a relatively recent discipline, having its origin in the crises of the 1970s and economic jolts of the 1980s. During the 1970s, the oil crisis, double-digit inflation, and rising unemployment consumed management's attention. Additional economic shocks further intensified the need for strategic planning: deregulation of various industries – airlines, railroad, telecommunications, and energy – and the influx of high quality and low-cost products from Japan – electronic products, steel, automobiles, and cameras. Today all large companies worldwide and an increasing number of small ones have some form of formal strategic planning process.

There were three main foci of this emerging strategic planning process: business mix or portfolio, future profit potential, and strategy.[3] The business portfolio focus stressed managing the firm's businesses like an investment portfolio. A business portfolio manager should function just as a stock portfolio manager who scrutinizes the performance of each stock in its portfolio, and – based upon performance against a required rate of return – decide to divest, keep, or increase investments. The second focus is examining each business's prospects for future profits. This focus is based on the idea that what is doing well in today's environment does not necessarily mean it will do well in tomorrow's environment. An analysis of the business's likely performance under different possible future scenarios should indicate whether it makes sense to stay in a given business in the long run. The third focus, strategy, represents a plan of action for each business to achieve its strategic objectives, and ultimately competitive advantage, given its available resources. There are different strategic game plans and approaches such as diversification, niche, cost leadership, and innovation. Given the turbulence of the information age, additional strategic levers have been used.

Levels of Strategic Planning

There are three levels of planning which include corporate, business, and product planning. Corporate level strategic planning makes decisions about resource allocations for each business, division, and subsidiary. Given their resource allocation, each business in turn develops a business strategy. Finally, a marketing plan is developed for each product level (product line and brand) within the business unit. Corporate level strategic planning process (Figure 3.1) begins with establishing the mission, objectives and policies, and overall game plan that will serve as the planning framework for each business unit.

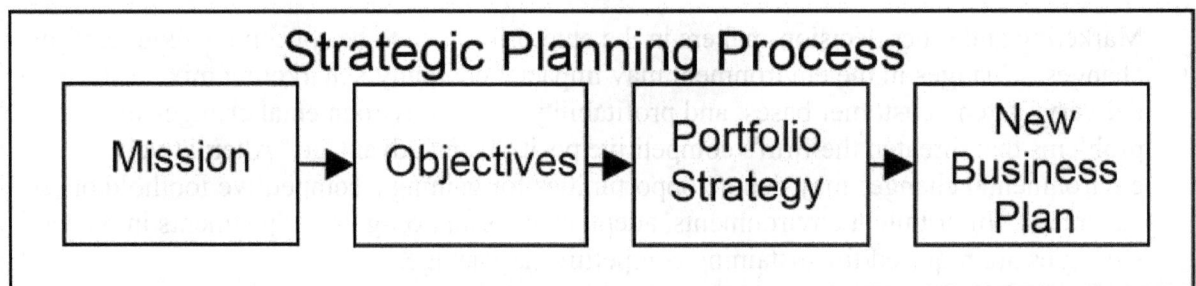

Strategic Planning Process

Mission → Objectives → Portfolio Strategy → New Business Plan

Figure 3.1: Strategic Planning Process

Mission statements answer the raison d'être questions of the corporation: In what business are we? Who are our customers? In what business should we be? What is value to our customers? The mission also defines the competitive "playing field" on which the corporation will compete. This playing field is dimensioned in terms of four scopes: industry, market segment, vertical, and geographic. The industry scope concerns the different industries in which the corporation will operate. The market segment scope identifies the type of market or customers the corporation will target. The vertical scope addresses the degree to which the corporation will produce within versus outsource components and stages of the value chain. Geographic scope specifies the areas of the country and globe in which the corporation will compete.

The organization must have a defined reason for being in existence. This organizational purpose positions the goals, objectives and strategy of the organization. This chapter describes the key components to the strategic direction development process shown in Figure 3.2.

FIGURE 3.2: Strategic Planning Process and Organizational Purpose

It begins with creating the strategic direction for the organization. These strategies describe how the organization will differentiate itself from its competitors and why the customer would perceive this as an advantage. This organizational purpose provides the marketing manager with an understanding of the organizational focus. This strategic focus provides overall direction to the marketing managers as they generate insights and search for opportunities. The organization communicates its strategies and its success or failure at achieving its strategies through the balanced scorecard. Each member of the organization then has an understanding of where the organization is headed and how close it is to meeting its vision.

Section 2. Strategy Development for Competitive Advantage

"Do not repeat the tactics which have gained you one victory, but let your methods be regulated by the infinite variety of circumstances."
Sun Tzu

Strategy Development Process

The first step in the strategic direction process involves the development of the organization's strategy. A company can achieve success even if many aspects of its internal resource uses are inefficient as long as the organization has a strong strategy in place. Conversely, an organization with strong internal processes but a weak strategy will likely fail. The strategy development process provides for the development of the organization's strategies, the definition of key organizational structures, and the description of systems required to achieve the organizational objectives (Figure 3.3).

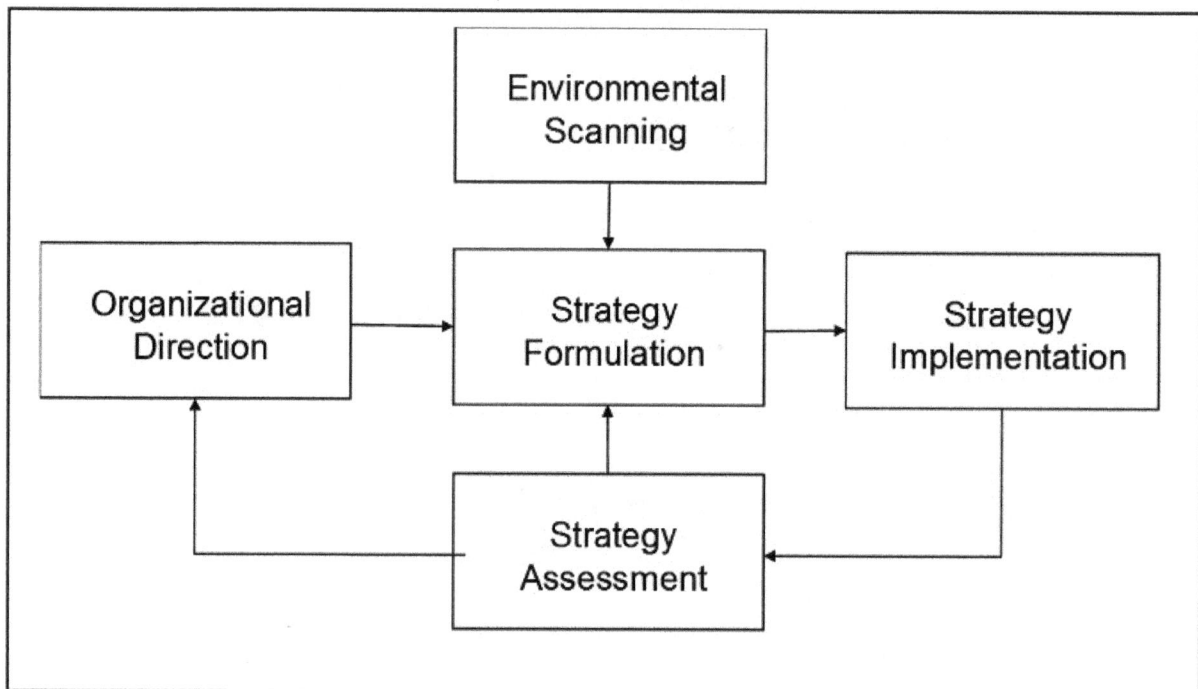

Figure 3.3: Strategy Development Process

These strategies should focus the organization on how the organization can perform different activities from competitors or similar activities to its competitors in different, unique, valuable ways. Strategy is the creation of a unique and valuable position, involving a different set of activities by making trade-offs in competing. Strategy is creating a strategic fit between an organization's activities and business environment. Strategy defines and communicates the organization's unique position by making trade-offs and forging fit among activities. Strategy is a long-term plan that integrates an organization's major goals, policies, and action(s). A well-formulated strategy helps firms allocate an organization's resources into a unique and viable posture based upon its strengths and weaknesses and anticipated changes in the environment. Strategies contain three elements: 1) goals to be achieved, 2) policies that guide or limit action, and 3) programs that accomplish goals.

90

The organizational strategy development process is used by the leadership team to create its position in the marketplace by focusing on an ideal vision of the future and is usually viewed as containing five distinct stages. Those stages include: first, creating an organizational direction; second, scanning the environment and understanding the customer; third, formulating the strategy; fourth, implementing the strategy; and fifth, assessing the strategy and providing feedback for continual improvement. To have an effective strategy development process requires input, resource, and information. Input is sought from a variety of potential stakeholders. These stakeholders include employees, customers, suppliers, government agencies, and others. The resources include the human resources, financial assets, various materials, internal processes, and machinery available to the organization to deploy in meeting its vision. The information is obtained from a variety of sources including internal transaction systems, industry organizations, market research, and government agencies.

Organizational Direction

The articulation of the strategic objectives provides overall direction for the organization. It is the responsibility of the organizational senior management to develop and create this direction and then to communicate it to the workers, known as top down strategic planning. The senior leaders of the organization must define the organization's vision, mission, strategy, goals, and objectives. Senior leaders need to understand the nature of reality first. Then, they must create a value orientation that takes into account such things as contribution, spirit, excellence, beauty, and joy and avoid an orientation toward rules. This organizational direction statement describes the future the marketing managers want to be part of and creates a sense of urgency for the organization to achieve it. Another form of strategic planning is known as distributed leadership or bottom-up strategic planning. According to this theory, it is the product managers and business unit leaders who are closest to the marketplace and best understand customer problems. For this reason these individuals should have some responsibility in developing the company's overall strategy.

Environmental Scanning

The process of scanning the environment provides the organization's leaders with insights and the knowledge required to understand the marketspace and creates the organization capable of competing and surviving in the global environment. The marketing managers must scan the environment and develop insights into the potential customers, partners, competitors, and macro-economic indicators.

Strategy Formulation

The strategy formulation phase of the process involves the development, evaluation, and selection of various strategies. To begin with, however, the leadership team must have developed the organization's vision, mission, and values. Then, the organization must assess its strengths and weaknesses. The marketing manager provides the strategy participants with information based upon the analysis of the organization's strengths and weaknesses and various opportunities and threats facing the organization. This critical assessment forms the basis for understanding the gaps that exist between the desired future state articulated by the organization's leaders and the current state of organizational operations. Only after this is completed can the strategy participants begin to develop the organization's goals, strategies, and objectives.

Strategy Implementation

During the strategy implementation phase the organization translates strategies into actionable activities. These activities involve the allocation of resources, communication of plans, reworking of job descriptions, and altering of processes. The strategy implementation must be more than just statements from the leadership team. The strategy implementation must have a clear deployment plan consisting of specific numerically measurable activities focused on achieving the defined strategic objectives.

Strategy Assessment

The strategy assessment phase involves the development of the measurements and control structure to report on the defined strategies. The emphasis is on reviewing the performance of the specific plans. The specific numeric measurements provide a quantifiable measure for the performance of the strategy. Comparing these values to the specified targets provides for the assessment and modification of the plan.

Strategies for Competitive Advantage

In the early part of the 20th century, businesses emphasized efficiency and productivity competitive levers such as cost, price, and product-differentiation. Thanks to the various Japanese management philosophies and practices, especially the total quality management movement, the competitive levers of this period are "prerequisites" for an enterprise to enter onto the information age's competitive playing field.

Enterprises facing the competitive market must emphasize different competitive capabilities. These capabilities require a different "mind set". To compete successfully in the information age, businesses must emphasize different sources of advantages such as time-based competition, market/customer-driven orientation, agility and mass customization, organizational learning/knowledge, total quality, and core capabilities.

Time-Based Strategy

In recent years, developing time-based strategies and competing on the basis of time has been capturing an increased amount of management attention. Time-based competition is a strategy of seeking competitive advantage by quickening the tempo of critical organizational processes such as new product development, processing customer orders, production processes, distribution processes, and after-sale service processes. Poor quality in procured materials, process capability, and process control can lead to inflated lead-times through rework and non value-added time. Improved supplier performance can help to reduce downtime and shortages associated with delivery delays. Just-In-Time purchasing calls for policies aimed as single sourcing and the awarding of long-term contracts, localized sources of supply, less frequent use of competitive bidding, and emphasis is on a close working relationship with suppliers.

The advantages achieved by time-based competitors enable them to grow faster and earn higher profits relative to other firms in their industry. Additional benefits include reduced lead-time, reduced inventory, reduced non-value-added cost, and enhanced global competitiveness. Time-based competition includes improved delivery speed, fast cycle capability, quick response, lead-time reduction, and throughput time reduction.

In order to effectively manage time and compete on the basis of time, optimization of the entire value chain is necessary. Time-based leadership is a critical source of sustained competitiveness, yet the problems associated with measuring lead-time signify that many firms are not managing lead-time effectively.

Customer/Market-Driven Strategy

Companies that are better equipped to respond to market requirements and anticipate changing conditions are expected to enjoy long-run competitive advantage and superior profitability. According to Stull, Myers, and Scott, market-driven companies are 31% more profitable, twice as fast to bring products to market, twice as likely to lead, and to have 20% higher customer satisfaction. In market-driven firms, the processes for gathering, interpreting, and using market information are more systematic, thoughtful, and anticipatory than in other firms.

Key steps in becoming market-driven include maintaining a customer orientation, developing a competitor orientation, and achieving inter-functional coordination.[4] A customer orientation implies that the firm has a good understanding of the target market. A competitor orientation implies that the firm has a good understanding of the long run capabilities of present and prospective competitors. Inter-functional coordination implies that communication and teamwork exist so that the utilization of company resources to create superior customer value occurs.

Agility/Mass Customization Strategy

Agility is defined as a firm's response to rapidly changing, continually fragmenting, global markets for high-quality, high performance, customer-configured goods and services. Agility is a concept reflecting the realization that the global competitive environment of the information age requires the provision of highly customized products to the specific needs of customers in narrow market niches. Mass customization is the strategic option chosen for agile firms.

The financial and accounting metrics for evaluating performance in the past were based upon:

- A one-dimensional price.
- The lowest unit cost that was the decisive determinant of competitiveness.
- Emphasizing efficiency that was a function of the direct inputs (cost of materials, labor, and manufacturing processes).

- Utilizing standardized pricing to determine product value.
- Single-instance sales transactions in which individualized customers were relatively undifferentiated.

In contrast, agile competition metrics must be multidimensional and incorporate pricing strategies that reflect differential value particularized to individual customers. Over the course of the relationship with the customer, the relative value of the physical, information, and service dimensions of the product, reflected in the original price, will have changed over time.

Organizational Learning / Knowledge Management

To provide customized products to narrowly targeted customers requires a plethora of information about those customers. Thus, organizational learning and the relevant knowledge that must be managed properly, are key critical enablers of agility-based competition. "Relevant knowledge", therefore, is the answer to the question, "What is the output or "product" of the organization learning processes?" "Competitive advantage" is the answer to the second question, "For what purpose is the organization learning relevant knowledge?". In turbulent competitive contexts, "organizational learning may be the only remaining source of competitive advantage."

Continuous organizational learning and effective knowledge management is increasingly necessary in order for organizations to maintain alignment with their competition. This alignment enables organizations to satisfy its customers and deal with its competitors. "An organization's capacity to improve existing skills and learn new ones is the most defensible competitive advantage of all."[5] Furthermore, as these environments become more turbulent, organizational learning and knowledge management becomes a strategic imperative for survival and competitiveness. The knowledge advantage is a sustainable advantage. Hence, the turbulent competitive environment compels organizations to build internal environments that foster organizational learning, knowledge management, and innovation in order to achieve any combination of the key sources of competitive advantage.

Nevertheless, knowledge management literature has underscored the "entangled relationship" between the organization's people as knowers and organizational knowledge. Whereas "information" is understood as "purposeful and relevant", "knowledge" exists within people as a function of "values, framed experience, contextual information and expert insight".

In summary, through the medium of business cultures that emphasize knowledge management and organizational learning, people can "learn to learn" and "learn to value learning" and utilize their learning to convert knowledge resources into knowledge assets.

Core Competencies

The true source of a corporation's competitive advantage comes from its core competencies. By conducting a core -competencies analysis a corporation is able to determine the functions best done within itself and which functions should be outsourced. Those functions determined to be held within are the activities which the corporation does extremely well and add real or perceived value to the company, thus becoming its competitive advantage. Core competencies are defined as the collective learning in the organization, especially those that coordinate diverse production skills and integrate multiple streams of technologies. In essence, core competencies represent a bundle of skills that are of value to customers, which are unique to a corporation and, therefore, difficult to imitate.

Competitive Advantage: A Moving Target?

Achieving a competitive advantage at one point in time does not guarantee that a firm will stay competitive forever. As other firms begin to imitate a business's strategy, its competitive advantage erodes. As competition becomes more intense, management must search for advantages that can improve a company's competitive position. To compete, the firm needs to define other domains of competition such as new levels of automation, new materials and technologies, innovative product features, and/or skillful management and expansion into developing markets.

Integrating the methods for improving competitive performance is one of the major challenges facing enterprises in the turbulent information age. Competitive advantage will increasingly rest on marketing's ability to better manage knowledge about the critical elements in the environment. Those elements include potential and existing customers, potential and current competitors, emerging technological innovations, potential and current markets around the globe, strategic business alliances formed by competitors and available to the corporation, regulatory and political issues in various governments, and regional and country economies, and finally environmental and resource issues.

Linking Strategic Planning to Marketing Management

Strategic planning is directly linked to marketing management. Figure 3.4 shows the linkages between strategic planning and marketing management. Just like any other functions in the organization, marketing should support the organizational goals and strategies developed in the strategic planning process. Strategic planning focuses on strategic control that examines whether the organization whether the company is pursuing best product/market and channel opportunities. Strategic planning is in the domain of top management. Strategic plans are translated to an annual business plan that examines whether the planned results can be achieved. The annual plan control is the joint effort of top and functional management. Various functional managers are controlling strategic component. Marketing managers examine how well resources are utilized in each element of the marketing strategy. Marketing strategies are developed to achieve the desired effect on demand. To implement marketing strategies, marketing managers develop marketing plans and programs that include target market and marketing mix decisions.

Figure 3.4: Strategic Planning vs. Marketing Management

Section 3. Relationship Marketing Strategy

> *"Marketing is not an event, but a process ... It has a beginning, a middle, but never an end, for it is a process. You improve it, perfect it, change it, even pause it. But you never stop it completely."*
> Jay Conrad Levinson

Customer relationship marketing strategy utilizes various CRM solutions to acquire, warehouse, and analyze customer and firm activity data and to generate customer analytics from these data. The customer analytics are used in acquiring new customers and retaining current customers through long-term relationship building. These analytics are also used to develop and design various marketing activities such as customized marketing communications to enhance customer relationships. A customer strategy comprises a set of strategic goals that will drive initiatives that can be applied to customers in identifiable segments to achieve the overall objective of sustained profitable growth. Typical elements of a relationship marketing strategy could be (1) rewarding best customers to improve loyalty, (2) re-ignition of dormant customers to reduce churn, (3) stimulation of occasional customers to stimulate more frequent contact, (4) cross selling to frequent low value customers to improve share of wallet, (5) reduction of cost to market, sell and serve to low value customers, and (6) migrate frequent customers onto lower cost channels.

To achieve these goals, various firms are implementing many different relationship marketing activities and programs. These activities and programs share some common components. Key common components of relationship marketing strategy include the following:[6]

- Marketing strategy building and maintaining long-term customer relationships.

96

- Management of creating both product (brand) value as well as customer value.
- The acquisition and intelligent use of customer data and business intelligence technology as well as generation and diffusion of customer insights to the appropriate stakeholders.
- The development and enhancement of long-term relationships with the right customers.
- Integration and collaboration to generate customer value.

Customer Relationship as the Key Driver

With the increased adoption of CRM initiatives, the marketing function experiences a dramatic change in its role and focus. Relationship marketing entails the shift in marketing focus from increasing the number and value of transactions to growing more effective and profitable relationships with multiple stakeholders. Relationship marketing is planning and implementing marketing strategy and programs on the basis of relationships with customers. It focuses on building customer value to increase customer retention. With this approach, firms can achieve potentially higher revenue and profit at lower cost by taking full advantage of existing capabilities of product development and lower customer acquisition cost. By focusing on customer relationships, marketing can obtain valuable knowledge about customers' needs through increased customer contact and customer involvement. This knowledge can be used to build future product and service delivery. Enduring customer relationship offers a wealth of opportunities for service and relationship enhancement. Relationship marketing will possess the following characteristics described in this section. While the detailed components of relationship marketing will vary depending on the products and industries, these characteristics represent most commonly accepted marketing practices adopting this approach.

Focus on Customer Equity

In developing and implementing marketing strategy, firms need to consider their objectives that need to be achieved from a successful marketing strategy. In a customer relationship marketing, customer equity introduced by Blattberg and Deighton can be an effective measure for success.[7] They defined customer equity as the sum of the lifetime values of the firm's customers. An example of such customer equity measure is customer lifetime value or driver analysis that derives customer equity drivers based on customer data.[8] Any marketing decisions made can influence customers' perception of a firm's product and brand affecting the customer lifetime value and customer relationship. Customer equity is composed of three key components.[9]

The three components are product value equity, brand equity, and relationship equity. These three components are managed effectively to influence customer equity such as customer lifetime value by responding quickly to changing customer needs, wants, and market trends.

Product Value Equity

Product value equity represents the customer's objective evaluation of the firm's product and/or service. Product value is the foundation of the customer's relationship with the firm. A firm's products and services must meet the customer's needs and expectations. Without the product value, the brand strategy or relationship marketing strategies would not work. Customers' perceived value can be determined by many factors including quality, price, service, and warranty.

Brand Equity

Brand equity refers to the customer's subjective assessment of the firm and its offerings. The brand equity is built through the creation of image and meaning attached to the brand or the firm. Brand serves many different roles. It acts as a symbol or identity that attracts new customers, reminds customers about the firm's products and services, and serves as the customer's emotional tie to the firm. Brand equity is formed over time driven by brand familiarity, brand image, and corporate ethics.[10]

Relationship Equity

Relationship equity represents the customer's view of the strength of the relationship between the customer and the firm. In the age of relationship marketing, a great product and brand may not be sufficient to hold the customer and grow the firm's profitability. Firms need to create a strong relationship that connects the firm to the customer. Relationship equity provides a means for a firm to make its customers to stick to the brand above and beyond the customer's objective and subjective assessments of the brand. Many marketing programs and actions enhance customer relationship equity. These programs include affinity programs, loyalty programs, community-building programs, and knowledge building programs. Affinity programs try to create strong emotional connections with customers. Examples of such programs are those offered by many credit card companies such as affinity VISA. Loyalty programs include many customer reward programs for specific behaviors of repeated purchase or patronage. Airlines, such as Delta Sky Miles program, are offering mileage points to redeem free tickets. These loyalty programs are becoming an integral part of many firms' marketing strategy. Community-building programs intend to increase the closeness of the customer with the firm by connecting the customer to a network of similar customers through Web portals and communities. For example, firms like Disney or Kodak create portal sites where the customer can share interests and activities. Knowledge-building programs create structural bonds between the customer and the firm. By creating a strong bond using the knowledge of the customer's preference or past purchase behavior, firms can make customers less willing to recreate the customer-firm relationship with competitor firms. An example would be Amazon.com making product recommendations and check out process easier for repeat customers. The relationship marketing programs allow firms to maximize the likelihood of repeated purchase as well as share of wallet and minimize the likelihood of brand switching and churning.

In developing a firm's relationship marketing strategy, marketing managers need to understand relative importance of the value, brand, and relationship equity to customers. Depending on the relative impact of these three components on customer equity, a proper strategic approach can be developed. It is expected that different market segments will exhibit differential importance of the value, brand, and relationship equity resulting different customer relationship marketing strategy.

Relationship marketing focuses on relationship equity rather than product or brand equity. This can be achieved by putting emphasis on the 'relationship' rather than the 'transaction'. In this sense, customer relationships are considered as the most critical assets of a firm. This implies that a firm must manage customer relationships just like other assets of a company. This implies that customer relationships must be selectively managed and enhanced to improve customer retention and profitability. Under this marketing approach, customers are not viewed as a group or audience who receives and responds to a range of marketing and promotional activities.

Proactive Use of Marketing Analytics

With increased impact of e-commerce and on-line business-to-consumer (B2C) and business-to-business (B2B) transactions, customers are empowered to a level that has not been seen in the marketplace and marketspace before. Since customers are now faced with more choices, access to comparative information, and personalized options, they can easily switch brands and suppliers that can offer a better value in this buyer's market. This creates market trends of diminished loyalty and greater propensity of churning. Firms are responding to this disturbing market development with mass customization and quickly customizing and redeveloping their offers to gain a greater share of market. To continuously redefine their market offers, firms need to know their customers and competitors and use this knowledge proactively. Recent development in tools and technology allows firms to generate knowledge and share business insights derived from their marketing analytic systems across various functions and sub-business units. These shared knowledge and insights are critical in creating value for customers. Firms using these customer knowledge and insights proactively, for example, will seek to identify and remedy potential customer complaints before they become a major source of dissatisfaction leading to customer defection. Relationship marketing relies on the information and insights in the marketing analytics system to increase revenue through increased effectiveness in the front office activities of sales, marketing, and customer service. Marketing analytics system encompasses data warehouse, business intelligence, marketing analytics and CRM application tools. Data warehouse serves as a data repository of customer information. Business intelligence and CRM application tools define customer interface used for value-adding interactions with customers across different marketing channels and touch points. Proactive use of marketing analytics enables firms to retain memory of relevant customer encounter and use all past encounters with that customer in every future interaction with that customer. How well a firm can fulfill customer relationship-driven marketing depends heavily on this proactive use of marketing analytics.

Firms can effectively perform differentiation with the depth of customer analytics and breadth of communication versatility. Customers must feel that the firm knows them and treats them with high regard for their value and personal interaction history. This requires customer analytics powerful enough to provide an actionable, holistic view of the firm's customers. The holistic view allows firms to prevent churn, retain customers, and motivate customers to stay. With this customer holistic view, firms can provide preemptive offering of discounts or fee waivers to existing customers who are a risk of churning, refining target marketing campaigns to smaller customers or specific products. Firms can package certain products together with fixed pricing to sell more products and increase their profitability. It allows firms to cross-sell products likely to be purchased with other products.

Viewing Customer Relationships as the Primary Source of Sustainable Competitive Advantage

With the increased global competition and outsourcing business environment, firms are struggling to gain and sustain competitive edge over their competitors. Firms have derived competitive advantage in the past from various sources. These sources include manufacturing capability, product quality, price, innovation, and market knowledge. The dynamic capabilities approach of the resource-based theory stresses the ability of the firm to integrate, coordinate, learn and transform thereby developing capabilities on an ongoing basis.[11] Management's ability to develop unique capabilities and combinations of resources that are hard to duplicate are required for a firm to be successful in developing a sustainable competitive advantage. Relationships are built upon the creation and delivery of superior customer value in specific segments and markets on a sustainable basis. To sustain this competitive advantage of customer relationships, firms must assess the economic value of different market segments and adjust the level of market offerings such a way that firms can continuously realize satisfactory profit while offering superior value to targeted customers.

Adoption of the One-to-One Marketing Program

With increased market competition and firms' efforts to offer specific tailored solutions to customers, markets are fragmented into ever smaller segments. When this market fragmentation reaches to an extreme, segmentation reaches the level of individual customers. According to Peppers and Rogers, this changes the very nature of marketing.[12] Segments become meaningless such that they have no memories, no interactions, and no referrals. Instead, individual customers do all these things. One-to-one marketers harness those activities of individual customers and try to develop continuing relationships with customers. One-to-one marketing is defined as marketing activities in which dialogue and interactions occur directly between a company and individual customers or customer groups with similar needs. It accommodates the customer-centric view with the focus on the individual customer. Instead of focusing products and product differentiation, one-to-one marketing focuses on customers and customer differentiation. Thus, a company builds a one-to-one relationship with individual customer, and retains and enhances that relationship in a profitable and productive way.

One-to-One marketing can occur in two different forms; personalization and customization.[13] Personalization involves the company deciding which marketing mix will be suitable for the individual customer based on previously collected data, such as Amazon's suggestions for similar products after purchasing something. Customization involves the customer specifying their own preferences for a marketing mix such as NikeID, which allows the consumer to customize the graphics and design of their shoes. While both forms have the potential for greater customer satisfaction there is also the added draw-back of greater costs and for personalization in particular the potential for unwanted invasions of privacy.

Adoption of the one-to-one marketing program requires more than changing marketing and sales plan. It is a management philosophy and discipline that puts the customer at the heart of the business. This discipline applies to both the business customer and individual customers. For example, B2B firms are adopting this philosophy primarily through key account management strategies. Smaller customers and B2C customers are dealt with mass customized campaign management strategies.

This philosophy is based on the notion of collaboration, engaging customers with dialogue, and building trust. While customers share their needs and aspirations, and their problems and ideas, firms try to find mutually profitable solutions with customers. The implementation of the one-to-one marketing provides obvious benefits.[14] These benefits include:

- Business focus shifting to the most profitable customers,
- Shift to the lifetime share of the customer base rather than market share as a key performance indicator,
- Emphasis on retaining profitable customers as the cost of new customer acquisition is far greater than the cost of customer retention,
- Collaboration with customers offer a rich source of new product development ideas and increase the new product success rate, and
- Greater marketing efficiency due to the implementation of more targeted marketing program with in-depth knowledge of the individual customers.

The key to any business's future success is its existing profitable customer base. The creation of one-to-one relationship requires not only effective customer relationship marketing strategies and enabling tools, but also a fundamental change in the business's management philosophy, organizational culture, design, and support systems. The one-to-one marketing programs should be able to bring the level of customer intimacy that has been lost.

Section 4. Total CRM Based Relationship Marketing Plan for Relevance

"We see our customers as invited guests to a party, and we are the hosts. It's our job every day to make every important aspect of the customer experience a little bit better."
Jeff Bezos

Total CRM Based Relationship Marketing Planning Framework

Figure 3.5 provides the total CRM based relationship marketing framework.[15] This framework provides the formation, process, reaction, and effects of the complex network-based marketing plan and activities. It allows firms to achieve a stronger and more differentiated market position and provide better customer value that ultimately leads to competitive advantage. The framework starts with the recognition that total CRM efforts include three types of initiatives. These initiatives are traditional CRM, e-CRM, and social CRM. In each CRM initiative, different marketing strategies are evolving. Traditional CRM generates traditional marketing goals and strategies for the target customers. Traditional marketing leads to typical bricks-and-mortar marketing programs and tactics. E-CRM, on the other hand, generates e-commerce goals and strategies that are more technology-driven. The online marketing activities are implemented through a web presence by firms. Social CRM leads to social media goals and strategies achieved through an active social media presence by the firm.

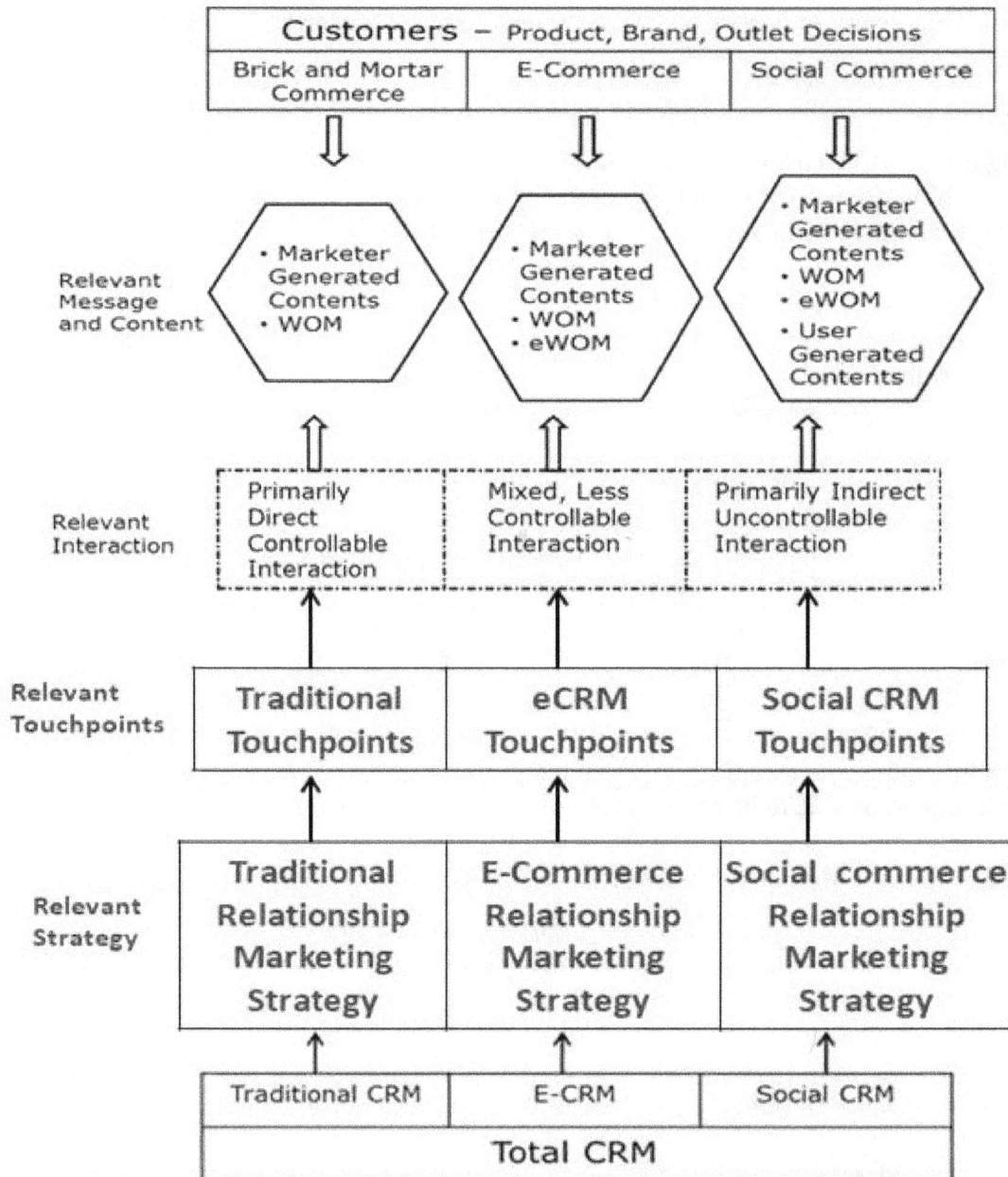

Figure 3.5: Total CRM Based Relationship Marketing Planning Framework for Relevance

The firm's relationship marketing efforts are directly linked to various touchpoints or channels utilized by marketing managers. The various types of touchpoint channels include traditional touchpoints such as television and newspaper, online touchpoints such as websites, and social media touchpoints such as YouTube and other social media platforms. In understanding the ongoing interactions and marketing communications, it is important to evaluate the nature of interaction and the type of messages exchanged in the interaction process. In the traditional touchpoints, the interaction is characterized as primarily direct from and controlled by the marketing manager in the firm. The main component of this traditional touchpoint is the content generated by the firm in the form of advertising and publicity. Traditional word-of-mouth (WOM) communication enters in this context. The traditional WOM communication involves inter-consumer communications pertaining to the organic exchange of product and brand-related messages with or without direct influence by the marketing managers through traditional means such as advertising and promotion as a component of traditional CRM efforts.

For the online touchpoints, the interaction is mixed and less controllable by marketers. Along with this generated content and traditional WOM communication, online touchpoint interaction generates e-WOM communication that includes online product evaluations and comments by e-retailers and e-shoppers. Firms develop e-commerce strategy to build effective online presence and manage customer relationships through eCRM activities. For the social media touchpoints, the nature of interaction is completely different. The interaction can be characterized as primarily indirect and uncontrollable by the firm's marketing managers. The message and content are also becoming more diverse. In addition to the marketer-generated content, traditional WOM, and e-WOM, user-generated content in the form of comments, blog postings, and video are increasingly dominant and important. This new user-generated content offers an opportunity for firms as they provide a new source of information and an avenue of interacting with visitors, prospects, and customers. At the same time, they offer tremendous challenges to firms that are not ready to adapt to the reality of social media applications and social network services.

As indicated earlier, the key premise of the Figure 3.5 framework is the transition from either traditional or e-commerce relationship marketing strategy to social commerce relationship marketing strategy. Firms need to develop and implement effective social media relationship marketing strategies in managing customer relationships. The next section discusses in more detail the nature and process of social CRM and related consequences in relationship marketing and customer relationship management.

Emerging Role of Social CRM Touchpoints

Market space is very dynamic and changing. This market space is becoming more and more controlled by the customer and virtual community opinion leaders. As such, firms must work to ensure that the information about its brands, products, and services can be searched, found, linked, communicated, engaged, shared, and involved. Why are these important issues? What is causing the "being relevant" requirement? What drives this change? Answering these questions requires using a new communications model and using a total customer relationship management perspective.

 What are drivers and inhibitors of interactive social media marketing? "Business-to-business (B2B) marketers see social media as an avenue to demonstrate thought leadership, generate leads, and obtain customer feedback."[16] So, understanding the various drivers and inhibitors to interactive social media marketing is a key requirement for these marketers. It has been determined that the drivers of interactive social media marketing include creating a community of fans, empowering opinion leaders, integrating digital strategies, trust, and use of technology. "Word-of-mouth marketing is not about giving customers talking points, as if they were brand spokespeople. It is about delivering an exceptional customer experience that makes customers want to recommend you."[17] It was shown that users do not have a high level of trust for firms, but rather they have a high level of trust for experts and 'people-like-me'. For the firm to avoid having trust become an inhibitor, the firm should become part of the conversation rather than trying to control the conversation.

Identified inhibitors of interactive social media marketing include a lack of knowledgeable staff, a lack of funding, management resistance, the inability to measure outcomes, and technical complexity. A lack of knowledge can lead to misconceptions and inaccurate decisions resulting in missed opportunities. These inhibitors to interactive social media marketing are, for the most part, things that the firm can control and address. The lack of a knowledgeable staff can be overcome by using consultants, by better hiring of new talent, or by training of existing personnel. The inability to measure outcomes can be associated with the use of incorrect tools or the lack of understanding of various reports generated by existing tools used by the firm. To overcome management resistance, the information professional can position the digital presence discussion in terms of return on investment and can position the discussion in achieving the overall organizational or marketing strategy.

Transition to Social CRM

"Social CRM is a philosophy as well as a business strategy, supported by a technology platform, business rules, processes, and social characteristics designed to engage the customer in a collaborative conversation in order to provide mutually beneficial value in a trusted and transparent business environment. It's the firm's response to the customer's ownership of the conversation."[18] The two key points in this definition are first, that the customer or user is actively engaged in a conversation with the firm and second, that there is mutually beneficial value. However, social CRM has a different 'holy grail'. Rather than one that is transaction-friendly and data-driven, the new holy grail is based upon 'a firm like me'. This concept is to match the trust opportunity where the user trusts 'people like me'. It has been reported that where online users do trust the firm, it occurs if and when the firm uses social media tools.

Facebook is one of the primary social media tools that can be used by firms. Yet, Facebook isn't a blunt instrument. It has great potential as a nuanced CRM tool if it is not abused. The firm should think long and hard about the context, sensibilities and the psycho-demographics of their intended audience. The firm should target carefully and make a compelling offer in a creative way that suits the social setting. Facebook has the potential to cement customer relationships if it is used thoughtfully.[19] The idea of thoughtful use goes back to the social CRM key points. Facebook should be used as a conversation tool and should be mutually beneficial to the user and to the firm.

Table 3.1 provides a list of key Traditional CRM versus Social CRM features and functions. Ongoing user interaction and engagement is important for the firm's performance and success. Social CRM helps firms to get closer to its customers.[20] Social CRM has two key characteristics that the firm can focus. The first characteristic of social CRM is the collaborative conversations with users that can create a mutually beneficial value where the firm joins the on-going conversations among existing customers and prospects rather than controlling the message and directing customer communications. The second characteristic of social CRM is when it is used to develop and utilize new forms of customer intelligence by combining the social data showing the nature of social conversations with existing customer information in order to generate insights regarding how to engage in conversations. Unique insights can be gained through intelligent monitoring of the social conversation. These two key characteristics of social CRM and social media can pose challenges and opportunities for firms. As customers use social media tools to connect with each other and share information, information travels much faster and more efficiently.

Traditional CRM	Social CRM

Definition:
    a philosophy & strategy supported by systems & technologies designed to improve human interactions
	Definition:
	    a philosophy & strategy supported by systems & technologies designed to engage the customer in a collaborative interaction that provides mutually beneficial value in a trusted &transparent environment

The organization seeks to lead and shape opinions about products, services & customer relationships	The customer is a partner from the beginning in the development and improvement of products, services & customer relationships
The organization focuses on products & services that satisfy customers	The organization focuses on environments & experiences that engage customers
Marketing focuses on processes that send targeted, highly specific messages to customers	Marketing focuses on building relationships with customers via activity & discussion, observations & conversations
Intellectual property protected with all legal might available	Intellectual property created and owned together with customers, partners, suppliers, & problem solvers
Technology focused on operational aspects of sales, marketing, & support	Technology focused on operational and social aspects of the interaction
Tools are for automating functions	Tools integrate into apps, blogs, wikis, podcasts, content sharing, and user communities

Table 3.1: Traditional CRM versus Social CRM Features and Functions

Firms may have difficulty in tracking, organizing, and responding to these interactive online and social media conversations. Social CRM can help redefine the way firms engage with customers and can redefine the very nature of marketing, sales, and customer service. It offers firms an organized approach to connect various organizational units to the social media sites and provide the opportunity to respond in near real time in a coordinated fashion. Firms can identify leads by listening to keywords that suggest a customer is getting ready to buy and then sending real time alerts to the sales teams to respond to that customer.[21] Firms can develop expertise in managing influencer relationships in social media sites for greater relevance. Through social CRM, firms can turn customers into advocates by talking to customers, engaging with customers, and collaborating with customers to solve customer problems leading to enlightened customer experiences.

Within the total CRM communication framework, social media can be managed from two different perspectives. For firms that do not have strong brand recognition and brand equity, they can consider social media as one of the many touchpoints. In this case, customers are interacting with social media as one of the many touchpoints of a firm. Social media is becoming increasingly important in the integrated touchpoint management process of a firm's relationship marketing efforts. Alternatively, firms can use social media as a component or tool in managing their brands. This approach can be used by firms that have strong brand equity or that want to build stronger brand recognition and loyalty. Social media sites are used to communicate, introduce, and promote new features and customer experiences with their brands. These two alternative perspectives are not necessarily contradictory but rather complementary. Therefore, both perspectives can be used simultaneously in managing online and social media sites. The next section describes in more detail these two alternative approaches of managing interactive online and social media sites.

Integrating total CRM Touchpoints

The multi-channel integration is an important task in managing relationship marketing efforts. The objective is to choose customer touchpoints and channels that will capture the attention of the target market and prove to be the most convenient for them. In today's world, firms have many different touchpoints and channels from which to choose. These various touchpoints include the following: (1) A traditional sales force, (2) Retail stores and other traditional outlets, (3) Telephones, including telephone, fax, and call centers, (4) Direct marketing, including direct mail, radio, and television, (5) E-commerce, including e-retail sites, banner ads, etc., (6) M-commerce, including mobile phones, etc., and (7) S-commerce, including social media sites and networks.

Most firms have chosen to use multiple touchpoints and channels to reach their prospects and customers. Thus, each of these divergent touchpoints and channels must be managed at the same exacting standards compared to each other. The firms must broadcast one unified face to its customers, while at the same time attracting the right customers to the right products and services. While this sounds straightforward, many problems can occur when trying to integrate marketing communications together throughout the entire firm. For a moment, consider the example of an automobile company. Originally, car companies sold only through their dealerships. However, as computer technology developed, direct marketing became a new method of selling exactly the right model car with the right color, and the right features to customers. This may have been a strong new channel for the firm, but it was seen as a threat by existing dealerships. This highlights a common problem between traditional "brick-and-mortar" (retail stores) and e-commerce (website) sales – channel conflict due to the fear that retailers will lose their customer base. Although this is a legitimate concern, if handled carefully, it can become an advantage to both the retail outlet and the firm. The firm must endeavor to create a solution that does not leave its retail outlet in the dark. Customers usually want to test drive the cars they are purchasing, so retail outlets add significant value to customers. If the car company can give monetary advantage to dealerships to direct customers online (i.e. referral bonuses) and use dealerships primarily as testing and distribution locations, then the company can better meet the needs of customers – getting the right product the quickest with the least cost. On top of the brick-and-mortar commerce and e-commerce sales, social commerce is added to the multi-channel management making the integration of various touchpoints more difficult and critical. For the relationship marketing success, firm must integrate all touchpoints and channels effectively to engage in relevant interactions with customers.

In all, there are four primary advantages that lead to the creation of synergy when integrating both traditional channels of distribution (i.e. retail stores), more direct models (i.e. internet, m-commerce), and newer indirect collaboration models (i.e., social media, social network service). The first primary advantage is the use of a common infrastructure. By using such elements as a common warehousing system or information technology systems or platforms, the firm can achieve cost savings in their dealings with customers through avoidance of redundant systems. The second primary advantage is that common operations can provide a benefit to the firm. An example of this is a common order processing system that allows for easy movement between channels for customers. A third source of synergy can come from the use of common marketing and sales programs. By using promotions for multiple sources through the same media, customers will be able to self-select the proper method for themselves. Finally, the touchpoints and channels used by common buyers can also be used as a synergy building CRM base for the firm. Simply put, the firm needs to find a way to balance its customers' desires for convenience (online), immediacy (nearby stores), interaction, and collaboration (social media).

Total CRM Based Comprehensive Relationship Marketing Plan

The importance and the process of developing a marketing plan were discussed earlier. With the increased use of e-marketing components, firms are developing a separate e-marketing plan or integrating e-marketing components into their existing marketing plan. Digital marketing plan is a strategic document that aims at achieving marketing objectives via web-based electronic medium. Digital marketing plan often represents a sub-set of firm's overall marketing plan that supports the general business strategy. The general process of developing digital marketing plan is similar to that of the traditional marketing. However, the components of the digital marketing planning process are quite different and distinct from traditional marketing.

The next section provides a comprehensive marketing plan that integrates the new digital marketing components with the traditional marketing plan. The comprehensive marketing plan integrates the traditional CRM, eCRM, and social CRM activities for customer equity. Table 3.2 presents various components of a comprehensive marketing plan that can include both the traditional and e-marketing components. Along with the five steps of customer relationships, various relationship marketing strategic components can be developed.

Relationship Marketing Steps	Customer Relevant Product Solution Strategy	Customer-Focused Service strategy	Traditional CRM Touchpoint Strategy	eCRM Touchpoint Strategy	Social CRM Touchpoint Strategy
Identify					
Initiate					
Build					
Develop					
Maintain					

Table 3.2: Comprehensive Relationship Marketing Plan Components

In creating a comprehensive marketing plan, firms must begin with a detailed outline of necessary components to ensure a well-structured and thorough plan identifying all aspects related to the strategic business unit (SBU). In broad terms, the content of the comprehensive marketing plan should include the following with variations and expansions based on individual company needs. For each step, specific CRM initiatives and relationship marketing programs can be implemented.

The outline of a total CRM based marketing plan is presented below. The digital marketing components are shown in italic bold to highlight the digital marketing components.

1. **Executive Summary**

2. **Introduction and Background**

     a) Company Mission/Objectives and SBU Objectives
     b) Market Definition and Product and Brand Background
     c) Degree of Digitization of Products and Services
     d) Problems/Issues
          i) Strategic (Traditional and **Digital Marketing**)
          ii) Tactical (Traditional and **Digital Marketing**)
          iii) Other
     e) Preferred Outcomes
          i) Performance Criteria
          ii) Ethical/Stakeholder Concerns
          iii) Internal and External Constraints and Factors

3. **Situation Analysis**

     a) Company Background and Assessment
          i) Firm and Vision
          ii) Principal Sources of Business and Competitive Advantage
          iii) Position and Trends in Current Markets
          iv) Recent Marketing Activities, Effectiveness and Capacity
     b) Industry Analysis (Traditional and **Digital Marketing Activities**)
     c) Demand and Customer Analysis (Traditional and **Digital Customer** Behavior)
     d) Customer Relationship Index and Scorecard
     e) Competitor Analysis (Traditional and **Digital Competitors**)
     f) SWOT Analysis (Traditional marketing and **Digital Marketing** components)
          i) Strengths
          ii) Weaknesses
          iii) Opportunities
          iv) Threats
          v) Critical Success Factors
     g) Problems and Opportunities (Traditional marketing and **Digital Marketing** components)

i) Current Markets
ii) Current Products and Services
iii) Potential Targets
iv) Salient Needs and Wants
v) Customer Relationship Metrics and Possibilities
h) Online Presence and Interactivity Assessment
i) Website and Social Media Site Audit
(1) Website Design, Layout, and Content
(2) Website Usage and Navigation

4. **Total CRM based Relationship Marketing Strategy and Program**

a) Objectives and Goals (Traditional marketing and **Digital Marketing** objectives and goals)
b) Customer Relationship Roadmap (Traditional marketing and **Digital Marketing** components and goals)
i) Customer Relationship Strategy
Traditional marketing and **Digital Marketing** CRM components
ii) Customer Lifetime Value Segmentation
iii) Customer Experience Map
iii) Customer Experiential Targeting and Positioning
c) Total CRM driven Relationship Marketing Programs for Relevance
ii) Customer Relevant Solution Product Strategy
(1) Traditional Product Strategy
(2) Digital Product Strategy
- Digitization Strategy of Products and Service
- Web-based Customer Service Strategy
- e-Branding and Online and Social Media Brand Management
iii) Relevant Customer Focused Service Strategy with Supply Chain
(1) Traditional Value Chain and Channel Strategy
(2) Digital Channel Strategy
- Channel Disintermediation Strategy
- New Direct Channel Strategy
- Online and Social Media Customer Service Strategy
v) Relevant Integrated Touch Point Management Strategy
(1) Traditional CRM Touchpoint Management Strategy
(2) eCRM Touchpoint Management Strategy
- Search Engine Optimization Strategy
- Digital Media Advertising Strategy
- E-mail Marketing Strategy
(3) Social CRM Touchpoint Management Strategy
- Social Media Marketing Strategy

Marketing Organization and Implementation

a) Budget
b) Organization

c) Control
      i) Qualitative Measures
      ii) Quantitative Measures
d) Contingency Plan
e) Summary of Recommendations

Appendices

The importance of a marketing plan cannot be stressed enough. Marketing plan creates direction to achieve goals. The firm must analyze its current strategy for the purpose of updating, or to create a completely new marketing plan. The purpose of a marketing plan is fourfold:

1. It compels the workforce to look at past organizational decisions and outcomes to effectively make future decisions.

2. It forces the workforce to evaluate the external environment and changing conditions that impact the firm.

3. It helps to determine goals and objectives while offering direction on implementation to achieve these goals.

4. It enables approval for funding to follow new projects.

In creating a marketing plan, one must begin with a detailed outline of necessary components to ensure a well-structured and thorough plan identifying all aspects related to the strategic business unit (SBU). Goals and objectives must be identified along with expected obstacles and variables. In broad terms, the content of the marketing plan should include the following, with variations and expansions based on individual company needs. The contents for a marketing plan focus on customer equity. This new approach in developing a marketing plan can ensure that a firm can achieve higher business performance such as profitability through customer relationship enhancement. The marketing plan components are as follows:

1. Executive Summary
2. Introduction and Background
3. Situation analysis
4. Total CRM Based Marketing Strategy and Program
5. Marketing Organization and Implementation
6. Appendices

Situation Analysis

A situation analysis, or an examination of the current situation, must be done prior to strategy formulation and implementation. This includes both internal and external elements with respect to the company and can be done in a number of ways. Generally accepted formulation of a situation analysis is through environmental scanning. This includes all attributes of the product or service, the current target market, and all components of the supply chain.

Environmental Scanning

Both internal and external environmental scanning is necessary to factor together all influential variables. This is done through a SWOT (strengths, weaknesses, opportunities, and threats) analysis among other methods. It is important to remember that a SWOT analysis is most effective when it involves input from a cross section of key managers allowing for as broad of a perspective as possible.

External Environment

The external environment includes competition, trends, economic conditions, segmentation and targeting, buyer behavior, legal limitations, political influences, and other factors. The analysis used for the external environment includes market and industry analysis, need analysis, channel analysis, and competitive analysis. With the advancement of customer relationship-driven marketing, current customer relationship management activity index and scorecard assessment emerges as an important area of external environment.

Internal Environment

The internal environment focuses on the firm's strengths and weaknesses. These include products and customers, logistics and operations, technology assessment, and human capital assessment.

Combining the elements of external and internal environments, the firm needs to redefine and to refocus its strategic choices for relationship marketing. A firm can identify problems and opportunities that are relevant for customers, markets, and customer relationship management.

Total CRM Based Marketing Strategy and Program

Strategic development is a vital and lengthy portion of the marketing plan. It is likely based on a three-tier system: marketing mix, marketing strategy, strategic marketing management.

Goals and Objectives

Objectives are defined as what the company is trying to accomplish. For example, a company may want to enter new markets, increase efficiency, or create a new product category. Objective development seems simple enough, however there are guidelines that must be taken into account. They must be challenging but attainable, measurable, fit the company's goals and resources available, are not conflicting, have the ability to change with the environment, involve the workforce and provide accountability, and effectively communicate objectives and ways of implementation to all those involved. To meet objectives, goals must be set. The definition of goals in this context is the details associated with the objectives.

It is important to keep the organizational goals and vision in mind when creating the marketing strategy. Imagine a goal of increasing sales by 15 percent. A strategy used to ultimately achieve the goal could be a monthly promotion that is also used to create or update a customer database. The strategy will include many steps and future planning. All elements of marketing and advertising that will likely increase the chances of goal attainment must be examined and utilized.

Customer Relationship Roadmap

Under the customer relationship marketing, a customer relationship roadmap needs to be developed before implementing the marketing strategy. This road map refines traditional market segmentation and targeting by using marketing analytics. Using customer insights generated from customer data, firms segment customers using customer lifetime value and other metrics. Value propositions are developed with the customer relationship enhancement in mind. Experiential targeting and positioning strategy is derived based on the customer experience mapping and customer equity consideration.

Total CRM Based Relationship Marketing Programs

Many important factors must be examined when creating the marketing strategy. Examination of the point of evolution on the product life cycle, the market attractiveness, product/brand positioning, and customer relationship scorecard are essential to create an effective and practical strategic plan. Before developing marketing programs, customer relationship strategy needs to be developed first. Marketing strategies and programs must support a firm's specific customer relationship management strategy set for various customer groups and segments.

Marketing strategy decisions are made primarily to increase customer retention and loyalty. The relationship marketing requires firms to fully adjust and customize marketing mix components to meet the specific customer segments in order to provide relevant perfect customer experience leading to strong long-term customer relationship. Beginning with product, existing and new products are managed to create customer solutions for the most profitable segments to enhance their retention and loyalty. It is important to provide customer focused service with effective supply chain and distribution channel management. Firms need to manage and integrate various customer touchpoints for consistent relevant customer experience. Traditional CRM related touch points are promotional contact points such as personal selling, sales promotion, advertising, and public relations. In addition to these traditional CRM touchpoints, firms need to manage eCRM and social CRM touchpoints that are becoming critical determinants of customer experience. Firms must provide customer relevant websites and social media sites for relationship marketing.

Control and Ratios

Liquidity ratios help a manager to understand the financial ability for debt payment. Liquidity is typically measured through the current ratio (current assets/current liabilities) and acid-test ratio ([cash + securities + receivables]/current liabilities). Average receivables and inventory turnover illustrate how fast you sell your inventory and how often you receive payment for your sales. Profitability measures determine how successful the firm is in comparison to its potential. Profitability ratios include asset earning power, ROE, profit on sales, investment turnover, and ROI. In assessing the impact of the firm's marketing programs, marketing managers need to consider customer impact, market impact, and impact on the value of the firm in addition to financial impact.[22]

Presentation and Implementation

The formal presentation of your research and customer relationship-driven marketing plan is important for three main purposes. The presentation can aid in the approval of funding for a project, can communicate the project to shareholders, and can make all stakeholders and employees aware of the marketing initiatives. This also assists in implementation by making those involved aware of the newly formulated strategies. Along with this, constant strategic evaluation and alterations are necessary.

Total CRM Based Relationship Marketing Template

Template 3.1: Current Relationship Marketing Activity and Impact Map

Template3.1 lists a firm's current relationship marketing activities and their business impact as well as customer impact.

Relationship Marketing Activity Initiatives	Business Impact				Customer Impact		
	Reduce Cost to Serve	Productivity Enhancement	Renewable Revenue	One-to-One Relationship	Acquisition	Enhancement	Retention
Churn Detection/Prevention							
Behavior Prediction							
Customer Profitability and Value Modeling							
Cross-Selling and Up-selling							
Touchpoint Optimization							
Personalization / Customization							
Event-based Marketing							
Other							

Real World Application Cases

Case 3-1: Ocean Spray[23]

Ocean Spray is the leader in bottled and canned juice drinks and is owned by cranberry and grapefruit growers. The company employs approximately 2,000 individuals and ranks in the top 50 U.S. food and beverage companies. Their market research partner, Information Resources, Inc. (IRI), is the leader in Business Performance Management services to retail and healthcare industries. IRI provides innovative software along with market models to maximize a business's operations in their marketing, sales, and operation divisions.

Ocean Spray and IRI have renewed as well as expanded their contract. The purpose of the contract expansion is to obtain specific market information in order to reduce their reaction time to respond to new trends. IRI boasts a 75,000-member panel and uses this to provide in-depth consumer information and behaviors. This enables Ocean Spray to rely on one sole partner for their marketing information needs.

Ocean Spray's objective for this partnership is to increase their understanding of consumer motivations, behaviors, and preferences as well as using this information to increase the speed of knowledge-based decision-making. They will also improve their data mining and analytics while improving both their convenience store channels and retailer performance.

Case Questions

1. What type of customer insights can you generate from information provided by IRI?

2. How does Ocean Spray's market information help marketing planning?

3. While IRI provides Ocean Spray with valuable market information, Ocean Spray cannot just rely on IRI for effective customer information management. What additional information and information management practices are needed for Ocean Spray to develop its total CRM based marketing plan?

Case 3-2: Giant Eagle[24]

Giant Eagle is a grocery chain operating in multiple states. Giant Eagle is very careful to only bring technology into the company that supports their existing corporate strategy. The mission statement addresses the importance of customer satisfaction, stating that to "provide service and products that meet or exceed our customers' requirements at all times" is a top priority.

Every aspect of the company's technology impacts the consumer whether directly or indirectly. Some examples of this include the Advantage Card, AdvantagePay Program, and self-checkout lanes. The loyalty card enables Giant Eagle to collect information, and then use this information to highly personalize marketing campaigns. The production-planning technology also impacts consumer's shopping experience by ensuring product availability as demand fluctuates from hour-to-hour, and day-to-day. This planning must take into account past information as well as external forces. This is especially critical with freshly prepared foods such as their bakery and meat departments.

In order to ensure correct inventory, Giant Eagle uses handheld wireless devices to communicate efficiently. Orders are taken and tracked via the wireless devices, and a knowledge management system has also been implemented to encourage sharing of ideas. This has proven beneficial through creating a positive corporate culture while improving processes. Giant Eagle sees the need in continuous improvement of technology to create a competitive advantage and has a team devoted to this.

Case Questions

1. What type of strategic models or concepts should Giant Eagle use in determining its future growth strategy? Be specific.

2. Giant Eagle is customer-focused as well as employee-focused. How might this increase customer satisfaction?

3. What additional programs would you recommend to Giant Eagle to further acquire new customers and grow existing customers?

Chapter 4. Customer Lifetime Value and Customer Portfolio Management

Section 1. Business Portfolio Management

"The best and most effective brands of the future will be built around knowledge."
Lord Puttnam CBE

Traditional Business Portfolio Model

The firm has to analyze its business units and decide which businesses to grow, maintain, abandon, and harvest. Various analytical frameworks and models have been used for traditional portfolio analysis.

Boston Consulting Group (BCG) Model

This model is known as the growth-share matrix and is the most widely cited standardized approach to marketing planning. In this approach, a firm classifies all of its strategic business units (SBU) in the business portfolio matrix (see Figure 4.1). The vertical axis, which is the market growth rate, represents the annual growth rate at which each market of the SBU is growing. The horizontal axis, representing the relative market share, shows the market share for each SBU relative to the share of the industry's largest competitor. The circles in the matrix depict the growth/share standing of a firm's various SBU. The size of the circles is proportional to the SBU dollar sales.

The BCG model is divided into four cells. Each cell represents a different type of business. The cell labeled "question marks" is low-share SBUs in high-growth markets. Firms can turn these question marks into market leaders by increasing market share with cash. Alternatively, firms can phase out these SBUs. The cell labeled "stars" represents high-growth, high-share SBUs. These SBUs require cash to support their rapid growth. Their growth will slow and they will eventually become cash cows generating cash and supporting other SBUs. The cell labeled "cash cows" is businesses that have a high relative market share but a low annual growth rate. As the name suggests, these SBUs produce significant amounts of cash for the business. With the large market share of cash cows, the business benefits from economies of scale and high profitability. Since the growth rate has slowed, the business does not have to invest in expanding capacity. Cash generated by cash cows can be used to finance high growth businesses (i.e., stars). Dogs are SBUs that may generate enough cash to maintain themselves. Yet, they offer little promise of large sources of cash for the firm. The BCG model provides an overall assessment of the long-term health of the corporation with respect to cash balance. The limitations of this approach include its inflexibility, the assumption of market share affecting cost, and cash-flow focus.[1]

The New BCG Model

In many ways the BCG matrix has begun to lose its relevance in today's fast paced society. Unlike the 1970's when the BCG matrix was created, businesses must now reevaluate their business models much more frequently. One cause of this is that market share is no longer as great of an indicator of market performance and competitive advantage as it once was. One study found that cash cows have experienced a significant decline in profitability as a result of a changing market. The Boston Consulting Group now proposes that the growth share matrix must be applied with greater speed and efficiency and because market share is no longer as important a factor they suggest the need for a replacement measure of competitiveness on its horizontal axis.

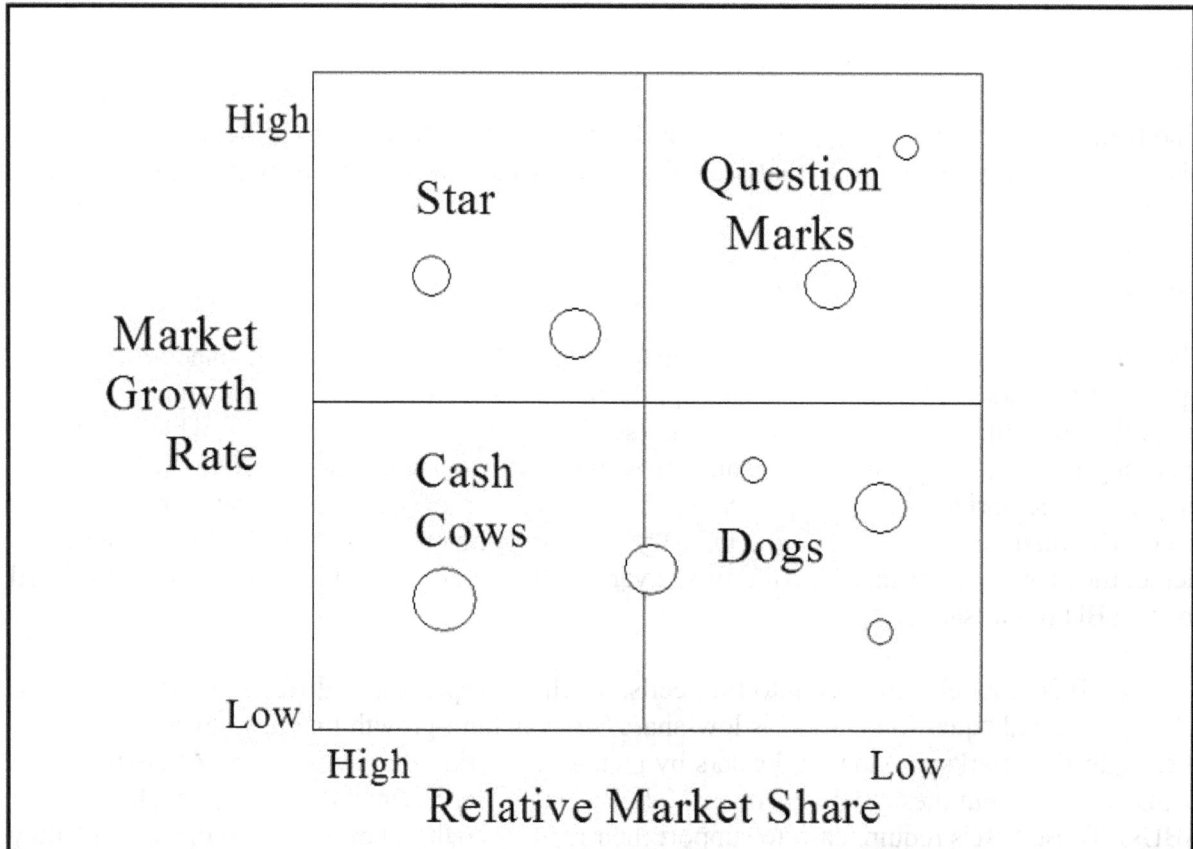

Figure 4.1: The BCG Growth-Share Matrix

The Boston Consulting Group Proposes four practical imperatives for the new way in which the growth share matrix should be applied which are acceleration, balance exploration and exploitation, select rigorously, and measure and manage portfolio economics of experimentation. *1) Acceleration* suggests that companies must increase their strategic planning cycles to match the speed of the environment. *2) Balancing exploration and exploitation* proposes that companies should increase their number of question marks and test them quickly and economically, focus on efficient use of cash cows, and move quickly to increase divestment from and decrease exit barriers to dogs. A third suggestion is to *3) select rigorously* by quick selection between investment and divestment of question marks through the use of data sources and predictive analytics. Finally, the Boston Consulting Group advocates the importance of *4) measurement and management* of costs and profitability for question marks and stars so that potential failures will be acceptable.

Figure 4.2 shows an example of a BCG growth share matrix map. In calculating relative market share and market growth rate, five product groups were treated as strategic business units (SBU). Using four percent of the market growth rate as the midpoint, skin care and shaving products SBUs are classified as stars. The oral care and hair care SBUs are classified as cash cows, while the deodorant SBU is classified as a dog. The BCG matrix suggests that this company needs to enter new business opportunities to maintain or increase growth. Within a few years, the shaving products SBU will drop to the cash cow category because its growth rate is decreasing. Eventually, the SBU's growth rate will dip below four percent. The oral care and hair care SBUs will eventually become dogs because competitive pressures eventually will reduce the market share. The current matrix shows that this company is generating a positive cash flow through their two cash cows SBUs and one star SBU which is expected to become a cash cow SBU soon.

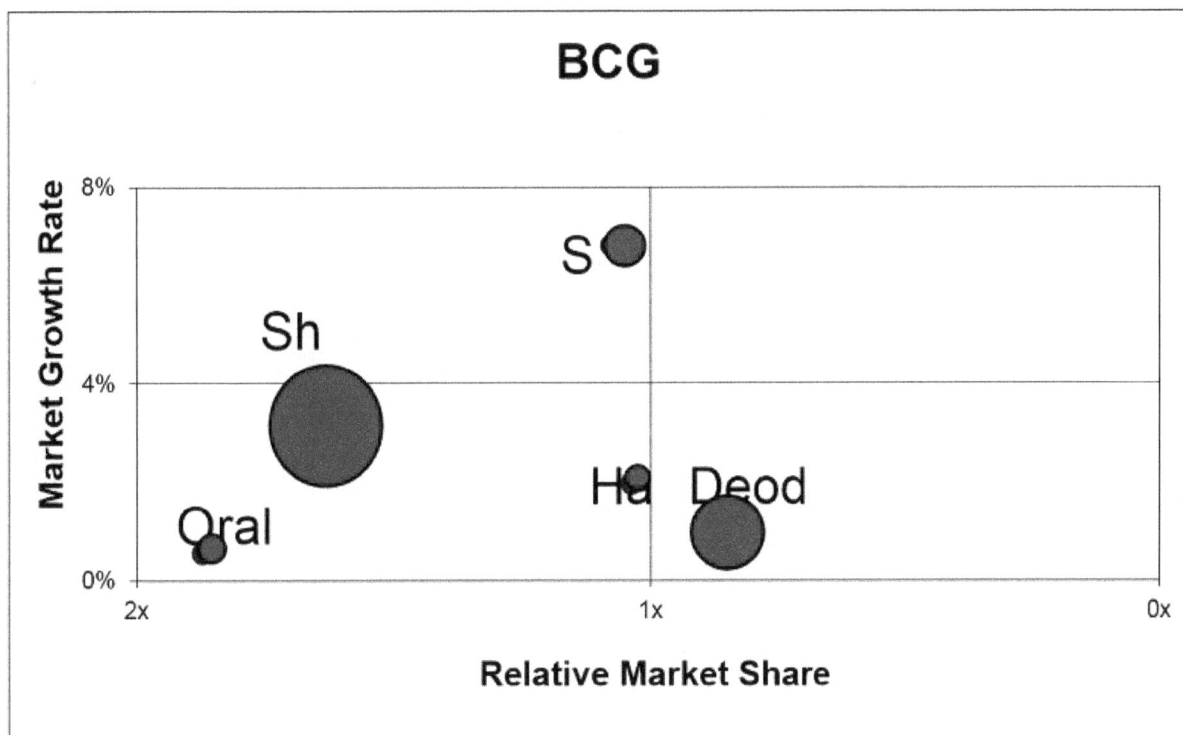

Figure 4.2: BCG Model

Management's job is to project a future growth-share matrix showing where each SBU is likely to be. By comparing the current and future matrices, management can identify the major strategic issues facing the firm. The task of strategic planning is to determine what role each SBU should play in achieving the overall corporate growth goal and allocating resources accordingly. For each SBU, management can decide whether to build, hold, harvest, or abandon the business. Management should also determine which strategic alternatives to choose in pursuing sales or profit growth. The basic premise of the BCG approach is to ensure adequate cash flow for the long-run health of the firm. Defensive strategies are usually more short-term based, and offensive strategies emphasize long-term strategic growth.

PIMS Model

The Profit Impact of Marketing Strategy (PIMS) model provides an intra-firm analysis of the relative profitability. Began in 1960 at General Electric, this model was developed on the premise that the pooled experiences of diversely successful and unsuccessful businesses will provide meaningful information about the determinants of business profitability. The PIMS database, comprised of over 450 participating firms, was analyzed using regression analysis. The regression analysis related market selection and strategic characteristics with profitability.[2] Table 4.1 shows the regression analysis results using return on investment (ROI) and return on sales (ROS) as the dependent variables.

Profit Influences	Impact on	
	ROI	ROS
1. Real market growth rate	0.18	
2. Rate of price inflation	0.22	0.04
3. Purchase concentration	0.02**	0.08
4. Unionization	-0.07	
5. Low purchase amount and ...		
➤ Low importance of purchase ***	6.06***	1.63
➤ High importance of purchase	5.42	2.10
6. High purchase amount and ...		
➤ Low importance of purchase	-6.96	-2.58
➤ High importance of purchase	-3.84	-1.11**
7. Exports minus imports (in %)	0.06**	0.05
8. Customized products	-2.44	-1.77
9. Market share	0.34	0.14
10. Relative quality	0.11	0.05
11. New products (% of sales)	-0.12	-0.05
12. Marketing (% of sales)	-0.52	-0.32
13. R&D (% of sales)	-0.36	-0.22
14. Inventory (% of sales)	0.49	-2.09
15. Fixed capital intensity	-0.55	-2.10
16. Plant newness	0.07	0.05
17. Capacity utilization (in %)	0.31	0.10
18. Employee productivity	0.13	0.06
19. Vertical integration	0.26	0.18
20. First in first out (FIFO) inventory valuation	1.30*	0.62
R^2	.39	.31
F	58.30	45.1

Note: All coefficients, except those starred, are significant at ($p < .01$).
* Significance level between .01 and .05. **Significance level between .05 and .10.
*** Products for which the typical purchase amount is low and the importance of the purchase to customers is low.
ROI = Return on Investment
ROS = Return on Sales

Table 4.1: Multiple-Regression Equation for Return on Investment (ROI) and Return on Sales (ROS) for the Entire PIMS Database

Firms can compare their actual ROI and ROS with those predicted for that business segment by PIMS database model. The PIMS model can be used as a benchmarking tool or as a diagnostic device to identify what stage of performance outcomes are consistent with a business's market position and strategy.

GE Multi-Factor Model

To overcome the simplicity of the BCG model, General Electric planners developed the market attractiveness-business strength matrix. Figure 4.3 shows the structure of the matrix. The horizontal axis, representing the market attractiveness, is based on various relevant factors such as market size, growth rate, customer satisfaction level, profitability, and technology. The managers are allowed to select the most appropriate factors. They then derive a summary measure by combining the relative importance of each factor with an evaluation score of each factor for a given market. The vertical axis, which is the business strength, considers many appropriate factors for the given decision context. Examples of these factors are size, growth, market share by segment, customer loyalty, margins, distribution, technology skills, patents, marketing, and flexibility. Although the GE matrix approach offers richer and more broadly applicable information than the BCG model, its measures can be more subjective and ambiguous when applied across business units. The results can be very sensitive to the definition of the product market.

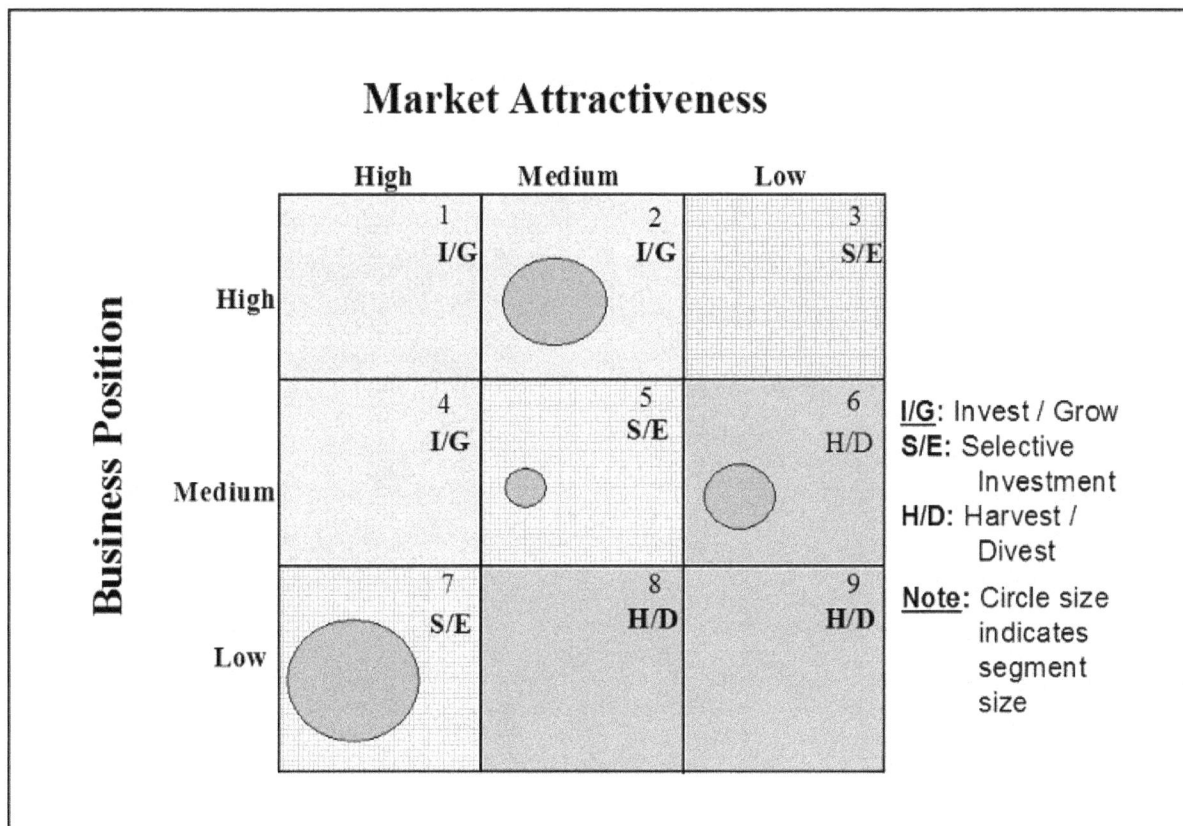

Figure 4.3: The Market Attractiveness - Business Position Matrix

123

Strategic implication of the analytic solutions described earlier is providing directions for the firm in determining which strategic categories to focus and making selective investment decisions. The matrix shows how firms make investment and growth decisions based on the portfolio analysis. For example, the three segments (Segment 3, 5, and 7) are designated for selective investment and earning. Segment 3 will utilize a "Protect / Refocus" strategy. Under this strategy, firms will defend strengths, refocus to attractive segments, evaluate industry revitalization, and monitor for Harvest/Divest timing. For segment 5, firms can employ segmentation and contingency plans to recognize vulnerability in this segment. Segment 7 can take an opportunistic approach by riding the market, seeking niches, and specialization, and increasing strength (e.g. Technical Acquisition).

The Risk Matrix

Shell Chemical developed the risk matrix by introducing environmental risk into portfolio analysis.[3] The risk matrix approach incorporates environmental risk as a separate axis in the model. Figure 4.4 shows the risk matrix model. Environmental risk is based on the seriousness of environmental threats and the probability of their occurrence. For example, managers can select the right business opportunities considering a firm's strategic direction. A firm pursues high growth as its strategic goal, it should be willing to take high risk and choose a business opportunity from the "very high risk" and "attractive" cell. Similarly, if a firm wants to maintain stability, it could choose an opportunity from the "medium risk" cell with "average profitability".

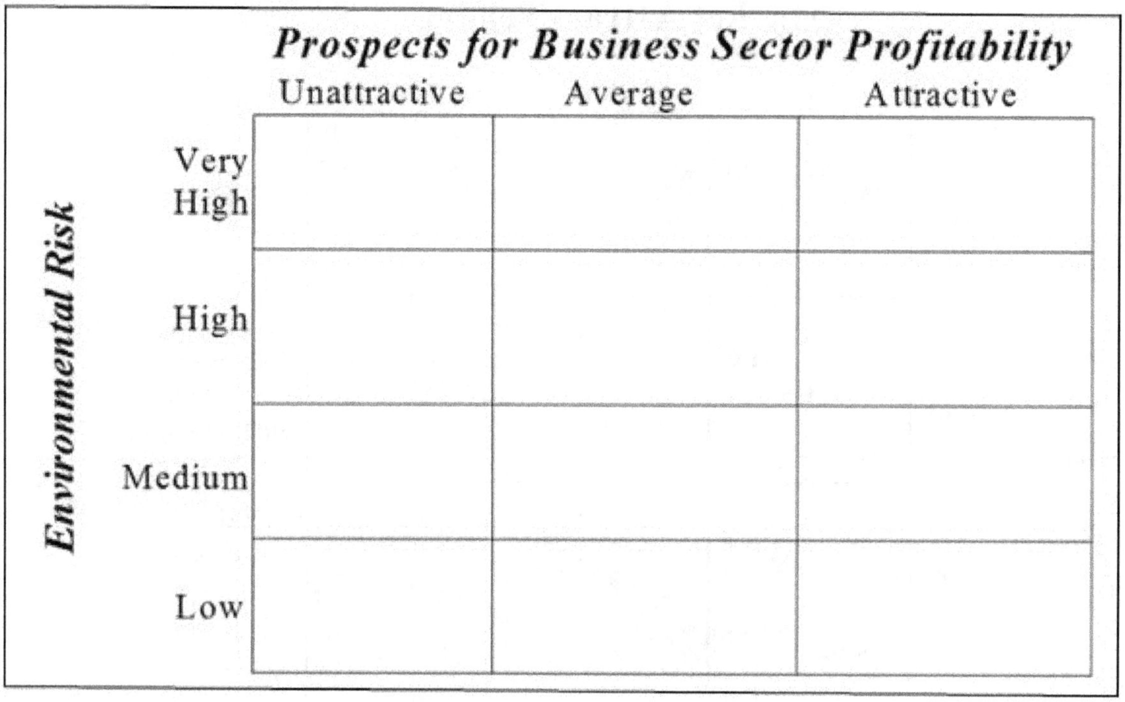

Figure 4.4: Risk Matrix

Business Growth Strategy

After assessing the overall business positions using the portfolio matrix approaches, firms need to consider various growth strategies to achieve the growth objectives set at earlier stages of the planning process. Figure 4.5 shows alternative growth strategies available for firms. Figure 4.5 presents a matrix detailing where firms can achieve growth.

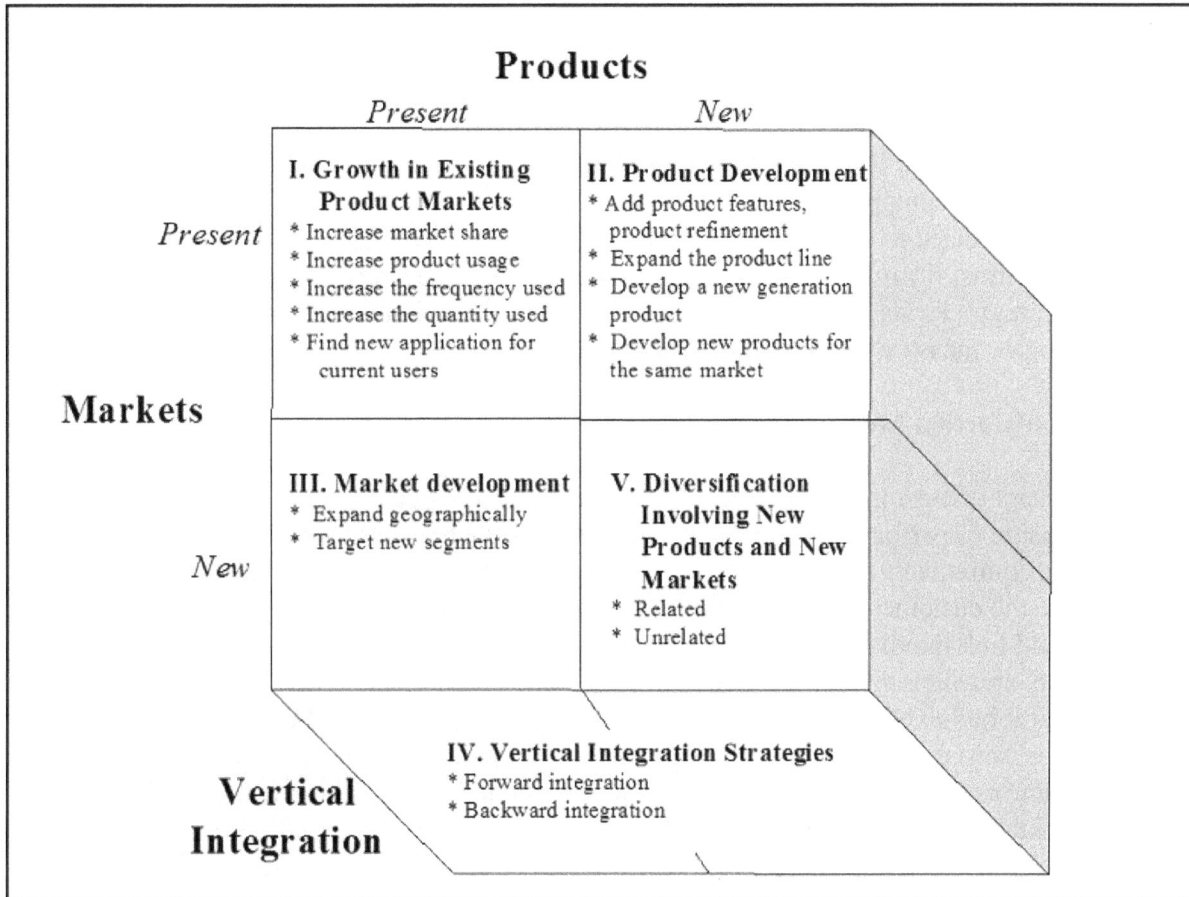

Products

Present   *New*

Markets

Present

I. Growth in Existing Product Markets
* Increase market share
* Increase product usage
* Increase the frequency used
* Increase the quantity used
* Find new application for current users

II. Product Development
* Add product features, product refinement
* Expand the product line
* Develop a new generation product
* Develop new products for the same market

New

III. Market development
* Expand geographically
* Target new segments

V. Diversification Involving New Products and New Markets
* Related
* Unrelated

Vertical Integration

IV. Vertical Integration Strategies
* Forward integration
* Backward integration

Figure 4.5: Business Growth Strategy

The growth strategy can focus on two factors: market and product. Firms can achieve growth by penetrating current market with existing products. They can increase market share, product usage, frequency of use, or quantity used to further penetrate the market. Alternatively, firms can develop new markets or uses for their existing products leading to market development strategy. Under this strategy, firms expand geographically or expand into new market segments. Product development strategy focuses on new products in currently served markets. This strategy involves product feature addition, product-line expansion, or development of new generation products. Adding products to a company's existing portfolio can reduce risk by spreading dependence of revenues over different markets and balancing the effects of the market environments of each product as product life cycles differ. As a product advances through its life cycle, investments can increase or decrease depending on internal and external factors to improve overall company performance. This is all part of the company's strategic plan, and limited budgets effect all product lines. This emphasizes the need for both short-term and long-term strategic planning. When considering an entrance into a new product market, a company must analyze the impact on competitive advantage, revenue growth, profits, and stock value. Firms can also diversify into new business arenas by introducing new products into new markets. This strategy is typically implemented by exporting or exchanging assets, skills, or resources to establish themselves in an unrelated business. The vertical integration strategy involves supply chains and acquiring controls over suppliers or distributors.

Section 2. Customer Value Driven Strategy

> *"The best way to predict the future is to create it."*
> Peter Drucker

Firms that are better equipped to respond to market requirements and anticipate changing conditions are expected to enjoy long-run competitive advantage and superior profitability. In market driven firms, firms are focusing on customer value in developing and implementing marketing strategy. Firms have used various customer value related metrics that are either indirect surrogate measure or direct measure of value.

Customer Satisfaction Measurement

With the concept of customer orientation, firms are developing customer satisfaction as a key criterion measure of performance. A good customer satisfaction measurement system should meet several requirements and have the necessary components.[4] There are three desirable properties are the customer satisfaction measurement system should possess. The first property is that it should link internal perspectives and processes with customer perceptions of product or service quality and subsequent perceptions of satisfaction. The second property that it should possess is that it be linked to key customer behaviors such as complaint behavior and customer retention. The third property is that it should reflect the underlying changes in product or service quality and not just random fluctuation. The measurement process begins with a design of a customer satisfaction survey. The questionnaire items should be specifically linked to the underlying benefits customers derive from the product or service. Survey results are used to develop customer satisfaction index (CSI). The next step is statistically analyzing how these desired benefits are related to overall customer satisfaction. Statistical analysis can derive the individual impact of each benefit on overall customer satisfaction. The final step is relating the satisfaction index to performance measures such as customer loyalty and financial returns.

Customer Value Analysis

Customer value can be a solution for identifying a common metric of strategic marketing decision and should be linked to performance.[5] Customer value analysis requires assessment of market-perceived quality and market-perceived price. Using these two market-based measures, the customer value index can be calculated. The variable names are defined in Table 4.2 with the equations immediately following. The value map can also be developed using the relative price ratio and the market-perceived quality ratio.

Variable Name	Variable Description
CPSS	Competitor's Price Satisfaction Score
CQS	Competitor's Quality Score
CVI	Customer Value Index
FPSS	Firm's Price Satisfaction Score
FQS	Firm's Quality Score
PW	Price Weight
QW	Quality Weight
RIP	Relative Importance of Price
RIQ	Relative Importance of Quality
ROQS	Relative Overall Quality Score
RPCS	Relative Price Competitiveness Score
RPCS	Relative Price Competitiveness Score

Table 4.2: Customer Value Analysis Variables

Where,

$$CVI = (ROQS \times QW) + (RPCS \times PW)$$

$$ROQS = \frac{FQS}{CQS}$$

$$PW = RIP \qquad QW = RIQ \qquad RPCS = \frac{FPSS}{CPSS}$$

Figure 4.6 shows the value map of various businesses. The value map can present the value positioning of each of its businesses. By evaluating value positioning of its businesses, a firm can assess the overall position of its businesses in the market. Managers can develop strategic marketing decisions in order to change or improve value positions of key businesses. It also shows who is likely to gain market share. Firms tend to gain market share when they are below and to the right of the fair value line. Firms need to make linkages between customer value measurements with performance measures. These linkages will vary by markets, products, and industries. The next section illustrates an analysis of the value measurement with key performance measures.

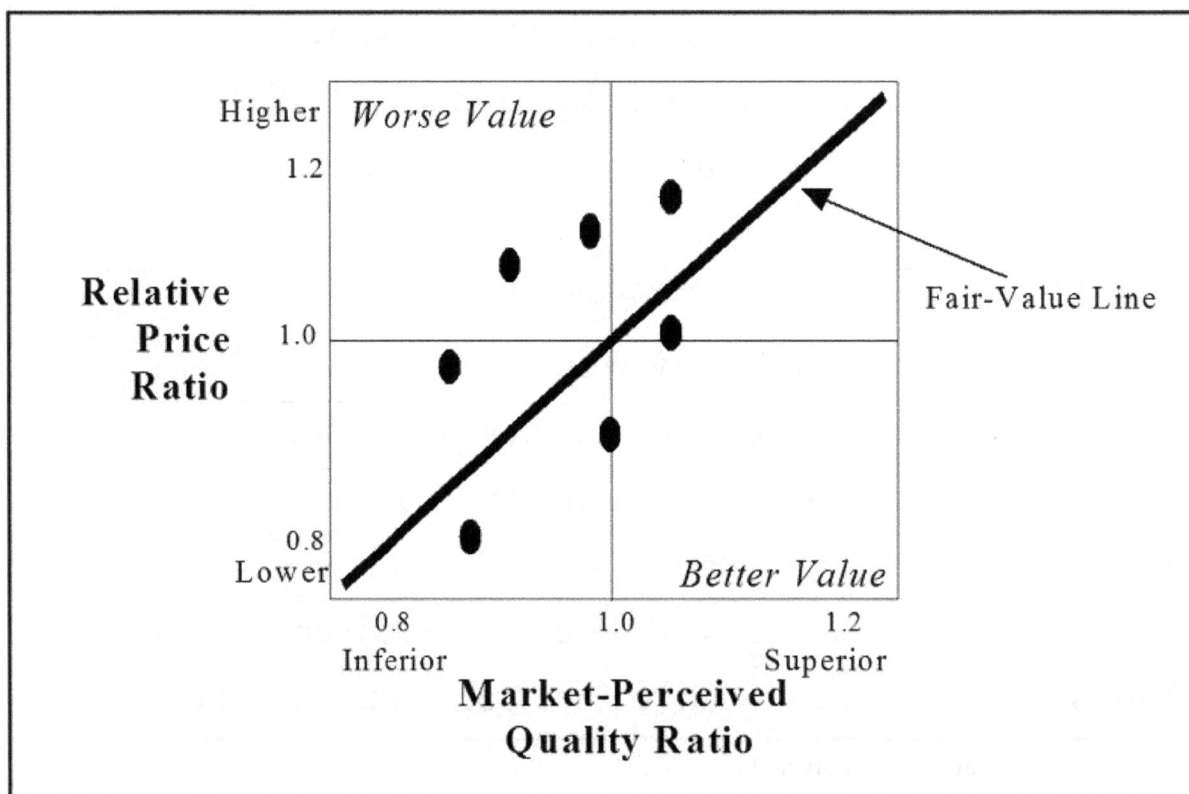

Figure 4.6: Value Map[6]

Figure 4.7 shows a value map of the skin care product line. The map is developed using the relative price ratio and the market perceived quality ratio. Each product item is positioned in the value map showing the value positioning of each of its products. By evaluating the value positioning, a firm can assess the overall position of its businesses in the market. Managers can develop strategic marketing decisions in order to change or improve value positions of key businesses or product lines. Products in the RHN and SS product lines show high customer value, while products in the FV and SP product lines show low customer value compared to competitors. Managers can expect growth in market share in the RHN and SS product lines but expect a loss of market share for the FV and SP product lines. The map can be used to develop brand management decisions based on the expected role of each brand in achieving target performance.

Strategy determination offers positioning of a business in a market so that the firm can control and influences all the forces in the market to pursue value and growth. The insight generated from this process can guide firms as to how the business will be managed in the future.

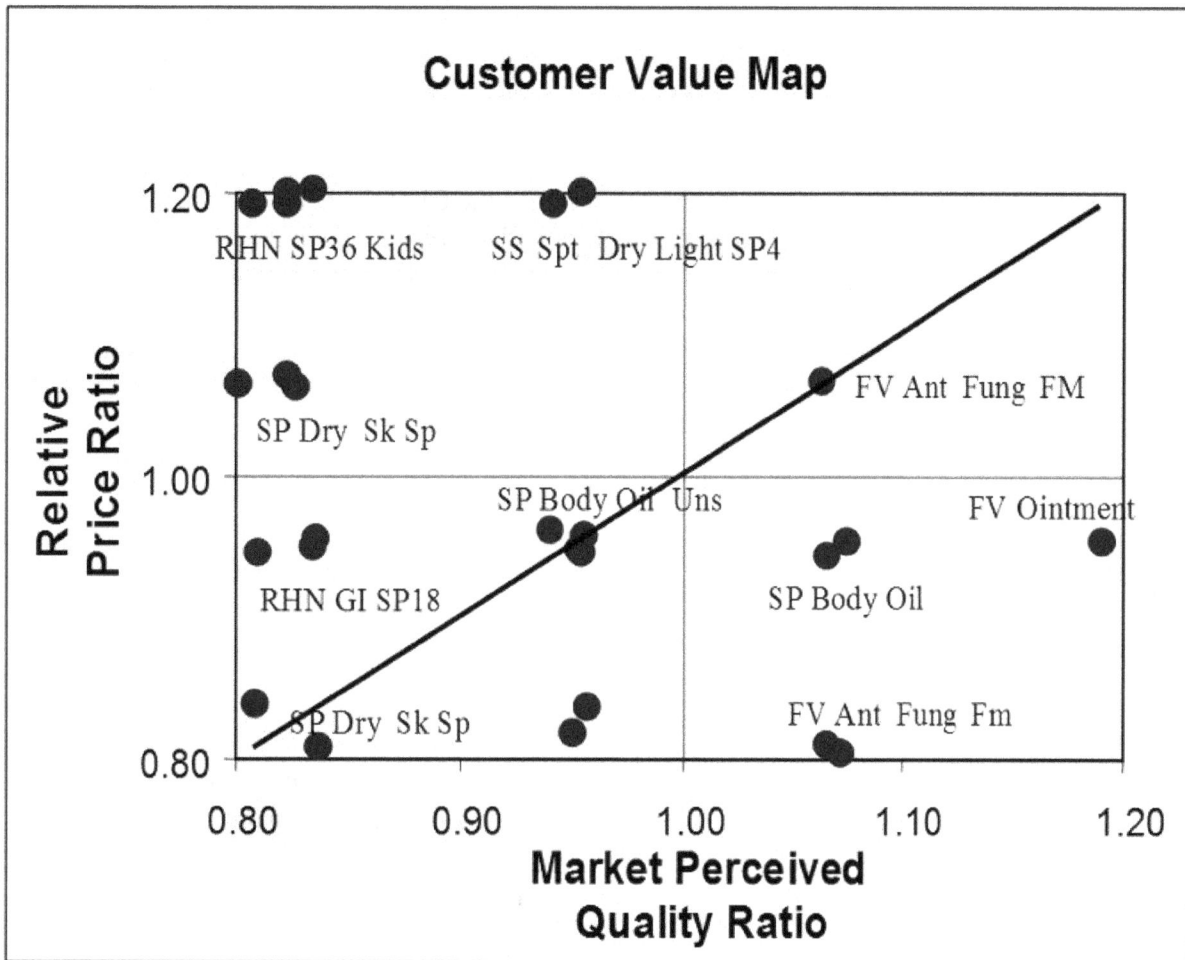

Customer Value Map

Figure 4.7: Customer Value Map Application Example

Section 3. Customer Lifetime Value Approach

> *"Make your product easier to buy than your competition, or you will find your customers buying from them, not you."*
> Mark Cuban

In customer relationship marketing, the traditional segmentation approach could also be used to serve customers better and build stronger customer relationships. However, the segmentation process is done differently. Market segments are not based on typical segmentation variables such as demographics or psychographics. Rather segments are based on customer lifetime value as well as on patterns and insights generated from detailed analyses of customer behaviors and purchases.

Customer Life Time Value

The basic prerequisite for the relationship marketing is knowledge of individual customer lifetime values for the customer base. Customer lifetime value (CLV) is rapidly gaining acceptance as a metric to acquire, grow, and retain the "right" customers in relationship marketing. The various components of CLV include purchase frequency, contribution margin, and marketing costs: however, the various CLV components can vary depending on the industry. Some of the antecedents of purchase frequency and contribution margin (e.g., marketing communications) are under the manager's control and affect the variable costs of managing customers.[7]

Knowing the individual CLVs of existing customers and the CLV distribution in the customer base along with psychographic and socio-demographic data for the relevant customers would allow firms to make efficient allocation of marketing resources to manage customers. The lifetime value is defined as the value of the customer for any customer and customer segment x and calculated by subtracting the future lifetime costs (CC) from the future lifetime revenue (CR). The following shows the formula for calculating the lifetime value of a customer.[8] Individual customer lifetime value for customer x (CLV_x) is as follows:

$$CLV_x = \sum_{t=1}^{n} \frac{(CR_n - CC_n)}{(1+i)^n}$$

Where;

- CR is the future life time stream of revenues from that customer or segment,
- CC is the future lifetime costs for a predicted relationship lifetime from time t =1 to n,
- i is a discount rate,
- $1/(1+i)^n$ is a function yields the net present value.

In applying this formula, marketing managers can make forecasts of lifetime duration based on previous experience with that customer and other similar customers. In addition, lifetime revenues of customer x, CR_x can be calculated. For time t = 1 to n and for products q = 1 to m, the lifetime revenues of customer x, CR_x is as follows:

$$CR_x = \sum_{t=1}^{n} \sum_{q=1}^{m} V_{qt} - P_{qt}$$

Where;

- V is the volume of products,
- P is the price of products.

The future lifetime revenues (CR) vary from customer to customer and depend on various factors. Customers vary in the number and mix of products purchased over time[9] and the size, growth, and distribution of share of wallet over time.[10] The future lifetime costs (CC) can be calculated by adding product costs and costs to serve the customer. The future lifetime costs are typically allocated proportionally to sales volume or value. As firms realize that some customers are far more costly to serve than other customers, activity-based costing can be used to determine appropriate allocation to customers of costs to serve.[11]

Lifetime value has been calculated in many ways. Firms have used sales revenues, contribution, gross profit, and net profit. In terms of time, some firms focus on what the customer will contribute in the future. Other firms use what the customer has contributed in the past. Some other firms consider both the value of past and future purchases. In order to get a lifetime value, sales revenues need to be adjusted by a profit margin as well as additional considerations that include other related purchases like services, opportunities for cross-selling and up-selling, and reference value. Customer life time value represents the net present value of the future profits over the lifetime of the customer relationships. For the correct customer life time value calculation, the total expected profits over a customer's lifetime are adjusted by a discount rate and other factors such as related purchases. Customer lifetime value need to be calculated to the detailed segmentation level that is the most appropriate for the firm. Although it may be difficult to accurately quantify future customer relationship benefits, customer lifetime value is the critical backbone of relationship marketing.

Customer Value Modeling

In using value metrics in relationship marketing, firms can use widely varied value metrics. Firms in different industries may use different value metrics. The value metrics commonly used are customer's life time value (LTV), potential value, competitive value (also known as wallet share). Regardless of the level of customer value being modeled, customer value modeling is only accurate as long as the customer data is rich and the analysis is statistically robust. There is risk of making erroneous decisions. Value modeling for customer profitability requires the extensive processing and detailed data and specialized profitability-modeling tool. The benefit of value modeling is the ability to quantify current or future profitability and identify value-based segments. Value modeling allows firms to score a customer based on his/her relative worth to the company over time. The value of future customers can be assessed with data that captures the characteristics of past prospects and a measure of the profitability of the customer. Challenges of using customer profitability and value modeling are the fact that current profitability is only a piece of the revenue puzzle with widely varied value metrics.

Value Based Segments

The profitability of customers varies widely depending on the degree of customer granularity, that is, at the customer segment, micro-segment or one-to-one level. The key in relationship marketing is building close relationships with customers who are highly profitable or have the potential to become profitable. Firms need to identify the appropriate level of segments that can be profitable. For true understanding of customer profitability, firms need to calculate the true costs of serving individual customers. For this purpose, firms should be able to assign all costs that are specific to individual customers. For better understanding of customer segment profitability, firms can rank customers into various groups.

A customer value typology can be developed. For example, firms can classify their customers as gold, silver, and bronze customers based on certain customer metrics such as customer lifetime value. Alternatively, firm can classify customers into most valuable customers, second-tier customers, below zero customers, etc. Most valuable or gold customers represent customers with the highest actual lifetime value and are the target customer group for customer retention. Second-tier or silver customers are those with the highest unrealized potential. They are a source of great untapped profitability. Below zero or bronze customers are those who will never be likely to be profitable due to the high cost of serving the customer and limited profitability.

Once value-based segments are identified, firms face more practical issues regarding various value segments. Many firms experience the gold level (highly profitable) customers can transition to bronze level (unprofitable) customers. For this group, firms must find out how many and why they follow the transition and what firms can do to prevent the transition. On the other hand, firms may see the bronze level (unprofitable) customers can transition to gold level. Firms need to find how to encourage this transition. For customers having a much higher potential value than a current value, firms must determine the least expensive action that will transition him/her to the state of higher value that represents the potential.

It is important for firms to understand and leverage customer knowledge in order to Identify and expand relationships with profitable customers. While the benefits of using detailed customer information in marketing, sales and service are well understood, customer data, shared within the firm in a timely fashion, is a valuable input to demand forecasting, new product developed, reporting and strategic planning. Customer information is rapidly becoming a company's most important asset. Each customer must be analyzed and potentially treated uniquely. Firms need to acquire customers that have the potential to become profitable. Customer lifetime value analysis and value modeling can direct firms their relationship marketing strategy regarding customer acquisition, retention, cross-selling and up-selling across different customer segments. Customer life time value analysis and value modeling are critical foundation for relationship marketing.

Customer Analytics for Customer Value Modeling

The customer is the most important force in any firm. The goal of the firm, then, should be to give the customer what they want, when they want it, and the way they want it. Relationship marketing helps the firm implement customer-centric strategies. Relationship marketing allows a firm to identify and target their most profitable customers. Firms can focus on retaining these people as lifelong customers. Customer analytics enables real-time customization and personalization of products and services based on the customer's wants, needs, buying habits, and life cycles. Customer analytics provides functionality for relationship marketing and fulfillment, sales support, and customer service and support. Key objectives include customer loyalty, attrition management, lifetime value analysis, churn, and response.

Customer analytics helps firms identify and target profitable customers for sales incentives and customer reward programs with the objective to help the firm focus on customer retention and customer loyalty. Customer analytics provides information on the distribution of the customer base to the general population. Customer analytics allows marketing managers to develop value-based customer classification by providing the value of a customer in a long-term customer retention perspective. The core of these analytics is calculating various measurement metrics such as lifetime value of a customer.

Customer analytics can be used to classify customers into various value based segments such as gold, silver, and bronze customers. Alternatively, high, medium, low, and subzero categories can also be used. These analytics solutions are used to identify loyal customers and evaluate their worth to the firm, calculate the threshold level of special offers, and develop detailed customer retention strategies for a particular type of customers. Firms are using these analytic patterns and models to increase retention rates, average order value, and profits per customer over time. The same information can be used to reduce defection rates, churning, and interactions with the least profitable customers. Some customers cost more than they contribute to the firm. Unprofitable customers tend to place many small orders, habitually ordering products or service and then returning them, or contact customer services and tie-up call center lines. The analytics model can identify these customers and provide managers tools to remedy this undesirable situation and to increase marketing efficiency.

The emphasis on customer retention in relationship marketing generates various metrics measuring the impact of customer care programs and actions. One important task is quantifying the expected results of relationship marketing programs and activities. Using the database of multi-year revenue history of customers, a firm can calculate the expected revenue from a new customer. The analytics can also provide a model that measures the financial profit from increasing customer retention. Customer lifetime value can be used to derive expected profit from customer retention. Using this model, a firm can calculate the break-even point of customer care costs compared to increase in revenue due to retention of loyal customers. Customer care programs can affect the retention rate and customer satisfaction. Although improved customer care increases retention rate and profits, the cost of offering the improved customer care should be considered.

Customer analytics can be used to develop the customer value matrix (CVM) that involves understanding the customer base with respect to revenue and risk. The firm should segment the customer base by profitability to enable improved customer relationship management. The segment should be assigned a value for revenue (high / low) and a value for risk (high / low). This information can be useful in developing marketing strategies. The customer value matrix (2x2) categories can be created. Customer analytics can help the sales team by tracking customer contacts and other events of customers for the purpose of cross-selling and up-selling. Customer analytics can help a firm provide a consistent customer experience and superior service and support across all touchpoints. It assists customer service representatives in helping customers who are having problems with a product or service by providing relevant data and suggestions for solving their problems.

Customer Equity Management

Important determinants of firms' market value include the firm's potential for acquiring and retaining customers or other stakeholders and the value of its brands or its human capital. The value potential of current and future customers is becoming of central importance. The firm's ability to acquire and retain attractive customers is ultimately crucial for the firm's success in a competitive market. Blattberg and Deighton (1996) have coined the term Customer Equity (CE) for this value potential. Customer equity can be defined as the sum of the discounted cash surpluses generated by present and future customers (within a certain planning period) for the duration of the time they remain loyal to a firm.

Customer equity is represented by future profit stream generated over a customer's lifetime. Firms will focus on growing customer equity and its market value just like any other valuable assets of the firm. Growing customer equity puts emphasis on identifying the most profitable customers and on developing these relationships. This, in turn, increases the asset value of the total customer base and the firm's market value. In many cases firms will determine that some customers are expensive to obtain and keep but this may not always be the case. Customers that are expensive to obtain in the beginning may prove just as profitable in the long run. Research suggests that there is no direct correlation between profitable customers in the long run and the initial costs of obtaining and retaining them. Customer equity represents the tendency of the customer to stick with the brand beyond the subjective and objective evaluation of the brand.[12] Customer equity represents the strength of the relationship between the customer and the firm. Key drivers of customer equity include customer relationship programs such as loyalty programs and affinity programs. Customer equity can create structural bonds between the customer and the firm. These structural bonds would make the customers less likely to switch to competitors and create the stronger customer-firm relationship than your competitors. Customer equity allows firms maximize customer's repeated purchase, retention, and the value of a customer's future purchases.

Relationship marketing adopts this management approach of acquisition and retention, geared to individual lifetime values of current and future customers with the aim of continuously increasing customer equity. Increasing customer equity through acquisition and retention geared to individual lifetime values of current and future customer's impacts on all levels of marketing:[13]

- Possible new and existing customers,
- Core processes for acquisition and retention as well as supporting steering processes,
- Value drivers and control variables to safeguard effectiveness and efficiency in these processes,
- Long-term financial target figures of a company,
- Investor relations.

The key for creating customer equity is effective and efficient management of individual customer relationships corresponding to the respective value potential. The following describes specific steps to take to effectively manage individual customers for customer equity creation:[14]

1. Determine and integrate industry-specific direct and indirect CLV drivers. Direct CLV drivers are factors that directly affect the amount of the customer lifetime value. Direct CLV drivers include volume of base transactions, repeat purchase frequency, extent of cross-buying, value of word of mouth activities, costs for acquisition mail campaign, and complaint behavior. Indirect CLV drivers affect the customer lifetime value as a result of their effect on the direct drivers. Indirect CLV drivers are customer satisfaction, brand attractiveness, process efficiency and other relevant influencing variables. Both direct and indirect CLV drivers need to be integrated in a single customer database and data warehouse for customer analytics.

2. *Operationalize general CLV and customer equity calculation models.* This step requires integration of associated algorithms and models into the data mining and marketing analytics procedures and store the resulting operationalized model in the analytics warehouse.

3. *Determine customer clusters.* Using the CLV drivers and values include in the customer database, firms need to identify customer clusters that translate into segments with similar needs, preferences, and purchase patterns. Various clustering procedures and models can be used in this step.

4. *Estimate of the average customer retention duration.* For the identified customer segments or clusters, firms need to estimate or calculate the average duration of customer retention.

5. *Calculate individual customer lifetime values.* In this step, firms calculate individual customer lifetime values for the customer base, determine the mean value and standard deviation of the CLV in the different segments, and select customers/segments with negative CLV.

6. *Determine cluster characteristics.* Considering the lifetime values of various clusters, firms need to identify utility structures typical for the segments. For example, conjoint measurement can reveal attached utilities of various product attributes for those segments. Firms can also understand distinctive utility and socio-demographic variables of the clusters. Firms can identify further clustering of potential customers in segments each with similar values for direct CLV drivers. Each cluster is further assessed for the estimate of average acquisition probability. Using these steps, marketing managers can determine the firm's current customer equity for its current customer portfolio. Various relationship marketing strategies can be developed and implemented to increase customer equity in many firms. The relative importance and emphasis given to customer equity compared to brand equity should vary depending on the segments' CLV, preferences, value drivers, and purchase patterns.

Section 4. Customer Portfolio Management Strategy

> *"Far better it is to dare mighty things, to win glorious triumphs, even though checkered by failure, than to take rank with those poor spirits who neither enjoy nor suffer much, because they live in the gray twilight that knows neither victory nor defeat."*
> Theodore Roosevelt

While business portfolio management is used to improve product or brand focused resource allocation, relationship marketing shifts the focus from managing a portfolio of business opportunities related to product type or brand to managing a portfolio of customers. Firms are now required to continually monitor the type of customers they have and effectively manage which customers to retain, acquire, grow or even divest to maximize long-term profitability and growth of the revenue stream.

Customer Portfolio Management

Firms need to balance the customer portfolio to increase long-term profitability of a firm. Effective customer portfolio management requires balancing short-term gains through customer retention and long-term profitability through new customer acquisition. For example, suppose a bank decided to stop targeting younger, less profitable loan customers based on lifetime value calculations.[15] However, firms need to be careful using this type of activities. First, this bank may be making this decision based on incomplete information. They have to consider the fact that these young, less profitable customers may evolve over time into older, more profitable customers. Lifetime value metrics may be incomplete in the sense that they do not capture this potential dynamism in a customer over time.[16] It is also possible that by dropping these less profitable customers, a firm may lose the economy of scale that allows the firm to generate profits from larger customers. Therefore, firms need to consider costs associated with providing customer value accurately.

The critical component of customer portfolio management is determining how a firm should manage an entire portfolio of relationships at different levels of cooperation to create value.[17] Relationship marketing requires building portfolios of relationships to increase a firm's return on relationships. In making relationship portfolio decisions, firms need to consider the firm, customer, and industry characteristics because the portfolios are relationships continually evolving over time.

Relationship portfolio decisions should focus on how to build value for a firm across an entire portfolio of customer relationships. Depending on the nature of the exchange relationships, the nature and processes of value creations are different. The various type of value creation is determined by customers' capabilities and problem-solving behavior as well as suppliers' capabilities and resource-allocation decisions. Different type of value creation processes will create the different types of relationships and different profit mechanisms. A firm's marketing strategies should consist of an entire portfolio of customers at different relationship levels.[18]

From a customer's problem-solving perspective, the formation of satisfaction, trust, experience, and commitment corresponds to the customer's willingness to engage in an exchange relationship. From a firm's resource-allocation perspective, the delivery of parity value, differential value, and customized value should be compatible to the firm's ability and motivation to create the type of relationships with their customers. Ideally, firms want to have customer relationships progress over time to closer and closer forms of value creation. In many cases, the progression of relationships may be different.

The progression of these relationship levels should vary by firm, customer, and industry. For example, a firm will pursue closer relationships with customers who have the greater lifetime values. Customers would pursue closer relationships if a firm offers more customized product or service offerings that meet their particular needs. On the other hand, customers are likely to switch because of the abundance of substitutes if the intensity of competition is high in that particular market segment.

A closer customer relationship creates a stickiness that lowers the likelihood of customer switching.[19] Closer relationships offer various benefits and advantages to the firm. The advantages include; a) increasing the competitor's cost to induce switching,[20] b) lowering the probability of switching, c) creating the premium value for the firm, d) increasing customer purchases, e) lowering the cost of serving the customer, and f) lowering the price sensitivity due to higher switching cost.

A firm's capability to learn from and about its market and customers is directly related to the process of customer relationship development and how value is created in its customer relationships. Firms differ in the way they deploy resources in developing relationships and create marketing capability to learn and to create a competitive advantage. Firms should make strategic decisions whether to allocate resources to build relationships through cooperation to increase the lifetime value of customers. The attractiveness of different types of customers in a customer portfolio varies depending on the industry and the proportion of service components of a product offering. In industries in which the products are primarily commodity goods, there should be greater value created by just having customers in the portfolio regardless their level of closeness to the firm. For firms that offer products containing a large proportion of service components, the creation of closer relationships that leverage the lifetime value of customers should be more important. A critical decision in customer portfolio management is how to allocate resources to attract customers and move relationships to higher forms of value creation to maximize profits and develop a sustainable competitive advantage. This type of decision requires an understanding of the dynamics of value creation and the profitability of the different types of relationships over time. In every market segment and time period, firms must decide whether to incur the costs required to create or maintain different levels of customer relationships for their customer portfolios.

The overall value of a firm's customer portfolio is an aggregation of the contribution from individual exchange relationships over time. Product-driven or brand-driven marketing focuses on creating brand relationships and partnerships by providing value to customers. Brand relationships are built upon brand concepts and create loyalty through repeated purchase. Partnerships are created for business-to-business customers by sharing resources and increased commitments. Relationship marketing focuses on accumulated value creation of a customer portfolio not on an individual value of customers. As the accumulated value created in a customer portfolio may be dominated by different type of relationships, managers should be careful in terminating business relationships with customers that are less profitable on an individual basis. Managers must assess overall composition of their customers with different type of relationships to effectively manage customer portfolio and build sustainable competitive advantage. Customer portfolios can be used to determine resource allocation and marketing strategy decisions. Considering value metrics such as customer lifetime value in a firm's customer portfolio, firms can determine which customers are worth acquiring and retaining for long-term customer relationship.

Customer Acquisition

Customer acquisition plays a critical role in managing customer portfolio. Customer acquisition focuses on how to acquire more attractive customers at a lower cost utilizing various existing and new channels. Firms need to determine which customers to acquire by considering the customer acquisition costs across different channels and cost variability of customer segments. For each segment, firms can evaluate the attractiveness and customer equity by considering number of existing customers, number of acquisition target customers, cost of acquisition, account retention rate, and profit per customer per year. Using these metrics, the expected profitability of the average customer in each segment and the overall profit potential of each segment can be calculated. Firms also need to consider how acquisition costs vary across different channels. In addition, customers acquired from different channels may be different in characteristics and behaviors. Improving acquisition activities require firms to acquire more customers, acquire more attractive customers, or acquire them at a lower cost.

Customer Retention

Many firms recognize the importance of customer retention in maintaining the current customer portfolio and short-term revenue stream. An increase in customer retention can have a significant positive effect on profitability. Firms need to find customer retention activities that of high value to customers with low cost to serve them. The reasons retention can have impact on profitability are the following. First, cost of acquiring new customers are significant and take years to turn them into profitable customers. Second, as customers are more satisfied with a firm and have stronger relationship, they are more likely to increase share of wallet that is the proportion of purchase customers are making on that product category. Third, loyal customers are less likely to defect and switch to competitors. The established relationship is valued especially in business-to-business markets by customers when switching costs are high. Finally, loyal customers are more likely to be advocates and refer others helping firms acquire new customers with much lower acquisition costs.

The emphasis put on acquisition and retention may vary depending on the nature of products sold, relationship portfolio, and individual firm circumstances. It is important to balance these two relationship marketing activities, customer acquisition and retention. As retention is considered critical for profitability, firms need to develop ways to improve customer retention in addition to well-designed customer acquisition strategy. Firms need to understand current customer retention rates and profitability by segment. To assess customer retention, customer retention overtime for various products and services by market segment can be measured. Firms also need to assess profit potential for each market segment. Marketing managers need to identify the root cause of defection and design customer retention programs that can provide solutions to customer problems and resolve the root cause of defection. Firms need to implement relationship marketing strategies that can increase retention rates and enhance long-term customer relationships.

Total CRM Based Relationship Marketing Template

Template 4.1: Value Metric Based Customer Segment

Template 4.1 identifies value-based customer segments using various value metrics.

Value Metrics Used	Value Classification/ Segments	Segment Profile	Relationship Marketing Benefits Sought
Metric 1 = Life Time Value	Gold		
	Segment A		
	Segment B		
	Silver		
	Segment C		
	Segment D		
	Bronze		
	Segment E		
	Segment F		
Metric 2 = Potential value	Gold		
	Segment A		
	Segment B		
	Silver		
	Segment C		
	Segment D		
	Bronze		
	Segment E		
	Segment F		
Metric 3 = Competitive Value (also known as Wallet Share)	Gold		
	Segment A		
	Segment B		
	Silver		
	Segment C		
	Segment D		
	Bronze		
	Segment E		
	Segment F		
Metric 4 = Other	Gold		
	Segment A		
	Segment B		
	Silver		
	Segment C		
	Segment D		
	Bronze		
	Segment E		
	Segment F		

Template 4.2: An Example of Current Relationship Marketing Program Implementation

Template 4.2 shows an example of a firm's current relationship marketing programs implemented for the various value based segments.

Value Classification Segments	Relationship Marketing Programs Currently Offered	Touchpoints (Departments) Involved*
Segment A	Special handling for shipments	E
	Special entertainment by company executives	C, I
	More liberal payment and discount terms	C, I
	Greater availability of SKUs or product volume	C, I
	More flexible advertising of return policies	C, D
	Liberal interpretation of warranties and service policies	C, E, I
	Special phone numbers or people to call	A, C
Segment B		
Segment C		
Segment D		
Segment E	Surcharges on smaller orders	C
	Slower service- or sales-response time	E, J
	Strict enforcement of payment terms	I
Segment F		

* Touchpoints (Departments) Involved
(a) Call center; (b) Web site; (c) Marketing; (d) Co-op advertising; (e) Customer service; (f) Direct mail; (g) General management; (h) Product management; (i) Sales; (j) Support; (k) Service and repair

Template 4.3: CLV Calculation Example

Template 4.3 shows an example excel sheet for calculating the customer lifetime value.

	A	B	C	D	E	F	G	H
1		Total	Retention	Total	Variable	Net	NPV at	Ten Year
2	Year	Customers	Rate	Revenue	Costs	Profit	10%	LTV
3	1	1,500	50%	$ 53,850	$ 40,000	$ 13,850	$ 13,850	$ 54.95
4	2	750	55%	56,925	25,000	31,925	29,023	$ 101.57
5	3	413	65%	31,309	14,575	16,734	13,830	$ 119.49
6	4	268	70%	20,351	7,875	12,476	9,373	$ 135.27
7	5	188	72%	14,245	5,631	8,615	5,884	$ 141.31
8	6	135	75%	10,257	4,535	5,722	3,553	$ 147.78
9	7	101	77%	7,693	2,985	4,708	2,657	$ 156.74
10	8	78	78%	5,923	2,137	3,786	1,943	$ 159.73
11	9	61	78%	4,620	1,714	2,906	1,356	$ 159.05
12	10	47	78%	3,604	1,357	2,247	953	$ 159.11
13	11	37	78%	2,811	1,045	1,766	681	
14	12	29	78%	2,193	745	1,448	507	
15	13	23	78%	1,710	635	1,075	343	
16	14	18	78%	1,334	512	822	238	
17	15	14	78%	1,040	395	645	170	
18	16	11	78%	812	312	500	120	
19	17	8	78%	633	235	398	87	
20	18	7	78%	494	175	319	63	
21	19	5	78%	385	146	239	43	
22	20	4	78%	300	105	195	32	
23						$ 110,179	$ 84,672	

Note: The longer your customers stay with you, the more they tell you about their lifetime value. Each year you succeed in retaining a customer, you can reassess their LTV for the next ten years and compare it to that of new customers you acquire.

Real World Application Cases

Case 4-1: Best Buy[21]

Best Buy's CEO, Brad Anderson has initiated a program for firing unprofitable customers while embracing profitable customers. He refers to these consumers as "devils" and "angels" respectively. Although 'devils' customers are unwanted, care must be taken not to upset these customers as they can spread negative word of mouth to other customers.

Sales records and existing databases are examined to separate customers. More appealing merchandise is stocked to fit the needs of profitable customers, while intense promotions are reduced and devils are cut from marketing lists. Best Buy's strategy of separating angels from devils has taken place in about one out of every six stores. Higher operation and overhead costs are being realized but costs per store are expected to decrease as the strategy is perfected.

Best Buy's plan to restructure their stores to target particular customers instead of having a universal standard is taken from the theory that a company should consider itself a collection of customers and not a collection of product lines. Each store will focus on two of the five value-based customer groups depending on the demographics of the store's location. Warranties and other services are also pushed to increase profitability, and store clerks are participating in increased training to recognize angels and learn how to effectively sell to them.

Case Questions

1. What specific factors should Best Buy include in calculating its customers' lifetime value? Identify value-based segments for Best Buy and describe their typical customer profiles.

2. What is the impact of Best Buy's new marketing strategy on its customer portfolio? What negative outcomes may arise from Best Buy's angel-devil strategy? What recommendations would you offer to Best Buy in managing its customer portfolio?

Case 4-2 WalkMe[22]

WalkMe has a broad target market, expanding across multiple verticals and companies, including small, medium and enterprise firms. The firm's buyer personas vary widely posing many problems in terms of sales and marketing. The significant challenge for WalkMe is evaluating lead conversion potential for a highly varied leads as well as the different perception of a quality of lead between the sales and marketing teams. The variety of leads has different prospect business sizes. In addition, a long business-to-business (B2B) sales cycle presented a problem of measuring and optimizing marketing and advertising campaigns in real time. The firm needed to find an effective way of lead prioritization that is acceptable for both its marketing and sales teams.

WalkMe developed an AI-driven predictive scoring model integrating the firm's Salesforce CRM to provide "fit scores" to each lead. The scoring model calculated the fit scores based on several factors such as the lead company's firm data (industry, revenue, employee count, job openings, etc.), technology related factors (technologies the target companies were using), web and social presence, technology vendors, patents, trademarks, and more. The model provides different score calculations and rules for the varied clients. The model categorizes the inbound leads in decreasing order of conversion potential. WalkMe can use this information to optimize its advertising bidding around keywords that drive the highest scoring leads. Using the system, WalkMe targeted about 2,000 top leads out of the total 78,700 leads with 318 leads conversion, bringing in total revenue of $10.3 million. The top 39% of infer-scored leads contributed to 79% of the firm's "won" revenue. In addition, WalkMe had a 2x increase in meetings scheduled.

Case Questions

1. What are some problems that may develop through the use of such a scoring model? How can these problems be avoided?

2. Any customer scoring model must be based on customer lifetime value. How can the scoring model incorporate the potential customer's lifetime value or wallet share?

Chapter 5. Customer Experience Management for Relationship Marketing

Section 1. Understanding Customer Experience

"The possible solutions to a given problem emerge as the leaves of a tree, each node representing a point of deliberation and decision."
Niklaus Wirth

Relationship marketing is built upon the concept of customer experience. While many researchers and practitioners define customer experience over time, customer experience involves the strategic management process of a customer's entire experience with a product or a firm.[1] Customer experience is more broadly defined to include all aspect of a firm's offering. Customer experience refers to every aspect of a firm's offering such as the quality of customer care, advertising, packaging, service features, and reliability.[2] Customer experience is considered as the internal and subjective response customers have to any interaction with a firm and brand. Customer experience represents the internal and subjective response customers have to any direct and indirect contact with a firm. Direct contact is typically initiated by customers and related to actual purchase, use, and service. Indirect contact refers to unplanned encounters of customers such as word-of-mouth communications, news reports, blog posts, and reviews. Experiences can be inherently personal, existing only in the mind of a customer. As experiences are formed by customers' interpretations of interactions, experience is shaped by both controllable factors and uncontrollable factors by the firm. Experiences are formed every time a customer interacts with multiple touchpoints that are any part of the product, service, brand, or firm at various points in time.

Customer experience is viewed as a multidimensional concept that contains five types of experiences.[3] The five types of experiences are sensory (sense), affective (feel), cognitive (think), physical (act), and social-identity (relate) experience. The sense experience is related to the five senses of customers creating customer value through sight, sound, touch, taste, and smell. The feel experience refers to customers' inner feelings and emotions. Customer experience is formed through affective experiences that range from moderately positive moods linked to a brand to strong emotions of joy and pride. The degree of affective experience depends on the nature of product and degree of a customer's attachment and purchase involvement to the brand or product category. The think experience is related to the customer's intellect through which firms can create value for customers. The act experience is related to behaviors and lifestyles. This experience creates value for customers by showing alternative lifestyles or alternative ways of doing business. The relate experience is related to social experiences. This experience creates customer value by providing a social identity and sense of belonging.

The nature of customer experience is holistic. Customer experience comprises multiple interactions across touchpoints. Customer experience can be characterized by the three dimensions of physical complexity, digital density, and social presence.[4] Physical complexity is related to what customers encounter in their interaction at various touchpoints. The physical dimension includes the arrangement of furnishings, equipment, and spatial arrangements that enhance functionality, convenience and a sense of comfort, ambient elements and cultural resources.

Digital density represents information density in the interaction. Firms are adopting digital technologies, such as mobile, location-based, virtual reality, digital twins, block chains, AI, wearable technologies, neuroscience, and business process automation, as well as machine-to-machine interactions through the Internet of Things (IoT) to improve customer interaction and enhance customer experience. Digital technologies allow firms to respond to digital demand and achieve complexity handling, high information availability, high reach, frequent interactions, and faster speeds of transactions. This allows firms to offer highly customized product offerings and personalized service to profitable customers. Digital technologies can help firms engage with customers more effective with increased interactivity and rich information exchange between the firm and customers.[5]

Social presence refers to interactions among actors such as customers and employees through different interfaces which are both human and non-human in nature. Firms need to understand customers' social environments and meet their expectations by facilitating customers' interactions with other customers. Customers can influence other customers and can co-create experiences with the firm through the density of social presence.

It is important for firms to design and deliver unique experiences by responding to customers' ideal experiences with comprehensive view of the customer experience over time that integrates all elements of customer experiences. Building relationships with customers involve all types of touchpoints that are traditional as well as new emerging web based and social media driven touchpoints. Firms need to integrate a variety of touchpoints to create a relevant total customer experience leading to strong customer relationship. For successful relationship marketing, firms must understand and manage all facets of customer experience and related touchpoints effectively.

Customer Touchpoints

Many firms consider touchpoints as the critical moments when customers interact with the firm and its offerings. Depending on the customers, different touchpoints may be preferred or used by customers. Touchpoints can be classified into four different categories. These categories are brand-owned, partner-owned, customer-owned, and social/external/independent.[6] Brand-owned touchpoints are any touchpoints related to the brand. They include firm-controlled touchpoints such as traditional and online advertising, websites, loyalty programs, and sales force. Partner-owned touchpoints refer to touchpoints that are jointly designed, managed, or controlled by the firm and one or more of its partners. Partners can be marketing agencies, multichannel distribution partners, multivendor loyalty program partners, and communication channel partners. Customer-owned touchpoints are touchpoints that are initiated and managed by the customer or third party and cannot be completely controlled by the firm or its partners. With the increased use of online product reviews and social media by customers, customers are becoming co-creators of value and can share important usage experience or express opinions about the brand experience. Social/external touch points are those touchpoints related to others in the customer experience. Customers are influenced by external and other touch points such as peer influence, comments or videos posted by others, and third-party evaluations. These sources can be either independent or sponsored by the firm. Regardless of the nature of the source, these touchpoints are having increased influence throughout the customers' experience journey.

Touchpoints can also be understood by the elements involved. The touchpoint elements include atmospheric, technological, communicative, process, employee-customer interaction, customer-customer interaction, and product interaction.[7] Atmospheric element refers to the physical characteristics and surroundings customers experience when interacting with any part of a firm or brand. Technological element is related to a customer's direct interaction with any form of technology during an encounter with a firm or brand. Communicative element is the one-way communication from the firm to the customer, including both promotional and informative messages. Process element refers to the actions or steps customers need to take in order to achieve a particular outcome with a firm or brand. Employee-customer interaction involves the direct and indirect interactions customers have with employees when interacting with any part of the firm or brand. Customer-customer interaction involves the direct and indirect interactions customers have with other customers when interacting with any part of the firm or brand. Product interaction is the direct or indirect interactions customers have with the core tangible or intangible product offered by the firm.

Business customers interact with touchpoints in a B2B context that encompasses all verbal and nonverbal contacts leading to customer experiences. B2B touchpoints include various forms of interaction involving different actors from the supplier firm, the customer firm, or partner firms. Within each firm, touchpoints are represented by different functional and organizational units, as well as individuals operating diverse hierarchical levels.[8] In addition, in B2B setting, different actors who are acting either at the individual level or group level may engage in different touchpoints at different stages of the customer journey.

Meaningful touchpoints change over the course of a customer's life. Not all touchpoints are of equal value to customers. Service interactions can be more important if the core offering is a service. At each touchpoint, the gap between customer expectations and actual customer experience can influence customer satisfaction and customer delight. The understanding of customers' experience with all relevant touchpoints enables marketing managers create products and services that can delight customers and increase customer retention and profitability. The narrow focus on maximizing satisfaction in a particular touchpoint can create a distorted picture of higher satisfaction and diverts attention from the customer's end-to-end journey.[9] In evaluating the interaction with a touchpoint, firms must understand the context of the customer interaction, root causes of interaction, and try to improve interactions upstream and downstream of the interaction process. Firms must manage the entire touchpoints collectively. Effective management of the entire touchpoints can provide firms enhanced customer satisfaction, reduced churn, increased revenue, and greater employee satisfaction.

The Customer Experience Journey

It is important for firms to understand the customer experience journey. Customers can interact with various touchpoints at all stages of the customer journey. They develop customer experience through all touchpoints and encounters that are either interactions directly linked to a firm or through indirect and unplanned interactions by the firm. Customer experience can be formed over time and is considered a journey during the complete purchase cycle. In understanding customer experience, firms need to capture how customers interact with multiple touchpoints, moving through the customer experience process during the complete purchase cycle. For effective relationship marketing, understanding the customer experience journey serves as the prerequisite. Through the evaluation of the customer journey, firms can assess the customer's preferred options and choices for touchpoints in multiple purchase phases. The customer journey provides a foundation for defining what is most important in a customer's experience. Customer experience journey reveals value that customers place on different levels of performance for each element of the experience. In addition, customer experience journey can provide customers' minimal expectations for each element and their perception of the firm's performance versus that of key competitors. In evaluating the customer journey, it is important to meet with the customer and pare down the list to the most critical issues. The customer experience journey also reveals whether the current experience level deviates from the ideal customer experience and what are the causes of the gap. The understanding of the experience gap provides directions for relationship marketing strategic choices.

Customer Identification for Customer Experience Mapping

In evaluating the customer experience journey, one condition for success is the proper identification of target customers. This is because the customer experience can vary widely depending on the customer. To correctly map customer experience and develop the appropriate experience-based marketing strategy, firms need to identify the type of customers they are interested in mapping the experience. As the subsequent marketing strategy and tactics depend on the customer experience map, the target customers that are profitable and worth long-term relationships must be selected for experience mapping and analysis.

Firms need to create a system that enables them to identify customers as individuals each time firms come in contact with them. To identify as many customers as possible, firms can use customer identification information that can separate one particular customer from another and track transactions and interactions with the customer over time. In identifying customers in a consumer market, firms first take an inventory of all customer data already available in an electronic format. Firms need to locate customer-identifying information that is currently "on file" but not electronically compiled. If repositories of customer information not digitized, then digitization need to be done. Database not considered useful for this purpose includes invoicing system, warranty-service system or complaint handling system data. In identifying business customers, customers can be purchasing managers, contract approvers, or actual end users in a B2B market. Identifying end-users in business markets can provide a convenient method of establishing reordering system of supplies. Firms can identify business customers through questionnaire or request form for end user manual of technical products, regular service time with end users, register information for installation, and built-in machine intelligence.

Typically available customer identification sources are billing and invoicing records, sweepstakes and context entry form, warranty records, coupon redemption and rebate forms, customer comment and research data, sales force records or other field personnel, repairs and service records, local or regional mailings and promotions, loyalty user card/frequency program, user groups, clubs, and affinity groups involving your firm or product, magazines or newsletters serving your industry, cooperative ventures with retailers, resellers, and distributors, other alliances with companies close to the customer, "list swaps" with others in industry, mailing list brokers and industry data providers. In deciding on a customer identifier, the important issue is how to "tag" your customers' individual identities. Name can be used for consistency. Movable data across different business units need to be selected. Common data gathering standards suggest the following identifiers that include account number, vehicle identification number, membership card, phone number, social security number, combined data-name/address, personal password. Firms can use the following practical information categories for customer data management.[10]

First category of 'current facts and figures' include (1) sales figures, per customers; by month, year to date, with comparisons to prior periods, (2) products ordered; by item or sku number, by category, by sales volume, (3) ship to locations; number of customer locations, units, or subsidiaries, (4) purchase frequency, (5) service/repair frequency; by product, by location, by incident type, and (6) payment and credit history; timeliness, creditworthiness, credit limits.

Second category of 'imputable and computable customer data' contains (1) data hiding behind the current facts and figures, (2) increase or decrease in dollar volume, purchase frequency, skus, (3) number of product end users in an enterprise, (4) number of business units, divisions, or subsidiaries, (5) number of purchases at each unit (from invoices, shipping records, purchase order), (6) seasonality of purchase, (7) unique sales or servicing costs, (8) ancillary services sold.

Third category of 'observable customer data' includes (1) fan or foe, (2) product knowledge and using a firm's product wisely, (3) referral potential and whether to serve as an enthusiastic reference, (4) "power of pen" representing buying roles played, (5) company health showing the degree of being energetic or growing.

Forth category of 'obtainable customer data' for business customers includes (1) company characteristics such as sic code, growth vs. peers, new product plans, profitability, industry reputation, (2) benchmarking value such as reputation, and (3) inherent opportunities that can Influenced by this initial adoption

The ability to identify intuitively sound actionable customer segments is important. If you can't segment your customers using relevant customer identifiers, a customer strategy is meaningless and customer relationship marketing impossible. If you can't explain your segments with the appropriate customer value metrics, no one will understand it, and relationship marketing may not work. Firms need to examine what customer identification data is available and to determine the level of customer segments that will be possible. Once the customers in the target segment are identified for customer experience map, firms can proceed to mapping the total customer experience journey.

Customer Experience Mapping

One way to understand the customer experience better is to map out the customer experience journey at various touchpoints throughout the entire experience process. As discussed earlier, touch points are all interaction points where the firm has direct or indirect contact instances with the customer about the product or service over time. Customer experience map offers a valuable tool for diagnosing key touchpoints between the firm and customer from the moment contact is made with a potential customer through the maintenance of an ongoing relationship.

A customer journey map is a diagram that illustrates the engagement steps that a firm's customers are involved in. The journey can involve the engagement regarding a product, an online experience, or a service or any combination.[11] The customer journey map shows a timeline that involves first engaging with a customer through certain touchpoints such as advertising or in a store; then buying the product or service, using it, sharing the experience with others in person or online; and then upgrading, replacing, or switching to a competitor. A customer journey map can have a unique component or process depending on the nature of the product or service. The journey map can be centered around the conventional sales funnel or online purchasing.

One approach to develop the customer journey map is by evaluating the various stages of a framework of actions, motivations, questions, and barriers. For each stage, firms need to assess why customers are taking certain actions, for what motivation, what type of questions or barriers they may have. For the 'actions', firms need to evaluate what customers are doing at each stage and what actions are taken to the next stage. In this case, firms can identify what touchpoints customers are using in interacting with the firm. For the 'motivations', firms need to find out why customers are moving to the stage and what emotions they have, what attributes they value. For the 'questions', firms can evaluate what things or issues prohibit or delay customers move to the next stage. For the 'barriers', firms need to assess what barriers stand in the way of moving on to the next stage.

Mapping B2C Customer Experience

B2C customer experience can be mapped with the customer journey that focuses on product, brand, or service. Consumers as B2C customers tend to follow the experience journey involving three stages: pre-purchase, purchase, and post-purchase. The B2C customer experience process can include three steps following the purchase and usage cycle of a consumer.

The customer journey includes pre-purchase to purchase to post-purchase stage.[12] In each stage, customers are in contact with various touchpoints that are either completely controllable or not completely controllable by a firm. The first stage of pre-purchase includes all aspects of the customer's interaction with the brand, category, and environment before making a purchase. This stage is characterized by customer behaviors such as need recognition, search, and evaluation that encompass the customer's entire experience before purchase. The second stage of purchase involves all customer interactions with the brand and its environment during the purchase process. This stage includes customers' making product or brand choice, ordering, and payment activities in both offline and online purchase environment. Marketing strategy and tactics can influence this purchase stage. The third stage of post purchase includes customer interactions with the brand and its environment after the actual purchase. This stage involves actual usage and consumption, post purchase engagement, service requests, and disposal and is related to the customer's experience while using and consuming the product and service. Customers' experiences are expressed and shared through various actions taken by customers such as repurchase, positive reviews, comments posted on the firm's social media by the customer, product returns, and complaints. This stage is critical in relationship marketing as this stage is related to customer loyalty, customer retention, and long-term relationships with customers.

Mapping B2B Customer Experience

In mapping the B2B customer experience journey, firms need to consider the unique characteristics and nature of B2B transactions. B2B customer experience is formed through multiple interactions with different employees in different positions and diverse functional units. In mapping B2B customer experience, firms need to consider the four critical factors: relationship types, control of touchpoints, function and hierarchical level, and stage of the customer journey.[13] Relationship type deals with the nature of business relationship to be either transactional or relational. Relationship type is determined by the nature of product or service as well as the number of customers in the customer portfolio. The customer experience map should reflect the type of customer relationship to be captured. Control of touchpoints refers to who primarily controls various touch points. In B2B setting, touchpoints can be controlled by the customer, supplier, partner, and external actors. The function and hierarchical level of the customer is related to the organizational design of the customer. The stage of the customer journey deals with the processes a customer goes through across all stages and touchpoints. In B2B setting, not all touchpoints are under the control of the firm. Those touchpoints not controlled by the firm can be indirectly controlled by influencing those entities that has the primary control over those touchpoints.

B2B customers' experience journey involves a set of relational processes to meet the customer's business needs. The B2B experience journey typically includes four distinct but interrelated stages: pre-bid engagement, negotiation, purchase and implementation, and operations and after sale service.[14] Each stage involves different types of touchpoints and interactions among the firm, customer, partner firms, or other actors. In the pre-bid engagement stage, purchasing department of the customer firm interacts with various touchpoints such as sales rep, selling firm website, and related blog sites for the procurement opportunities. Partners and consultants are also playing as touchpoints for customers providing relevant information such as business, market or technical requirements. In the negotiations stage, the buying team in the buying firm determines the specification and interacts with various touchpoints of the qualified suppliers and other actors. After receiving bids, B2B customers again interact with the selling team for contract negotiation of terms and conditions. In this stage, multiple contact points consisting of different hierarchical levels and firms are involved. In the purchase and implementation stage, B2B customers interact with the selling firm and selling team consisting of sales, purchasing, and engineering. These various touchpoints serve as contact points for the buying team of the buying firm contributing to the B2B customer experience. In the operations and after sale service stage, B2B customers interact with various touchpoints such as service technicians, online service platform, and online marketplaces for components or spare parts. These touchpoints include the selling firm, partner firms, and other external entities involving both traditional and digital touchpoints.

Section 2. Customer Experience Management

"I don't care what you believe, just believe in it."
Shepherd Book

Customers interact with firms through various touchpoints in multiple channels and media. It is important for marketing managers to have a comprehensive view of the total customer experience. Customer experience management involves the process of strategically managing a customer's entire experience with a product or a firm. It deals with how a firm and its product and service offerings can be relevant to a customer's life. Firms connect to the customer at every touchpoint and need to provide coordinated and consistent customer experience throughout all touchpoints. Customers can receive delightful experience relevant for their purchase and usage situations.

Managing Customer Experience

Customer experience management focuses on capturing and managing what a customer thinks about a firm at various touchpoints. The overall experience quality can be derived from relative importance of various touchpoints and quality of experience of various touch points. The captured customer experience information is the immediate response of the customer and can be used by marketing managers to create fulfillable expectations and experiential promise regarding products and services. By evaluating the gaps between expectations and experience, firms can create new product offerings to strengthen customer relationships. To better understand and manage customer experience, firms need to identify various patterns of interactions with customers. The patterns of customer interaction include past, present, and potential patterns. Past patterns represent recent experiences of customers. These past experience patterns can help firms improve transactional experiences, find experiential trends, and identify emerging issues. Present experience patterns focus on current relationships and experience issues. These present experience patterns can reveal consistent and deeper state of relationship and other factors. Potential experience patterns intend to identify future opportunistic experiences desired by specific customers with unique problems. Each experience pattern can provide firms with different insights, be used to enhance customer relationships, and develop relationship marketing strategies.

Providing a seamless and consistent experience to customers is critical for customer retention and improving customer experience. Firms must consider the cost of serving the customer as well. Improvement must be made for customers or customer segments that show the profit potential. As customers interact with multiple touchpoints, the customer experience must be considered collectively by covering all channel interactions. These touchpoints are where the customer actually experiences the brand and firm. Firms need to carefully develop customer experience management strategy to offer an outstanding or near-perfect experience at an affordable cost. There are many aspects and activities involved in achieving an outstanding or near-perfect customer experience. The starting point is to fully understand the customer experience throughout the customer journey. With this understanding, firms can develop a touchpoint channel design that offers the greatest value to the customer and firm. This involves evaluating the value and costs of different channel structures for certain customer segments and determining the touchpoint channel strategy that provides the near perfect customer experience and the greatest customer retention and loyalty for the firm.

The experience-based relationship marketing strategy should improve the customer experience, increase account coverage, improve revenue growth, lower the cost to serve the customer, and enhance customer retention. In addition to the expensive common customer retention tactics such as upgrade offers, discounted rate plans, and intercepting defectors, firms can use customer experience as an important lever for reducing churn and building competitive advantage[15]. It is important for firms to identify key journeys that matter most and deciding where to begin the transformation. Firms can identify the most significant journeys and the pain points within them that represent the critical shortcomings damaging customers' experiences. Firms need to focus on supporting journeys not just touchpoints to deliver outstanding customer journeys. Firms focusing on customer journey transition from siloed functions and top-down innovation to cross-functional processes and empowered, bottom-up innovation.[16]

B2B Firms are increasingly recognizing customer experience management (CEM) as a key source of competitive advantage and especially as a strategic response to commoditization.[17] Managing B2B customer experience requires a multidisciplinary approach in which multiple functions and network partners cooperate to manage the customer experience. Managing touchpoints within such a network of actors is a critical characteristic of experience management in B2B settings. B2B firms must be able to manage customer interactions across different touchpoints, which can reside within or outside the firm.

Due to the involvement of multiple actors and entities, B2B firms can have varied controls over different touchpoints as they cannot influence completely what actors will do in a particular interaction. Customer experience management in B2B markets involves interactions that are unique and multi-directional. B2B interactions occur among various actors at the individual level or across groups such as selling team and buying team. Individual and group experiences interact each other in B2B setting.

Customer Experience Management Steps

Customer experience can be managed with the following five steps.[18]

The first step is to analyze the experiential world of the customer. In this step, firms need to analyze socio-cultural context of consumers or business context of business-to-business customers that can influence the experience of customers. In conducting experiential analysis, firms need to identify the precise target customer for the planned experience. Firms need to track the entire experience along all the touchpoints between the customer and the firm throughout the experience process of pre-purchase, purchase, and post purchase of usage and disposal. The goal of experience tracking is to understand how an experience can be enhanced for the customer throughout the experience process. Firms need to focus on finding out which touchpoints customers want or prefer to use, and at each touchpoint what information customers want and what experience they desire. The focus is how customers' experiences are addressed currently at each experience stage by the firm and its competitors.

The second step is building the experiential platform that is considered as the key connection point between strategy and implementation. This platform describes the desired experience and the value customers can expect from the firm and brand. It also includes a value adding concept that can be implemented in the style and content of the brand, interface, and innovation elements.

The third step is designing the brand experience. Brand experience includes (1) experiential features and product aesthetics, (2) appealing logos, signage, packaging, and (3) appropriate experiential messages and imagery in advertising as well as website and social media site design and user interfaces. Firms need to use a common implementation theme of the experience such that all customer touchpoints communicate a consistent and relevant experience to customers.

The fourth step is structuring the customer interface. The customer interface must reflect the experiential platform identified in the third step. As the customer interface include all types of dynamic exchanges and contact points with the customer, firms need to structure the content and style of the user interface such that it gives the customer the desired information and service in the right interactive way. The customer interface must be designed to provide experiential consistency over time and coherence across various touchpoints.

The final step is engaging in continuous innovation. Firms must be engaged in continuous innovation that can improve customers' personal lives and business customers' work life. The goal in this step is to convince customers that the firm can continually create and deliver new and relevant experiences. By creating new and relevant experiences, firms can acquire new customers, retain existing customers, and build customer equity. A firm's innovation efforts need to be planned, managed, and commercialized to improve the customer experience.

Section 3. Customer Experiential Targeting and Positioning

> *"Facts are stubborn, but statistics are more pliable."*
> Mark Twain

Traditional Segmentation and Targeting Approach

Deciding which customers/markets to target is a problem that marketing managers at any firm face at some point. Market segmentation and targeting analysis is the process of dividing an entire market into different segments and then deciding which markets to target or which potential segments the firm will focus on.[19] This can depend on lifestyles, demographic areas, common needs, interests, characteristics, and much more. This is important to determine the other marketing activities such as price, distribution, promotion, and product. Each segment needs to be approached in different ways. A problem marketing managers could face when deciding which markets to segment and target is identifying the right approaches.

Customers who are profitable and want or need a product or service that the firm offers are ideal candidates. Successful implementation of the marketing strategy requires a detailed understanding of those customers and how they are segmented. Marketing managers can come across the problem that they may be marketing to the wrong customers or to the wrong markets. Targeting the wrong customers wastes the firm's marketing dollars and decreases overall profit.

Knowing different techniques to target the right customers at the right time with the right touchpoints will help ensure the firm has a competitive advantage.

The marketing objectives in segmentation and targeting are to reduce the risk in deciding where, when, how, and whom a product or service will be marketed to as well as to increase efficiency by directing the most resources and marketing initiatives toward the designated segment(s). Some benefits of effective market targeting are better serving customers' needs and wants, purchasing power by price differentiation, attracting additional customer groups, sustainable customer relationships, and higher market shares. Even with a limited product range it can seem possible to target a variety of customers. Just using different forms, bundles, incentives, or promotional items associated with the product can make it effective in different markets.

Finding the right customers involves profiling.[20] A profile is defined as a collection of information about a single customer.[21] In understanding customer needs, requirements, preferences, and interests, two alternative approaches to profiling have emerged: personal profiling and social profiling. A personal profile can be developed based on personal information provided by each individual customer through traditional and web-based survey responses, product registration, and/or web click-stream activities. A social profile can be developed by profiling the community to which that individual belongs. In social profiling, preferences are identified through common interests of the community that a customer or consumer belongs and the interacting members in that community. When a product or service is found by a member of the community, every member in the community with a similar profile is alerted to the available information. For example, Amazon.com uses social profiling by offering reviews of a book by other readers and providing book recommendations based on purchase patterns of purchasers with similar social profiles.[22]

The social profile can be used to determine customer needs, requirements, preferences, and interests as well.[23] These common types of profiling originated in the catalog industry. RFM (Recency, Frequency, Monetary) factors are used to segment customers based upon their buying behavior and are used to identify high-value customers.[24] The recency factor is defined as the number of months since the last purchase; the frequency factor is defined as the value of the number of purchases made; and the monetary factor is defined as the value of the total dollar amount of the purchases made. So, RFM factors provide a view of customers based upon the last time they purchased, how often they purchased, and how much they purchased. Thus, profiling enables marketing managers to identify consumers and demographic groups. Profiling can help marketing managers identify the interests and preferences of specific individuals as well.

Using Customer Analytics for Segmentation and Targeting

Marketing managers are facing an important marketing task of developing and implementing a successful market segmentation scheme for a given product or service. Such effective segmentation provides strategic guidelines for the firm and helps marketing managers make various marketing decisions. It also helps firms to determine the right product-market relationship. The analytic question relevant to this task is how to identify groups of customers who are relatively homogeneous with respect to their responses to market offerings. It is important for marketing managers to answer the analytic questions of how to group potential customers into homogeneous groups that are large enough to be profitable. This type of decision must be data-centered and focused on a fact-based decision-making process.

In market segmentation, targeting, and positioning decisions, it is important to identify specific product markets or segments showing exceptional growth or decline. The important task of marketing managers is to select which segments the firm will indeed target. A firm should choose an option that best serves the structure of their firm. Obviously, a small firm will not be able to cover the entire market or perhaps even provide several products. A large firm, on the other hand, may be able to do whatever it wants. Segmentation is used to identify segments or groupings within variable categories. Segmentation is an analytical procedure by which predictor variables are split into subgroups that impact or explain variation in the target variable. It is used to gain more detailed knowledge of cause and effect between variables and the target. Applications include response profiles, customer profiles, profit profiles, and process profiles. Marketing managers could explore the question, "Does age or income level really influence the consumer's purchasing habits?". If the analyst discovers this to be true, then the analyst can ask, "What are the significant segments that require further analysis?". However, with the segmentation technique, the analyst is unable to perform sensitivity analysis or to conduct forecasting of future events.

How can the marketing managers use the segmentation technique? The marketing managers can use the decision tree algorithm to decide which consumers should be focused on. For example, the marketing managers can segment all customers by age (0-25, 25-55, 55+), by gender (male, female), or by region (North, East, South, West). The marketing managers can identify exceptional customers who do not fit well into their expected group. As such, segmentation can be data-driven or market-driven. Data-driven segmentation uses characteristics that are determined to be important drivers of the firm. Market-driven segmentation uses techniques such as cluster analysis or factor analysis to find homogenous groups. An example of market-driven segmentation is "life stages". Life stages are patterns that change over time. The consumers are clustered into groups defined by demographics such as age, gender, and marital status as they progress through various life stages. To select the right target markets for the firm's products, marketing managers may ask questions such as "Which market segment should we target for the new and existing products?" or "Who are those that belongs to the selected target markets?" or "How can we know a potential customer that follows the behavioral pattern or responses of different target market segments?" Marketing managers need to generate analytic solutions to these questions.

Marketing managers face the task of target marketing that involves directing marketing activities to those customers who are most likely to respond. With the increased adoption of relationship marketing tools, firms are required to build and maintain customer databases. These databases keep detailed records of customers and can be combined with other relevant data to be used for targeting. Targeting involves selecting customers who are worth pursuing and are more valuable than others. To resolve this targeting task, marketing managers need to ask analytic questions that are related to identification and selection of profitable customers. Marketing managers want to know who the profitable customers are and which are more likely to respond to the firm's marketing efforts. They are interested in classifying customers into segments such as most profitable to least profitable and predicting responses to marketing activities such as promotions. Marketing managers also want to identify factors that determine the responses such as product purchases. Targeting decisions are related to analytic questions of how to classify customers and predict the class category of new or potential customers who share similar response and behavior patterns.

One form of directed learning algorithm is the classification model.[25] In this directed AI learning model, the algorithm can be developed to map an input and output. Directed classification models map a set of input features to a discrete class label. The input can take many different forms such as numerical values, categorical values, text, image, video, and others and is then converted to some meaningful features. The output can be a discrete class from a pre-defined set of labels. In AI powered classification algorithms, input can be a binary variable such as purchase versus no-purchase and the output can be interpreted as the probability of target class. AI classification algorithms can use the user-generated classifiers to build the AI model. In this case, typical user-generated classifiers are rule-based classifier or the classification results generated from the user-generated classification tools such as k-means clustering or neural networks. As the AI algorithm updates the classification model with new data and learns new knowledge, the model can be improved to achieve higher efficiency, updated to reflect the customer changes, or reformulated to gain different insights. AI algorithms can identify which customer segments need to be targeted and find better match customers for the firm's products and brands.[26] In business-to-business marketing, an important task is identifying and qualifying potential leads for further action. AI can make the account selection process more efficient by building a model that identifies accounts of existing and new customers based on the predefined attributes. The AI-driven model can help salespeople give access to a large number of ideal prospects and make more accurate choices when prospecting based on fact-based decisions.[27]

Marketing managers can develop and train machine learning algorithms based on the user driven classification models, the firm's big data, and other external data. AI powered classification algorithms can build actionable customer segments by using an advanced machine-learning engine and develop personas based on big data that includes past and current real-time customer interactions of the firm's all touch points, typical segmentation variables such as psychographic and demographic variables, macro trends, and geo-specific events. AI algorithms can crunch huge amount of data and generate marketing insights customizable to customers' behavioral patterns of various customer segments. Using these AI generated insights, marketing managers can identify more clearly which customer segments to target, better match products with customer segments, and increase revenue for various customer segments with more effective relationship marketing.

Marketing managers can use AI powered classification algorithms to reach their customers with the level of personalization and targeting at the granular level. With AI and machine learning, marketing managers can develop and implement dynamic segmentation.[28] Dynamic segmentation applies AI to a firm's segmentation and targeting tasks in order to consider that customers' behaviors are changing and taking on different personas. Dynamic segmentation can group potential customers with real-time data instead of outdated data for targeting. For business-to-business marketing firms, AI can be used by marketing managers to filter out customer firms from its list of prospects and help firms for effective targeting and customization.

Customer analytics involves gathering data about customers and their relationship with the firm in order to improve the firm's future sales and service and lower cost. As websites have added a new and often faster way to interact with customers, the opportunity and the need to turn data collected on customers into useful information has become increasingly apparent. Customer analytics can provide customer segmentation groupings (at its simplest by dividing customers into those most and least likely to repurchase a product); profitability analysis (which customers lead to the most profit over time); personalization (the ability to market to individual customers based on the data collected about them); event monitoring (when a customer reaches a certain dollar volume of purchases); what-if scenarios (how likely a customer or customer category that bought one product to buy a similar one); and predictive modeling (comparing various product development plans in terms of likely future success given the customer knowledge base). Data collection and analysis are viewed as a continuing and iterative process; ideally, over time business decisions are refined based on feedback from earlier analysis and consequent decisions.

Experiential Positioning and Experiential Value Promise

After determining the target market segments, marketing managers must develop an appropriate value proposition for each target market segment. The value proposition states how a firm's product or service is differentiated in the mind of its target customers. This is why a customer should buy the firm's product rather than its key competitors' product offerings. Ideally, the value proposition for a market segment must be built around the value drivers or benefits sought by the target segment. Each value proposition is designed to meet the unique needs of the various target market segments. In relationship marketing, the positioning approach is used to better serve customers and to build stronger customer relationships. Market positioning can be developed based on typical positioning variables such as value drivers or benefits sought. However, in relationship marketing, the positioning process can be done differently using experiential positioning.

Experiential Positioning

Experiential positioning utilizes customer experience as well as patterns and insights generated from detailed analyses of customer behaviors and purchases. The experiential positioning represents what the brand or firm stands for the customer experience. Although it is similar to traditional positioning, the difference is its focus on experiential dimensions of the positioning statement. The positioning statement must include useful multisensory strategy components that are relevant and directly related to customer experience. The experiential positioning is the image driven depiction of the experience that the brand stands for. The experiential positioning needs to be updated or modified according to the changing desired experience of the target customers. Firms need to respond to changes in the environment and communicate the experiential positioning to the customer. In addition, firms need to communicate their commitment to delivering a certain experience for their customers at every touchpoint. In this endeavor, firms need to differentiate its experiential positioning and focus on the relevant aspects of the customer experience.

Experiential Value Promise

The experiential value promise describes what the experiential positioning will do for the customer.[29] It shows what type of experience the customer can expect from the firm. In specifying experiential value promise, firms can identify the types of experiences such as sensory experience or affective experience. In many cases, the experiential value would be hybrids of several types of experience leading to holistic experiences. This experiential value promise can guide marketing toward customers and help managers develop innovative new offerings. It is linked to financial expectations and customer equity.

Firms that implement experiential value promise successfully will gain customer loyalty and profitability. Today, experiential positioning plays the pivotal role for strategic position of a firm. Experiential positioning focuses on the integration of customer experience, knowledge for finding and keeping customer to grow customer lifetime value and customer equity. It also plays an important role in helping firms to keep existing customers and to make them loyal. Firms should know leaving customers' reasons and finding ways of keeping them by evaluating customer experience. Therefore, experiential value promise can play a critical role in customer retention by better recognizing the right customers and enhancing their loyalty. Effectual customer preservation starts with right experiential positioning and experiential value promise for the target customers. Firms ought to collect customer experience as well as customer profile that include all demographic information, communications and interactions, and purchasing information. This data/information, together with customer experience assessment allows firms to measure the productivity and the profitability of every customer. Firms can then make plans and policies proportionate with the customer's profitability.

Total CRM Based Relationship Marketing Template

Template 5.1: Value Based Segments

Template 5.1 identifies various value based classification segments. In this example, the classification scheme is gold, silver, and bronze.

Value Classification Segments	Current Value	Potential Life Time Value (LTV)	Current Experience Level	Key Pain Points Identified
Gold				
Segment A				
Segment B				
Silver				
Segment C				
Segment D				
Bronze				
Segment E				
Segment F				

Template 5.2: B2C Customer Total Experience Mapping over the Experience Journey

Template 5.2 tracks B2C customer experience level offered by your firm and identify key pain points for each value based segment over the customer experience journey.

Value Metrics / Value Classification Segments		Stage 1 (Pre Purchase)		Stage 2 (Purchase)		Stage 3 (Post Purchase)	
		Experienced Delight Level [1 = Very low; 5 = Very high]	Key Issues / Problems Identified	Experienced Delight Level [1 = Very low; 5 = Very high]	Key Issues / Problems Identified	Experienced Delight Level [1 = Very low; 5 = Very high]	Key Issues / Problems Identified
Metric 1	Gold						
	Value Segment A						
	Value Segment B						
	Silver						
	Value Segment C						
	Value Segment D						
	Bronze						
	Value Segment E						
	Value Segment F						
Metric 2	Gold						
	Value Segment A						
	Value Segment B						
	Silver						
	Value Segment C						
	Value Segment D						
	Bronze						
	Value Segment E						
	Value Segment F						
Metric 3	Gold						
	Value Segment A						
	Value Segment B						
	Silver						
	Value Segment C						
	Value Segment D						
	Bronze						
	Value Segment E						
	Value Segment F						
Metric 4	Gold						
	Value Segment A						
	Value Segment B						
	Silver						
	Value Segment C						
	Value Segment D						
	Bronze						
	Value Segment E						
	Value Segment F						

Template 5.3: Customer Experience Gap Analysis

Template 5.3 identifies customer experience gap for value based segments.

Value Metrics / Value Classification Segments		Current Touchpoints	Current level of Experience Offered [1 = Very Low; 5 = Very High]	Minimum Experience Requirements [1 = Very Low; 5 = Very High]	Optimal Experience Requirements [1 = Very Low; 5 = Very High]	Experience Gap [Currently Offered minus Optimal Requirement]
Metric 1	Gold					
	Value Segment A					
	Value Segment B					
	Silver					
	Value Segment C					
	Value Segment D					
	Bronze					
	Value Segment E					
	Value Segment F					
Metric 2	Gold					
	Value Segment A					
	Value Segment B					
	Silver					
	Value Segment C					
	Value Segment D					
	Bronze					
	Value Segment E					
	Value Segment F					
Metric 3	Gold					
	Value Segment A					
	Value Segment B					
	Silver					
	Value Segment C					
	Value Segment D					
	Bronze					
	Value Segment E					
	Value Segment F					
Metric 4	Gold					
	Value Segment A					
	Value Segment B					
	Silver					
	Value Segment C					
	Value Segment D					
	Bronze					
	Value Segment E					
	Value Segment F					

Template 5.4: B2B Customer Total Experience Mapping over the Experience Journey

Template 5.4 tracks B2B customer experience level and identify key pain points for various interaction entities over the customer experience journey for a gold segment A customer

Value Metrics / Value Classification Segments (Gold: Value Segment A)		Stage 1 (Pre-bid Engagement)	Stage 2 (Negotiation)	Stage 3 (Purchase and Implementation)	Stage 4 (Operations and After Sale Service)
B2B Customer Interaction	**Touchpoint**	Experienced Delight Level Key Issues and Problems	Experienced Delight Level Key Issues and Problems	Experienced Delight Level Key Issues and Problems	Experienced Delight Level Key Issues and Problems
Other Buying Team Members	Personal				
	Email				
	Phone call				
	Video call				
	Website				
	Blog				
	Social Media				
	Other				
Sales Rep	Personal				
	Email				
	Phone call				
	Video call				
	Website				
	Blog				
	Social Media				
	Other				
Other Selling Team Members	Personal				
	Email				
	Phone call				
	Video call				
	Website				
	Blog				
	Social Media				
	Other				
Partners and Consultants	Personal				
	Email				
	Phone call				
	Video call				
	Website				
	Blog				
	Social Media				
	Other				

Real World Application Cases

Case 5-1: Carhartt[30]

Carhartt utilizes the traditional model of selling through wholesalers. With great products and a strong brand, Carhartt has the potential for strong growth as a leading retailer. The challenge is to connect every customer with the products they are looking for, because the firm is a step removed from the end customer. When growth was ahead of expectations, it took the firm too long to serve its wholesale customers and that trickled down to the end customers. This exposed a replenishment problem that had to be solved. In the past, the firm relied heavily on a spreadsheet-based approach to determine how the digital merchandising strategies were performing. Due to so many different systems used to collect the data, it took at least a full working week to build the reports. Creating a granular view of one of the categories could take even longer.

The real task is making decisions and taking actions at the people and process level from suppliers to sales channels with data signaling to guide it. In the world of fashion, trends can surge up and subside in a matter of days. It can take a week to identify that trend missing out on a significant opportunity. To help the firm get in front of fast-changing customer preferences, Carhartt needed to accelerate and enhance the analytics processes to achieve broader transformation, affecting all the downstream processes related to replenishment decisions. To realize its goals, Carhartt needs to adopt solution that can deliver real-time information on business performance to merchandisers and marketers. The firm needs to build algorithms that consider a huge range of factors from economic indicators to weather, even down to micro factors like changing retail store footprints and automatically generate demand forecasts at the SKU level. For replenishment optimization, the firm needs to achieve the speed of turning insight into action.

Watson Commerce Insights brings tremendous change to the way Carhartt works particularly for the merchandising teams. Instead of spending a long time pulling in data from multiple different systems to identify changes in product demand, AI-driven systems provide a single analytics hub that contains all the information needed with the customization capability for each team member. The analytics hub provides information regarding which of the strategies are working and which strategies are not working. The integrated solution delivers insights in a proactive way allowing the firm to make necessary adjustment for lift conversion and to respond quickly and confidently to the trend of sales decline.

By constantly monitoring its business data for emerging trends, Carhartt can act faster than ever to capitalize on new opportunities. The firm can quickly identify the source of a surge in website traffic and quickly adapt marketing and merchandising strategies. By taking timely actions like making the in-demand product on the homepage and purchasing related search terms, the firm can make it easy for customers to buy leading to increased revenues. The firm is harnessing AI to help accelerate its decision-making at times when every hour counts to making well-informed merchandising decisions. Using the solution's intelligent sequencing capability, the firm designed rules to automatically move products that are trending to the top of their page and reposition products where inventory is running low further down their page saving valuable time that the firm can spend on deeper analytics. The firm achieved record-breaking conversion rates during the holiday period. Deeper insight into inventory is helping Carhartt to deliver better experiences to its customers. With a range of separate analytics systems throughout the business having AI capabilities, the firm can learn what our customers want and find the best way to offer it to them.

Case Questions

1. How did Carhartt combine its assessment of the trend with its strategy to adapt to fluctuating consumer preferences and changes in demand?

2. Who are primary target customers of Carhartt? In recognizing the importance of customer relationship-driven marketing, what should Carhartt do to increase customer lifetime value and provide the revenant level of service?

Case 5-2: Belle Tire[31]

An auto service firm, Belle Tire has a unique goal of nurturing customer loyalty through many products with long-life spans measured in years, not months. When customers come in with their vehicle, they may not return for an extended period of time because of the long lifecycles of its products. Belle Tire has the challenging task of gaining deeper insight into the needs and preferences of its customers. Although Belle Tire has rich data on customer purchase histories, the firm does not have a practical way of harnessing this data. The firm adopts generic, catch-all email campaigns instead of a high level of personalized service on its digital channel. This caused Belle Tire to use the same voucher code for every recipient for a discount campaign. Belle Tire has limited control over pricing and limited campaign success as the firm cannot provide customized product offerings of many different types of products and services with particular brands. After gaining insights into their customers as individuals, Belle Tire could deliver the right message at the right time to the right customers. To achieve this goal, Belle Tire adopts a fresh approach.

Belle Tire builds a lasting engagement approach using AI powered segmentation for targeted and personalized email campaigns. AI powered segmentation allows firms to implement a micro-segmentation strategy.[32] Micro-segmentation can automatically create and present micro-segments and determine the optimized strategy. It utilizes various data sources, analyze data, and auto generate micro-segments, and generate message and offer variants. Belle Tire can design and execute targeted campaigns with unique offers for each recipient, tailored based on individual behavior. Belle Tire can automatically suppress promotions to customers who purchased new tires for a defined period after the transaction or target personalized messages with offers relevant to their most recent purchase. Belle Tire can use predictive analytics to drill down into the firm's big data and gain a deeper understanding of its customers' needs. Belle Tire offers a unique coupon code based on the customer record and dynamically adds the code to the email repeatedly. Belle Tire can gain competitiveness and nurture long-term customer loyalty with the automated approach to customer engagement on the digital channel. Belle Tire can deliver more relevant, timely and compelling communications to smaller micro-segments.

Case Questions

1. Describe the new strategy Belle Tire is attempting. What are the advantages and disadvantages to attempting this new direction?

2. What is the likelihood of success for this new segmentation strategy? Which type of performance would be impacted most by the new strategy?

3. What type of marketing planning should Belle Tire use to develop marketing strategy based on the new segmentation strategy?

PART III. TOTAL CRM BASED RELATIONSHIP MARKETING STRATEGIES

"The best advisors, helpers and friends, always are not those who tell us how to act in special cases, but who give us, out of themselves, the ardent spirit and desire to act right, and leave us then, even though many blunders, to find out what our own form of right action is."
Phillips Brooke

In Part III, the customer relationship management framework developed in Part II is applied to design relationship marketing strategies and programs. The marketing models, marketing analytics, and specific marketing programs are discussed in detail in each of the following areas: customer solution driven product strategy, customer focused service with supply chain management, and traditional promotion decisions as well as digital CRM related to eMarketing and social media marketing. Each chapter illustrates how marketing managers can build customer equity and increase marketing performance utilizing traditional CRM, eCRM, and social CRM based marketing programs.

Chapter 6 introduces customer solution driven product strategy that include new and mature product management issues and the strategic implications of product strategy. Various existing product strategies and new product development for relationship marketing is explored and importance of building brand equity is analyzed. The chapter concludes with a discussion of brand loyalty management that can be used to build customer relationships.

Chapter 7 discusses providing a customer-focused service to build customer relationships with value chain participants. The key topics include supplier chain and channel management and customer service performance management. Multi-channel marketing concepts are also introduced.

Chapter 8 discusses traditional promotion touchpoint management decisions. Various traditional promotional touchpoints are reviewed. The effects of IMC are detailed and the sales force performance model is created. Various integrated marketing communications and customer touch point management programs are introduced. The chapter concludes with a discussion of how these programs can be used to build and grow customer relationships.

Chapter 9 discusses how marketing messages and meanings do not flow uni-directionally but rather are exchanged among members of the customer network. Customers are transforming from passive spectators to active participants. Issues related to digital presence, digital content management, and managing e-CRM related touchpoints are discussed. The chapter ends with eMarketing strategy for relationship marketing.

Chapter 10 discusses how to manage social CRM touchpoints for relationship marketing. Five stage model of social media relationship marketing is presented first. Managing social media network is discussed. The chapter concludes with the discussion of how social media touchpoint management strategy can be used to enhance customer relationship management.

168

Chapter 6. Customer Solution Driven Product Management

Section 1. Customer Solution Driven Approach

> *"Take a lesson from the mosquito. She never waits for an opening – she makes one."*
> Kirk Kirkpatrick

To keep a competitive advantage in highly volatile and competitive global markets, firms need to examine their product strategies. As new product development and managing a product over its product life cycle is an integral part of a firm's business success, managing existing and new products is a formidable challenge to marketing managers of firms of all sizes and in all markets. Volatile environments will mandate marketing managers be more systematic and effective in their strategic and tactical decisions to develop, plan, and market new and mature products and services.[1] The changes in the business environment dictate that a firm needs to continually change its product line to retain existing customers and attract new customers.

With heavy emphasis on Research & Development (R&D), U.S. firms are spending millions of dollars in this department. The competitive race in R&D has led to a proliferation of new technologies, products, and services. The shortened product life cycle led to fast product development generating more new products for the market. Many of these new products, however, are in the form of modification, reformulation and extensions of the existing product line.[2] This emphasis on the continuous innovation in U.S. firms has generated increased new product introductions but lessened market success. The strategic direction taken by firms to focus on continuous innovation has influenced the performance of firms. Understanding the critical issues in managing new and existing products is very important. In this chapter, we introduce solution driven approach for new and mature products and its strategic implications.

Before discussing product strategy and performance, it is necessary to define the product or service. A product or service includes not only physical attributes (intrinsic attributes) but also intangible attributes (extrinsic attributes). Physical attributes define functional features of the product. For example, for a car the physical product or functional features would refer to whether it is made with front-wheel drive or 4-wheel drive, whether it is a 4-door sedan or a sports utility vehicle. For a computer, the physical product would be its operating system, processing speed, and memory capacity. These characteristics or attributes are actual components of the product and determine the functionality of the product. Extrinsic attributes, on the other hand, include packaging, price, brand name, and country of origin. When customers evaluate products, brand names such as Mercedes-Benz, Lexus, and Tide communicate quality, value, and high product image. In customers' minds, these products are differentially positioned as being a brand name they can trust, and they are, therefore, willing to pay a premium price for these particular products. In addition, warranties offered, deliveries, and other related services are important determinants of purchase and usage behavior. These different components all make up the product. Understanding the role of these components in purchase decisions is important to the marketing manager in making decisions with regard to new product development and managing existing product lines. With the shift to a customer relationship management perspective, firms are increasingly focused on providing better product solutions that can enhance customer experience and customer retention instead of improving individual product features or functionalities. Solution-driven product management builds on the customer experience journey. Firms identify the pain points of customers by analyzing the entire customer experience. Firms then manage existing products and develop new product and services to enhance customer experience and provide near perfect customer experience and satisfaction. Firms that adopt the customer solution driven approach will focus on relationship management and customer equity in managing existing and new products.

Customer Relevant Solution

Firms focusing on relationship marketing need to understand and incorporate customer experience in developing and deploying customer solutions. Traditionally, many firms try to develop a superior product and service before considering customer relations. A solution is a customized and integrated combination of products and services for meeting customer needs and enhancing customer experiences. A solution can be viewed as relational processes that involve defining and understanding customer needs and experiences. This solution also involves processes of customizing products and services as well as providing post-deployment customer support. Solution marketing aims at solving customers' problems and enhancing their experience by resolving key pain points encountered by customers at various touchpoints. Solution marketing can offer firms a new avenue of growth, new ways to differentiate, and a new way to attain higher customer loyalty. Firms developing solutions must define their own capabilities and use them to create better customer experience. Firms can increase responsiveness, offer better service, improve quality, and reduce costs with the solution marketing approach. Under this approach, all customer exchanges are considered interactive with the objective of developing a stronger long-term relationship. The exchange process is characterized by co-creation of value with the customer and providing solutions to customers. The strategic focus is on winning customers by creating and delivering superior customer solutions and enhanced total customer experience. Quality of customer-firm interaction is valued over quality of internal processes and firm offerings.

As the value to customers is not determined by a single product, firms must offer a stream of products tailored to their particular needs through management of existing and new products. In the age of relationship marketing, firms must offer superior customer value by becoming a trustful partner in a long-term relationship with customers. Firms continually adjust products and services they offer to increase customer retention and profitability. Next section discusses managing existing products and developing new products as a component of customer solution.

Section 2. Managing Existing Product for Customer Relationship

"We will be victorious if we have not forgotten to learn."
   Rosa Luxemburg

In order to manage existing products, a marketing manager needs to look at the overall product mix for profitable customers. The product line depth and width typically define the product mix.[3] The number of product lines a firm's product mix determines product line width. Accordingly, the addition of a new product line can increase product line width. The addition of a new product line results from the introduction of a platform product or an innovative new product. The number of products in each product line determines the product line depth. Adding modifications or line extension products can increase the product line depth. In assessing overall product mix, it is necessary to evaluate the performance of each product's items and lines as well as how they serve value based customer segments for customer retention and loyalty. To assess product performance, the sales growth of each product or product lines must be evaluated. The results of this sales/contribution analysis can be used in assessing in which stage of the product life cycle the product items are.

In understanding existing product of your firm, a product comparison table can be developed. Table 6.1 shows which competitors are competing with your firm in the major product line or categories. This table can give you an overview of your firms' existing product portfolio and the product portfolio of key competitors. Firms focusing on relationship marketing assess their product portfolio in the perspective of managing customer relationships rather than increasing market share or sales revenue.

Current Product Portfolio Map	Your Firm	Comp 1	Comp 2	Comp 3	Comp 4
Product A	X	X	X		
Product B	X	X	X	X	
Product C	X	X		X	X
Product D	X	X	X	X	X
Product E		X	X	X	X

Table 6.1: Product Line Comparison

Product Life Cycle Management

Product life cycle is one of the most commonly cited marketing planning tools. The basic premise of a product life cycle assessment is to ensure a firm's long-term existence by maintaining a balanced product line with a mix of old and new products. Adequate mixes of products that are at different life cycle stages ensure both the reduction of risk and a continuous cash flow so those mature products will support the growth and development of new products. Ideally, a firm has a product mix that includes items at each of the four stages of the life cycle: introduction, growth, maturity, and decline. The dollar contribution assessment can be used to determine the life stages of each product. Each product can be located in a given stage of its life cycle by comparing its performance, competitive history, and current market position with the typical known characteristics of a particular stage of the life cycle.

In determining the stage of the life cycle of a product, many different performance and industry-related measures can be used. Sales and market related performance measures such as sales-growth change, sales, and profits for similar products in industry, number of years the product has been on the market, change of price, probable replacement new products, and history of similar products can be measured. Marketing managers must assess the industry-related measures such as profit history, number of competitors currently in the market, and number of competitors that have dropped out.

These measures help the marketing managers determine the stage of the product life cycle. Increasing sales, new competitors, high profits, increasing distribution, and a relatively new product, for example, can characterize the growth stage. Declining sales level, competitors dropping out of the market, price drop, and increased marketing costs suggest that the product has reached the maturity stage. Each product of the product mix can be assessed for the stage of life cycle. Appropriate marketing strategies can be developed according to this analysis. Table 6.2 shows key characteristics, objectives, and marketing strategies for each of the four stages of the product life cycle.

	Stages in the Product Life Cycle			
Characteristics	Introduction	Growth	Maturity	Decline
Marketing Goal	Attract innovators and opinion leaders to the new product	Expand distribution and product line	Maintain differential advantage as long as possible	Cut back, Revive, or Terminate
Industry Sales	Increasing	Rapidly increasing	Stable	Decreasing
Competition	None or small	Some	Substantial	Limited
Industry Profits	Negative	Increasing	Decreasing	Decreasing
Customers	Innovators	Resourceful mass market	Mass market	Laggards
Product Mix	One or a few basic models	Expanding line	Full product line	Best-sellers
Distribution	Depends on product	Rising number of outlets/ Distributors	Greatest number of outlets/ distributors	Decreasing number of outlets/ Distributors
Promotion	Informative	Persuasive	Competitive	Informative
Pricing	Depends on product	Greater range of prices	Full line of prices	Selected prices

Table 6.2: The Characteristics of the Traditional Product Life Cycle

In assessing product performance, the sales growth of each product or product lines can be evaluated. Figure 6.1 shows "net sales % growth" and "profit % growth" of the five major product lines in the southern region of a firm. The results of this analysis are the sales/contribution of the major product groups. The southern region shows both negative sales and profit growth indicating that all five product groups are not doing very well in terms of sales and profit growth in that region. The results imply that management should make a drastic change in their marketing strategy to stop this downward spiral of sales and profit decline. Firms need to develop customer experience mapping and identify key problem areas of various touchpoints of the customer experience journey to find the source of this sales decline.

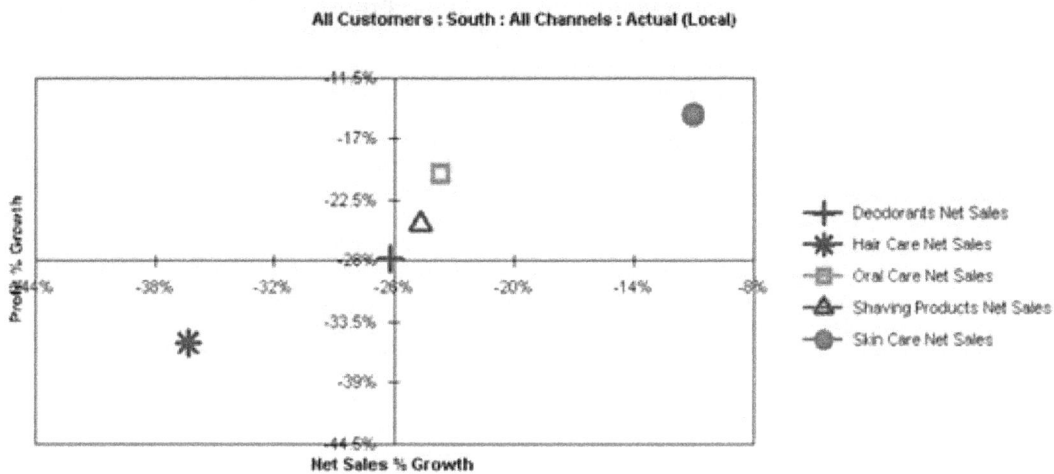

Figure 6.1: Sales Contribution Analysis

Marketing managers can assess whether the products offered in each regional market are the right solutions for target customers. Based on this analysis, firms can modify the product depth and width for existing products. If some critical product solutions are missing, firms may need to consider introducing a new product for that particular customer segments.

Market Share Strategies

Based on the performance information generated, the marketing manager can determine market-share strategies. Market share has been the most attention-getting marketing variable in managing products. Market share can be assessed by creating "share by market" chart. An example of the chart is presented in Figure 6.2. In this chart, major key competitors and their respective market share in each market segment are listed. This chart shows which brands or companies are dominating each market segment.

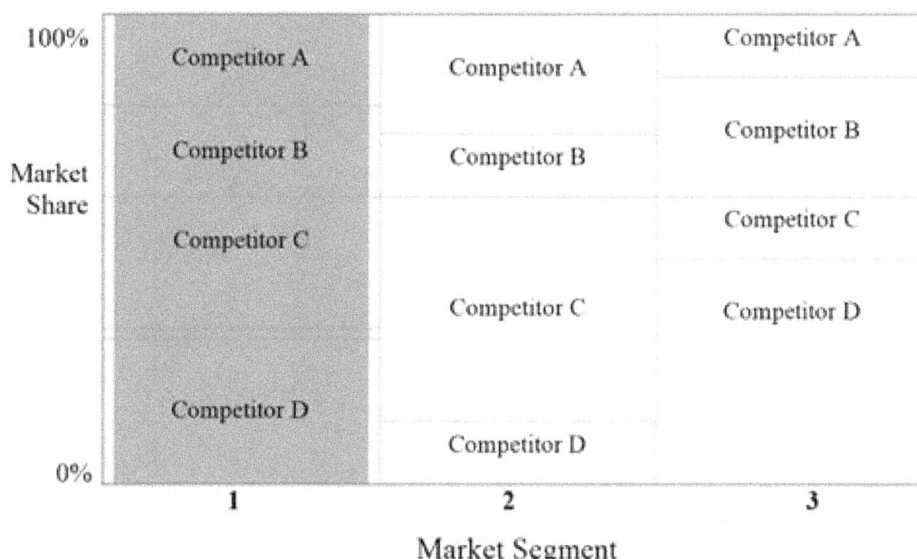

Figure 6.2: Share by Market Chart

After evaluating market share diagram, firms also need to perform product gap analysis to identify where product gaps exist in various market segments. Figure 6.3 presents a product gap analysis of a firm. In Figure 6.4, ease of use and price are the two factors defining the positioning map.

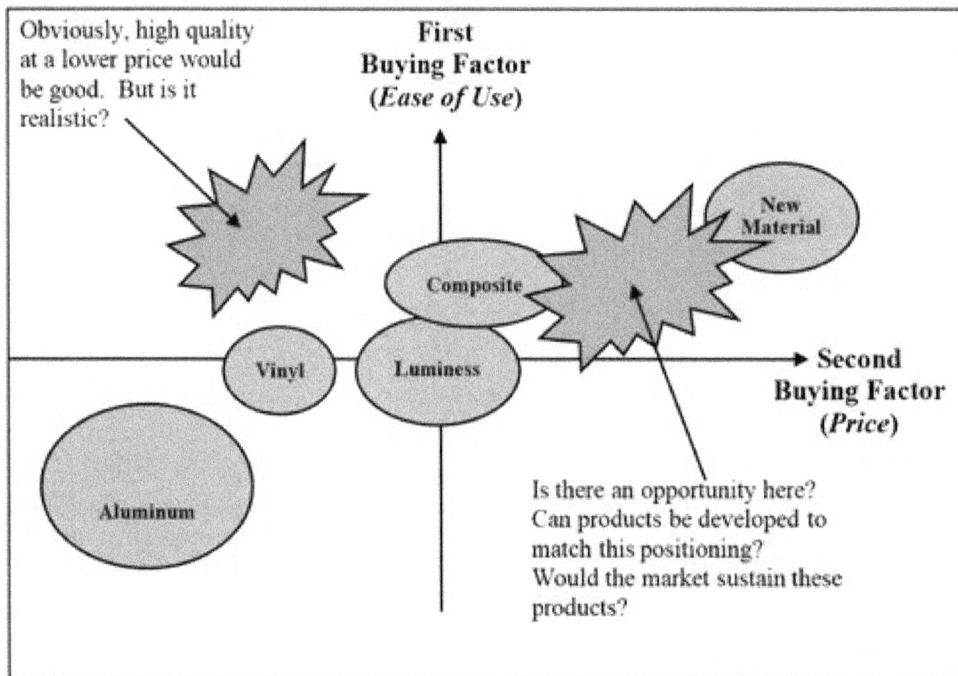

Figure 6.3: Product Gap Analysis

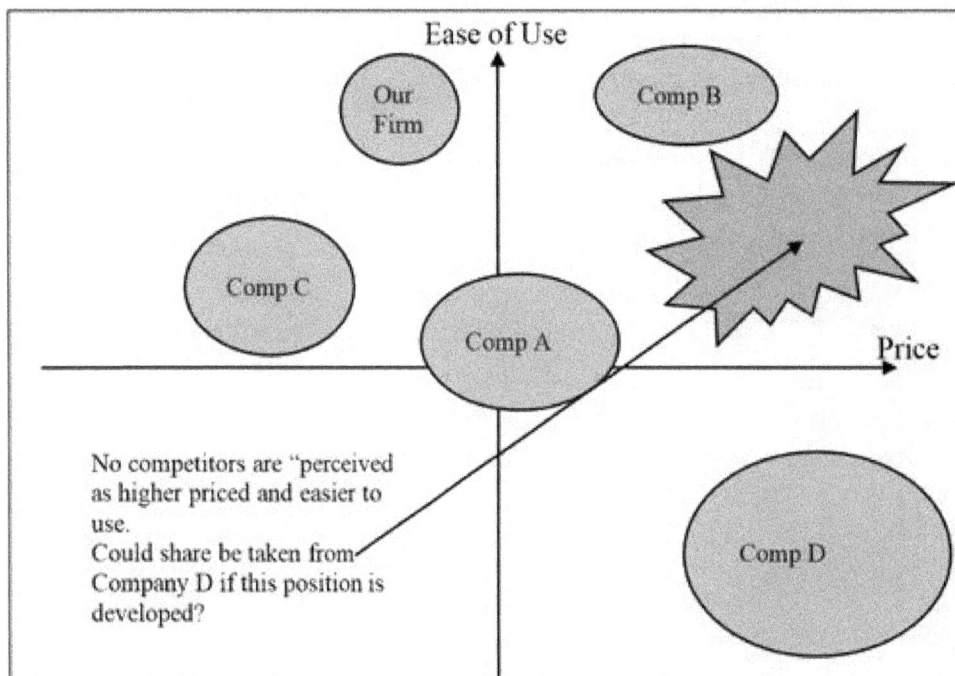

Figure 6.4: New Opportunity in Competitive Positioning Map

174

In the figures, marketing managers can identify various potential new product development opportunities in the competitive positioning map. A competitive positioning map puts various competing brands and product types on a map defined by key market factors. It is generally believed that a higher market share leads to higher profitability. There are four strategic choices in making market share decisions. The four strategy choices are gaining share, holding share, harvesting, and abandonment.[4]

Gaining share strategy

This offensive strategic option requires the right market conditions and resources. Gaining share is not always possible or desirable as this option can be quite risky and expensive. The gaining share strategy, therefore, can be used only when the market condition is right and the firm is ready to commit resources to take full advantage of the opportunity of market share growth. The right market condition for marketers wanting to use the gaining share strategy is high growth of the market.

In a growing market, building shares is easy and attainable. Also in a growing market, the competition is less fierce and less likely to result in price competition. Gaining share strategy can be pursued with a definite competitive advantage that competitors cannot fight or overcome in a short time period. When a firm introduces a breakthrough product through a discontinuous innovation project, this new product creates a window of opportunity to gain share from an existing product. Shares can be gained through increased promotion or service, improved product quality, service quality or customer value, and innovative positioning or satisfying customers.

Holding Share Strategy

This defender strategy requires holding or maintaining a market share that a firm has already gained. It is known that retaining a current customer is much cheaper and easier than attracting a new customer. To hold your market and customers, commitment should be made to a specific area or market. To hold shares, firms can use various tactics such as price cutting in selective markets, heavy promotion, focusing cutting edge innovation, or customer relationship management (CRM).

Harvesting Strategies

The harvesting strategy is used to generate cash from products that face imminent decline. This strategy is used when the business or product still can generate income but does not warrant further investment. A marketing manager needs to assess the future prospect for the product or service and the expected decline of business with reduced reinvestment. The essence of the harvesting strategy is to reduce costs. Cost savings can come from many sources, such as marketing and R&D cost savings. Cutting services or reducing the number of product offerings are other routes for harvesting.

A firm may seek to sell or abandon the business or product. This strategy should be used if the product or service shows a poor market position or is inconsistent with the company's strategic base of businesses. These four strategies are directly related to the way marketing managers manage the product mix of a company. The decision to maintain, add, or delete product items is strategic in nature. In relationship marketing, this strategic decision must be based on the customer portfolio management. Firms also need to consider which product items are offering solutions to which value based segments. At the same time, the decision to increase or decrease support for certain product items is tactical. This is accomplished through resource planning and allocation. Marketing managers need to make these strategic as well as tactical decisions based on objective evaluations of product items and product line performances.

Understanding Existing Product Affinity with Market Basket Analysis

In implementing relationship marketing, firms need to consider cross-selling opportunities. It is important to identify products purchased together by various value based customer segments. To understand which products are purchased together for product recommendation and cross-selling, marketing managers can perform the market basket analysis. The market basket analysis is also called affinity analysis or association rules method. Market basket analysis aims to discover which group of products tends to be purchased together using customer transaction data. Market basket analysis can show customer preference patterns and provide answers to the question of which products are ordered or purchased together. Using customer transaction databases, association rules are identified to determine dependencies between purchases of different items. Association rule modeling begins with generating an item set of collection of items selected from all items in the transaction database. Item sets can include two, three, or more items. An association rule identifies two subsets in each item set using an 'if-then' format. One subset, the antecedent, is considered as preceding the other subset and represent the 'if' part. The other subset, the consequent, represents the 'then' part. In market basket analysis, the item sets consists of the antecedent and consequent.

Association is an approach that measures the probabilities or likelihood of the occurrence of a particular event given the occurrence of other events. This marketing analytics technique looks for patterns of repetition in the data. It scans the data looking for an association between one set of items and another set of items. Market basket analysis is one example or outcome of this approach. Market basket analysis explores the probability or percentage occurrence that a consumer who purchases product A and B will also buy product C. Association analysis can be used for determining cross-selling and up-selling opportunities. It can be used to identify the purchasing patterns of customers. The firm can use this information to determine where to place items that are associated together in a display area. Common associations include wine and cheese, batteries and toys, pencil and paper, and beer and diapers.

The association algorithm considers each attribute/value pair (such as product/bread or region/Midwest) as an item. An item set then becomes a combination of items in a single transaction. The algorithm scans through the data trying to find various item sets that tend to appear together in many transactions. For example, a frequent item set may contain Product =

"Mountain Bicycle", and Option = "Water Carrier". Each item set also has a size, which is defined as the number of items it contains. In this example, the size for this item set is 2. Often association models work against datasets containing nested tables. A nested table example could be a customer table followed by a nested purchases table. If a nested table exists in the dataset, each nested key (such as a product in the purchases table) is considered an item. The association algorithm finds rules associated with item sets. A rule in an association model looks like A, B=>C. In the model, A, B, and C are all frequent item sets. The '=>' symbol implies that C is predicted by A and B.

Association rules are generated to identify all possible combinations of items in the customer transaction database, which can be a single item, two items, three items, and so on.[5] As the generated association rules can be very large, managers need to select frequent items sets that occur often in the database. To determine which item sets can be chosen as the frequent item sets, managers can use the selection criteria of support, confidence, and lift ratio.[6] The rule is evaluated based upon these three criteria.

The first criterion, support, refers to prevalence of an item set. Support is the number of transactions that include both the antecedent and consequent item sets. The support measures the degree to which the data supports the validity of the rule. If a marketing manager sets the minimum support criterion of 0.01, then any item sets that exceeds the criterion of 0.01 will be the frequent item sets and will be included in the next phase of analysis. A support criterion of 0.01 suggests that one in every one hundred market baskets must contain the item set. The support helps the marketing manager by indicating how many transactions use this rule. The goal is to have a relatively high support number for the rule.

The confidence criterion refers to the degree of predictability of the if-then rule. This criterion is an estimate of the conditional probability of the consequent, given the antecedent. Confidence can be calculated by dividing the number of transactions with both antecedent and consequent item sets with number of transactions with antecedent item set. For example, out of 10,000 grocery store transactions, 3,000 include both milk and bread, and 1,200 of these include jam purchases. The association rule is "If milk and bread are purchased then jam is purchased on the same shopping trip." This association rule has a support of 12% (1,200/10,000) and a confidence of 40% (1,200/3,000). While high value confidence indicates a strong association rule, confidence can be high if both the antecedent and consequent have a high level of support although the antecedent and consequent are not associated. The probability threshold is a parameter that determines the minimum probability before a rule can be considered. The probability is also called "confidence." While confidence is necessary condition for association but it is not sufficient to conclude the association. Therefore, mangers need to evaluate the final criterion of lift ratio. Lift ratio assess the strength of an association rule. Lift ratio is calculated by dividing confidence with benchmark confidence assuming independence of consequent from antecedent. The benchmark confidence is number of transactions with consequent item set divided by number of transactions in customer database. In earlier grocery store transaction example, 2,500 transactions contain jam purchases out of 10,000 transactions. The benchmark confidence is 25% (2,500/10,000). Lift ratio of this rule is 1.6 (40%/25%). As the rule is considered useful if the lift ratio is greater than 1.0, this association rule of 1.6 is considered as a useful rule. The importance examines the usefulness of the rule. It is a way to examine the importance of the causality of the data. For example, all computers require a power supply. By knowing that a power supply has been selected doesn't help in determining the model of the computer. Yet, the probability is 100% that if you have a power supply, you will have a computer. No useful information is given to marketing managers.

With the increased importance of customer relationship marketing, marketing managers have more opportunity to engage with customers. In interacting with customers, managers can provide personalized recommendations based on other customers who purchased a similar set of items. They can do cross-selling or up-selling of products or services associated with an item that customers are considering. An important task of marketing managers is determining what type of products to recommend or cross-sell to a particular customer. In other words, which items are co-purchased with the first item purchased by that customer? Managers are interested in knowing whether certain items are consistently purchased together. With increased online or mobile purchase by customers, managers need to decide in online store front design which items to display or recommend to online shoppers when they are examining an item or putting an item in the shopping basket. Marketing managers focus on selling more products or services to existing customers through cross-selling or motivating them to trade up to more profitable products with cross-selling and up-selling. Marketing managers want to know which products will increase a customer's overall profitability by selling the right product to the right customers.

Section 3. Managing New Product Solution for Customers

"To conquer the enemy without resorting to war is the most desirable. The highest form of generalship is to conquer the enemy by strategy."
Ancient Chinese Warlord

With increased global competition and rapid technological changes, one of the major challenges facing marketing managers is generating new product ideas, turning ideas into new products, and launching them successfully in the market. New product managers have been pressured to produce more new products faster yet at lower costs. In responding to this demand, firms generate more product-line extension products than innovative new products. The type of new products generated by firms is directly related to the growth strategy pursued by them. Figure 6.5 shows new product types that are typically generated by firms. With the solution marketing approach, firms must determine the types of new products to develop based on the product or service solutions most needed for the targeted value based segments.

Firms can pursue different types of new product development strategy. Figure 6-6 shows the four phases of product development focus. While product-driven strategy is initially pursued, most firms move toward market-oriented strategy, then market-driven strategy, and finally customer-driven strategy. Relationship marketing firms are more likely to adopt the customer-driven strategy in new product development. In the customer-driven strategy, the focus is on developing and maintaining the closer relationships with profitable customers. Product development efforts are directed toward offering product solutions for retention and acquisition of the most profitable customers.

Increasing Technological Newness

Product Objectives	No Technological Change	Improved Technology	New Technology
No Market Change		*Reformulation* Change formula or product to optimize cost and quality	*Replacement* Replace existing product with new one based on improved technology
Strengthened Market	*Remerchandising* Increase sales to existing customers	*Improved Product* Improve utility to customers	*Product Life Extension* Add new/similar products based on new technology
New Market	*New Use* Add new segments that can use present products	*Market Extension* Add new segments by modifying present products	*Diversification* Add new markets with new products developed from new technology

Figure 6.5: Type of New Product Developments

PHASE 1: <u>Product Driven Strategy</u>
     Less Inventory / Lower Cost
     Operations as Planned
     Production Cost / Stock Levels

PHASE 2: <u>Market Oriented Strategy</u>
     Quicker Adaptation to Change / Shorter Throughput Time
     Data Accuracy
     Throughput Time / Total Operating Cost

PHASE 3: <u>Market Driven Strategy</u>
     Competitive Advantage / Quicker Adaptation to Market
     Competitive Edge
     Market Share / Sales Volume / Number of New Products

PHASE 4: <u>Customer Driven Strategy</u>
     Closer Relationship with Customers
     Relationship with Customers
     Customer Satisfaction / Value Added

Figure 6.6: Four Phases of Product Development Focus

Successful new products or services can provide long-term competitive advantages to firms. Timely, cost-effective new products and services are needed to produce a sustainable competitive advantage. In achieving competitive advantage in new product development, cost and quality have been important requirements for new product success. In the 1990s, faster new product development and innovativeness of new products are becoming critical in winning the new product development game. Flexible new product development is also gaining attention for successful new product development. The power of new products includes improving gross margin and building revenues, serving as a competitive weapon, providing competitive differentiation, and increasing stock prices. Leading companies in global markets generate about fifty percent of their sales from products introduced in the past five years. With shortened product life cycles, new products are imperative to maintain market leadership and survival of a firm. A typical new product management process can be diagramed and presented in Figure 6.7.

New Product Management Process

As shown in Figure 6.7, the new product development process involves direction setting stages and new product development stages. In direction setting stages, new product blueprints provide an overall plan or guide for new product development. The next step is conducting a new product diagnostic audit. This audit presents a report card on historic new product performance. The audit also uncovers the factors leading to success and failures. Considering the audit results, firms establish appropriate foundations for new product development. These foundations are the expertise of people, the technology and research bases, and the innovative corporate culture. At the same time, firms map a new product strategy. The new product strategy typically involves evaluation of the financial growth gap, strategic role of the product, and market screening criteria.

New product development stages include the idea generation stage; the concept development and evaluation stage; the product design and technical development stage; and the commercialization stage. When following these stages, firms customize a new product development process by adjusting typically recommended processes. The most commonly recommended new product development practices are simultaneous development, concurrent and team-based development, fast new product development, quality function deployment (QFD), and design for manufacturing and assembly. These new product development practices involve specific management decisions regarding how to manage new products and innovation of a firm. Due to dramatic changes in the market environment and the emphasis on flexible new product development, effective marketing analysis is becoming an absolute necessity in making an intelligent decision with respect to new product development.

Today's Digital consumer reacts faster and demands new products with greater intensity. For this reason, a company's competitive advantage now lies with its speed in innovation and imitation. Based on research, the Boston Consulting Group determined that the most successful Fast-Moving Consumer-Goods Companies (FMCG) will develop new products within 15 months with existing product renovations taking as little as 5 months to bring to market. Benefits of adopting this strategy can include; longer sales life which can lead to as much as a 60% increase in first year sales, larger market share, lower development costs, greater accuracy in forecasting, and increased agility in reacting to customer feedback.

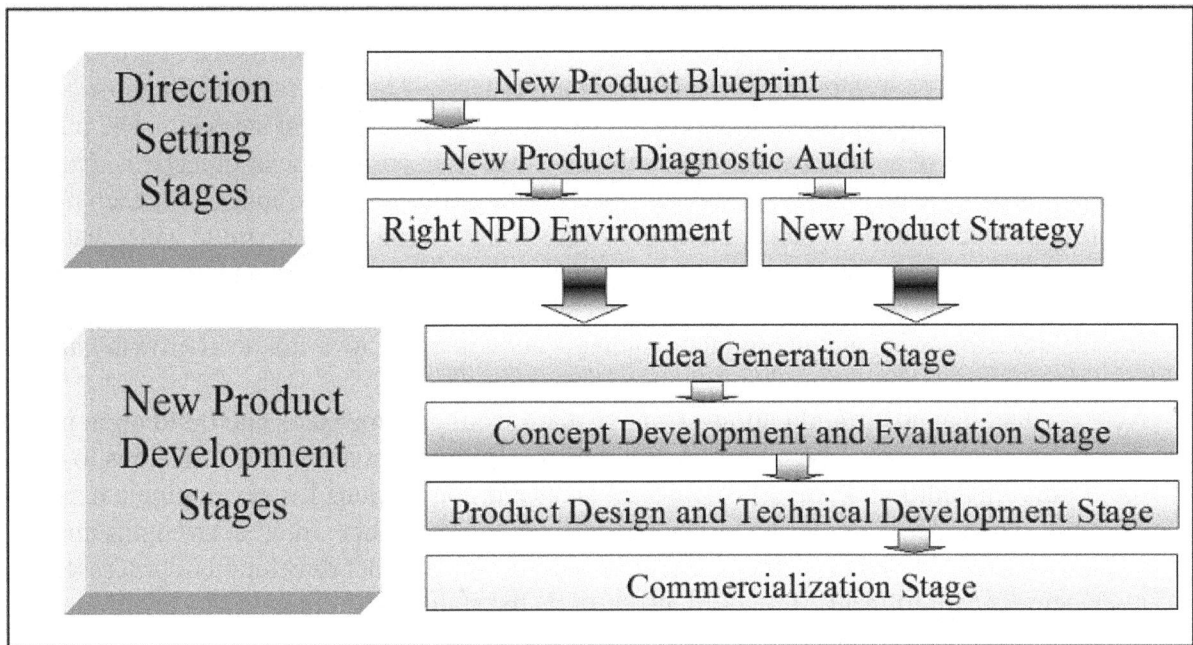

Figure 6.7: New Product Management Process

According to the Boston Consulting Group, a company can become faster by adopting a holistic approach that draws on multiple segments of the organization to achieve three key imperatives including standardize, prioritize, and mechanize. A standardization of operations can lead to clarity and routine and in turn increased speed. This should include clear project start and end points; having a project leader with authority across the entire process; a schedule with detailed descriptions of each step in the process; and clearly defined checkpoints in which products must pass specific criteria and never revert back to once completed. In order to prioritize, some projects must be given extra resources in order to accelerate their development. This prioritization can include project completion forecasting, added funding, skipping other projects at bottlenecks, and minimizing controlling parties to shorten decision approval delays. Finally, mechanization of a company's processes through support tools such as end-to-end IT support, knowledge support tools, and automated decision support tools can lead to greater agility and speed. Ways to improve mechanization include; creation of a toolbox or template of all existing designs held by the company allowing designers to utilize materials already approved by regulatory requirements thus shortening approval time, installation of a tracking system to improve strategic planning, and standardized reporting for the development process.

The next section presents performance based marketing analysis that can provide decision support for new product development.

New Product Diagnostic Audit

The new product strategy provides directions for innovation management and product development efforts. The new product strategy allows management to focus on the market categories, ideas, and concepts that match specific strategic roles assigned to each product. The new product strategy can help managers identify acceptable categories, new product ideas, and reduce development time and cost. The new product strategy is developed based on the product innovation charter, resource base, and new product development process. The new product strategy development requires understanding the detailed new product financial growth gap, financial objectives, strategic roles, and screening criteria. The new product diagnostic audit can provide the background for determining the new product development strategy. The product strategy consists of a definition of the financial growth gap and financial objectives that new products are expected to meet. Strategic roles are the expected contribution that each new and existing product is to provide the company. Screening criteria can determine which categories and new product concepts are most attractive to pursue. The new product strategy defines how new products contribute to meeting the financial growth objectives of the company. The next section describes what a new product diagnostic audit is and how a financial growth gap results.

New product diagnostic audit allows firms to learn from past mistakes and build upon previous new product successes. The audit shows areas of improvement as well as directions to take in the future. In addition, it identifies problem areas and foundations for developing a new product strategy. The audit examines historical new product performance, internal strengths and weaknesses relative to competitors, effectiveness of new product development processes, and top management commitment. The audit also reports the state of the company's new product program.[7] The audit can:

- Quantify past new product revenue, cost, and profit performance by comparing actual to original product forecasts.
- Delineate underlying causes and rationale for new product program successes and failures.
- Classify all new product development projects into the types of new products (new to the world, new to the company, line extension, revision or improvement to an existing line, cost reduction, repositioning, and licensed / joint ventured / acquired new product) by risk level.
- Determine the survival rate of new products.

Financial Growth Gap

Based on the diagnostic audit results, the financial gap for new products can be identified. Senior management can determine whether revenue target is attainable in consideration of the company's new product performance record. The growth gap analysis provides the portion of financial growth expected to come from new products as a part of new product strategy formulation.[8] The first step in determining the growth gap is to examine the past revenue and profit growth of the existing core business. Then the next step is to calculate the total revenues and profits that the new products are expected to contribute to a company's growth during a specific time period (e.g., 3 to 5 years). A five-year gap can be developed by building up the revenue projections estimated from each growth model. Percentages or absolute-revenue projections are applied to each growth model. The analysis can then reveal the relative importance of new products to alternative growth models.

In filling the financial growth gap, marketing managers first complete a technology assessment. Technology assessments may include assessment of product technology and process technology. In assessing technology, managers have to generate key critical questions related to technology. These questions include "Do our product and process technologies give us a competitive edge in the market?", "Do our technologies support our business goals and objectives?" "Are our product technologies aligned with market demands?", and "How can we leverage the opportunities created by our technology?". Answering these questions would require various activities and generation of analytic questions. The analytic questions would probe current technology status (including costs and productivity), technology scanning (competitive and lead-edge) for new materials, processes, applications and capabilities, new patent analysis, and technology benchmarking. The objectives of this process are to assess current product, process and IS technology capabilities relative to the market, to determine if our IS/ product technology is providing us with a competitive edge, to identify current technology situation relative to "state-of-the-art" practices for speed, flexibility and ease-of-use, and to determine industry trends in technology and likely effect on your firm

New Product Development Performance

Multiple measures of the outcomes of the new product development process have been widely used by firms. The measures of the outcomes can be separated into two groups. The first group is indicators of the project level success, while the second group is indicators of the overall success of the new product development programs. New product success has been measured primarily at the project level by financial measures such as return on investment or sales. Other financial measures are whether the product's profitability exceeded the minimum and the actual profit in dollars or return on investment. Non-financial measures of new product success include perceived success and failure, ratio of clear-cut successes to clear-cut failures, and meeting new product objectives. New product performance measures are typically compared to new product objectives set in the planning stage of product development. The product objectives include role objectives such as percent of sales and corporate profit derived from new product projects as well as performance objectives such as success rate of the new products, number of new product ideas to be considered, number of projects entering development, and minimum acceptable returns for new product projects.

Project-level success measures can be grouped into three categories. Those groups are customer-based success, financial success, and technical performance success. Customer-based success includes customer satisfaction, customer acceptance, market share goals, revenue goals, revenue growth goals, unit volume goals, and number of customers. Financial success includes met profit goals, met margin goals, return on investment, and break-even time. Technical performance success includes competitive advantage, met performance specifications, speed to market, development cost, met quality specifications, launch time, and innovativeness. Among these various performance measures, the utility of each performance measure depends on the type of projects a firm is involved in (See Table 6.3).[9] For example, Table 6.3 shows that for products new to the world or to the company, customer satisfaction, customer acceptance, revenue goals, profit goals, and competitive advantage would be useful measures for project performance evaluation.

	Low	Newness to the Market	High
High	**New-to-the-Company** C1: Market Share Revenue or Satisfaction F1: Met Profit Goal P1: Competitive Advantage		**New-to-the-World** C1: Customer Acceptance C2: Customer Satisfaction F1: Met Profit Goal or IRR / ROI P1: Competitive Advantage
Newness to the Firm	**Product Improvements** C1: Customer Satisfaction C2: Market Share or Revenue Growth F1: Met Profit Goal P1: Competitive Advantage	**Additions to Existing Lines** C1: Market Share Revenue / Revenue Growth / Satisfaction / Acceptance F1: Met Profit Goal P1: Competitive Advantage	
Low	**Cost Reductions** C1: Customer Satisfaction C2: Acceptance or Revenue F1: Met Margin Goal P1: Performance or Quality	**Product Repositioning** C1: Customer Acceptance C2: Satisfaction or Share F1: Met Profit Goal P1: Competitive Advantage	**Project Strategy**

Legend: C1: Customer Measure #1; C2: Customer Measure #2; F1: Financial Measure #1; P1: Performance Measure #1

Table 6.3: Most Useful Success Measures by Project Strategy

For projects involving product improvement or line-extension type of products, market share goals, revenue growth goals, profit goals, and competitive advantage offer more utility in evaluating project performance. Overall program level success can be measured by development program ROI, new product's fit with business strategy, percent profits from new products, success/failure rate, percent sales from new products, overall program success, program hit 5-year objectives, product's lead to future opportunities, percent sales under patent protection, and percent profit under patent protection. For these various success measures, the utility of each success measure depends on the type of business strategy a firm is pursuing. If a firm is pursuing a proactive innovation strategy, percent profits and sales from new products provide an effective measure for its new product development program. Firms using a reactive innovation strategy find that program ROI, new products fit with business strategy, success/failure rate, and overall program success measures are more useful in evaluating their new product program success.

Evaluating New Product Sales

In making new product development decisions, marketing managers run into a situation where either test market data or similar previous product launch data are available. It is important to have an accurate assessment of the market and sales potential in the business analysis stage and the commercialization stage of new product development. After numerous prototyping and testing cycles, management is satisfied with the product's functional performance. At this point, the new product is ready to test in a realistic customer setting with a given brand name, packaging, and a preliminary marketing program. Market testing is performed to learn the reactions of customers and dealers to using, handling, and purchasing the products. Market testing can offer valuable information about market potential, product defects, and market program effectiveness. Test markets can provide a reliable forecast of future sales of new products. If the test market sales do not meet the expected target level, the company will drop or modify the product. Many new products that are line extensions and minor modifications of existing products will not achieve the objectives set for them and will be withdrawn within two years of their introduction. To minimize these costs, firms need methods that will better forecast the sales of new products before they are introduced into the market. There is also a need for methods that will give firms diagnostic information so that they can identify potential problems with the product and improve its chances for success in the market.

Many pretest market forecast and analysis models have been developed and widely used in the past decade.[10] Commercially available packages include BASES and ASSESSER to name a couple. What is needed is how to track and monitor products already introduced to the market. The following analysis shows what type of diagnostic information can be obtained by analyzing performance data of product items introduced in the past year and sales forecasting. Figure 6-8 shows dollar sales by product introduction year. One commonly used criterion for evaluating new product program is the percent of sales from products introduced in the past five years. Sales from products introduced in the past five years represent over 37 percent of total sales indicating an average new product development program.

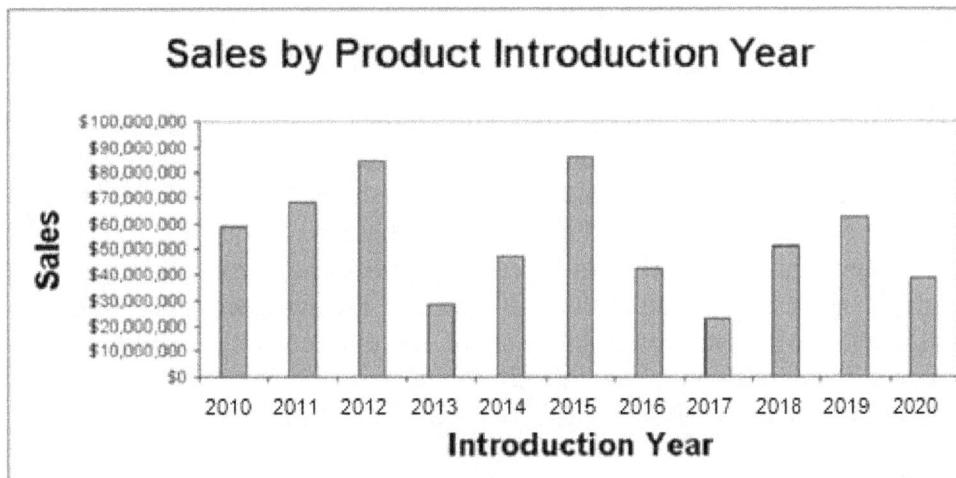

Figure 6.8: Sales by Product Introduction Year

New Product Design and Development

If your company has a product or service that everyone needs and no one else offers, it's easy to be the best. Unfortunately, that's not a reality for most firms today. To succeed in the real world, firms need every advantage they can get. Many CEOs agree that the way to win is to develop and manage their firm's new products. From a brand management perspective, brand valuation is a strategic tool that brings together market, brand, competitor, and financial data into a single, value-based framework within which the performance of the brand can be assessed, areas for improvement identified, and the financial contribution of the brand to the firm results quantified.

By combining strategy, analytics, and valuation to determine the expected impact of brand investment on the top and bottom line, marketing managers need to make decisions regarding the expected change in product features. Strong new products usually enhance business performance by influencing three current or prospective key stakeholder groups: customers, employees, and investors. They influence customer choices and create loyalty; attract, retain, and motivate talent; and lower the cost of financing. The influence of new products on current and prospective customers is a particularly significant driver of economic value. The relevant and differentiated new products consistently help shape attitudes and experience, therefore, purchase behavior, making products and services less substitutable and demand more sustainable.

What differentiates firms from their competitors is their ability to also provide a rich and insightful new product analysis, delivering value to the firm beyond the raw numbers alone. Product attribute analysis helps firms better understand the drivers of business and brand value. Understanding how value is created, where it is created and the relationship between brand value and business value is a vital input to strategic decision making. Determining product attributes shows what makes products distinct from other products. Attributes can include size, color, flavor, and packaging. From a consumer's perspective, these attributes are what determine the consideration set and influence the ultimate purchase decision. From a retail perspective, product attributes help define how aisles, departments, and shelve sets are organized. Manufacturers use attributes to help define their product's competitive advantage.

Some problems marketing managers face when dealing with product attributes is, "What kind of message does the brand give?" and "Does the brand and product create customer loyalty and emotionally connect with the target market?" Marketing managers need to know if the target market is aware that they are being targeted and does the brand share the uniqueness of what the firm offers and why it's important? Managers would want to know if their products have what it takes to succeed in today's increasingly competitive marketplace. Knowing why the brand or product is of value will explain what types of problems it can solve for customers and if it is even something customers will care about or want/need. When people think about the firm or product, what are the feelings and associations managers want them to have? Are they unique? Can the firm "own" them? What are the functional benefits that the firm delivers to its customers? What are the emotional benefits that only the firm delivers to its customers? All of these questions have to do with what value can the brand or product give and is it relevant to who is being targeted.

The most important task marketing managers face is developing a product that meets the needs of target customers. With the high new product failure rate, marketing managers must identify product opportunities and develop the right new products for market success. For this important task, marketing managers need to determine the customer preferences and how customers value the different product attributes. In addition, managers want to know the trade-offs customers are willing to make among the different product attributes and features a firm can develop. Typical analytic questions marketing managers want to answer is which set of product attributes are optimal for the target market segment(s). While firms have information about available product attributes to be incorporated in the product, managers need to identify as precisely as possible the product attribute combination for the target segment. The key is determining the importance of various product attributes as well as relative importance of individual attributes.

AI Powered New Product Design and Development

AI can influence the entire process of new product development. By analyzing big data with advanced analytics, AI can find innovative patters in connected sources of big data, identify potential product improvement features, and generate new innovative product ideas. The impact is particularly important in new product design, product pretesting, and product launch decisions.[11]

AI can synthesize all available information and suggest numerous variants of a design for further evaluation. AI can discover creative and innovative new technologies by identifying patterns using big data and assess impacts of various product traits. AI can suggest optimal product traits that are most likely successful in the market. AI-powered learning model can evaluate behavioral data about how customers used a firm's products and help marketing managers to solve the customer pain points in product usage situation.

AI powered models can evaluate a range of traits as well as a wide range of structured and unstructured data stored in a firm's big data and discover relationships at the traits level without pre-populated or pre-specified structure. Both directed and undirected AI powered models can provide a new avenue or direction of new product development with the flexibility of input data. These models can provide more accurate information regarding product potential by building dynamic and adaptable models that account for changes in initial traits and relationships of inputs and outputs. AI helps marketing managers to perform robust digital testing, automated user testing, and predictions of prototypes before product trials.[12]

AI powered product design allows firms develop generative design algorithms, use virtual prototyping, and perform model-based simulation by complementing human problem-solving capacities with machine learning and automation capabilities.[13]

In addition to recommending the optimal product traits, AI can also recommend product market launch considering the constraints of suppliers, existing distribution channels, and market conditions.[14] These AI powered models can be designed to collect their own data to enable scaling though the learning cycle.[15] As a result, AI can reduce new development time and costs significantly as well as the quality of design of products.

While AI models can help firms in product design and development, AI can offer new opportunities for creating autonomous self-learning products.[16] Self-learning capability through machine learning can reduce the development time and strengthen the customization of products through self-learning of the particular customer's usage data.

Relationship Enhancing New Product Development

One great way of improving relationships with customers is through product development. To increase their value, firms often turn to customers to help them generate new ideas. Unfortunately, this methodology does not always work. Customers may not have the motivation or creativity to come up with truly innovative new ideas. However, there are a couple ways around these problems.

The first method around the motivation problem is to only use "lead users" during idea generation. Lead users tend to be consumers who are in fairly extreme conditions and are looking for solutions to their current dilemmas. These individuals can be motivated to join in the process predominantly due to their desire for innovative products, although additional incentives may be necessary. After company teams have identified problems consumers are seeking answers for, a select number of ten or so lead users should be invited to the company to help create the plan for the new product. These individuals should be teamed with only a few company employees to allow for the greatest amount of collaboration between the customers.[17]

Another good method to use to generate creative ideas is to create a virtual network for customers. Through discussion groups, not only will you get feedback about current products, but you will also get ideas on how products can be improved, as well as brand new ideas for products. Since customers are talking with each other, the company can get an idea of how top customers are all reacting to new ideas. The challenge comes in ensuring that this information is monitored and used by the company itself.[18]

Additionally, sometimes the customers the company should target are not their direct customers, but rather their "customer's customers," or the end users of a product. For example, consider Hewlett Packard. When the company determined they wanted to create "service-provider-in-a-box systems" for their customers who are application service providers (ASP), they talked to the ASP's target customers (like oil exploration firms and electronics design companies). Through talking with the end users of the product, the company was able to develop a new product called e-utilica that sold well to its own customers.[19]

One other method of new product development is focusing on creating new experience for customers. Innovations can improve the lives of consumers and business customers by providing new solutions. The new solutions can provide an image of relevance to customers. The firm can be seen as relevant with innovations. As innovation can influence the customer experience, firms can capture the customer experience early on and incorporate it in new product development. Firms need to seek breakthrough innovation that can create a desirable customer experience. The customer experience captured throughout the entire experience journey needs to be incorporated into the product development process early on. The customer experience can be incorporated into every stage of product development process. For example, the customer experience needs to be analyzed in the market assessment stage. With the analysis results, firms can generate experiential solutions and test the experiential appeal of the concept in concept testing in the idea generation stage. Firms can incorporate the experience in product specification in product design and test the customer's usage experience in product testing. Innovation can impact add-on selling.

Product Bundling and Unbundling

One method of improving customer relationships by adding product value is through bundling. Bundling is defined to be the sale of two or more separate items in one package. Chances are, customers have seen (and purchased) many bundled products. From packs of DVD's to Personal Computers to value meals at fast food chains, many companies use this technique to improve value for both the customers as well as themselves.

There are two basic types of bundling strategies. First, there is the price bundling strategy. In the price bundling strategy products are grouped together, but not integrated, by the company as a means to increase sales. Because no additional value is created beyond the costs of the original products, these bundles must be sold at a discount price to entice customers. Examples include a case of beer or season tickets to the opera. Price bundling can be quickly enacted by the company as a short-term method of earning profit.[20]

Within the pricing bundling strategies, there are multiple ways of grouping products. If products are determined to be better alone than together, then the company engages in "unbundling." If the company creates a product that is only sold within a bundle (for example, a toy in a McDonald's Happy Meal), then that is an example of "pure bundling." Finally, some products are sold both within bundles and sold separately. This is an example of a "mixed bundling" strategy.[21]

The second bundling strategy, product bundling, is different from price bundling in that the products are integrated in some way. Put another way, the company is differentiating itself through bundling, thus making product bundling a part of the longer-term relationship marketing strategy. Product traits that the firm may try to deliver as product bundling include compactness (integrated stereo systems), seamless interaction (PC systems), non-duplicating coverage (one-stop insurance), reduced risk (mutual fund), interconnectivity (telecom systems), enhanced performance (personalized dieting and exercise program), or convenience from an integrated bill. While the consumer's reservation price representing the highest price customers will accept is equal to the price of the component products in a price bundle, a product bundle raises their reservation price, as the new product is more than the sum of its parts.[22] Product bundling can be the product solution offered to customers for better experience.

Unbundling an integrated bundle or system provides an alternative way of attracting and building stronger relationship. Many business customers want to purchase components and integrate them into a certain desired configuration that best serves their needs. This allows customized product configuration, installation, and customer service. As markets are becoming increasingly competitive and fragmented, the need for this customized product solutions emerged. Firms with the customer relationship in mind would offer this customized product configurations or solutions to build customer relationships.

Section 4. Managing Brand Loyalty

> *"Ordinary people can spread good and bad information about brands faster than marketers."*
> Ray Johnson

After introduction, the new product will follow the product life cycle. In managing existing products, an important decision to make is how to manage brand name and brand image of a firm's products. While brand loyalty is important to have, brand equity is becoming an invaluable asset for businesses to maintain and achieve. Behind this emergence of the brand equity is the value and function of brands. Several perspectives reveal the function and value of the brand to consumers and firms themselves.[23]

To consumers, brands identify the source or maker of a product. Brand image is formed in a consumer's mind based on past experiences with the product and its marketing program. Most importantly, brands have a special meaning to consumers. Brands also communicate quality. Brands, therefore, reduce search cost and play an important role as a choice heuristics in purchase decision. Brands also serve as symbolic meaning to consumers. It is generally believed that consumers choose a product whose image is similar to their self-image. This concept of image congruence is often used to develop brand images for new products or to reposition existing products to effectively fit the target market. Brands can reduce risk in purchase decisions. There are many different types of risks that consumers perceive when purchasing products. Several of those risks are:

- *Financial*.......... The product can incur more overall expenses than expected.
- *Functional*........ The product does not function as expected.
- *Physical*.......... The product can harm the physical well being of the user or others.
- *Psychological*.. The product influences the mental well being of the user.
- *Social*.............. The product can hurt the social image of the user.

Although there are many different ways of reducing risk, choosing a well-known brand or remaining loyal to a brand is the most commonly adopted is one of the risk reduction strategies of consumers.

Brands also provide important functions to firms. Brands can help firms to simplify product handling or tracing for the firm. A brand name can be an intellectual property and provide legal protection for unique features or aspects of the product. Brand names can be protected through registered trademarks. Investments on a brand name can be an asset because a brand can differentiate a firm's product from competitors' products. With certain quality connotation, brands can be used to develop marketing strategy. Brand loyalty ensures a certain percent of the market share and creates a barrier of entry to the market for new firms. Branding becomes a powerful tool and legal property that helps firms build a competitive advantage in a highly competitive and volatile market. In many mergers or acquisitions, brand name is valued more than the physical assets, and contributes to goodwill. Brand names receive much attention from senior management due to these bottom-line financial reasons.

Firms create and maintain a brand name through their marketing programs and other activities. The branding process involves several steps in consumer's mind: brand recognition, brand knowledge and preference, and brand loyalty. Branding involves creating mental schemata about products or services in consumer's mind. Brand differentiation can be achieved through actual differences in benefits or features, and through intangible positioning images. Brand names can be created for a variety of products and services. Branding can be applied to physical goods including commodities and high technology products, services, retailers and wholesalers, people and organizations, sports, art, entertainment, and geographical locations. Creating a leading brand in a product category offers significant financial and perceptual benefits. While leading brands such as Coca-Cola or Kodak enjoy brand leadership for a long period, some leading brands lose their brand leadership due to inadequate or inappropriate responses to changes in business environment. At every level of the branding process, firms need to continually monitor brand images and to measure the brand equity of their products. Many models in the past have been developed to accurately assess the brand equity.

Brand Equity Model

Aaker Model

The Aaker model consists of five categories of brand assets and liabilities linked to a brand.[24] The five categories are: (a) brand loyalty, (b) brand awareness, (c) perceived quality, (d) brand association, and (e) other proprietary assets such as patents and trademarks. These five categories of brand assets provide value to customers by enhancing the customer's processing of information, confidence in the purchase decision, and use satisfaction. They also provide value to firms by enhancing efficiency and effectiveness of marketing programs, brand loyalty, brand extensions, trade leverage, and competitive advantage. In this model, two concepts play critical roles in building and managing brand equity. The first concept is the brand identity that communicates a unique set of brand associations that consumers hold. Brand identity can be built around four perspectives: the brand as product, the brand as organization, the brand as person, and the brand as symbol. The other concept of importance is brand system that considers a brand as a member of a system of brands. This model takes the customer-oriented perspective emphasizing the importance of brand awareness and association.

PowerGrid Model

While the Aaker model was developed in the academic research stream, an industry-based model, PowerGrid model, is a commonly used tool for assessing brand equity. Young & Rubicam, one of the world's largest advertising agencies, developed the BrandAsset Valuator based on a world-wide survey of consumers. This model contends that successful brands are built by consumers acquiring, in sequence, cumulatively specific brand perceptions: Differentiation (D), Relevance (R), Esteem (E), and Knowledge (K). First, consumers need to recognize differentiation of your brand from all other competing brands. Differentiation is measured by the perceived distinctiveness of the brand, which represents brand strength.

According to this model, brand strength is an important predictor of future performance and market potential. Next, consumers should have a relevant perception of your brand. Relevance represents a brand's personal appropriateness and is strongly tied to the level of market penetration. Consumers having both differentiation and relevance perception will hold the brand in high regard and move to esteem perception. In other words, consumers will have high esteem for a brand that can create relevant differentiation in their mind. The final stage is knowledge where consumers have an intimate understanding of the brand and for what it stands. Consumers having both esteem and knowledge for a certain brand will put the brand in a high brand stature. Brand stature indicates a brand's presence in current market. The evaluation of these four brand perception measures can show the current and future status of a brand.

Based on the brand strength and brand stature, the PowerGrid was developed. PowerGrid is a two (high and low brand strength) by two (high and low brand stature) dimensional grid representing a visual analytical device. Figure 6.9 shows the cycle of brand development in the PowerGrid model. Brands start as a new brand in the lower left corner of Quadrant I. They then can move up to reach high brand strength entering the upper left quadrant. This, Quadrant II, is characterized by emerging brands. Successful brands move to the upper right area of Quadrant III. In this quadrant, firms enjoy brand leadership. If improperly managed, a brand can lose its leadership position and be pushed to Quadrant IV. This quadrant indicates potential weakness with loss of the brand strength. Also noted in the model is that the PowerGrid of a brand can be country-specific. A true global brand like Coca-Cola enjoys a position consistently in Quadrant III around the world.

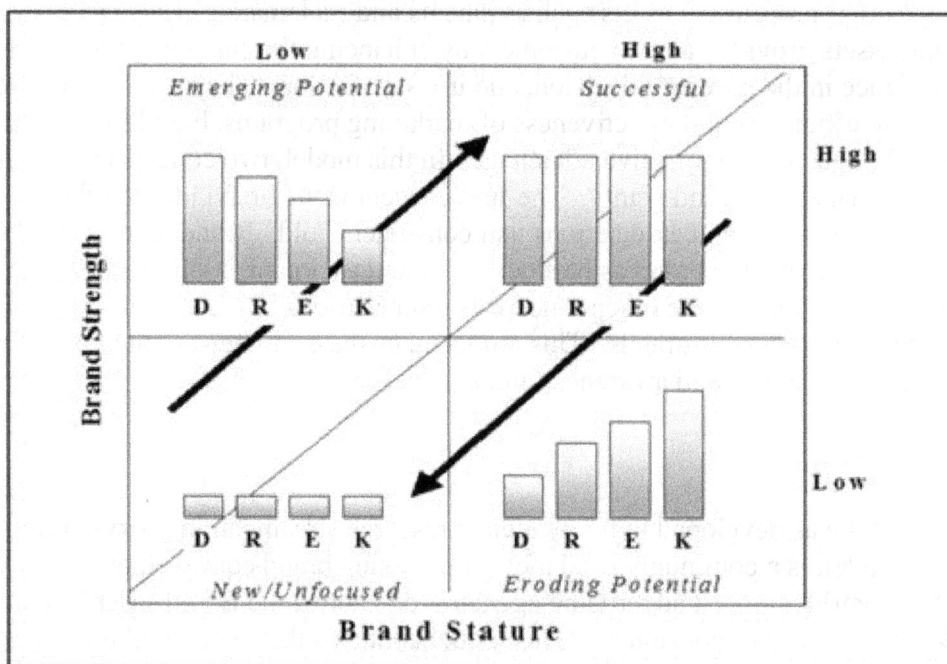

Figure 6.9: The Power Grid Showing How Brands Grow and Decline

Figure 6.10 shows an example of the power grid application with the 11 brands of a personal care product firm showing their brand strength and brand stature. The PowerGrid chart shows that three brands are in Quadrant I including Fulton for Women. Two brands in the Fulton Fraser Hair Line are emerging as potentially successful brands. Five brands are listed in

Quadrant III representing brand leadership. Three brands belong to Quadrant IV indicating loss of brand strength. Marketing or brand managers can make resource allocation and brand management decisions based on this guided analysis. The PowerGrid presented here represents the total market of the firm, and similar charts can be developed for different regions of the U.S. and international markets.

The Power Grid

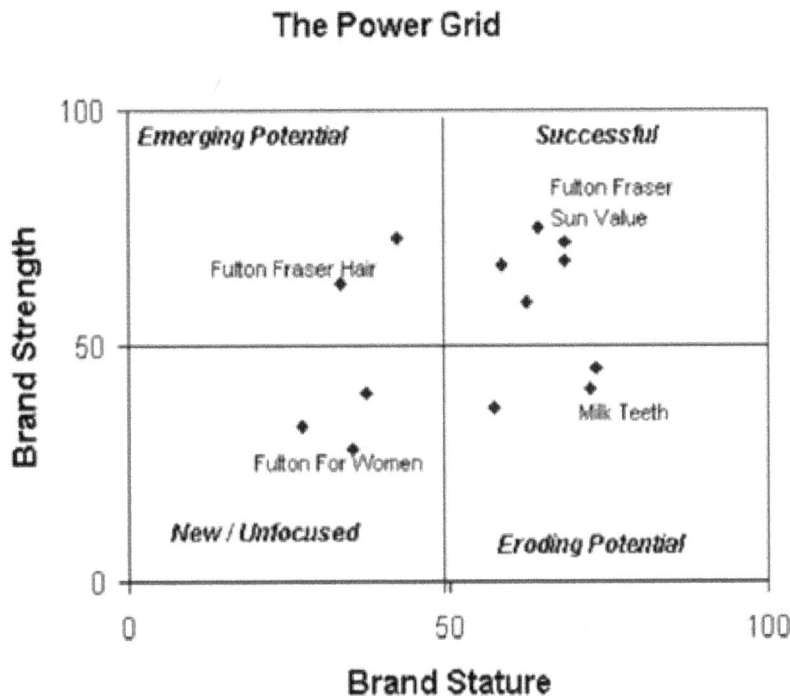

Figure 6.10: Power Grid Model

Brand Equity Report

In establishing a brand equity measurement system, creating a brand equity report is an important step. With the initial preparation of formalizing the company view of brand equity into a document, firms can combine the tracking survey results and other relevant performance records into a regular report of brand equity. This report is prepared to inform managers of what is happening with a brand (market level information) and as well as why it is happening (consumer level information such as consumer perceptions on key attributes and benefits). Of particular interest is market level information that can signal the problem areas or potential opportunities with respect to a particular brand. Market level information typically reported includes: product shipments and movement through channels of distribution; relevant cost breakdowns; price and discount schedules where appropriate; sales and market share information broken down by geographic region, type of accounts, or customer types; profit performance broken down by geographic region, type of accounts, or customer types.

Figure 6.11 and Figure 6.12 show the market level information of a brand equity report. The market level information can signal the problem areas or potential opportunities with respect to a particular brand. The first chart shows dollar sales of various brands in the current and prior year. In this chart, for example, managers can quickly identify a fast growing product, which in this case is Fulton Fraser Skin Value. Three other brands exhibited sales growth. These brands include Dippit, Fulton Fraser Family Care, and Nice-n-Brite. These products signal potential growth opportunities. On the contrary, many brands suffered a setback. Of particular concern is Fulton Fraser Hair that shows the largest decline in sales compared to the prior year. This signals a potential problem with these brand hair care products.

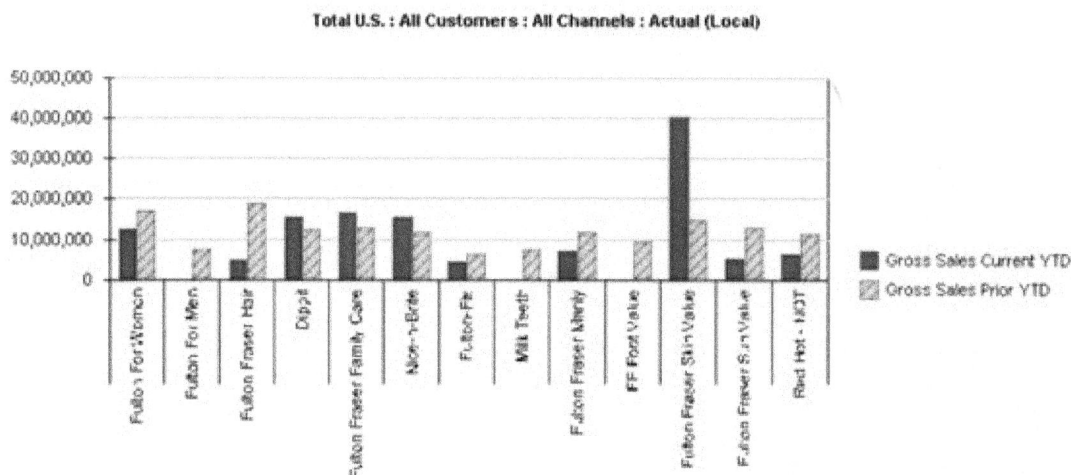

Figure 6.11: Brand Equity Analysis by Product for Sales Year-To-Year Changes

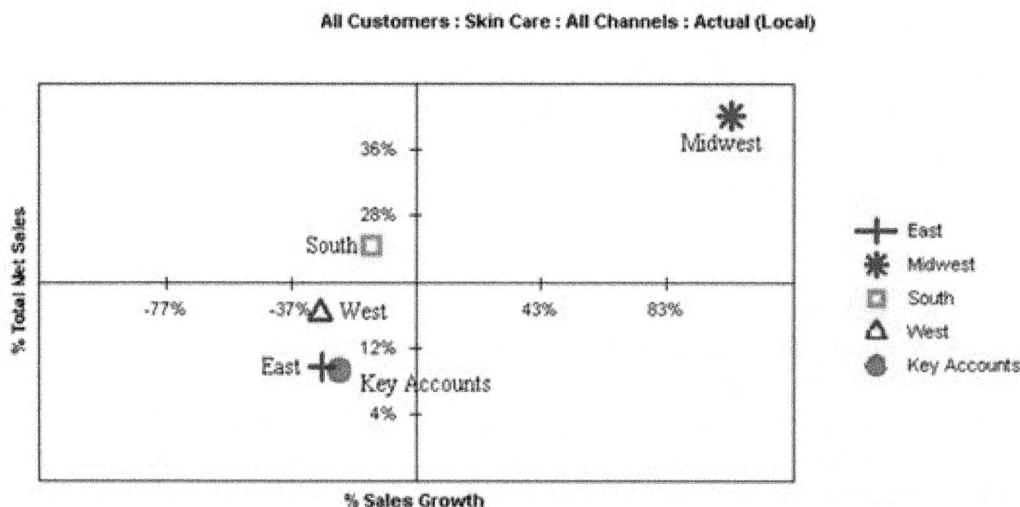

Figure 6.12: Brand Equity Analysis by Customer for Sales Growth

Brand Management with Social Media

What a brand does is far more important than what a brand says. "A brand is an individual's emotional response to an organization's product or service. Branding is important because people rely on their gut when making choices. Branding is a promise between the product and the consumer. Consistent delivery on that promise creates trust. Trust promotes consumer loyalty. Consumer loyalty leads to advocacy by opinion leaders."[25] So, what is the brand? Key to answering that question is to focus on defining the one differentiating and powerfully compelling quality that makes the brand. It is important to unify the brand by developing

194

branded touchpoints that establish trust. However, remember, if price is the only point of differentiation, the organization is not building a brand. The organization is just selling a commodity.

In Figure 6.13, the communications channel is illustrated. It highlights that the organization can control various communication media such as television and radio, but not necessarily uncontrolled communication such as user reviews, blogs, and word-of-mouth can also influence the perception of the brand. This highlights the uncontrollable nature of social media's influence on brands.

The cool branding ingredients include authenticity, uniqueness, innovativeness, excitement, and self-image congruity.[26] Brand coolness is a gestalt. The brand coolness index (BCI) includes the brand affect, the brand trust, the brand loyalty, and positive word-of-mouth. The BCI framework has antecedents such as advertising, endorsements, scarcity, social influence, and utility. The BCI has consequence of brand trust, brand loyalty, advocacy, purchase intention, brand affect, premium price, and satisfaction. "Not having a social media presence sends a message about your brand's relevancy with the connected customer."[27]

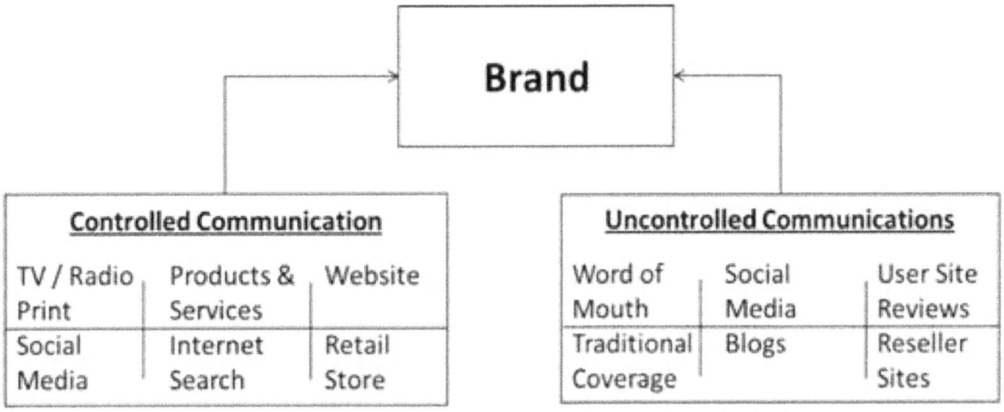

Figure 6.13: The Brand Reality – Controlled Versus Uncontrolled Communications

"Thirty-four percent of people post opinions about products and brands on their blog."[28] The goal is not to control the conversation. "The goal is to inspire, enable, influence, and engage. The goal is to create opportunities for people to feel ownership of the brand. Sixty-nine percent of companies participating in a study by London-based intellectual-property firm Marks & Clerk said they regard social media as the next big threat to protecting their brands online. In particular, 73 percent said that being online today risks exposing a brand to "unfair or inaccurate treatment" – largely via the unrestricted commentary that dominates online. Eighty-one percent said the web fosters a culture in which a brand's intellectual property is likely to be exploited. In addition, respondents directed most of their ire at Google. Approximately 58 percent said that they believed the search engine organization had grown too powerful. Also, when asked whether, in the name of healthy competition, it was fair to be able to buy a rival's trademarked brand name as a keyword in online search marketing, nearly 63 percent of individuals surveyed answered not at all. Firms must be actively involved in interactive online and social media marketing to develop and protect their brands. In addition, this emerging social media networks can offer a new opportunity for organizations to reach target markets in a cost effective manner.

Designing Brand Experience

Brand experience can be designed and delivered to customers to enhance customer relationship. Firms can design the brand experience by specifying the product experience, the look and feel of the brand, and experiential communications.[29] The product experience includes important experiential product features in addition to the functional attributes of the product. The product experience must demonstrate how a product works and include an elegant solution that shows its simplicity, uniqueness, or intricacy. This experience also includes the aesthetic appeal of the product representing its design, colors and shape. The brand needs to offer the experiential value as well as functional value. The look and feel component includes the visual identity, packaging, and other visual elements such as graphic design of websites. Experiential communications focus on how brand related marketing communications can be used implement the brand experience. Experiential communications provide relevant context for the customer. Brand experience can have significant impact on customer acquisition and retention.

Co-branding

For any firm, the decision of what the firm's product offerings should be is a major decision. The firm must determine what broad groups of products it will produce, as well as how many individual products it will market within each group. There are two primary advantages to customer attraction and retention from a diversified product line. The first advantage is that not all customers have the same preferences. By tailoring individual products to different groups, the firm can appeal to a larger share of potential customers. The second advantage is that a larger product line allows the customer to make his or her own price discrimination decisions. If the customer is unwilling to pay for additional quality or features, the business will not have lost the customer. Additionally, more discriminating customers will also be served, which creates value for the customer (through having the "better" product) and to the firm by being able to charge a slightly higher margin for the higher end products.

However, as always, there is a potential risk to the firm. If the firm has a product line that is too large, cannibalization is likely to occur. This means that the sale of one product detracts from the sale of another similar product. The greatest danger for the company is the effect cannibalization can have on its high-end products. Upon seeing a low quality product at a low price, a customer who may normally buy the high quality product may instead make a more economically-driven decision and buy the less expensive product. To diversify product line, firms are using various product-line extensions to specifically meet certain customer needs and provide the right product solution. The type of product line extension strategies include vertical line extensions (adding other versions of products), horizontal brand line extensions (adding complementary products), and new product-market brand extensions (entering other product-markets with the brand reputation).

Another strategy to build stronger relationships is to develop a co-branding. Co-branding achieves the potential synergy of two brands that share common market space and customer base. An example of such co-branding is creation of Trix Yoplait yogurt. Another example is 'Intel Inside', which is an example of ingredient co-branding.[30]

Total CRM Based Relationship Marketing Template

Template 6.1: Product and Service Solution Roadmap

Template 6.1 captures how well a firm is managing customer experience in terms of product mix and guides managers with the identification and development of new product or service solutions for relationship marketing.

Value Classification Segments	Current Value	Potential Life Time Value (LTV)	Current Products/ Brands offered	Current Experience Level	Key Pain Points Identified	New Product or Service Solutions Needed
Gold						
Segment A						
Segment B						
Silver						
Segment C						
Segment D						
Bronze						
Segment E						
Segment F						

Real World Application Cases

Case 6-1: Honda[31]

As automobiles are becoming a multi-faceted combination of mechanical parts, electronics and in-vehicle software, Honda R&D must continuously adapt their development processes to handle these complexities. As many design problems actually occur early in the development process and are known to the development team only in the latter stages, Honda performs many reworks at the end phase of automobile design. The task for Honda is to improve the precision of the conceptual design phase to minimize revisions later. Honda wanted to find out what its designers' major pain points were and how they hoped to change automotive development. When design problems arise, the firm documented those issues. However, the forms are managed in an unstructured data format with descriptions of problems written by different individuals. These unstructured documentations are systematically hard to analyze.

Honda built a machine learning model to analyze the unstructured data in the counter measure request forms. Honda created a chatbot user interface where Honda designers could set up appropriate tags to classify problems and search on them. This search capability helped identify past issues to reduce some of the design reworks the team currently encounters. The AI system solutions and AI models can recognize and classify the firm's documents and give them appropriative tags. Because AI learns from experience, the system will grow up like an expert engineer and engineers can ask it for whatever information and knowledge is needed. Honda R&D revolutionized automobile development.

Case Questions

1. What are Honda's advantages and disadvantages of using the new product development processes?

2. What is unique about Honda's new process? How this new process can facilitate building customer equity and customer driven new product development?

Case 6-2: JORI[32]

JORI deals with the generation of consumers who have grown up with the Internet. The firm used to present customers with a static physical or online catalog with pictures and descriptions. As the furniture-buying experience is constantly changing, the best catalogs and the most fully stocked showrooms are not sufficient enough to keep up with the growing and changing expectations of digitally-native consumers. The new generation of consumers are used to viewing products online before they go into a shop to buy. Even with this rise in online shopping, consumers still want to see and try out new furniture before their purchase. They also want to personalize and customize furniture to their own unique tastes. JORI offers furniture collection with the customization ability to mix and match components. However, customers find it increasingly difficult to understand all the possible options for a piece of furniture, and what the final design would look like. The sheer volume of customization options can overwhelm both shoppers and salespeople. JORI has created a way to provide the best shopping experience and merge it with a personalized design encounter.

JORI decided to create an online 3D configurator to allow consumers and salespeople alike to build, visualize and customize 3D models of furniture. The firm is creating a solution where the customer can submit a photo of a fabric they like and can cross reference it with the firm's system to find something similar. The system uses existing business rules to guarantee that the output will be comfortable, attractive and technically possible to manufacture. Customers can use the solution online or in-store to access the full range of customization options and visualize exactly how their finished items will look. The system allows in-store sales advisors to create the perfect item for a customer with accurate pricing no matter how complex the chosen options and speeds up the order-to-delivery timetable.

Case Questions

1. What are JORI's advantages of using the new system? What performance metrics can be improved by this new system?

2. In recognizing the importance of customer relationship-driven marketing, JOTI want to focus more on customer equity than brand equity. How the new model can help JORI build customer equity?

200

Chapter 7. Providing Customer-Focused Service with Supply chain

Section 1. Touchpoint Optimization for Customer-Focused Service

"You don't win until you conquer the little flaws. You don't beat these great ones until your form is perfect. This is true in all of life. A flaw in a product can ruin a business. A personal failing, a little one, can ruin a person's life. Don't be content with mediocrity -- strive to live up to the greatest within you."
Bob Richards; Pole Vaulter & Two-Time Olympic Gold Medalist

Customer touchpoint management deals with customer Interface issues. The dynamic exchange of information and service that occurs between the customer and a firm can occur in person, over the phone, online, or in any other way. The types of exchanges include in-store face-to-face, field sales force, service personnel, and others (consulting, counseling, and entertainment). Personal but distant exchanges can occur via phone or text messaging or in writing. Electronic exchanges are exchanges or interactions on an e-commerce site, social media sites, or via e-mail or other methods. These various touchpoints need to be coordinated such that they can provide the most appropriate contact points for perfect customer experience.[1] Firms optimize various touchpoints considering the life time value of the customer and cost to serve them.

Touchpoint Optimization

Touchpoint optimization refers identifying the right touch point for customers offering the right message to the right customer at the right time. Firms need to determine customers' interaction preference and decide how to engage with customers. Touchpoint (optimal channel) management focuses on optimizing a company's "inbound" touchpoint channels with its "outbound" means of customer interaction. The goal is choosing the best approach for each.

Touchpoint Categories

There are many different touch points customers can interact with the firm and brand. These touchpoints can be physical and virtual. They include outlets, sales force, telephony, direct marketing, e- commence, and social commerce. Outlets are retail stores, kiosks and other physical outlets where customers can experience products and services directly. Salesforce includes all sales outlets such as field account management, manufactures representative, service and sales representatives. Telephony includes all interactions and customer contacts through traditional telephone, fax, call center contacts, and mobile devices. Direct marketing touch points are direct mail, radio, traditional TV, and others. E- commerce touch points include web-sites, e-mail, SMS and text messages, and online advertising. Social media touch points include all customer interaction and engagements through various social media platforms.

A customer touchpoint strategy can be developed by recognizing that different customers want to interact with different touch point channels. Their touch point channel preferences may also vary depending on the customer relationship cycle and customer characteristics. To utilize the full range of viable touchpoint channels to serve customers, firms are adopting relationship marketing strategies such as an integrated multi-channel strategy. A multi-channel strategy offers firms the ability to respond to customers' channel preferences and propensities of use for better customer relationships. During the typical sales cycle, firms need to offer customers different touch points to meet their changing needs. In each stage, customers have interactions using various touch points of their preference and choice with the firm and brand. For successful relationship marketing, firms need to understand the nature of customer encounters and what customers want to achieve with a specific encounter. All touch points must be integrated throughout the sales cycle to provide the perfect customer experience and create the strong long-term relationship.

The key issues in structuring the customer interface and integrating its touchpoints are the following. First, firms must provide the appropriate mix of essence and flexibility. Essence refers to key operations, interactions, and exchange while flexibility concerns about making the interface fresh and up-to-date. Second, the right mix of style and substance must be provided to customers. Style is related to the manner of expressing essence and flexibility. Substances are tangibles associated with it. Third, the right timing of customer interface is important. Firms need to determine how customer contacts should be phased over time. The right strategy need to be established regarding contact initiation, duration, key transition points, when customers leave, and how to get him/her back. It is critical for firms to interconnect interface touch points for coordination and consistency.

Coordinating Customer Touchpoints for Customer-focused Service

Customer service is integral to relationship marketing success. It provides the primary means of contact with the customers and becomes a critical customer touchpoint that can impact customer experience and customer retention. Customer service can be coordinated by many different ways. Customer service can be organized by product line or by multiple lines of business or by multiple products. The most common way of service coordination is service centers. This approach shares a common customer information system and requires routing customer changes. Service centers should be equipped to deal with multiple lines of business or multiple products. As firms add new channels, coordinating the service activity across these independent channels becomes very important. In order to gain the benefits associated with top-quality customer service, the firm must have a mechanism to coordinate customer-oriented service processes across multiple channels.

This service coordination can be provided in several ways. First, if service centers are organized by product line (such as a cable service center and a cellular service center for same communications company), then all service centers should share a common customer information system and can route customer changes as required. Common customer information systems across service centers provide a strong benefit to the customer. Customers wanting to update their name and address information, for example, can call one location to facilitate the change. The called location takes the information and is able to make the change for all centers or can pass the information to the other centers. Where possible, service centers should be equipped to deal with multiple lines of business or multiple products. However, if the firm does have multiple service centers or service channels, all customer-oriented service processes should be coordinated across all the disparate service centers.

Coordination practices for multiple channels require the ability for one center to transfer the customer and their related information to another center. Call centers should facilitate the transfer of customers. A single customer-level identifier should be used across all channels. Some coordination practices for multiple channels are the following. Firms that have multiple service centers should provide the ability for one center to transfer the customer and his or her related information to another center, rather than requiring the customer to make another call. Call centers should facilitate the transfer of customers with telephony systems that can directly transfer customer and account information, rather than requiring the caller to reenter or repeat name account numbers. A single customer-level identifier should be used across all product and service channels to provide seamless information transfers. Common training programs should exist across service centers for non-product-specific processes such as customer greeting and customer name change processes. Independent service centers should conduct regular meetings for cross-line-of-business service representatives to discuss issues and coordination mechanisms. Published guidelines should exist for common customer-oriented processes.

Service options should be offered to sales representatives and customers alike. Such options should also include call centers, traditional retail standalone centers (such as branches, phone stores, or agencies), multipurpose retail stores (such as Radio Shack, which also carries cell phones), in-store kiosks (cell phone displays in a mall or grocery store), and Internet-based self-service mechanisms. In evaluating customer service success, the following measures can be used. Some mechanism coordinates service measurements and incentives across multiple service centers. Customer satisfaction is included as a service objective and is actively measured. The ability of service representatives to handle all customer issues in one call is included in performance measures as are cross sales and retention saves. Traditional performance measures are adjusted to accommodate customer-oriented measures. For example, the acceptable call handle time could be increased, or the acceptable number of rings/hold time could be increased if required.

The relationship marketing plan should provide the following types of best-practice policies at each channel. Valued customers are identified at all service points and are treated accordingly. Service representatives are empowered to conduct customer save activities and improve customer experience where necessary. Service representatives are provided with training that enables them to become relationship managers rather than product-level service providers. Service representatives are trained to recognize retention issues. Service representatives are provided with adequate sales training. Service representatives are trained to recognize the appropriate time to solicit additional information or attempt product cross-sell activities. This would include how to recognize customer signals.

The customer service functions are integral to customer relationship success because they provide the primary means of contact touchpoint with the customers. Customer service is a tremendous opportunity to positively influence the customer's feeling about the firm and to increase customer satisfaction and loyalty. Service management is an effective and non-intrusive way to collect information about the customer that can be used in all aspects of customer relationship marketing and strategy development. Customer service activity coordination requires a mechanism to coordinate customer-oriented service processes across multiple service channels. It provides the contact mechanisms that can be leveraged to implement relationship marketing strategies.

Section 2. Managing Distribution Channels as Customer Touchpoints

"Daring as it is to investigate the unknown, even more so is to question the known."
　　　Kaspar

The key participants in the value chain include the suppliers, the internal manufacturing organization, the distribution channels and the customers. Distribution channels are the important contact points for customers. They are critical customer touchpoints that can significantly influence customer experience leading to retention. Each part of the value chain is important and the entire value chain must be managed in its entirety. A critical aspect of the value chain management is the measurement of performance. Measurements let the managers see the problems developing and potential opportunities for improvement.

Two terms associated with value chain management are physical distribution and logistics. Physical distribution is defined as activities associated with collecting, storing, and physically distributing the product to buyers. These activities include packaging, warehousing, inventory management, and outgoing transportation.[2] Logistics is defined as the process of planning, implementing, and controlling the efficient, effective flow and storage of goods and services, and related information from point of origin to point of consumption for the purpose of conforming to customer requirements.[3] These activities can determine the level of customer satisfaction in the demand chain. If a business is to be market-driven, it must sustain certain types of capabilities.[4] One of these capabilities is the "outside-in" process. These processes allow the organization to foresee changes in markets through the development of sound relationships with suppliers, channel members, and customers. These processes enable the firm to gather and interpret information regarding technological advancements, competitors, distribution channels, and customers. They act as market sensing and customer linking mechanisms.

In the household and personal product industry segment, packaging, ingredients, and other manufacturing costs account for just 50% of the retail price consumers pay. The remainder of the costs is allocated to advertising and marketing costs, distribution expenses, and the manufacturer and retailer's operating profits. Value chain management has been an overlooked source of competitive advantage for many firms. This is an area that can benefit from efficiency improvements. There is a tangible expense of carrying inventory that can be recognized. There is a belief that the value chain can concurrently lower costs, increase service to achieve differentiation, and influence customer experience.

In managing value chain, marketing managers need to ask key questions to understand the role and impact of value chain on relationship marketing. They would want to know how good their firm is in terms of value chain management and customer service. Marketing managers must answer such questions as "what type of strategy does logistics and value chain capabilities allow them to deploy?" and "what competitive edge does value chain structure provide them with?" In addition, they would want to know what are the trends in logistics and value chain management in our market and how could we match these trends in the future given our value chain and logistics capabilities today to provide perfect customer experience. Key activities and analytic questions to be utilized include assessment of current customers' channel preference and requirements, determining logistics and value chain costs, assessing capabilities and determining gaps relative to channel needs and requirements, determining total lead time from a customer order to the product/ service delivery, and reviewing against competitors. The goal of this type of evaluation is to analyze logistics and value chain so that marketing managers can anticipate processes and technologies required to support customer requirements in the future. Specifically, firms must determine effectiveness of their logistics and value chain activities, how to produce and deliver the product/service more efficiently relative to the competitors, alignment of logistics and value chain activities with their relationship marketing goals, and the flexibility to react to marketplace versus our competitors.

Value Chain Processes

The key components of the value chain and their interaction with customer satisfaction and business performance are best illustrated in Figure 7.1.[5] In the supply and distribution processes, the transportation cost varies based on time, cost, occurrence of damage and/or lost freight, and frequency of delivery. The use of warehousing facilitates supply mixing. Key warehousing activities include receiving, data entry, put away, and picking. Finished goods inventory investment may account for fifty percent of the company's asset base.[6] Since consumers are demanding product line variety and are often unwilling to postpone delivery, it makes the correct placement and control of specific items essential to customer satisfaction. Packaging is used to prevent damage and to facilitate efficiency during storage and movement of the product.

In the spanning processes, order processing are the activities that take place from the time the firm receives an order until the customer physically receives the order and payment is secured.[7] Information dissemination provides for the means for teams to respond resourcefully to the environment. It facilitates real-time, cost-effective adjustments in inbound materials flow, product volumes and mix, distribution schemes, and delivery timings. Businesses are looking for the combination that yields the best competitive advantage.

Channel Management Decisions

Firms have several key channel management decisions to make and tasks to perform. Channel management decisions can have a direct impact on customer experience and determine the availability and quality of distribution channel touchpoints. These tasks are not performed just once but rather are continually evaluated as the market environment and competition change and evolve. The major channel management categories or activities include:

- Reviewing the channel alternatives,
- Deciding on the most appropriate channel structure,
- Implementing the channel structure,
- Managing and evaluating the channel performance.

Value Chain Processes

Supply Processes	Distribution Processes	Spanning Processes
• Transportation	• Transportation	• Purchasing
• Warehousing	• Warehousing	• Order Processing
• Inventory Control	• Inventory Control	• Information Dissemination

Organizational Flexibility

- Advanced Technology
- Involvement
- Participative Management

Capacity to Satisfy Customers

- Price
- Product Line
- Quality
- Order Fill Rate
- Cycle Time
- Order Information
- Frequency of Delivery

Performance

- Customer Satisfaction
- Financial Performance

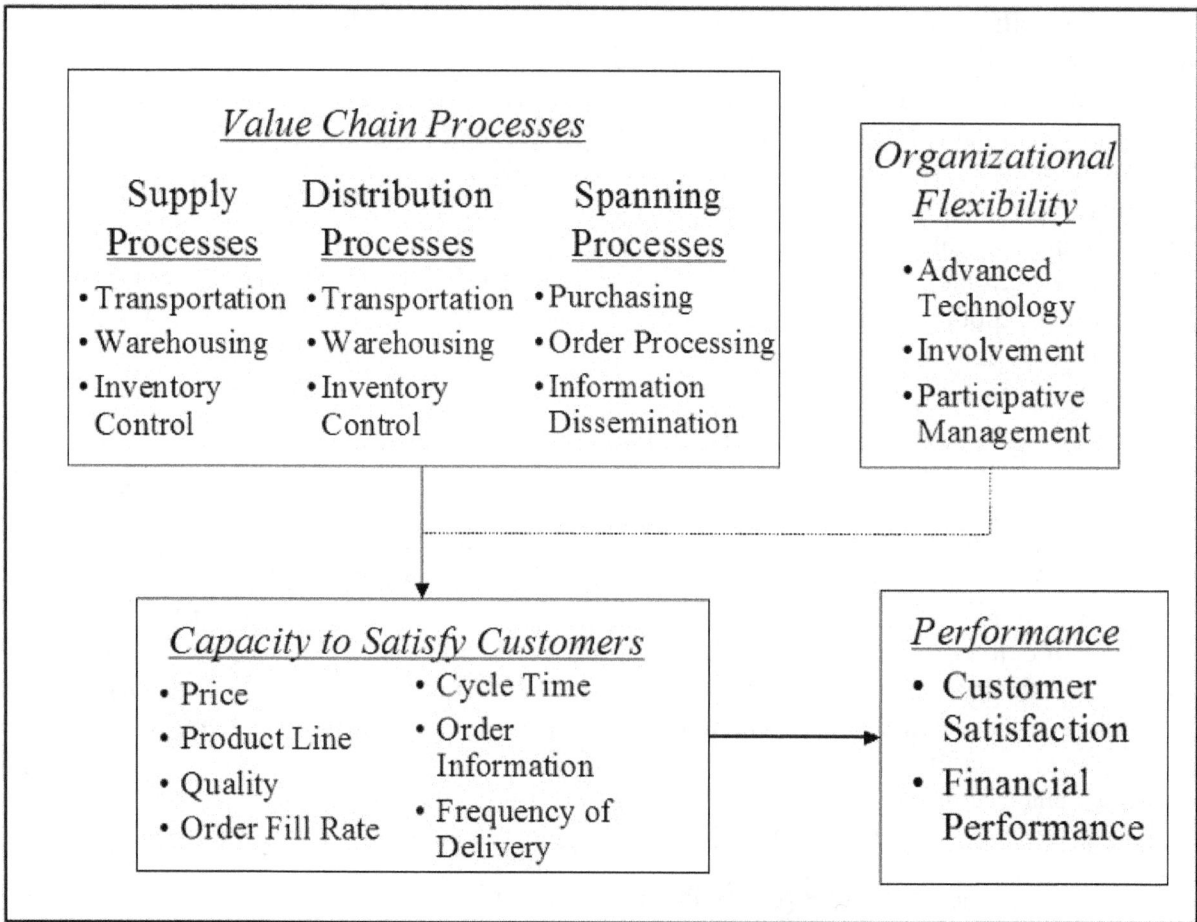

Figure 7.1: The Role of Value Chain in a Market-Driven Organization

The channel manager must constantly review the various channel alternatives and decide on the most appropriate structure. The channel manager can choose between utilizing a direct channel structure and focusing on an indirect channel structure to sell the firm's products. A direct channel has no intermediary levels between the company and the consumer whereas an indirect channel can have multiple levels of intermediaries. These intermediaries can include jobbers, distributors, and brokers. The Internet has presented itself as a new direct channel that the firm can utilize. Each channel brings various issues and conflicts forward as well as the associated benefits.

A number of channels exist to distribute the product. Types of channels are based upon various requirements. The specific institutional form utilized by the firm classifies one type of channel. Examples of this form include supermarkets, wholesale clubs, and mass merchandise outlets. Another type of channel is the direct sales, delivery channel, and online storefronts. This channel links directly to the customer. Each channel has its requirements for advertising, transportation of the product, and form of selling.

The appropriate channel structure and channel strategy involves understanding these benefits and issues. An initial assessment of the expected sales, costs, and profitability can help rank alternatives. This analysis must be tempered with the organization's strategy, the product's technical complexity and requirement for service and support and the assessment of the environment. The firm must determine if the channel members can change with the market conditions. The firm must also assess the level of control over the marketing process that they are willing to give up. Because of their proximity to the customers, channel members can exert control over various marketing decisions.

In making channel decisions, marketing managers can use the impact guided analysis framework. They can start by identifying key managerial questions that must be answered for effective channel management. Key questions include: a) What are the different channels to reach an end-user?, b) What value is added at each step?, and c) Could some customers be better served with an alternative channel configuration? Key activities involve identifying market distribution channel per segment and mapping current distribution channel links from the firm to the end users, "first buyers" and segments and factors that strongly influence "first buyers" purchase decision. In addition, marketing managers may need to identify trends in each channel of distribution (% of volume, price, long term trends, future channel evolution), and reasons for changes. They also need to compare their current distribution channel mix in cost and volume to the market and identify any discrepancies and analyze what value is added along each step of the distribution channel (from the raw material suppliers to the final consumer - Value chain analysis), and determine needs per channel segment. The goal of the channel analysis is to understand current and future sourcing and distribution practices within each segment of the market and understand the value added at each step of the distribution channel. Specifically, channel analysis can help marketing managers to:

- understand where products/services are sold and how they move along the value chain,
- understand the amount of value added at each step in the distribution channel as well as the costs and services provided by the channel member,
- determine the reasons certain channels are preferred over others.

The outcome of the channel analysis is marketing managers' complete understanding of the channel trends and thorough channel value chain analysis results. Various managerial insights and solutions can be obtained from this type of analysis. For example, marketing managers can understand the percent of business in volume and dollar amount and its evolution over the last year. They can also identify major channel trends such as large retailers are gaining share from traditional contractor channels and retailer "installed sales" is expected to continue to help retailers gain share from all channels. They may also reveal that channel needs vary depending on the type of customers. Major accounts may prefer marketable brand name and product variety, while distributors value service reliability, product size, database marketing. On the other hand, retailers may value service reliability, marketable brand name, and support for stocking programs (SKU). These insights can be used in maintaining and modifying existing channels and in designing new channels as customer touchpoints.

Distribution Channel Evaluation

Once the channel structure is determined and implemented, it must be continually evaluated to ensure the objectives that were set are being met. To evaluate the channel, various analytic dimensions and performance measurements must be determined and the required data collected and analyzed.

Dimensions that can be used to evaluate the channel and the channel members include segmentation by market and by product. The market analytic dimension is useful in highlighting which geographic segments within a distribution channel are profitable and are providing the expected sales revenue. The market dimension may be defined by company regions and sales districts or by regions, states, counties, cities and/or metropolitan statistical areas (MSA). The product analytic dimension is useful in determining which brands, product lines and products provide expected revenues and profits through which distribution channels. This information, along with the non-quantitative information provided by the channel member, can be used in making decisions about product additions and deletions, or about required promotions and pricing strategies. Figure 7.2 provides a hierarchical view of the channel being evaluated based upon sales with the high-level market dimension and the high-level product dimension providing supporting information. The channel manager may want to reverse the analysis and examine channel within product within market. Each analysis may provide the channel manager with unique insights.

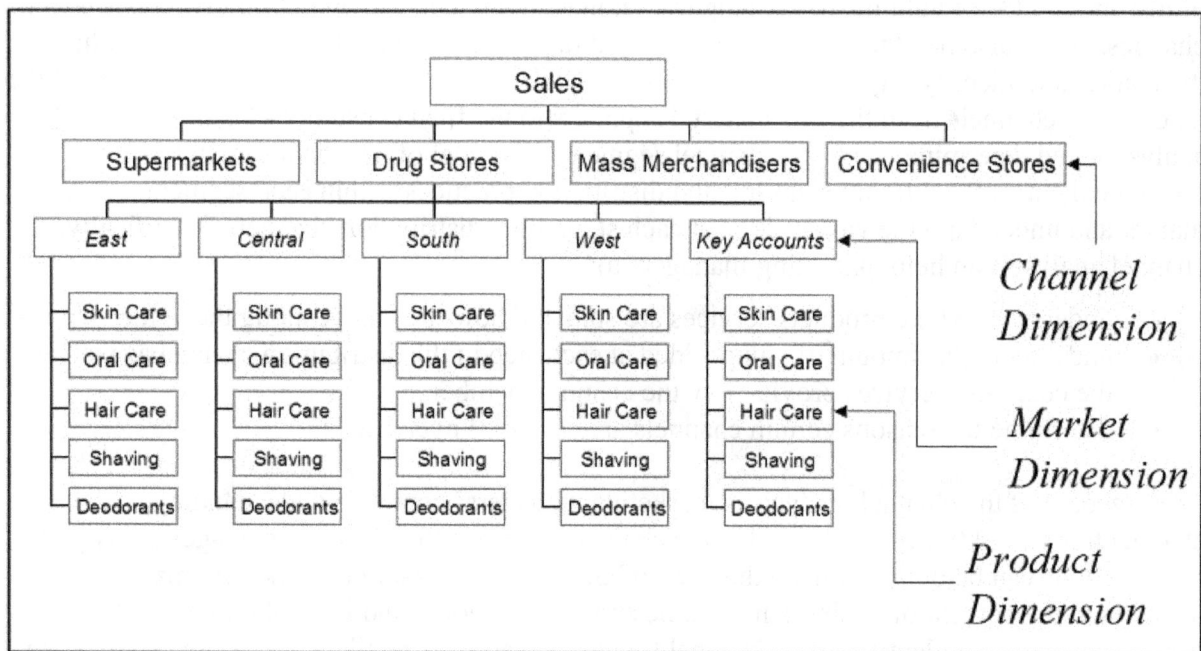

Figure 7.2: Channel Analysis by Market and Product

The channel manager can evaluate the channel members based upon performance against various established standards. The various standards used could include an annual budget, a monthly forecast, or strategic, multiyear performance plan. The performance measures used include:

- Amount of damaged goods.
- Amount of lost goods.
- Cooperation with company promotions.
- Delivery time.
- Market growth rates.
- Relative profitability.
- Replenishment time.
- Sales by time period.
- Service to the customer.

The various costs of the channel, the sales revenues produced by the channel, and the asset investments required in the distribution channel can all be used by the firm to determine the relative profitability and performance of the channel. Understanding the costs, revenues, service levels, and investments required aid the channel manager in identifying which channel should be used.

Performance Measurement

An assumption used by marketing analysts and managers is that the corporate strategies and objectives have already been developed. The performance measurements discussed and used are in support of those strategies and objectives. Measurements include customer satisfaction, service level, cost, Return-on-Investment (ROI), Return-on-Sales (ROS) and profitability. These measurements are classified as effectiveness measurements, that is, how well the process is accomplished or as efficiency measurements, that is, the least usage of resources by the process.

Figure 7.3 illustrates the relative performance aspects of the various channel alternatives. This chart shows sales volume, net sales, and selling profit for each type of retail institution. The type of retail institutions used by this firm includes convenience stores, drug stores, mass merchandisers, super markets, and Internet sales outlet. Super markets are the primary retail outlets for this firm with 79.9% of sales volume, 76.8% of net sales, and 77.1% of selling profit. Convenience stores generate 8.9% of net sales and 8.8% of net profit, but only represent 3.4% of sales volume. Products sold through convenience stores seem to generate higher net sales and profit relative to volume indicating the high-end nature of products or customers. Drug stores are third in generating sales volume, net sales, and selling profit, followed by Internet and mass merchandisers.

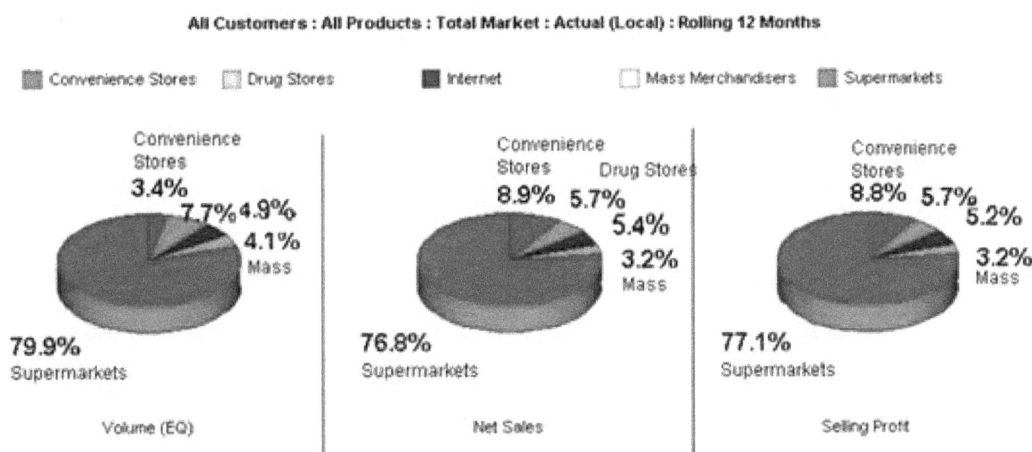

Figure 7.3: Channel Performance

Channel Evaluation Models

Various models exist that can be used in evaluating the performance of the channel and the channel members. In this section, three models are reviewed. Those three models are the:

- Strategic profit model.
- Contribution model.

- Net profit model.

The strategic profit model (SPM) is an analytic tool that can be used to focus the organization on common objectives. The SPM combines elements from the balance sheet and the income statement to produce three distinct ratios that can be used to evaluate organizational performance and to compare it to other firms in the industry. Return on net worth (RONW), return on assets (ROA), and net profit margin (NPM) are the three ratios that are linked in the SPM at the organizational level.

Figure 7.4 illustrates how the elements of the balance sheet and income statement are combined to produce the required ratios. Asset Turnover is computed by dividing sales into total assets. This ratio helps management understand how efficiently they are using the firm's assets to produce sales. Net Profit Margin is computed by dividing the net profit into the sales. This helps management understand the amount of from each sales dollar that is retained by the firm. The Return on Assets ratio is computed by multiplying the net profit margin by the asset turnover ratio. This ratio helps management understand how well operations are using the firm's resources. Financial Leverage is computed by dividing total assets by the net worth. This ratio helps management ensure that the firm is providing an adequate return to attract and keep investor's funds. Return on Net Worth is computed by multiplying ROA by the financial leverage.

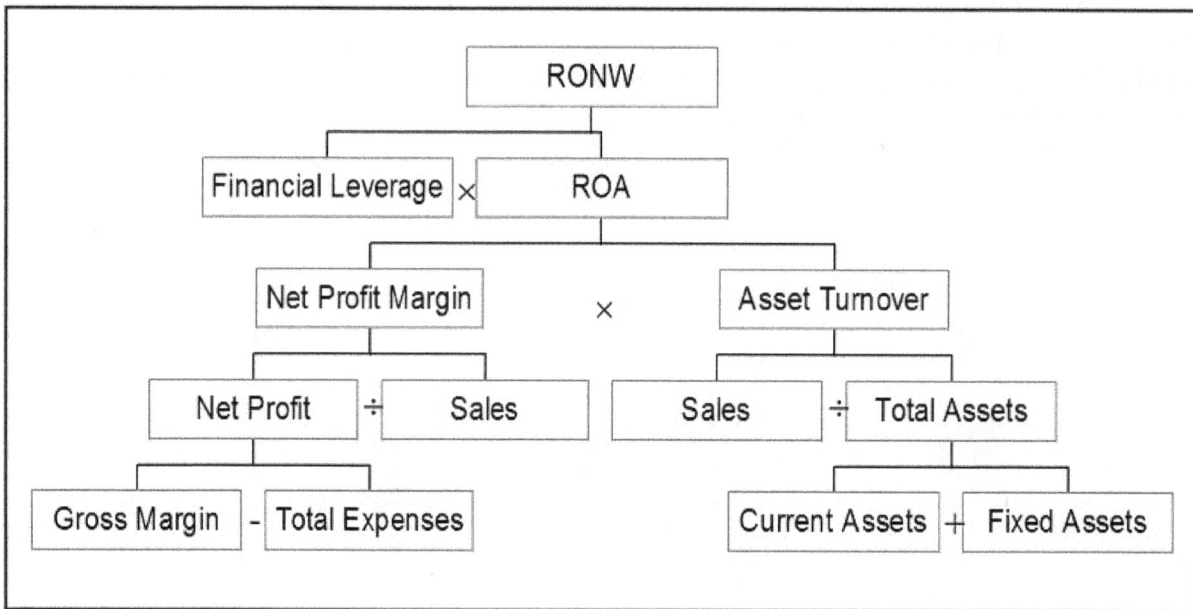

Figure 7.4: Strategic Profit Model

The second model is the contribution model. This model identifies the contribution of each channel member to the organization. The first step in calculating the contribution is to identify and classify the various cost elements. Costs are classified as variable or fixed and direct or indirect. Fixed costs are those costs that do not change in the short run. Variable costs are those costs that are a function of some activity, like sales. Direct costs are those costs that are incurred in support of the channel member. Indirect costs are those costs that exist regardless of the channel member. The channel manager has to use the variable direct costs, fixed direct costs, variable indirect costs and fixed indirect costs in the analysis. Variable direct costs include those costs that are directly related to volume like sales commission, discounts, allowances, and free goods. Fixed direct costs are any other costs that can be traced directly to the channel member including those associated with training, advertising, promotion, internal sales salaries and expenses to support the channel member. Variable indirect costs are those costs associated with the production of the product mix. Fixed indirect costs cannot easily be traced to channel member and include costs like management salaries and factory overhead. Table 7.1 provides an analysis of three channel members.

	Mass Merchandisers	Brokers	Distributors	Total Firm
Gross Sales	$50,000.00	$100,000.00	$150,000.00	$300,000.00
- Variable Indirect Costs	$30,000.00	$55,000.00	$97,500.00	$182,500.00
Variable Gross Profit	$20,000.00	$45,000.00	$52,500.00	$117,500.00
- Variable Direct Costs	$10,000.00	$20,000.00	$30,000.00	$60,000.00
Gross Contribution	$10,000.00	$25,000.00	$22,500.00	$57,500.00
- Fixed Direct Costs	$2,000.00	$3,000.00	$4,000.00	$9,000.00
Net Contribution	$8,000.00	$22,000.00	$18,500.00	$48,500.00
- Fixed Indirect Costs				$30,000.00
Net Profit				$18,500.00
Contribution Percent	16%	22%	12%	16%

TABLE 7.1: Product Contribution Statement by Channel Member

The third model is the net profit model (Table 7.2). This model is based upon the idea that most of the organizations cost are shared costs and that each channel should be charged with its fair share of these costs.

	Direct	Brokers	Distributors	Total Firm
Annual Sales	139,937,320	428,831,956	91,545,633	$660,314,908.00
Gross Margin Percentage	57%	57%	56%	57%
Gross Profit	79,299,233	242,447,080	51,715,740	$373,462,053.00
Selling Expenses	6,918,637	21,407,615	4,621,761	$32,948,014.00
Promotional Allowances	8,015,778	24,474,013	5,272,625	37,762,416
Cash Discounts	2,090,137	6,397,978	1,360,462	9,848,577
Advertising	2,338,669	7,153,270	1,532,080	11,024,020
General and Administrative Expense	98,662,454	301,879,956	64,502,668	$465,045,080.00
Operating Profit	33,695,130	102,962,033	21,759,332	$158,416,495.00
Operating Margin Percentage	24%	24%	24%	24%

Table 7.2: Net Profit Model

Each of the models presented tells the channel manager something. Each model has strengths and weaknesses associated with it, yet the true benefit is in performing the analysis as the channel manager begins to uncover insights at various steps in the analysis. The models used external comparison of other firms, internal comparisons with the entire organization and peer-to-peer comparisons with channel members.

Managing Supplier Relationships

The supplier-buyer relationship is undergoing a tremendous paradigm shift. Firms are aggressively seeking ideas and ways to obtain competitive advantage. They are seeking ways to reduce costs, improve quality, and decrease the time to deliver products and services to customers. Suppliers are in the unique position to help businesses achieve these objectives through changing the traditional adversarial relationship into a strategic partnership. It has become an entire value chain effort.

Changing Role of the Supplier

The traditional business buying process involved buyers determining which products and services their firms needed to purchase and then finding, evaluating, and choosing among alternative suppliers. The requirement for these products and services was based upon the derived demand of consumer goods being sold. It was a very formalized process driven by professional purchasing agents. However, technology, specifically the Internet, is changing how the purchasing process is being conducted.

This change is more than just using current technology. The paradigm for dealing with suppliers is also changing. The supplier of the 21st century will deal with far fewer but far larger buyers. Each party in the purchasing process will become more dependent on the other. Long term relationships between the supplier and the buyer will develop.

With manufacturers significantly reducing their supplier ranks and with the continued emphasis on cost reduction, suppliers have to question the profitability and viability of this new relationship. This newly evolving relationship doesn't come at the expense of the rate of sales growth for the supplier, and thus the suppliers can still reduce their costs. [8] The cost reduction achieved by the suppliers comes from better inventory utilization and a reduction in selling, general and administrative overhead. It appears that the lower demand uncertainty achieved by the closer working relationship with the manufacturer allows the supplier to improve the effectiveness and efficiency of its operations. The suppliers have the ability to remain profitable.

For the changing supplier relationship to work, however, policy changes at the manufacturer's level are required. These include evaluating purchase orders based upon quality and delivery instead of price, establishing long-term contracts with suppliers, and sharing information on a variety of areas. These policy changes must ensure that a greater level of trust between buyers and suppliers evolves. The benefit of these changes is in a reduction of buffer inventories and elimination of formal paperwork.

A key policy change involves information sharing. Information sharing between the members of the value chain is required. The information sharing is a two way street with the customers providing, for example, sales projections and the supplier providing, for example, shipping information. This information sharing is extremely important to the manufacturer. They need confidence in the ability of suppliers to deliver the material.

To achieve the required delivery of material and reduction of inventory buffers, the concept of JIT purchasing has evolved. The JIT purchasing concept requires policies aimed at single sourcing, the awarding of long-term contracts, localized sources of supply, less frequent use of competitive bidding, and emphasis on a close working relationship with supplier.[9] The benefits of this concept are reduced inventory levels, fewer bureaucratic controls, and reduced incoming inspection. It is evident that the supplier-buyer relationship has two sides. The performance measurement on the buyer's side details the supplier selection criteria. Various tools and techniques show to the supplier how to make JIT purchasing.

Supplier Performance

With the changing role of the supplier-buyer relationship, different measurements are needed to help manage and control the new purchasing process and evaluate the various suppliers. Three commonly used performance measurements are the percent of orders that were shipped late, the percent of items that were rejected, and the delivery lead-time. The delivery reliability can be measured as the average percent of late deliveries. Item quality can be measured as the average percent of unacceptable quality lots shipped in the last year.

Delivery performance has two key dimensions: reliability and speed.[10] The reliability dimension is the delivery of the product when promised, neither early nor late. The speed dimension is defined as the delivery of the product in the shortest time from the point of the order to the point of the receipt by the customer. Time is a key component in these capabilities. The time component is the time to deliver the product and, more importantly, the time to understand the production constraints and tradeoffs and then to commit to a delivery date for the customer. Many measurements can be used for the supplier performance criteria. The performance measurements can be categorized into those related to the product, those related to lead-time, and those related to the supplier firm.

Supply chain management requires a strategic vision aimed at developing a supply base with the best suppliers, and continually driving improvement in these suppliers through long-term arrangements, benchmarking measures, and progression down the learning curve. A key tool in developing partnerships is a well-developed vendor certification and measurement system that strives to reduce the supplier base. The fact that purchasing consumes the majority of the lead-time promised to customers signifies that a high priority should be assigned to managing critical suppliers.

Most firms use intermediaries to bring their products to the market. To accomplish an objective of quickly and efficiently bringing products to the market, they create distribution channels. A distribution channel is defined as a set of interdependent firms involved in the process of making a product or service available for use or for consumption by the consumer.[11] To the manufacturer, these intermediary firms have both advantages and disadvantages that must be recognized and evaluated. These firms represent a partial loss of control for the manufacturing firm yet they provide the firm with greater efficiency in making products available to market.

The channels that are ultimately created will move the goods and services from the production line to the purchasing basket of the ultimate consumer.

Value Chain Strategy for Customer Relationships

Firms are adopting various value chain strategies to build customer relationships. These strategies can enhance customer experience as customers interact with the distribution channels per their preferences. Customers have different channel preferences and requirements. Firms need to make the appropriate channels available to customers for retention, loyalty, and profitability.

Channel Migration

In traditional distribution, the primary goal was the reduction of shipping expenses. At the most basic level, shipping individual parcels, there is no advantage to using a transshipment center. However, when multiple heavy or large units are being sold in the same region, there is a reduction in cost for the company by shipping truckloads rather than individual packages. Depending on the size and weight of the objects being shipped, managers must make the decision between using parcel delivery to customers, less-than-full truck shipping, full-truck-load shipping, or hire their own private fleet.

However, the only benefit brought to customers using this system is the minimization of costs, which may allow the company to lower the costs of the products they sell. There is little to be gained from a long-term relationship standpoint under this old method.[12] Still, the use of distribution centers may be necessary for the company. Customers with low purchasing power or those who require only small lot sizes may place a higher emphasis on low cost than quick distribution. The company can manage these customers through layers of distribution channels to give them that lower cost at the expense of service level. Provided this is the expectation of customers, this method may be the correct one.[13] However, customers buying larger lots with greater purchasing power may require flatter distribution networks. Additionally, these customers may require highly customized products, making it hard to stock the shelves of retail stores with all the necessary products. For these customers, direct marketing may be the best answer.

In all, there are four main factors which are important to consider when choosing a distribution strategy to fit with customer expectations: lot size, waiting time, spatial convenience, and variety. Lot size and waiting time have already been discussed. Spatial convenience reflects the ease with which the customer purchases the product. A customer with a high emphasis on spatial convenience would require an intensive distribution channel, perhaps including direct-to-customer models such as door-to-door sales and online marketing. A customer with less emphasis in this area may find enjoyment in shopping at a mall for the good. Either way, the marketing strategy must fit with the product.

The final dimension to consider is variety. With today's fast-paced modern lifestyle, many customers expect/need their products to be all in one centralized location. These customers need high variety of unrelated products. When customers are willing to spend more time on the purchase, then they expect a high variety of similar goods in a product line. The first case is analogous to a discount retailer, while the second case more fits the mold of a specialty shop.

To create value for the firm and customers, firms can migrate customers to profitable channels. If you identify customer segments with less lifetime value, you can direct them to inexpensive channels such as self-service Web or automated customer service.[14]

Multi-channel Marketing

Firms are becoming highly successful for customer contacts and service due to new prominent marketing channels: text messaging, websites, email, and instant messaging. In addition to these new forms, there are also the more traditional methods of phone and mail. While each of these methods alone can provide benefit to the firm, there is more benefit to be gained through careful selection and use of multiple channels. Known as multi-channel marketing, this strategy can help the company generate prospects and reach customers in a method convenient for them.

For example, a person may call a 1-800 number when they see it advertised on their TV. The information collected at the call center will initialize a second step in the communications process, which could involve an email or a letter.[15] As another example, consider a retail organization with online sales. It has been proven by researchers that customers who have positive experiences tied to a physical store will be less price sensitive online. Thus, a relationship is made more solid through the use of more than one channel of distribution.[16]

As an example of using effective channels, consider the case of Nestle. Normally, in order to generate sales, marketers need to work very hard in lead generation. Through their use of surveys and email, however, they receive high response rates that average about 5 - 10% for posted (mailed) surveys and 10 - 20% from email. Together, the two channels provide the company with a wealth of leads which to work with further.

When planning to use multi-channel marketing involving both a direct channel and a retail channel, there are several steps in the planning process. First, the company needs to plan how customers will be segmented. Will it be based on how close they are to a retail store? Or will it be more focused on customer risk aversion, switching costs, life time value, or price sensitivity? Next, current customers should be assigned to each segment, and a profile should be made for each to determine not only how to best serve them but also how to attract new customers in the same segment.

After this step, the company should make use some kind of predictive model to determine the probability of customers to buy from specific chains. From here, it is time to create the marketing communications strategy. For this strategy, the marketer needs to determine:

- What types of customers are the most valuable (these are often not customers in one segment; rather, they are customers that use a certain combination of segments)
- Which is the channel (or channels) that these customers are both most likely to use and most prefer to use?
- How much will these customers be impacted by shifts in marketing communications?

215

- What are the costs of changing?

Once all of this has been done, the company is free to assign new and potential customers to these segments. As the firm experiences either success or failure with their strategy, the firm should continue to update their information and techniques to create the best possible marketing communications mix.

Multi channel retailers, for example, can develop a channel choice prediction model by using enterprise-level data to assess and predict customers' channel choices over time. This knowledge can be used to manage channels more effectively. As prior channel choices influence current channel choices when customers make repeat purchases, marketers' knowledge of customers' prior channel choices can guide channel management strategies.

Omni-Channel Marketing

Omni-channel marketing takes a holistic view of all channels offered to the consumer and supply chain members allowing consumers switch from one channel to another in their buying experience.[17] For example, consumers may find a product or service in one channel, place order with another channel and delivery from a third channel. In this case, different types of channels refer the way product or information is transferred. Omni-channel marketing covers all phases of the customer's experiential journey and pursues information availability and consistency across all channels involved in the customer's journey. Firms are putting together a combination of many types of channels to match how customers want to search, buy, and return product and services.[18] Omni-channels can provide a seamless shopping experience regardless of the channels used and maximize customer relationships. Thus, firms are managing all available channels and touchpoints such that customers can have consistent and near perfect experience across channels and touchpoints. Firms utilizing omni-channel marketing unifies the total collection of available platforms and touchpoints into one integrated choice environment and create platform and message consistency across the firm.[19]

Section 3. Customer Service Satisfaction

> *"If we do not learn that we are competing in a global economy, that we have to be more competitive than ever before and we have to produce world class quality products and services and we have to add value to our customers, we will not make it."*
>
> John Wallace; The Wallace Company

The customer is the reason for business; they are the most important people in any business and the purpose of work. Customers are human beings with desires, feelings, and emotions. They come to companies with their needs and wants and deserve to be treated in the most courteous and attentive manner that the firm can provide. They are not a statistic or a non-entity, for if the customer is not satisfied, the rest of the firm's performance is moot.

Determining what is customer satisfaction, especially customer service satisfaction and experience, understanding why it is important, and, ultimately, how to measure it, can be a daunting task. Yet, a firm can develop a competitive advantage by understanding customer needs and providing value-added products and service to meet the identified needs.

Defining Customer Satisfaction

Although the concept of customer satisfaction is fundamental, it has been the subject of considerable debate and controversy in the marketing literature. Customer satisfaction has evolved from being defined as simply an attitude to a multifaceted concept of expectation and perception. It must be remembered, however, that customer satisfaction involves both the customer of the product and/or service and the provider of that product and/or service. In this section, the anecdotes and stories of several business leaders begin to shape the importance that customer satisfaction has upon the firm.

Carl Sewell, owner of Sewell Cadillac in Dallas, Texas, believes in lifetime customers. He focuses his attention on the details of how to turn a one-time buyer into a lifetime customer. In his story, Customers for Life, he emphasizes that one's actions with the customer should be viewed as part of the lifelong commitment. Each interaction should be made as pleasant as possible. He states that if you need to be motivated to do this, recall that they are a $332,000 customer.[20]

Jan Carlzon, president of Scandinavian Airlines System (SAS) looks at myriad customer interactions with his firm through various touchpoints. He describes these interactions or routines as "moments of truth". A "moment of truth" is defined as an interaction between an employee of the firm and the customer of that firm. He states that for SAS there are over 50 million "moments of truth" each year. These are the opportunities to demonstrate to the customer the employees' and the firm's commitment to providing outstanding customer service. Customer satisfaction or dissatisfaction is earned at each "moment of truth" and it is through the collection of these "moments of truth" that the customer becomes delighted.[21]

Gayle Hamilton, an area manager for the Pacific Gas & Electric Company, states that "I never let a day go by without spreading the word that our customers are what we are in business for. I try to ask each account representative about what our customers are telling them about our services."[22] Customer satisfaction is the first item on her staff meetings. She uses these meetings and its position on the agenda to demonstrate the importance she places on customer satisfaction.

Stew Leonard, owner of Stew Leonard's, a grocery store in Norwalk, Connecticut, states that something terrible happens when customers fail to say WOW! -- nothing. At Stew Leonard's, they look at each customer as a potential $50,000 asset. An average customer spends $100 per week, $5,000, per year, $50,000 in 10years. Constant focus on customer service through surveys, suggestion boxes, policies, and employee training ensures that the customer always says, "WOW!" This focus has Stew Leonard's earning $3,000 in business per square foot, well above his competitors.[23]

Tom Peters describes the point of sweating the details. The manufacturer's product speaks louder than any other communication or advertising message and surveys have shown that a dissatisfied customer will tell up to seven other people of their problems and is unlikely to purchase the product or service again.[24]

These anecdotes and stories help provide life to the importance of customer satisfaction from the firms' perspective. Achieving customer delight is in the details of the product, business processes, and interaction with the employees. It must be viewed as a long-term survival issue with its benefits occurring over time. Achieving customer delight is in demonstrating the importance of customer satisfaction and in listening to the customer and customer touchpoints. It is in making the customer say "WOW!" that customer satisfaction is ultimately achieved and near perfect customer experience is provided.

Yet, stories and anecdotes do not help firms improve customer satisfaction. Improvement requires a proven methodology to develop understanding of customer issues, a framework to interpret results, and a process to implement corrective actions. A key step in the improvement process is the measuring of customer satisfaction. As firms find it increasingly more difficult to establish sustainable, technology-based competitive advantages, management will have to direct additional attention and resources to the value-added service component.[25] The key to understanding what services to provide and the customer's satisfaction is through timely, continual measurement. Customer satisfaction must be performed on a customer's terms and must emphasize the intangible aspect.

Customer satisfaction is:

$$CP \approx \frac{D}{E}$$

where the variable CP means customer perception, D means delivery, and E means expectation. This is a simple concept to highlight that customer satisfaction is a function of how well the firm delivers on its experiential promises given the expectations that the customer has. It is important to remember that customer satisfaction is not about achieving "happy scores"; it is about understanding wants and needs and exceeding customer expectations. To completely understand the variety of customer wants and needs, it is important to measure everyone's satisfaction in the value chain – all direct and indirect customers – and all members of the distribution channel – dealers, retailers, and wholesalers.

Customer Satisfaction Measurement Model

Many tools exist to measure customer satisfaction. The two tools to be focused on as part of value chain management are the Kano diagram and the ServQual instrument. The Kano diagram is used to highlight the excitement attributes that can be used to increase the numerator, delivery, in the customer perception equation. The ServQual instrument is used to close the gaps between expectation and customer perception.

Kano Diagram

The Kano diagram is used to classify attributes by focusing on their impact on customer satisfaction. In the Kano diagram, the level of satisfaction with a product is measured against the product's performance relative to the competition. The attributes or benefits are categorized as threshold characteristics, performance characteristics, or excitement characteristics.[26] The Kano diagram is shown in Figure 7.5 and highlights the relations between the characteristics and customer satisfaction.

Threshold attributes are those characteristics that provide diminishing returns once the basic expectations have been satisfied. These are the must have attributes and are the admission ticket the organization must have in order to compete in the marketplace. An example would be an accurate billing system or timely payment of commission checks.

Performance attributes keep adding to the customer satisfaction as more of them are provided. In effect, there is no saturation for these characteristics. The performance attributes are labeled need attributes and tend to be segment-specific. Typically, organizations focus on these attributes when they develop their competitive strategy.

Excitement attributes are unexpected benefits. These characteristic produce the Stew Leonard's "WOW!" Excitement attributes are the nice-to-have attributes. It is important for the organization to monitor its competitors for their use of the excitement attributes and to match them when possible. It is also important for the organization to develop their excitement attributes as strategic advantage elements.

Tom Peters states that the organization should add at least ten value-increasing "differentiators" to each product and/or service every 90 days. Adding ten differentiators every 90 days can only be accomplished if the organization clearly understands its customer's wants and needs. An outstanding customer satisfaction system is required.

ServQual Model

ServQual is a tool to determine customer requirements and measure customer service qulaity. It was developed over a multi-year, multi-industry research study. ServQual is a measurement tool. It looks at the "gaps" in the customer delivery system. Figure 7.6 details the five gaps in delivering value to the customer. The first four gaps are gaps or shortfalls within the firm. The fifth gap is the shortfall that is perceived by the customer. By clearly understanding and addressing each of these gaps, the firm can ensure that it is delivering a defined level of service to its customers. Once all the gaps are closed, the customer's expected and perceived level of service should match.

The first gap in the model represents the gap between the customer's expected level of service and management's perception of the customer's expectations. It is management's perception that must change. The focus must be on ensuring that management clearly understand and easily acquires accurate information about the customer's expectations. Market research can be used to close this gap. Linking customer complaints to the failing process and conducting transaction based surveys are but two of the many research tools that can provide information for improvement. Combining this information with the tools and models presented in the previous chapters can provide the analyst and manager with new insights. Yet, this research is effective only if it is first understood and then acted upon. Sharing the information with the customer contact teams is important.

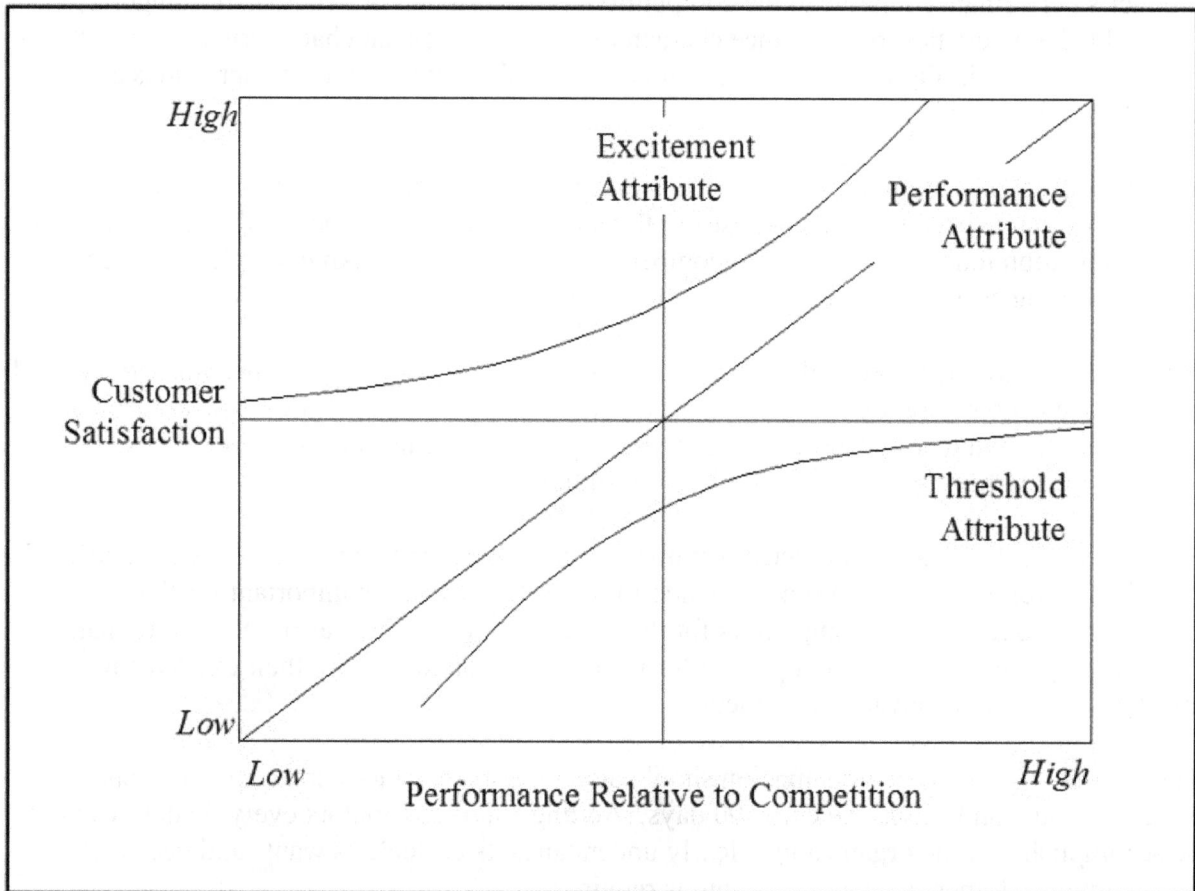

Figure 7.5: The Kano Diagram

The second gap presented in the model is the gap between management's perception and the standards set for the organization. The standards and goals are entirely under the control of the firm. To close this gap requires the team delivering the service to believe that they can deliver the service to the highest standards set for them. As discussed in the supplier section, the firm's policies must be subject to change. It requires the commitment of management to deliver quality services. Stew Leonard has a three-ton granite block at the entrance to his store that states, "Rule 1: The customer is always right. Rule 2: If the customer is ever wrong, reread Rule 1." There is no question about his commitment. LL Bean prominently displays "What is a customer? A customer is the most important person. A customer is not dependent on us, we are dependent on him. A customer is not an interruption of our work; he is the purpose of it. We are not doing a favor by serving him; he is doing us a favor by giving us the opportunity to do so. A customer is not someone to argue or match wits with. Nobody ever won an argument with a customer. A customer is a person who brings us his wants."

The third gap presented in the model is the gap between the specifications and the delivery. This gap points out that just having the specification is not enough. The firm must have a work force willing and able to perform at the defined levels. The work force must feel that they have control over the situation, that they are empowered to deliver the high level of service required. Indirectly, this is affected by the analyst and manager, who together, chose the market or market segment that the firm is serving. If the segment demands certain characteristics, and the firm is unable to meet them, the segment should not have been chosen.

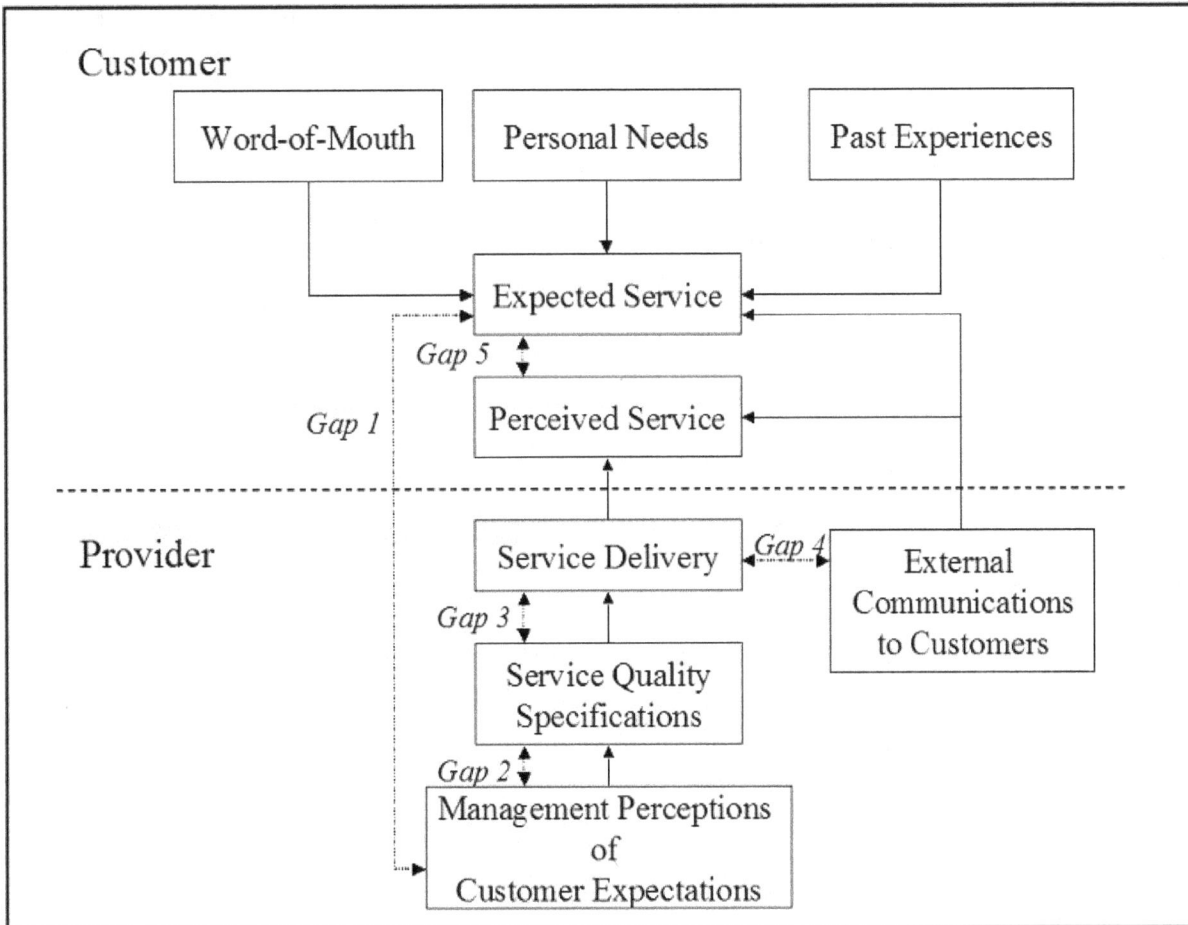

Figure 7.6: Conceptual Model of Service Quality

The fourth gap presented in the model is the gap between the delivery to the customer and the customer's perception of the service to have been received. It is a gap between what is promised and what is delivered. It is a result poor communications. The poor communications can between various departments in the firm or because of the advertising to the customer. By clearly understanding the price elasticity of the product, when an advertising campaign supplemented with a price reduction is introduced, an adequate supply can be ensured to be available in the channel. By understanding the impact of advertising, the potential demand by region can be anticipated.

By closing gaps one through four, the firm can reduce variation in delivery of the service. Now the firm can focus on addressing gap five. Gap five is the gap between expected service and perceived service. The factors that affect expectations include what they have heard from others, what their needs are, what their past experience has been, and what they have heard from the firm. The importance of understanding service quality is because many firms are using services to differentiate their products. For the differentiation to be positive, the firm must understand the measurement requirement. The dimensions identified are listed in Table 7.3.

The customer was the third part of our value chain management discussion. Continually improving customer satisfaction requires management focus. In managing customer satisfaction, it is important to match internal process performance numbers with external sources. While a 99% ship on time record sounds good, it is important to ask the customers if it is. Ask your customers – maybe they wanted delivery sooner but marketing said "No. This is my best date." Therefore, you are shipping and measuring a date that customers are already angry about. You think they are happy with your performance, but no repeat business occurs.

ServQual Dimension	Dimension Definition
Tangibles	The appearance of the physical facilities, equipment, personnel, and communication materials.
Reliability	The ability to perform the promised service dependably and accurately.
Responsiveness	The willingness to help customers and provide prompt service.
Assurance	The knowledge and courtesy of employees and their ability to convey trust and confidence.
Empathy	The caring, individualized attention the firm provides its customers.

SOURCE: Delivering Quality Service by Valarie Zeithaml

Table 7.3: Service Quality Dimensions

What value-enhancing thing can you add to your products to delight your customers and bring them ever tighter into the distribution channel? Remember that you never win an argument with a customer. The key points stressed in this section include:

- Keep score!
- Know who your $332,000 customers are – Treat them that way!
- Don't focus on an average, focus on the worst 10%.
- Survey customers quarterly at a minimum.
- Measure intangible – that is where the differentiator will occur.
- Listen, Listen, and Listen again.
- The key members in the value chain were the various suppliers, the distribution channels members, and the customers.

Understanding Customer Satisfaction with Text Data

Marketing managers need to understand how customers express their opinions after product purchase and to know the level of a customer's satisfaction. In the past, customer satisfaction measures are obtained by structured survey. With the emergence of websites, social media and blog sites, customers are expressing their feelings through these digital information sites. The digital information exists in text data form and provides valuable information and insight for marketing managers. The big data generated through online website as well as social media sites contain a large amount of text data.[27] Marketing managers need to analyze text data and understand the frequency and sentiment of these text postings. The key questions marketing managers have are: Who are generating these online postings? What types of postings are generated by whom? Which social media platforms are generating what type of postings? All these questions can be answered by performing text analysis.

Increasingly, marketing managers have to deal with unstructured data as a part of the big data firms are gathering and analyzing. Unstructured data can be in many forms such as text, audio, and video. Among these sources, text comprises the largest amounts of unstructured data. Most common text data are customer feedback provided as their post-purchase behavior. The traditional sources are responses in survey, focus group transcripts, customer complaints received in call center and customer service operations or emails received from customers. Recently, text data are obtained from website, blog site, social media platforms such as Twitter or Facebook. Customers are also providing text data through various communities where interactions among participants are exchanging opinions and information. Firms are encouraging their customers to engage with various touchpoints of the firm to provide product or service feedback in their own words. Managers are facing the task of processing unstructured text and having to derive meaningful insights for better decision making. When marketing managers receive the large amount of text-based feedback from their customers, they need to figure out what customers are talking about and whether their feedback is positive or negative. Managers have to answer the analytic questions such as what are the main themes or issues discussed in customers' complaints or praises and how often these complaints or praises are made for which products or services. In addition, managers need to evaluated the nature of sentiment and understand the degree of positive or negative comments and responses. Firms need to effectively utilize text data sources to generate the necessary knowledge to make better decisions. To effectively analyze text data, firms are increasingly using text mining analytics performed by marketing managers using artificial intelligence (AI).

For example, IBM Watson provides a number of AI-driven text analytics tools for marketing managers. IBM Watson 'Natural Language Classifier' uses machine learning to analyze text and label or organize data into custom categories. With natural language processing and machine learning, IBM Watson can categorize text with custom labels to automate workflows, extract insights, and improve search and discovery with higher accuracy using less trained data. IBM Watson allows marketing managers to classify short text input into predefined classes using machine learning algorithms. Marketing managers can create and train a classifier to classify texts into predefined classes. Watson knowledge component offers natural language understanding function that provides advanced text analysis using natural language processing. In addition, Watson's 'Knowledge Studio' can discover meaningful insights from unstructured text.

AI can also perform sentiment analysis on social conversations and assess the feelings and evaluations of the firm's products and brands. AI-driven tools can provide sentiment analytics using natural language processing capabilities. For example, IBM Watson 'Empathy' can provide marketing managers with customers' text tone, emotional state, and personality characteristics using text information provided by customers. AI generated sentiment analytics can be combined with the firm generated sentiment analytics to evaluate customers' positive and negative feelings and emotions toward a firm's brands and products. These insights can be used in making marketing decisions related to a firm's products and brands. In addition, IBM Watson offers 'Tone Analyzer' that can analyze emotions and tones in what people write online, such as tweets or reviews through social listening and predict whether customers are happy, sad, or confident. It can also monitor and analyze service conversations of the firm with customers. With AI-driven analytics, marketing managers can respond to customers appropriate and at scale. This information can be integrated to chatbots to build dialogue strategies with customers based on the detected customer tones. IBM Watson 'Assistant' can build conversational interfaces into any applications and more than a chatbot. Most chatbot tries to mimic human interactions that can frustrate customers when a misunderstanding arises. IBM Watson 'Assistant' knows when to search an answer from a knowledge base and when to direct a customer to a human representative.

Section 4. Providing Customer Focused Service for Customer Relationship

"We are approaching a new age of synthesis. Knowledge cannot be merely a degree or a skill ... it demands a broader vision, capabilities in critical thinking and logical deduction without which we cannot have constructive progress."
Li Ka Shing

Call Center Management for Customer-focused Service

In many ways, call centers are one of the most crucial touchpoints for firm to build strong relationships with customers. According to a study, a large percentage of business interactions in America occur in call centers.[28] Clearly, with all of these interactions, the call center has a significant impact on how customers view a company and the relationship that is formed between the two.

The strength of the relationships formed or maintained through these interactions are primarily determined through the service level received by the caller. Poor service and/or a slow response time will result in a loss of goodwill, good service experience, and eventually sales as well. Exceptional service will increase customer's perception of the firm. Thus, the more workers at the call center, the more the firm will get in stronger relationships. However, the cost of labor is by far the most significant cost of operating a call center. Thus, there is a definite trade-off between cost and reward, thus, the firm must strategize as to how they want to serve their customers. To offset some of these issues, phone cueing is often used to better direct calls. Still, customers only have so much patience, and will hang up after a certain period of time. This leads to more than lost revenue; this may lead to a ruined relationship with a customer.

Another important set of variables to conceptualize when designing the firm's call center system is what is called the "service-profit chain." This chain is a multi-step chain that relates a firm's financial performance with customer and employee satisfaction. At the beginning of the chain, the support services and policies set forth by the firm determine an employee's level of satisfaction. When satisfied, employees create value for customers, who in turn become first satisfied, then loyal, and finally contributes strongly to a company's profitability and growth. In support of this, studies find that employee and customer perceptions of quality are highly correlated. Besides the direct route through the service-profit chain, information can be brought up the chain expediently through the contact employees who serve them. As they are on the front lines, these individuals are at the forefront to identify changing trends and notify the firm of these issues.[29] So, can employees be satisfied? In this context, empowerment or extensive rewards may not be necessary to keep employees happy. Instead, the following correlations are considered to have an impact on employee satisfaction in call centers. First, employees tend to treat customers the way management treats them. Thus, if a motivating, energized person is the supervisor of these individuals, the results will be positive for all involved. Second, team support is necessary. With the intense interactions call center employees have on a daily basis, they need support of others to unwind. Third, effective technology not only is a boon to workers, it allows them to work more efficiently, saving on time and money.

Firms recognize that customer support is critical to both keeping existing customers and acquiring new ones. It is important to perform customer support effectively. Call center technologies can effectively alleviate some of the repeat work and increase efficiencies. These technologies allow firms to creation of trouble tickets for customer complaints and provide tracking of trouble tickets from the seminal call through its resolution. Service staff can search data base for similar calls and resolutions while a customer is on the phone. It can also generate call patterns (categorize calls by type, time-to-resolution, escalation percentages, and average call duration). The focus is on customer happiness (soothing the customer) and establishing the process of ensuring that the complaint is recorded and post facto analysis and comparison.

Transition to Cross-channel Contact Center for Customer Service Enhancement

Firms are converting call centers to more integrated customer contact centers for relationship marketing. The biggest source of inefficiency in a contact center is the time spent in getting complete customer information. When customers call they expect the agent to have instant access to details of *all* their interactions with the company. This information, however, usually resides in multiple systems within the firm. One other source of inefficiency is acting on a customer request that involves fulfillment of some sort, such as an order for check books or for setting up the voice mail service on a subscriber's cell phone. Today's contact centers must be a call center, e-contact center or multimedia contact center. The purpose is to provide a personal customer service experience that is individualized to each customer's needs and questions. These allow customers with Internet access to contact customer service representatives through e-mail, online text chatting or real-time voice communications. These contact centers require integration of all customer service functions and change in the culture of customer service representatives. They must be more technically knowledgeable to handle all forms of contact and be able to provide a highly personalized experience that satisfies customers.

A cross-channel contact center must possess two vital capabilities of (1) common incident tracking, reporting, and histories across all channels and (2) use of a common knowledge base across all channels. Unified contact centers deliver competitively superior service at dramatically reduced cost. Each channel becomes more efficient and, over time, more customer interactions are driven to the least expensive and most scalable channel: the Web. Multichannel contact centers also provide companies with clearer insights into their customers' top concerns. These insights are enormously helpful for improving customer care, driving the development of successful products and services, and formulating high-impact relationship marketing strategies.

The transition to a true cross-channel contact center can provide several benefits to the firm.

1. Significantly Improved Customer Satisfaction

Cross-channel contact centers resolve customers' problems faster and provide them with consistent answers regardless of which communication channel they use. That makes them happier. This improved customer satisfaction has a direct impact on customer experience, revenues and profitability. Superior service helps you retain customers, which is more profitable than capturing new ones. Superior service also helps you outsell the competition - especially in markets where there aren't many other competitive differentiators. Superior customer service also means that your company doesn't have to compete on price alone. That premium pricing can have a substantial impact on profitability.

2. Substantially Lower Operating Costs

Cross-channel contact centers are far less expensive to run than separate customer service stovepipes. Calls get resolved faster because service representatives have more complete information about each customer and each incident. At the same time, multichannel contact centers drive a larger percentage of customer interactions away from the phone toward less expensive channels. If customers can get prompt, personalized service via email or chatbot, they'll have less reason to call. And if you take advantage of the superior knowledge-authoring capabilities of the multichannel contact center, even more customers will find answers to their questions by themselves on the Web, where the cost-per-incident approaches zero.

3. Superior Insight into Customers' Wants and Needs

Firms that implement multichannel customer service know more about their customers than those that don't. They can track on a weekly or even daily basis what customers are asking about by phone, email, the Web, and chat. They can respond to that information with better products and more effective marketing campaigns. They can also use that information to further improve service quality and experience, and reduce costs. Firms can immediately notice their customers are suddenly asking about something and the firm can quickly respond with relevant information content, an email broadcast, or advertisements with special offers. The sooner you can pick up on any such trend in customer queries, the better.

4. The Market Requires It

Even if your business strategy doesn't necessarily call for customer service that's competitively superior, unification of your customer service channels is still a must. That's because multichannel contact centers will soon become the norm in just about every market. According to a recent Forrester Research study, 80 percent of companies have made multichannel contact centers a strategic priority. As more companies create such contact centers, customer expectations will rise. You'll need to do it just to keep up. Otherwise, your customers will take their business elsewhere.

5. It's Very Doable

Cross-channel customer service requires some new thinking about how customer communications are managed and how knowledge bases can be most effectively leveraged. But it doesn't require a major IT infrastructure overhaul and it doesn't require exorbitant software licensing fees. That's because today's application hosting providers enable you to acquire all the functionality you need for your multichannel contact center via the Internet. Instead of deploying a complex customer service application in your own data center, you can get all the incident management and reporting capabilities you need right on your PCs using nothing more than your Web browser. Your hosting service provider manages all the software and underlying server infrastructure for you. You just customize your screens, reports, and content to meet your individual business requirements.

Contact Center Automation

Contact center automation features automate various communication processes such as call routing, contact center sales support, web-based self-service, customer satisfaction measurement, call scripting, and cyber agents. Firms can create support help desk that is made up of many geographically dispersed contact centers. This help desk can minimize the time a customer waits on hold for a customer service representative and remain open around the clock (24 hours). It also has the ability of the network to automatically route a customer call to a first available operator. The contact center can be used as a point-of-sale. This offers opportunity to generate additional revenues. Web based self service can play the roles of obtaining general information and tracking specific orders. It can provide FAQs and more choices, "Call me" button as well as live text chat, and customize service screens by customers. New customer satisfaction measurement can monitor customer satisfaction but detailed questions are often personalized to specific customers or segments. Responses are input into databases and included as part of customer profile. It can fine tune communications based on preferences and prioritize product improvements based on value-based segments. Based on customer predictive modeling of similar customers and customer intelligence, firms can provide CSR with a logical series of talking points and guiding a customer service representative through a dialogue with the customer. Online text chatting provides a real-time form of communication between customers and service representatives. Service representatives may be able to handle more than one text chat at a time. Customers can continue to view the website as they chat with a service representative and this allows the service representative to see what the customers are looking at as they pose their questions. Cyber agents are lifelike "representatives" depicted on a company's website as a real person. They combine the best of both personalization and advanced technology.

Total CRM Based Relationship Marketing Template

Template 7.1: Customer Service Gap Analysis

Template 7.1 identifies service gap experienced by customers for each value based segment.

Value Classification Segments	Value Metrics	Current Value [1 = Very Low; 5 = Very High]	Life Time Value (LTV) [1 = Very Low; 5 = Very High]	Potential Value [1 = Very Low; 5 = Very High]	Potential Life Time Value (LTV) [1 = Very Low; 5 = Very High]	Current Service Level [1 = Very Low; 5 = Very High]	Best Service Level [1 = Very Low; 5 = Very High]	Service Gap [Current service level minus Best service level]
Metric 1	Value Segment A	5	5	5	5	5	5	0
	Value Segment B	5	2	5	5	5	4	1
	Value Segment C	3	1	5	2	4	3	1
	Value Segment D	1	3	3	5	3	5	-2
	Value Segment E	1	5	1	1	3	3	0
Metric 2	Value Segment A							
	Value Segment B							
	Value Segment C							
	Value Segment D							
	Value Segment E							
Metric 3	Value Segment A	5	3	5	5	5	5	0
	Value Segment B	5	2	2	2	5	3	2
	Value Segment C	4	3	5	4	3	4	-1
	Value Segment D	2	4	5	4	3	5	-2
	Value Segment E	1	5	1	1	2	2	0
Metric 4	Value Segment A							
	Value Segment B							
	Value Segment C							
	Value Segment D							
	Value Segment E							
Metric 5	Value Segment A							
	Value Segment B							
	Value Segment C							
	Value Segment D							
	Value Segment E							

Template 7.2: Value-based Service Planning Model

Template 7.2 shows how to plan the optimal service level for each value based segment.

Segment Code:	1 SE1	2 NW1	3 SS4	4 MT1	5 SW2	6 LP3	7 JY2
Service Gap (Current service level minus Best service level)							
Service Tier (Solution driven = 4) (Service driven = 3) (Product driven = 2) (Commercial driven = 1)							
Call Center CSR							
Field Service Rep							
Account Manager							
E-Commerce							
Knowledge Sharing							
Targeted Incentives							
Volume Discounts							
Promotions							
Contact Center CSR							
Other							

Template 7.3: An Example of the Value-based Service Planning Model

Template 7.3 shows an example of the value-based service planning model applied to a firm.

Segment Code:	1 SE1	2 NW1	3 SS4	4 MT1	5 SW2	6 LP3	7 JY2
Service Gap (Current service level -Best service level)	- 1	0	2	-2	0	1	0
Service Tier (Solution driven = 4) (Service driven = 3) (Product driven = 2) (Commercial driven = 1)	4	2	3	4	1	2	2
Call Center CSR			X		X		
Field Service Rep		X	X	X		X	X
Account Manager	X		X	X			
E-Commerce	X	X	X	X	X	X	X
Knowledge Sharing	X	X	X	X		X	X
Targeted Incentives	X			X			
Volume Discounts						X	X
Promotions					X		
Contact Center CSR					X		
Other							

Real World Application Cases

Case 7-1: Dell[30]

Dell computers has long been a model for the PC industry, as well as any company wishing to engage in direct sales. The Dell model is based on direct sales of build-to-order machines through phone and online sources. This mass customization method became popular, and helped propel Dell computers from a minor player to among the top firms in the industry, especially in their favorite target segment, business customers.

However, that was ten years ago. During the past decade, many competitors have learned from the Dell model and have taken away some of the companies key competitive advantages. While Dell keeps firm control over its supply chain, it failed to realize that this alone could not keep the company at the top of the market. A telling quote by CEO Kevin Rollins alludes to the improper focus at the company. "There are some organizations where people think they're a hero if they invent a new thing," he said in 2003. "Being a hero at Dell means saving money."

Thus far, this attitude has only hurt the company. In keeping with the corporate goal of cost reduction, the company has made decisions that critics have said undermine customer service and product quality. While the company is now trying to regain consumer confidence through the investment of $115 million in service, it is too late for some business customers, who have already jumped ship from the company. Additionally, the company's main sales tactic (lure customers in with cheap computer deals, then convince them to buy the more expensive models) has been working poorly as of late. This can be attributed to the computing power of today's PCs; many customers feel they can get the level of performance they want from generic store models, and have no need for a customized product.

Another problem for the company is the increasing popularity of notebook PCs. While the company does sell them, their suppliers in Asia do not have exclusive contacts with Dell. Thus, other computer companies are using the same parts, and thus taking away from the Dell's claim of superior quality. While the some in the company would like to change tactics, there is a fear that admitting that the "Direct from Dell" PC no longer carries an advantage to customers would be disastrous to both buyers and Wall Street. The company has tried diversifying itself into Television sales, but they have yet to achieve the level of product sophistication the company needs.

There is a strange silver lining for the company, however. While Dell continues to have problems in America, they have recently had a lot of success in a previously weak country for them, Germany. Unit sales have risen 13.6% in the second quarter compared to the previous year, they have moved from 5th place in the market to 3rd, and they were one of only two companies in the top ten to achieve sales growth in this period.

How has this happened? Insiders point to freedom that was given to managers in Germany. The direct sales model in Germany closely follows that of its American counterpart, but managers have been allowed to double their sales force to better serve their corporate customers. Additionally, the managers learned that Germans prefer to buy their computers from native speakers (although they don't care if they have non-natives for tech support). Thus, when the company made a new center for small businesses and government sales, they chose the German city of Halle instead of the Slovak capital of Bratislava. This racked up major PR points for the company. Additionally, the German engineers and gamers enjoy being able to customize their own PCs, rather than the alternative: to buy identical discount chain PCs. Promotions for gamers especially have been met with success.

Case Questions

1. Dell is currently using a multi-channel strategy to market to its customers. What channels does Dell use? Comment on the effectiveness of this strategy.

2. How could Dell improve its direct sales model?

3. Dell is doing better in Germany than in most of its other locations. What can Dell learn from its successes in Germany? Can it apply these lessons elsewhere?

Case 7-2 Dollar Tea Club[31]

Dollar Tea Club is a small, subscription-based business headquartered in Toronto, Ontario. The firm offers low-cost tea subscription services that allow subscribers to sample a wide range of tea blends delivered to their home monthly without a contract. As the firm considers the ongoing satisfaction of its subscriber base as critical for the firm's success, Dollar Tea Club puts quality customer service as the top priority. Most of the firm's customers contact Dollar Tea Club through email, which is the main touch point of the firm. Anytime of the day the firm receives the emails containing similar questions regarding such topics as subscription plans, delivery coverage or brewing times. As the firm is overwhelmed with reoccurring customer questions delivered by email, Dollar Tea Club wants to provide consumers with the information they seek without needing to leave the company website. The firm wants to find ways to communicate with subscribers more efficiently, resolving issues and answering questions before the user had even left the website instead of copying and pasting the same answer into several emails.

Dollar Tea Club developed and launched a web-based chatbot to handle common customer questions. Dollar Tea Club develops a web-based chatbot that can answer consumer questions directly and provide context-sensitive product recommendations. Visitors to the firm's website can interact with "Teabot". Through a natural language interface, users can ask the chatbot about delivery timelines, obtain tea recommendations for specific events, and even have the chatbot tell them a tea-themed joke. Teabot also provides a tea suggestion based on the customer's preferences and answer user-specific questions in real-time. Using the AI based solution Teabot, most consumers of Dollar Tea Club can obtain immediate answers to many questions and receive tea recommendations leading to improved user experience and higher revenue. Almost 80 percent of the firm's email inquiries are now instantly answered online with Teabot.

Case Questions

1. How do customers benefit from Dollar Tea Club's web-based chatbot?

2. How would Dollar Tea Club's online marketing affect traditional and other online tea selling firms such as Teavana.com? What problems do you see with its strategy?

3. What is the impact of this online marketing strategy on dollar Tea Club's relationship with current and potential customers?

Case 7-3: Caffé Nero[32]

Each year Caffé Nero runs four quarterly campaigns revolving around two seasonal promotions (Christmas and summer), and two specific coffee-focused campaigns as well as a number of smaller product launches. The challenge for the coffee house was to make its customers more aware of these by providing personal, omnichannel engagement that would result in greater customer participation and increased revenue. Caffé Nero needed to provide more personalized, timely communications, increase awareness of seasonal promotions and turn online communications into increased loyalty and physical customer spend using the large database of customers that contains its existing customer base.

Caffé Nero deployed a three-point personalized communications strategy, based on segmenting with persona and behavioral mapping, which at every touchpoint provided Caffé Nero with more and more valuable data. Caffé Nero identified that its customers viewed visits to its stores as more of an experience than simply an amenity-based function. As such, it identified pre-paid card holders (existing and future), as a core focus for its marketing communications push. To turn its new customers and card holders into brand advocates, it used IBM Watson Campaign Automation to deploy a three-point personalized communications strategy, based on persona segmenting and behavioral mapping, which at every touchpoint provided Caffé Nero with more and more valuable data. In turn, this data enabled it to take an increasingly segmented and laser-focused approach to its future customer communications.

As soon as a Caffé Nero customer signs up to the database and pre-paid card initiative, a welcome email is delivered to start the engagement process. In addition to informing the customer about offers and opportunities, these initial emails gather personal information such as frequency of use and preferences that are pivotal to building on the persona mapping process. These automated messages allow Caffé Nero to engage with its registered customers on a regular basis, providing personalized information on existing card balances, but also informing customers of seasonal updates and new releases. Caffé Nero now sends triggered, real-time email reminders when its customers' cards are lower than £2, so they are less likely to run out of credit or miss that mid-morning coffee hit.

Case Questions

1. How do customers benefit from Caffé Nero's online marketing?

2. What specific marketing performance areas would be affected by Caffé Nero's online marketing? What problems do you see with its strategy?

3. How Caffé Nero's online marketing can contribute to building customer equity and increasing relevance to customers?

Chapter 8. Traditional IMC Touchpoints for Customer Relationships

Promotion is a marketing mix variable that can be adjusted easily and relatively quickly. Understanding the strategic impact of this variable will help marketing managers make sound promotion decisions. With increased global competition, more and more firms are forced to manage the promotional mix effectively to communicate with their customers. In this chapter, issues related to traditional integrated marketing communication (IMC) touchpoint management are discussed.

Section 1. Managing Traditional Promotional Mix

"Setting a goal is not the main thing. It is deciding how you will go about achieving it and staying with that plan."
            Tom Landry

Relationship marketing calls for more than developing a good product, pricing attractively, and making accessible to target markets. Firms need to position products in their target customers' mind by promoting them effectively. Marketing managers manage a complex system of integrated marketing communication and promotion. Firms promote their products throughout the value chain. Customers engage in word-of-mouth communication with other customers and publics providing feedback to other groups. Traditionally, promotion mix consists of four major tools: advertising, sales promotion, publicity, and personal selling. Recently, firms are adopting a variety of Web-based and social media based promotions as a part of their overall promotional mix.

Promotional Mix Decision and Performance

After determining the total budget, firms face the task of allocating them over the five promotional tools of advertising, sales promotion, personal selling, publicity, and Web-based promotion. Within the same industry, firms can differ in how they allocate their promotional budget. It is possible to achieve a given promotional objective with various mixes of advertising, sales promotion, personal selling, publicity, and Web-based promotion. Firms are continually searching for ways to improve promotional efficiency by substituting one promotional tool for another. As the Internet and World-Wide-Web become more popular, firms begin to increase expenditures on Web-based promotion. One promotional tool can be used to support other promotional tools. Many factors can influence the choice of promotional tools. These factors include nature of each promotional tool, type of product and market, push-versus-pull strategy, target customers, and product life-cycle stage.

Nature of the Promotional Tool

Each promotional tool has its unique characteristics and costs. Managers need to understand these advantages and associated costs in selecting them. Advertising is a highly public message and can repeat a message many times allowing customers comparison of the messages from various competitors. Advertising can present visual information about products and company. Advertising is an efficient method to reach geographically dispersed buyers at a lost cost per exposure. Personal selling is most effective in building up buyers' preference, conviction, and action. Personal selling offers interactive communication with immediate feedback and potential of developing long tern relationship with customers. Sales promotion can provide useful information, direct inducement to purchase, and added value to customers. It can induce a stronger and quicker response but is not effective in building long-term brand preference. Publicity is considered by customers as most credible source and can reach many prospects. Web-based promotion offers highly interactive environment with customer initiation and active voluntary involvement.[1] It can provide a large quantity of information and allow purchase a much lower price due to tax and cost advantages.

Type of Product and Market

The effectiveness of promotional tools varies between consumer and industrial markets. Consumer goods firms allocate most of their budget to advertising followed by sales promotion, personal selling, Web-based marketing, and publicity. On the other hand, industrial firms spend most of their promotional budget on personal selling, followed by sales promotion, advertising, publicity, and Web-based marketing. As more consumers and organizational buyers are purchasing products through electronic commerce, Web-based promotion will gain a larger share of promotional budget replacing traditional advertising or personal selling. The relative importance of promotional tools in consumer and industrial markets is derived from empirical studies such as ADVISOR project.

Push versus Pull Strategy

The promotional mix decision is heavily influenced by the choice of the push and pull strategy. Push strategy uses sales force trade promotion to push the product through the channels. Producer heavily promotes to wholesaler, then wholesaler promote aggressively to retailers, then retailers aggressively to consumers. A pull strategy requires a large advertising budget directed toward the consumer in order to build up consumer demand.

Target Customers

Depending on the stages in response hierarchy of target customers, promotional tools should be chosen. According to the AIDA model, one of the best-known response hierarchy models, the buyer passes through the stages of attention, interest, desire and action.[2] The cost effectiveness of various promotional tools varies at different stages of buyer response hierarchy. Advertising and publicity are most effective at awareness and interest stages, while sales promotion and personal selling are most effective at desire and action stages. Web-based promotion is equally effective for customers at interest, desire and action stages.

Product Life Cycle Stages

The promotional tools vary in their cost effectiveness at different stages of the product life cycle. In the introduction stage, advertising and publicity are most cost effective, followed by sales promotion and personal selling. In the growth stage, promotional expenditures for all tools are reduced taking advantage of increased sales due to word of mouth. In the maturity stage, sales promotion, advertising, personal selling and Web-based promotion all become more important. In the decline stage, sales promotion and Web-based promotion remain strong, advertising and publicity are reduced, and personal selling is minimized.

In making effective promotional mix decision, firms need to assess and evaluate current level of expenditures of the various promotional mixes and their effectiveness. The promotional expenditure level of various promotional mixes by market, product, and customers can provide valuable information in assessing the effectiveness of the promotional spending. The next section provides such an analysis and discusses the implications of the analysis results.

With the given total promotional budget, firms are allocating their money over different promotional tools. Figure 8.1 evaluates the proportion of the promotional budget expended for the four most heavily used tools for this firm. For this illustration, the Midwest region was selected. The pie chart shows that consumer promotion is most heavily used with 54.5 percent. Sales force is second with 32.9 percent. Advertising is 11.0 percent, followed by the free goods program with 1.6 percent. Similar analysis can be performed for other regions and products. This type of analysis provides managers a tool to assess promotional efficiency of various promotional tools in different market segments.

All Products : All Customers : All Channels : Actual (Local) : Rolling 12 Months

▦ Free Goods   ▨ Sales Expenses   ■ Consumer Promotions   ▢ Advertising

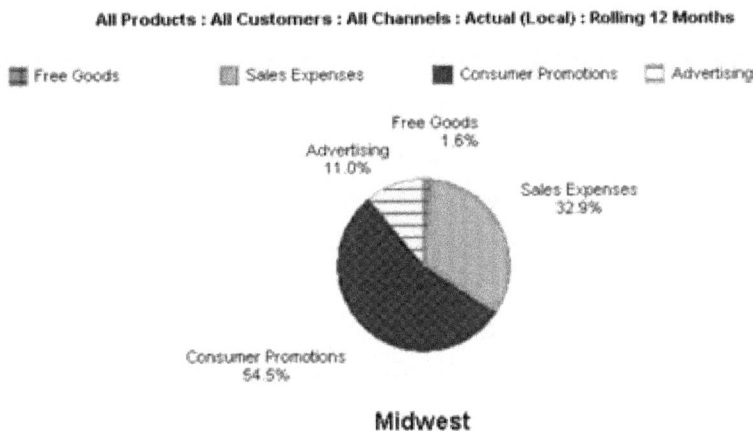

Midwest

Figure 8.1: Promotional Expense Allocation

Advertising Effect

Advertising is one of the promotional mixes that firms use to direct persuasive communications to target buyers. It is characterized by non-personal, one way, and paid form of marketing communication. It is quite effective in influencing customer attitude, purchase intention, and purchasing behavior. Advertising program is developed using a five-step procedure: objectives setting, budget decisions, message decision, media decision, and advertising evaluation. In developing advertising program, these five decisions should start with the target market. The most difficult step for most marketing managers to understand and perform is the advertising evaluation. Advertising effectiveness is hard to accurately measure especially on sales. This difficulty can be attributed to various characteristics of advertising effects. Advertising effects occur over time and can exhibit a long-term carryover influence. In addition, advertising effects may be non-linear and interact with other marketing mix variables.

237

Many advertising response models have been developed. In understanding the advertising response model, managers need to understand shape, dynamics, and an interaction.[3] Shape represents the long-term level of sales expected at each level of promotion. The shape can be linear, S-shaped, or non-linear. Dynamics shows the rate of increase or decrease of sales when advertising level is increased or decreased. It's important to evaluate the level of sales without advertising as well as the maximum sales with increased sales. Interaction represents the interactive effects of advertising with other marketing mix variables.

Considering the advertising effect, firms must decide how much to spend on advertising. Several common advertising methods have been identified and studied.[4] These methods are similar to total promotional budgeting method. The most commonly used method is the objective and task method with 74% industrial firms and 63% consumer product firms reporting the use of this method. Other approaches used are percentage of sales method and competitive parity method. In determining advertising budget, the factors to be considered are: stage in the product life cycle, market share and customer base, competition, advertising frequency, and product substitutability.

Section 2. Managing Integrated Marketing Communications as Customer Touchpoints

> *"We can believe that we know where the world should go. But unless we're in touch with our customers, our model of the world can diverge from reality. There's no substitute for innovation, of course, but innovation is no substitute for being in touch, either."*
> Steve Ballmer

Integrated Marketing Communication (IMC)

Traditional IMC focuses on using multiple sources of both traditional media and other means of communication to integrate all outgoing messages for consistency and synergy.[5] In this perspective, a firm takes firm driven inside-out perspective. Under customer relationship marketing, firms need to manage the firm-customer interface effectively focusing on customer focused IMC.

The IMC efforts are directly linked to various touchpoints or channels utilized by marketing campaigns. Touchpoints include traditional touchpoints such as television and newspaper, online touchpoints such as websites, and social media touchpoints such as Twitter and other social network services. In understanding the ongoing customer interactions and marketing communications, it is important to evaluate the nature of interaction and the type of messages exchanged in the interaction process.[6] In the traditional touchpoints, the interaction is characterized as primarily direct from and controlled by the marketer. The main component is the marketer-generated contents in the form of advertising and publicity. Traditional word of mouth (WOM) communication enters in this context. The traditional WOM communication involves inter-consumer communications pertaining to the organic exchange of product and brand-related marketing messages with or without direct influence by marketers through traditional means such as advertising and promotion.

For the online touchpoints, the interaction is mixed and less controllable by marketers. Along with marketer-generated contents and traditional WOM communication, online touchpoint interaction generates e-WOM communication that includes online product evaluations and comments by marketing firms and customers. For the social media touchpoints, the nature of interaction is completely different. The interaction can be characterized as primarily indirect and uncontrollable by the marketing manager. The message and contents are also becoming more diverse. In addition to the firm-generated content, traditional WOM, and e-WOM, user-generated content in the form of comments, blog postings, and video are increasingly dominant and important. These new user-generated contents offer an opportunity for firms as they provide a new source of information and an avenue of interacting with customers.

Marketing managers are facing a significant challenge in finding direct causes of sales increase. It is a difficult task to isolate the effect of any specific marketing activity on brand, customer, and sales. It is a difficult task to identify the influence of specific marketing action on customer behavior. One of the specific actions that has received significant attention is promotional campaign effect. Promotional campaign can be a component of integrated marketing communication and can be done through various promotional modes including traditional media such as newspaper, T.V. as well as digital media of web, social media, and mobile.[7] Regardless of the media used by firms, marketing managers need to evaluate campaign effectiveness. Firms need to evaluate the effectiveness of whole promotional campaign, specific advertising, or different advertising copy. At each customer level, firms also have to determine whether to send a promotional message to a particular customer, and which message to send if managers decide to send a message to that customer for relationship enhancement. In addition, firms can decide which customers not to send the message as those customers would purchase their products anyway.

Firms must answer what is the impact of promotional campaign and advertising on sales, brand and customers. Firms can use A/B testing with uplift modeling to determine which campaign is more effective. A/B testing refers to standard scientific experiment conducted to track responses of participants. This experiment allows managers to evaluate the direct cause of customer responses and product sales. Managers need to design an experiment that will provide accurate results.

Optimizing Total Integrated Marketing Communication Effectiveness

The linear optimization model can be used to develop a total IMC budget allocation model. The optimization model maximizes the objective function to achieve optimal IMC budget allocation for a firm. Marketing managers achieve maximization of customer contact and frequency using the optimization model. Additionally, IMC budget allocation can be made optimally using this model. Considering the firm's marketing strategy, available budget, and selected touchpoint and media availability, the linear optimization modeling can maximize the marketing objective set by marketing managers. Table 8-1 shows an example of a firm's IMC mix table. This table provides information regarding the touchpoint media type, expected number of customers reached, cost of campaign, time availability, and exposure quality rating.

Touch Point/Media Type	# of Customer Reach per Campaign	Campaign Cost	Maximum # of Effective Campaigns	Exposure Quality	Expected Campaign Profit
TV Campaign	1,000	50,000	5	40	60,000
Newspaper Campaign	1,300	10,000	10	30	15,000
Magazine Campaign	2,000	30,000	2	45	35,000
Radio Campaign	600	2,000	20	10	3,500
Ad word Campaign	1,500	3,000	5	15	7,000
Mobil Ad Campaign	3,000	5,000	10	25	8,000
Social Media Campaign	2,500	5,000	10	35	9,000

Table 8.1: IMC Mix Table

Machine learning algorithms can provide marketing managers the optimal solutions for decision making.[8] AI powered optimization offers various advantages over traditional A/B testing.[9] AI powered optimization has the following advantages over traditional A/B testing.[10] AI is faster and more efficient than A/B testing as traditional split testing is time consuming with several different variables and resource intensive. With AI, marketing managers can focus on strategic aspects based on the optimized solution continuously in real time. Another advantage is that AI enables marketing managers to experiment with a potentially infinite number of variables instead of a limited number of variables used in traditional A/B testing. AI also enables marketing managers to follow each individual customer and increase the effect of the firm's optimization efforts resulting in higher performance.[11] AI can help marketing managers in conversion rate optimization.[12] AI relies on two different methods to improve conversion rates by displaying persuasive message and enhancing A/B testing methodology to derive better results. AI with its machine learning capabilities constantly makes use of evolutionary algorithms, big data, and predictive analytics. AI can improve the productivity of A/B testing by delivering results with a fewer number of consumers and grasping the intricacies of multivariate testing faster with expedited testing cycles. AI powered tool can evaluate different elements of an ad from all parts of the consumer's purchase funnel and compares performance for different messaging and images.[13] Marketing managers can use machine learning for image and video recognition to break down different variables such as concept or copy and evaluate which variables influence performance. Marketing managers can create all the variations and test them using AI driven algorithms that continuously collect all user data and deliver the best option to each individual consumer.[14]

IMC Driven Relationship Marketing Strategy

Under relationship marketing, firms need to manage firm-customer interface effectively. In managing this interface, firms first find out how and what customers want to hear from your firm.[15] A firm's promotional campaign must target customer who both want to hear about the firm's particular offer as well as are qualified buyers. A firm sends promotional offers or messages only to those who are more likely to respond to them. This will increase hit rates and promotional effectiveness. In addition, this targeted approach can minimize the disturbance to customers. Firms also send messages only to those who are qualified for the offer. This would minimize customers' disappointments when they receive an offer and find out that they are not simply qualified for the offer. This will also save the cost of sending the offer to unqualified customers. The use of customer analytics and insights provide a win-win promotional strategy.[16]

The Multi-Channel MARCOM Process[17]

To effectively manage marketing communications to build customer relationships, firms need to identify relevant factors that differentiate among customers who use different channels and touch points. Using these models and analytics, firms can develop effective communication strategy for existing customers. Firms can also predict the right communication strategy for prospects and new customers. The multi-channel MARCOM process shows step-by-step procedures for establishing effective marketing communication in a multi-channel environment. The following shows these steps.

Step 1 is estimating a segment-level channel choice model. Managers need to identify variables to be included in the model. These variables are factors that drive channel choice, help classify prospects and customers into segments, and measure the efficiency of the marketing communication expenditures and activities. Factors typically included in the channel choice model are customers' price expectations, type of products to be purchased, convenience, switching cost, prior channel choice, and customer goals during his or her shopping experience. Variables that measure the number, nature, or dollar amount of communication expenditures also need to be included.

Step 2 is assigning each existing customer to a segment and profiling the segments. After the channel choice model is developed and estimated with existing data, developed customer analytics can be used to assign customers to a specific segment. A profile of each segment can be created along with the description of the demographics and historical behavior patterns of the segments. This profiling will help firms understand the customers who are using various types of channels and touch points. It will also help firms determine which prospective customers to target and which segment to assign new customers.

Step 3 is predicting the probability of channel choice over time. In this step, firms predict the customer's future channel choices and direct marketing communication activities accordingly. Various customer analytics models can be used for prediction.

Step 4 is developing a segment-specific communication strategy. In this step, firms can develop marketing communication strategy for existing customers knowing the probability of choosing certain type of channels and touch points. Marketing communication strategy can be developed in consideration of the following factors. Firms need to prioritize various market segments in terms of overall value and select the customer types that generate the most value to the firm. After careful assessment of the current marketing communication tactics used for this segment, firms should develop marketing communication strategy consistent with a customer's intrinsic channel choice preferences and tendencies. Another factor is the degree to which customers respond to marketing communication activities and the nature of the response. Finally, the costs associated with different marketing communication activities and expected returns need to be considered.

Affiliation and Lock-in

Promotion activities truly are an uphill battle in today's information-driven age. Today, the issue is no longer whether promotion activities can find a medium and an audience. Instead, the issue revolves around whether or not these messages will be heeded, ignored, or even perceived. Information overload is a major impediment to the marketers of today.

In order to stand out in one's promotion activities (especially on the internet), a company needs to gain some form of competitive advantage. Two methods to do this, which tend to work well together, are through the strategies of affiliation and lock-in.

Affiliation is more than caring for or adding value for customers. Instead, affiliation is making the decision to trust the customer by being upfront with information, even when it is potentially damaging for the company. While this may be counter-intuitive, the extra information provided to the consumer establishes a sense of fairness between company and customer. From this beginning, better customer relationships can be the long-term result. An example of this is Progressive Auto Insurance. Not only do they provide their own rates, but also they provide the rates of competitors regardless of whether their rates are higher or lower. This "customer centric" philosophy creates loyalty in customers.

If a company wishes to increase its affiliation with customers, there are several possible electronic methods of doing so. All of these strategies appeal to the decision maker's "cognitive dimension of loyalty." Three are listed below:

- Creating navigational services that solve problems, not just pushing products.
- Providing comprehensive information.
- Adding decision support software on content.

In addition to the three methods listed above, marketing managers are increasingly recognizing the importance of building 'community' of customers to create the sense of "belonging" to the brand or firm in the sense of human relationships. Many managers are seeking to create not just a set of customers who purchase their products but a community of customers who share information and experiences of the product or service with other customers and the firm. Customer communities provide participants a forum for exchange of common interests, shared experiences, tips, solutions, and relationship enriching dialogues.[18] Through these communities, firms can enhance the brand, gain increased involvement from customers, and create long-term relationships. Some examples of such communities include Pillsbury's website offering recipes and cooking tips and Microsoft Xbox video game community.

Lock-in is a different strategy associated with the "behavioral dimension of loyalty." In this strategy, customers can become economically forced to remain with the same company due to the cost of switching from one brand of product of website to another. From a marketing standpoint, these economically driven feelings can be further developed into customer loyalty through the use of some of the strategies given below:

- Building an installed base of customers.
- Capturing customer through product design and promotion.
- Leveraging customer commitment by selling complementary products.

Together, many of the most effective companies use these strategies in conjunction with each other to best enhance customer loyalty.[19] The affiliation strategy works best when customers are in the pre-buy information gathering stage, while the lock-in strategy works best to keep customers within the company after they have made their initial purchases.

Loyalty Programs

One subject for firms to consider when attempting to maximize customer loyalty through promotional means is the use of loyalty programs along with loyalty cards.[20] The loyalty programs encourage repeat purchases through a formal enrollment process and the distribution of benefits. Loyalty programs are used for both B2C and B2B customers. Examples of such programs include Hallmark's Gold Grown Card program, Harrah's Total Rewards, Cracker Barrel's Old Country Store Neighborhood program, and Verizon's Business Link loyalty program. Loyalty cards are cards that customers use to derive some kind of benefit from the company, usually monetary.

Those in favor of loyalty cards name some reasons why they are effective. First, the customer is making a conscious decision to associate themselves with the company. Every time the customer shows their card to get privileges, they are reinforcing the idea that they "belong" with the company. Secondly, these cards give benefits to customers, which keep them satisfied. These benefits can be in the form of savings, special shopping nights, or even access to a preferred service from the company. The value and savings customers receive from the company leads to feelings of reciprocity; in other words, customers feel obligated to patronize a store they feel they have derived value from.

From the data, it seems that the best way to enhance loyalty through the use of these cards is by offering significant discounts on promotional items. In exchange for the savings consumers are receiving, they are usually making larger overall purchases in a single trip than their counterparts who are not using loyalty cards. Additionally, loyalty cards can be made more effective if the company is willing to talk to companies in other industries to create loyalty cards for multiple companies. Because the multi-industry card means more for the consumer than would a card that is only good in one store, the customer is likely to (a) derive more value from the card, and (b) be constantly reminded of all the companies involved in the card every time they use it.

Loyalty programs need to be implemented selectively. These programs work best under the conditions when they support the brand's value proposition, add value to the product or service, and are targeted to high lifetime value customers. Firms cherish customer loyalty and develop various loyalty programs to discourage churn. Loyalty can be considered to be fragile and changing. In developing loyalty programs, firms must clearly define loyalty and how to measure it. Firms can define and measure loyalty in many different ways.[21] Loyalty can be defined as repurchase, frequency of repurchase, percentage of category purchase, retention, and quality of relationships. Different definitions may be appropriate depending on the type of product and industry. For example, retention rate can be important loyalty indicators for firms with time-limited contracts such as cellular phone service. Quality of relationships are important for infrequent purchase situations with products of high dollar value and long usage life. Firms need to develop marketing programs and select appropriate marketing channels and touchpoints to attract preferred customers and discourage undesirable customers. Firms should focus on customers who can be loyal. It is important to identify which customers can be loyal. Customers who are most likely to be loyal are those who have few options and value relationships with preference of avoiding switching. Some customers are difficult to achieve loyalty or too expensive to build loyalty. Common ways to build loyalty include offering a unique product or service, loyalty-focused segmentation and targeting, calling customers after sale to thank and offer custom options, educating the customer on use, staying in touch with customers through various touchpoints, and implementing incentive programs such as point system. Even with successful loyalty programs, some customers may be attracted to competitors and churn. In this case, firms must develop counter strategy for churning customers. To deter defection, firms need to detect early signs of customer defection and act quickly. Firms can use promotions and special offers to encourage continuity. If that effort fails, firms need to develop and implement win back programs that target customers who defected to competitors and are still considered to have high lifetime value.

Customization Strategy

Customization refers to the capability to customize customer communication based on knowledge of preferences and behaviors. Firms can provide tailored messages, recommend customized product/service offerings, and implement invitation marketing. Tailored messages are messages tailored to a particular customer or customer segment. Variable insertion can be use to insert the customer's name into the message. Personalizing content can be developed using detailed customer data such as customer profile data, past purchases, clickstream data and web survey response.

Invitation Marketing refers to delivering instantaneously direct messages to the customer via television or in-store digital displays. For example, upon entering a store, customers would "ask" for personalized ads by swiping their loyalty card in front of a digital signage promotional display, or by just walking up to it, in the case of a radio frequency identification-enabled card. Customers could use handheld devices, kiosks, or large-screen displays to retrieve information they may have saved while surfing the Web, such as product comparisons or shopping lists. In addition to tailoring offers to individuals, sensors could help retailers track the traffic in front of dynamic promotions. The format and content of the product messages and the videos on these displays could be changed in real time as customers linger and appear receptive to receiving more information. Firms that use new technologies to create relevant, real-time customer dialogues will likely be better positioned to keep up with their demanding and elusive customers, will outpace the competition in providing better customer experience, and will improve profitably in the years to come.

Event-based marketing is considered as time-sensitive marketing. It combines personalization with process design and ensures that the right action targets the right customer at the right time. This method is based on a clearly defined set of high-profile events. The goal is to react to customer events in near real-time, soon after the actual event occurs. It requires the use of complex data mining capabilities and understanding of possible events and their desired outcomes.

Automated campaign management allows firms to target smaller customer segments and increase the number of campaigns. This allows firms to ensure continuous interaction with as many customers as possible with personalization and customization in messages, frequency, and contact intervals.

Cross-Selling and Up-selling

Cross-selling is the act of selling a product or service to a customer as a result of another purchase. Up-selling motivates existing customers to trade up to more profitable products. Benefits are increased revenue by selling more to existing customers and being less costly than acquiring a new customer

Challenges of using cross-selling and up-selling is evaluating which products will increase, rather than decrease, a customer's overall profitability, and identifying the right candidate. Simply cross-selling an unprofitable product might actually render that customer less profitable than they were prior to the cross-sell. Right cross-selling means "selling the right product to the right customer". Not every customer is a good candidate for cross selling/up selling. Understanding the ways by which customers evaluate how and whether to respond to such relationship marketing activities is critical.

Section 3. Managing Sales Force as a Customer Touchpoint

> *"When you can measure what you are speaking about, and express it in numbers, you know something about it, but when you cannot measure it ... your knowledge is of a meager and unsatisfactory kind."*
> Hayes and Wheelwright

For obvious reasons, the sales area is also considered to be a high-impact relationship marketing area. As the primary distribution point for most firms, sales must rely on the customer information generated by marketing and on customer satisfaction fostered by service. The sales group typically generates and maintains the personal relationship that exists between the customers and the firm. In this capacity, the sales representatives are in a position to gather much useful information about the customers that can be passed onto the other business units as well in the context of relationship marketing.

245

Sales Activity Coordination

For effective relationship marketing, sales activity coordination is needed. Firms need to establish a mechanism for understanding, coordinating, and communicating multiple sales activities to the same customer. For better coordination, overall account managers who direct all sales efforts to each client need to be identified. The contact management systems need to be available across business lines.

Firms need to understand and implement best-practices for coordinating sales activity. Sales and deal teams are dynamic and flexible, pulling specialist resources as needed. Relationship managers understand the importance of recording sales contacts in the contact repository for use by all sales personnel. In the case of independent sales efforts across business lines, formal and informal communication mechanisms are mandated to ensure adequate communication on independent sales efforts to a single client.

Many firms have multiple sales channels. This is particularly true in firms that sell to other businesses, which is known as business-to-business (B2B) selling. Many corporate sales departments have sales representatives organized by product line and can have several individuals contacting the customer at the same time. Overall account managers who direct all sales efforts to each client, and they should have sales teams with product specialists from different areas within the company. In addition, the contact management systems need to be available across business lines, and sales representatives from one product line need to know which offers are on the table to a customer through another business line. In the perspective of relationship marketing, sales force is increasingly integrated as on touchpoint of many touchpoints used to interact and engage with a customer. For this purpose, firms are adopting CRM tools such as salesforce.com or Hubspot.com for better integration and coordination of sales with marketing and other functions. These tools include sales force automation feature as a key component of the tool.

Sales Force Automation

The relationship marketing considers sales as one of the several important touch points that customers may choose to use. With the redefinition of the sales role, firms are adopting sales force automation (SFA) either as an independent tool or a component of CRM system to improve the sales productivity of the firm, better serve the customers, and strengthen customer relationships. First begun in the 1990's, the goal of SFA is to put information in the hands of the sales force, and thereby allow them an advantage in interacting with both potential and current customers. Besides allowing a salesperson the ability to more easily track prospects and check customer information, the SFA allows the seller to track the effectiveness of price, promotions, campaigns, and other sales efforts the company is currently undergoing. By having access to this information, both the firm and the salesperson tend to be more profitable.

All SFA software systems have a few commonalities. The first of these is an application dedicated to contact management. At the basic level, this may simply be individual's names, addresses, phone numbers, and the like, but it is likely that the system will provide more information than that. More robust versions include marketing information about which individuals in a firm can be identified as key decision makers, as well as linked data in the salesperson's contact list with their calendars and other databases.

The next application usually found in a SFA system is used for activity management. In these systems, the general sales process is defined by the firm for the seller to follow. As a seller moves through the process, the database is updated and the next step comes up. While the seller may be used to certain transactions and may not need to be guided in routine sales, this software becomes increasingly useful for large sales events that require more planning. When action is needed to be taken by the seller, warnings pop up to alert them. Although this is not the most complicated software in a SFA package, it does help productivity through standardization. Activity Management Tools offer calendars that are optionally visible to fellow team members. They also offer the abilities to oversee activities within the sales process, automates both an individual and organizational to-do list, and streamlines team-selling and ensures company-wide consistency of the sales cycle. It assists in the planning of key customer events such as proposal presentation and product demonstrations. Activity management tool provides valuable post facto analysis of sales cycles and allows sales teams to examine the duration and procedures involved in critical tasks, and understand the success factors that contribute to closing a sale. Sales Process Management Tools offer sales methodology that can be usually be customized to the company's specific sales policies and procedures. It includes a sequence of sales activities that can guide sales reps through each discrete step in the sales process. The advantages are being not too sophisticated, effective training aid, minimizing human errors, and resulting in greater productivity for both individuals and entire teams.

Another function that all SFA software includes is account management tool. In many industries, a single sales rep may be responsible for a very large territory. This tool allows both the seller and the seller's manager to effectively keep track on the sales activity in each region. This allows managers the ability to assign the right sellers to individual customer accounts.

Next is the Opportunity, or Pipeline, Management system. The goal of this system is to turn leads into sales. At its most basic level, this should detail the opportunity, the company involved, team, status, etc. A more useful system, however, may get more in-depth about the customer and the environment. Information including the strengths and weaknesses of competing products and even the probability of a successful closed deal can be accessed by the sales force through these applications. This will allow the company the ability to discern which customers are worth attempting to form relationships with, based on both the characteristics of the customers and the strengths of competitors for their business.[22] Lead Management Tools is known as opportunity management or pipeline management. It provides foolproof sales strategies so no sales tasks, document, or communication falls through the cracks. It also allows salespeople to follow a defined approach to turning opportunities into deals and track customer history, monitor leads, generate next steps, and refine selling efforts online. It allows marketing or sales management to automatically distribute client leads to a field or telemarketing rep based on the rep's product knowledge or territory. It allows firms to track other prospect attributes such as known product interests, discretionary budget amounts, and likely competitors. It provides a real-world view of each lead and its likelihood of becoming a full-fledged sale by tracking leads against orders to provide a view of close rates and salesperson productivity.

One system that provides significant benefit to customers is the Quotation Management system. As soon as a seller agrees on a quote with the buyer, they e-mail it or use a firm's internet system to verify the quote is OK with their superiors. Thus, offers can be verified quickly and painlessly. The customer will not have to wait long for approval. Additionally, other company systems (for example, accounting) will be able to get information about the sales right away and update their systems accordingly.

Finally, every SFA has some sort of Knowledge Management system. This serves as a holding place of information and documents to make the lives of sellers easier. In these systems, the seller will be able to find such materials as "policy handbooks, presentation materials, forms, historical sales and market reporting, and industry and competitor analysis."

Firms develop sales force strategy to determine the size of the sales force and the allocation of the sales effort across product or customers. The objective of the sales force strategy is allocation of sales force and other sales expenses most efficiently to maximize the incremental sales. Firms need to understand and predict the net contribution and sales volume that would result from a particular sales force size and allocation policy. This understanding would lead to the determination of the optimal sales force size and the optimal allocation policy.

Sales force efficiency can be evaluated by various measures of sales force utilization. These measures include average revenue and cost per sales call, sales force cost as a percentage of total sales, and number of new or lost customers per period. These performances can be assessed by product, type of customer, and region. The analysis can raise useful questions or issues to be addressed by marketing managers. In addition, marginal analysis can also be performed using these measures. Marginal analysis focuses on allocating incremental sales effort to product and customers for which incremental effect will be the greatest. Therefore, marketing managers can assign each additional sales representative to generate highest incremental contribution. Firms can also determine both the optimal sales force size and the optimal allocation of sales force effort across products and customers.

Figure 8.2 shows the sales force efficiency measures across geographical markets. Various measures of sales force utilization have been used in assessing sales force efficiency. This analysis evaluates sales force cost as a percentage of total sales for different markets of the firm. The bar chart shows that sales force cost ranges from .7 percent to 4.6 percent. The Midwest region shows the highest sales expense of 4.6 percent while the eastern region posts the lowest expense rate of .7 percent. The southern region shows 2.1 percent, followed by the western region with 1.3 percent and key accounts of 1.1 percent. Interestingly for this firm, the Midwest region generates the most sales revenue with the southern region generating the second most sales. Based on the sales expense ratio, this firm needs to reevaluate both the optimal sales force size and the optimal allocation of sales force effort across regions and key accounts. Similarly, sales force efficiency can be evaluated by product and type of customer.

Figure 8.2: Sales Force Efficiency Measurement

Sales Management Tools

Sales management tools facilitate the sales managers to oversee tens or hundreds of sales teams. Managers can optimize individual teams according to critical mass and skill sets appropriate for the client or prospect leading to the Increase of the odds of closing the deal. It enables managers to set up sales teams and link individuals to accounts, regions, and industries by integrating Web sales data into analysis. Teams can be linked to headquarters specialists such as industry experts or product managers. This allows firms to track territory assignments, monitor pipelines and leads for individual territories, and provide a host of information on one account or many, freeing geographically-dispersed staffs.

SFA's benefits to internal and external customers are most apparent. Sales force productivity enhancement enhance customer relationship management and the corporate bottom line. For successful SFA program implementation, firms need to understand how SFA will help, and enlist salesperson as key stakeholders at the beginning of the implementation. Firms need to involve sales staff at all deployment steps and communicate the value proposition to the sales force up front.

It is important to communicate the value proposition to the sales force up front. SFA fails because it appears to be using the tools that provide no apparent net benefits. Firms need to communicate the benefits of automating key tasks, defining repeatable processes, integrating disparate data, knowing customers better. Firms should be able to quantify the value of these benefits in terms of potential revenue uplift or increased market share and show specific benefits pertaining to sales force. Firms should commit to allocating the funds recouped from the expected productivity gain into additional marketing and advertising campaigns, rendering their company's products and services more accessible. Firms need to invest in and enforce training and consider inherent sales processes packaged into SFA tools. Salespeople are especially reluctant to take time out to be trained on something they aren't convinced they need. Firms may consider combining SFA training with quarterly regional sales meetings to maximize sales staff time. Firms need to train sales managers before training sales staff and ensure addressing their concerns first. Successful implementation needs customization of tools and optimization of current sales process.

Sales planning focuses on customer needs and on the next best product to sell customers based on these needs. Sales management actively assists the sales force in understanding customer profiles and characteristics. Sales representatives have periodic account reviews with most customers. Sales training sessions address relationship management. Sales training techniques include solution-selling concepts such as active listening and problem confirmation before proposing products.

Many firms adopt SFA tools and approaches. SFA assists firms in the sales process, including maintaining and discovering leads, managing contacts and other sales-force activities. It can lighten the administrative load on the sales force. Important information about products and customers can be accessed in real time, allowing salespeople to keep current on company and client information. Customers may want human contact at some point throughout the purchasing process, especially with higher-priced items.

Firms are increasingly adapting. The remote-sensing solutions selling is utilizing remote monitoring tied to "permission-contact" plan. Internet-enabled sensors monitor product and service status of the products at the customer's location. This allows remote monitoring by aggregating sensor data in central repository using algorithms predicting equipment failure and optimizing maintenance cycles. The firm offers customers appropriate communication protocols that define frequency, recipients of maintenance reminders, real-time equipment failure response processes. This provides platform for fast-growth, predictable service revenues and near perfect customer experience.

Total CRM Based Relationship Marketing Template

Template 8.1: Sales Force Automation Impact Map

Template 8.1 shows the business and customer impact of sales force automation.

Impact SFA Functions	Business Impact				Customer Impact		
	Reduce Cost to Serve	Productivity Enhancement	Renewable Revenue Stream	One-to-One Relationship	Acquisition	Enhancement	Retention
Sales Force Automation Initiatives							
Sales Process/Activity Management							
Lead Management							
Sales and Territory Management							
Configuration Support							
Field Force Automation							
Contact Management							
Knowledge Management							

Template 8.2: Integrated Touchpoint Management Plan

Template 8.2 shows how to develop an integrated touchpoint management plan.

Relationship Marketing Program Initiatives	Existing Touchpoints				New Touchpoints		
	Contact Center	Sales force	Fax	Email	Web Access	Social Media	
Program A o Activities o Medium o Objectives o Performance Metrics o Process Change Required							
Program B o Activities o Medium o Objectives o Performance Metrics o Process Change Required							
Program C o Activities o Medium o Objectives o Performance Metrics o Process Change Required							

Real World Application Cases

Case 8-1: Eastman Kodak[23]

Eastman Kodak, a leading photographic equipment and products supplier, was in need of increased sales efficiency and more effective retail promotion. Their old system, IVR curtailed Kodak's ability to change questions within the system quickly, preventing the company from easily customizing its sales-call questions, product lines, and promotions for particular store chains. "We needed a new solution that would give us the ability to customize sales-call questions and promotions according to the needs of our customers and that would allow for more timely feedback from the field," says Sitarz, Account Manager of Eastman Kodak "and, ultimately, we wanted a sales automation technology that would let our field reps perform their jobs better."

"With more than 52,000 accounts, our biggest challenge had been making sure we placed the right account in the right territory with calls at the right frequency," says Sitarz. With the help of a mobile computing platform, on-site decisions can be made to suit each specific location. This allows for timely and accurate information to be collected. Suitable promotions can then be implemented with less lead-time. Part of that new system involved use of a fully scalable sales-merchandising application that links low-cost, easy-to-use portable Handheld PCs with the power and potential of the Web. Using the system, Kodak sales managers are able to input sales objectives, tell reps which promotions to use, and then they can quickly get feedback on results within 24 hours. Currently, more than 950 Kodak field representatives use the software program on the Handheld PCs, with more than 200 account and field managers accessing the reports online.

"As a general rule, members of a retail group should spend 85 percent of their time selling and merchandising and no more than 15 percent of their time capturing and recording information." "It focuses our sales reps on high-impact activities at retail and on program performance attributes we're concerned about – seeing the right stores, in the right rotation, for the right amount of time." With this new sales automation system, a salesperson's job is also more efficient freeing them from time consuming paperwork and increasing the amount of sales calls per day making each employee more efficient and valuable. Furthermore, when promotions are implemented, data can be accessed by managers within 24 hours. Inventories were also affected and out-of-stock merchandise was reduced. All information can now be streamlined making every aspect of Kodak's business more efficient, and thus, more profitable. Changes can be made in a timely fashion to improve Kodak's processes, and then feedback can be collected in the same timely manner.

Case Questions

1. How can the implementation of Kodak's new SFA system using a mobile computing platform improve overall company performance?

2. With such large amounts of information collected, how can Kodak sort through and use the information to improve sales performance? What is the most important type of information in this case?

3. In implementing such an SFA system, what type of difficulties or barriers would Kodak experience? What can Kodak do about them?

Case 8-2: BEHR Paint[24]

BEHR Paint Company offers more than 3,000 colors in its paint collection. As a leader in the do-it-yourself (DIY) market, the firm experienced the DIY consumer paint segment decline over the past 10 years, while the professional painters or "do-it-for-me" segment has been growing. BEHR Paint believes that this decline is due to consumers getting confused when it comes to picking the right color for their project. The DIY consumers are overwhelmed with choice, causing a kind of analysis paralysis and do not take on or complete a painting project because of their struggle to choose a color. BEHR Paint wants to provide consumers a customized service and specific answers uniquely geared to their needs by developing a personalized tool discovering the right color. BEHR Paint developed a Color Discovery tool which was very effective in helping people choose a paint color through the website. The tool used a series of questions and a chatbot format to narrow down a customer's choice to a set of three colors specifically selected for what they wanted to accomplish. However, the firm does not have scale to reach its target audience.

BEHR Paint is looking to reach and engage consumers on a 1:1 level with personal recommendations that make their interior paint color selection process easier. Since the process of selecting paint colors is a personal experience, BEHR Paint wants to provide a perfect way to offer personalized paint color recommendations at scale, helping to take the indecision out of the interior painting process. BEHR's AI-driven tool is believed to be more robust, personalized, reaching a broader range of consumers in the firm's target audience. BEHR can contain all interactions with the tool right in the app instead of placing a banner or display ad driving consumers to the firm's website. BEHR can get a lot more insight from the tool in addition to a much broader reach. By adding more questions than the firm previously had on its website, BEHR can collect more data and generate patterns in consumer interaction with the app. BEHR used these insights in improving the app and to understand what consumers are looking for in paint colors and choices. After consumers purchased and used BEHR paint, they provided the firm with online product reviews and shared their finished work on the firm's site and on social media creating the feedback loop influencing other consumers who want to take on similar projects.

Case Questions

1. How should Behr Paint indentify high life time value customers and choose who to offer discounts and promotions to and who not to offer?

2. What additional promotion strategies should Behr Paint use for their customers to build stronger customer relationships?

3. What marketing programs should Behr Paint implement to reduce customer defection?

Chapter 9. Managing e-CRM Touchpoints for Relationship Marketing

Firms are increasingly supporting more diverse digital marketing activities that encompass entertainment, information sharing, promotion, and crowd sourcing. For effective relationship marketing, marketing managers need to generate and evaluate a firm's website management issues. This chapter focuses on the digital site management for better customer experience and engagement. The key topical areas covered in this chapter are how firms manage their digital marketing presence. A firm's digital marketing presence can be achieved through digital websites.

Digital marketing involves managing the digital content, maintaining digital sites, and user engagement management. These components represent the digital content generated internally and externally, users' digital site ratings, and user engagement activities in those digital sites. They are critically important contact points for customers. The quality and interactivity of these touchpoints can influence customer experience and determine the likelihood of repeated purchase and customer retention.

The first important component is digital content. With the firm's websites, digital content is created by the firm, its customers, and other stakeholders. Marketing managers face the task of evaluating and managing the digital content for relationship marketing. Digital content management becomes increasingly important as customer interface for brand and customer service management. Marketing managers need to generate and evaluate the appropriate digital content and assess the quality and impact of a firm's digital content on customer relationship.

The second important task marketing managers face is digital site management. While users are engaged with the firm's websites, e-commerce sites, and social media sites, marketing managers need to understand how well the digital sites are performing and whether these sites provide the kind of user experience the firm is pursuing. It is important for marketing managers to assess how a firm's websites as well as social media sites are rated by customers. Marketing managers need to generate and assess a firm's sites ratings for effective management of digital sites.

The final task of marketing managers is evaluating digital site user engagement. It is important to understand how and why customers interact and engage with a firm's websites and social media sites. Although the vividness and interactivity of user engagements may be different, it is the activities generated and the individual engagement that make specific types of digital marketing initiatives valuable to the firm.[1] Marketing managers need to understand the quality of user engagement for a firm's websites as well as social media sites for customer relationship.

Section 1. Digital Marketing Presence

"Hence that general is skillful in attack whose opponent does not know what to defend; and he is skillful in defense whose opponent does not know what to attack."
> Sun Tzu

With the increased importance and influence of digital marketing, marketing managers are facing the not-so-familiar task of managing digital marketing activity. With the dramatic growth of e-commerce, online advertising, and social media, marketing managers must understand the nature and process of a firm's digital presence and how to manage digital marketing activities to enhance customer relationships. To understand the digital marketing task and generate the right analytic questions, marketing managers need to have the basic knowledge of the components and technologies driving the digital marketing activities.

Using websites and social media can be an effective way for firms to reach significant numbers of individuals. However, in order for firms to gain value from these digital sites and to reach the potentially interested individuals, the firms should do more than having a mere digital presence.[2]

Firms can enhance their digital presence by specifically focusing on monitoring digital marketing activities and managing their digital presence. With increased use of digital marketing, firms must discover ways to critically evaluate the effectiveness of their digital marketing activities in managing customer relationships. Digital marketing activity and its effectiveness is the results of a firm's plans and tactics for digital marketing which fosters the engagement of users for the firm's websites and social media sites.

A firm's digital marketing activity comprises the totality of activities generated by both internal and external users of the firm's websites and social media platforms (e.g., Facebook, Instagram, Pinterest, Twitter, YouTube). Digital marketing activities and tactics have the three key components of breadth, depth, and intensity.[3] Digital marketing breadth refers to how many different types of digital marketing activities a firm utilizes. This is necessary in helping firms understand which types of digital marketing activities to engage and allocate resources.

Digital marketing depth refers to the number of digital marketing tools and social media platforms in each specific type of digital marketing activities a firm supports. A firm can support multiple digital marketing tools and platforms for a digital marketing activity. The firm must determine which digital marketing tools and social media platforms to invest and to allocate resources for various digital marketing activities, as digital marketing tools and various social media platforms have become important components in the firm's marketing communications process. A firm's websites and social media platforms are permitting firms to engage with an individual or to dialog with various individuals without the restrictions of time, place, or medium.[4]

Digital marketing intensity refers to the degree of interactions and engagements generated in digital marketing tools and social media platforms. Intensity represents the number of occurrences or frequencies of the commonly identified user and firm engagement metrics relevant to selected digital marketing tools and social media platforms. Some firms concentrate on specific digital marketing tools such as blogs and generate significant number of posts while other firms choose to spread their efforts on several digital marketing tools to generate average metrics.[5] Firms are using digital marketing tools and social media platforms to support various strategic areas such as brand management, sales, new product development, customer service/support, customer acquisition, and customer retention.[6]

A firm's three digital marketing components (breadth, depth, and intensity) determine the firm's digital marketing presence through its websites and social media sites. Marketing managers need to manage the firm's e-commerce sites as well as their social media sites. This digital network management is becoming critical for a firm's marketing success. In managing the digital network, marketing managers need to understand and effectively manage a firm's websites as well as social media sites.

Section 2. Digital Marketing Content Management

"Education is what remains after one has forgotten what one has learned in school."
Albert Einstein

The important task of marketing managers in managing digital marketing is to understand and manage the digital contents posted by the firm, customers, and other visitors. The posted content exists in many different forms such as blogs post, videos, photos, and comments. The digital marketing content exists primarily in the form of text, video, and image. Marketing managers must evaluate what is posted regarding the firm and brands. It is important to evaluate the nature of the posted contents, the sentiment of the postings, and by whom they were posted. Marketing managers can respond effectively to those postings as well as various issues related to digital marketing content by generating and using the appropriate digital content analytics.

Important Issues related to digital marketing content include which online advertising and digital channels they need to use to post digital content, how to evaluate customer response to various digital marketing content, how to improve the quality of the firm's content marketing, how to choose and adapt digital content to the selected target customers, what is the right way of promoting the selected digital content, what types of digital content are generated by users, and what is the sentiment and nature of reactions generated by users.

Text Content

For the digital marketing content, marketing managers can utilize text analytics for customer text posts regarding the product, brand, and firm. One of the most significant developments in analytics field is text analytics. The text analytics is particularly important as digital marketing content exist in the form of unstructured data such as text. In order to evaluate text content, firms first have to capture any online content in text form. Digital content that exists in text form include blog post, customer comments, product and brand evaluations, and Twitter text. The captured text can be the input format for text analysis. The captured text can reveal customer insights such as what are the common issues or problems mentioned in the posts, what are the sentiments of the posted contents, and for which contents the participants' sentiments are positive or negative.

Marketing managers can use two types of text analytics for marketing decisions. These two types are the user generated text analytics and AI generated text analytics. The user generated text analytics can be generated by marketing managers using analytic tools and processes. Text mining tools can evaluate the tone, intent, and topic of a customer's feedback on a firm's brand. Organizations can evaluate which customers post reviews of what they buy and how these reviews are read or viewed by other customers and influence their purchase decisions.

AI-generated text analytics can be created using various AI analytics tools and services offered by many different firms. One such AI generated text analytics is provided by IBM Watson. IBM Watson provides a number of AI-driven text analytics tools that can be used by marketing managers. Watson "Natural Language Classifier" allows marketing managers to classify short text input into predicted classes using machine learning algorithms. This tool can categorize text with custom labels or categories to automate workflows, extract insights, and improve search and discovery using natural language processing and machine learning. Marketing managers can create and train a classifier to classify texts into predefined classes. Watson knowledge component also offers "Natural Language Understanding" function that offers advanced text analysis using natural language processing. In addition, Watson "knowledge studio" can discover meaningful insights from non-structured text.

Sentiment analysis can be also performed by AI analytics tools. AI-driven tools can provide sentiment analytics using natural language processing capabilities. For example, IBM Watson "Empathy" tool can provide marketing managers tone, emotional state, and personality characteristics using text information. AI-generated sentiment analytics can be combined with the user generated sentiment analysis results to evaluate customers' positive and negative feelings and emotions toward a firm's brands and products. These insights can be used in making marketing decisions related to a firm's products and brands. In addition, Watson offers "Tone Analyzer" to conduct social listening. Watson "Tone Analyzer" analyzes emotions and tones in what people write online, like tweets or reviews, and predict whether they are happy, sad, confident, etc. Using this tool and service, marketing managers can monitor customer service and support conversations and respond to customers appropriately at scale. Marketing managers can assess whether customers are satisfied, frustrated, and if agents are polite and sympathetic. Marketing managers can integrate these results with chatbot. Firms can enable chatbot to detect customer tones and build effective dialogue strategies to adjust the conversation accordingly.

Video Content

An important form of digital marketing content is video. The digital content of video can be generated by the firm or by users and customers. The increased popularity of social media video platform such as YouTube makes the video analytics a critical component of marketing analytics that marketing managers must understand and utilize in marketing decision making. Video is a key element of the website promotion. Online video analytics is way of measuring how viewers get to an online video and what they do when they watch it.[7] A video is any length of video stream, such as a movie clip, video advertisement, movie trailer, television show or full-length video. Video content especially if it is negative can have powerful impact on brand evaluation and customer experience.

Depending on the goal of video marketing, different types of measures are utilized. The following are list of video analytics and related goals.[8]

- *View count* – view count is the first measure of video analytics showing whether your video is drawing customers to the posted video reflecting the goal of 'reach'. It is important to focus on the deeper story of how videos are performing and resonating for your goals.

- *Quality* – the percent of a video that a viewer watched shows a firm's video 'quality' of views. This analytic indicate whether viewers find it helpful, stick around to watch the entire video, or lose them to a slow hook, or start wrapping up too soon. Although the level of engagement is important, firms need to consider whether viewers leave videos satisfied (e.g., get what they wanted or feel more educated).

- *Play Rate* – the percent of page visitors who clicked play and started watching, shows the 'relevance' of video indicating whether your video is in the best possible context.

- *Site Metrics* – site metrics can reveal user experience with your videos. Site metrics showing user experience include bounce rate (the number of viewers who enter your site and then leave without viewing other pages), time spent on page (visitors will spend more time on the page where a good video is embedded), and sign-ups, subscriptions and conversions (with embedded video, viewers' activity in your analytics showing how they're converting).

- *Word of mouth with social media* – keeping track of how viewers are sharing and discussing your content on social media and *what* people are saying about your video content.

- *Comments* – comments can be a great way to measure how strongly your content resonated in the user community.

- *Type of conversations* – when firms create a video to help answer a common question or solve a common problem, tracking how many support emails or calls you receive about that topic, or, the quality of questions you receive over time can indicate the 'clarity' of videos posted.

- *Trust* – the level of trust customers put on your firm or brand can be indicative of the level of success of posted videos.

Image Content

Image is another form of digital marketing content that can provide valuable marketing insights for marketing managers. Images posted on the website by the firm and customers can have ensuring impact on brand perception and firm image. In addition, the growth of image centric platforms like Instagram, Snapchat and Pinterest have made sharing images popular among customers. In addition, images in video can also have marketing implications. Firms are utilizing image analytics to extract meaningful information from photos and images in video for marketing decision making using digital image processing technology.[9] As a huge number of images and videos are posted online, they contain brands and products. Image analytics utilizes image recognition method that allows marketing managers to find images online containing a pre-defined search query or similar images.

The digital marketing content includes photos that can be brand products and logos without any mention of them in the posted text. In many posted images, a certain brand or brands are shown but they are not the main focus point of the post. However, the natural appearance of those brands or products in photos can help marketing managers understand the lifestyles and passions of their target audience. This information can be used by marketing managers for competitive intelligence, product development, influencer strategy, and organic reach.

Image analytics can complement text analytics as images can transcend language barriers; they can be more accurate than text, and they tend to be more personal.[10] Images can be universal and expand geographically for global brands and allows marketing managers to glance users' lives provided by the images they share. Image analytics provides many benefits to marketing managers. Image analytics offers deeper understanding of social media posts by providing the quality and context of social mentions. It also makes sentiment analysis more complete by evaluating the expression of a user's face with the posted text and context. It allows marketing managers readily spot and analyze user-generated content. Marketing managers can gain insights regarding how customers use products through lifestyle posts on social media. Image analytics allows marketing managers to identify both celebrities and non-celebrities' influencers sharing images of their lives revealing the firm's products and brands.

Image analytics can identify the firm's logo or brand image in social media posts. This is an instance of visual mention of the firm's products and brands.[11] A firm's logo can be identified in many different photos such as selfies, a photo with a celebrity, a photo in a particular location, a photo of a specific display such as billboard, real-time digital sign, sponsorship banner, phone booths, transport ads in taxis, buses, subways, and trains.[12]

Image analytics can provide all instance of image-based user-generated content that include the firm's logo and product through visual listening of social media. The user-generated content containing the firm's logo and brands can build brand awareness. This allows marketing managers the ability to monitor the actual brand exposure outside the channel and evaluate how much engagement and exposure the firm's brand is receiving. Image analytics can detect unauthorized use of the firm's logo and counterfeit brands through identifying similar images of the firm's logo and brands. AI powered image analytics can capture the user reactions when shown certain advertisements and content by collecting real-life and spontaneous facial reactions and expressed emotions.

AI Powered Digital Content Analysis

Marketing managers can use AI powered algorithm to determine recommendation scores that are based on the behavior summarized into a profile of the user. The output shows which products or hotels to recommend to a particular customer based on the relevance score. Cross-selling decisions can be made by marketing managers considering the recommendation score as well as marketing and strategic importance of the product. Once the AI-driven model is implemented, the algorithm in the AI-driven model can continuously update the model using the real time data from a firm's big data and optimize the model performance. This algorithm can retrieve a list of entities based on the relevance score based on the match to a query.

AI image recognition utilizes machine learning algorithm to recognize patterns in images and videos. AI image recognition and analysis allows marketing managers to perform visual search that performs the act of using search to find results that are visually similar to one another. Visual search has useful applications in marketing.[13] AI-driven visual search technology can recommend relevant products based on how they look rather than past behavior or purchase helping customer to find products of s similar or complementary style. Image recognition driven by AI allows marketing managers to find uses of brand products and logos by spotting where and how customers are interacting with their products visually without verbal or text references made by customers. In addition, AI image recognition can provide visual trends of target market. AI-powered image recognition can be used for images and videos to identify people and objects.[14] AI-image recognition algorithm can synchronize online content and store visits of customers by tracing customers' in-store visits and link these videos to those customers' profiles.

Section 3. Managing Digital Sites as Customer Touchpoints

"Leaders keep their eyes on the horizon, not just the bottom line."
Warren G. Bennis

Website Clickstream Management

For effective management of digital marketing, it is important to understand the structure and nature of web traffic. Web structure analytics provides the structure of websites. Marketing managers have the task of evaluating the clickstream of website users of the firm's sites. Managers need to understand how visitors reach the firm's websites and their visitor behavior patterns as a component of customer experience journey. Marketing managers must understand whether the firm's online web and e-commerce sites are performing adequately and provide the desired impact and outcomes. It is important to assess that the web and e-commerce sites are generating the amount of traffic of the right type of visitors and that the firm's web and e-commerce sites are providing the expected customer experiences using desktop, tablets, and mobile devices. Thus, a firm's web and social media sites are optimized for both desktop and mobile devices. Marketing managers need to understand how visitors come to their sites and what the traffic and navigation patterns of the visitors of their website and e-commerce sites are.

Web analytics can be defined as the measurement, collection, analysis, and reporting of internet data for purposes of understanding and optimizing web usage. A survey result shows that in-house web analytics expertise is more valuable than the technology itself. Web analytics can help firms better understand and manage their customers with the insights generated from web data analytics. Web analytics can provide a wide variety of insights related to shopping behaviors, customer purchase paths and preferences, research behaviors, and feedback behaviors.[15] Web analytics can provide information regarding how customers make online purchases. This information includes what search engine they use, what specific terms they enter, the use of bookmark, the referring sites, and many others. Web analytics can provide information on how customers arrive at their buying decisions, how they navigate a site, their preferences in purchasing, and search patterns regarding weekend deals. Understanding how customers use a site's research content can provide insights into how to interact with a customer. This can provide insights regarding which aspects or features of the site can add value to customers thus driving sales as well as which type of information such as product specifications or customer reviews is ultimately valued by customers. Web analytics can provide information regarding customers' feedback on product and services.

Clickstream data allows managers to see what actions customers are taking on their websites. As online purchase and e-commerce is becoming increasingly important, marketing managers must capture and evaluate clickstream data to stay competitive. Managers can analyze customers' behavior with the clickstream data. Managers can combine the individual visitor level information with any other data source. With clickstream data, personalization can be done on different customer touchpoints. Marketing managers can recommend relevant products or content tailored specifically to the customer who is browsing their website. Marketing managers can ensure that all customers can have consistent customer experience across all touchpoints.

Patterns can be used by the marketing managers to segment or cluster the firm's customers into those that perform a similar sequence of navigation to locate information or purchase products and services. Clickstream analytics can provide marketing managers with information regarding which pages are most frequently visited, which will be subsequently visited, which pages yield results, and the order in which these pages were visited by the consumer. Firms also need to know where the visitor comes from, which webpage the visitor first accesses and in what sequence the visitor accessed the pages on the website, how much time the visitor spends on each page and from which page the visitor exits the website, and what items the visitor adds to his/her shopping cart. The knowledge of customers' web behavior can help managers design and maintain websites to provide perfect customer experience for those using website related touchpoints.

AI Powered Digital Site Management

AI tools can monitor web sites, retail sites, social media platforms, provide automated customer service and engagement, and optimize content based on key insights derived from the AI-powered models. The undirected machine learning can analyze big data and find structures. The identified structures can be a network or graph generated from network or graph data such as communities in social networks or link structure of the graph such as page rank or click stream pattern. Marketing managers can use insights generated from real work networks analyzed by the undirected machine learning algorithm. AI powered algorithm can continually update data and utilize real time data to generate network information and insights for marketing managers. AI-driven algorithm maps a query into a sorted list of entities representing relevant queried items such as web page, images, videos, and products. The output is a list of entities sorted by a score. AI algorithms can be used for social media monitoring as well. AI monitoring tools can identify customer segments, show the trending phrases or topics, recognize thought influencers, and listen to specific mentions about the firm's products and brands.[16]

Marketing managers evaluate the firm's website and social media pages looking to understand the status of its online and social media presence. Firms are required to perform various analysis routines for recommendations and enhancements to the online websites and social media sites for better customer experience. To perform digital sites management task, marketing managers need to understand how well the firm's websites and e-commerce sites perform functionally relative to competition and whether the sites offer the consistent user experience to customers and stakeholders. Social media sites must provide the right place for engagement and interaction.

Authority Linking For Online Site Augmentation

Gaining authority for the firm website involves getting links from various authoritative websites to the firm's website. As the search indexing algorithm evolved, Google started analyzing the link text. The keywords or words contained in the link text started to become relevant. The words used in the link described information about the web page that was being linking to and therefore when the words used in the link text matched with the text found on the web page, the more relevant the firm's web page became for those keyword phrases. The next step in the evolution was when search engines started looking at the quality of each link. The search engines began to determine if the links came from a perceived low authority website or if the links originated from a perceived high authority website. Ultimately, the higher the website's perceived authority, the greater the value of the link that was provided. In addition, the age of the link became a factor in determining authority as the search engine algorithms determined that the longer a link stayed in place, the more 'serious' the linking website was about the website it was linking to. If the links came and went rapidly, then the search engine algorithm might infer something about the quality of the website being linked to or might infer that the link was an ad purchased. The core components of links that are relevant to the search engine algorithms include the anchor text, where the link appears, the type of link, the link style, the link age, and the linking website.

The identified link text is a significant component factored into the search engine rankings. Anything the search engine algorithms can ascertain about the content of the web page from external sources weighs heavily in determining the quality and relevance of the web page. The link text tells the search engine what the web page could be about and it tells the search engine that someone else determined that the web page contained relevant information. Linking to a website that gives users context to what they will locate on the website is important. Therefore, linking to a webpage should include keywords relevant to that website.[17]

Where the link appears on the web page provides a great deal of information for the search engines. Search engines assess the value of the link by its location on the web page. Links contained in the navigation section are weighted one way, whereas editorial links are considered more relevant and links placed in ad spaces are generally ignored. Editorial links (those actually linked in the web page's primary content area) are deemed the most valuable links. Linking actual text provides the search engines with more information as to what the destination site may be about. It adds to the web page's keyword focus from an external site.

Image links do not do that as well. In general, terms the longer the link remains in place the more power it sends to the linked page. News links will likely fade over time rather than build strength. However, with these exceptions, the link gains value over time. The website that links out plays a strong role in the value of the link itself. The higher authority the linking website has the more link value is passed. The page the link is on is also considered. A low-authority webpage on a high-authority website may not have as much value as a lower authority site linking out from its home page. The topic of the web page, how relevant it is to the topic site, can also be factored into how much relevance and weight the link sends out.

Linking is the mechanism that connects all the web pages on the internet. Links throughout the website permit users to navigate the website. All types of links can influence the search engine optimization results, helping determine where the organization's web site shows up online. Though the hardest to control, inbound links pointing to the website can make the biggest impact.

At its most basic, the concept is that if several high-quality sites are linking to your website, then Google and other search engines figure your website must be a popular, valuable resource and they will be more likely to show it higher in their search ranking results. However, it is not enough to just secure a couple of links. The Google PageRank algorithm looks at the pattern of links to the website as they build over time. The mix of links created out on the web pointing back at your web site should avoid skewing toward any particular type. A good mix that you can influence may include directories, press releases, and blog posts.

Professional organizations, online communities and forums, and directories can all provide quality links to the website. Writing and submitting press releases can help get news in front of more people and build links to the website. Building relationships online with bloggers can lead to linking back to the website by them. Active blogs with high visibility and large followings are important. As other sites grow in PageRank, the value passed to the website will also grow. When the content on the website is so fascinating, then people will want to tell others about it. This is the ultimate for building naturally growing incoming links.[18]

Links from popular, established websites usually carry the greatest value. That is because they have high PageRank from plenty of other people already linking to them. A link from CNN.com, for example, will carry much more weight than a link from a free press release distribution site. With authority linking, a firm's websites with high rankings in keyword search can give confidence and credibility to customers.

Section 4. eMarketing Touchpoints for Customer Relationship

> *"Opportunities multiply as they are seized."*
> Sun Tzu

E-Marketing Strategy

It is not any more a choice rather a mandate for firms to develop and maintain online presence. For the effective online presence, firms need to develop and maintain corporate websites, product and brand sites, e-commerce sites and social media sites. These online touchpoints offer a new way of interacting and communicating potential and current customers. Firms increasingly recognize the importance of developing effective e-Marketing strategy for better customer interaction and relationship management. E-marketing strategy comprises any marketing activities and programs related to online and social media touchpoints including all websites and social media sites. E-marketing offers various benefits, advantages, and disadvantages compared to traditional marketing. In developing e-marketing strategy, firms need to take full advantage of e-marketing efforts and minimize the negative impact of online marketing activities.

E-marketing offers various benefits to marketers and marketing managers. However, it is important to assess your business and evaluate whether your firm can achieve the e-marketing activities competitively and efficiently.

Global Reach: Websites allow firms to find new customers and markets globally making global reach possible. Firms can make information, digital goods and services available to anyone who has access to the Web anytime. Web also allows instant delivery and access to digital contents, goods, and services increasing customer value at a minimal cost.

The Syndication of Information: On the web, firms can sell the same digital goods or services to many different customers with minimal additional cost, who then combine them with other information, digital goods and services, and distribute them. The syndication process can be automated and digitized enabling the creation and expansion of syndicated networks. The technology of Really Simple Syndication (RSS) can be used to feed syndicated content to users who are interested in such contents.

Personalization: When firms link their customer data base to their websites, they can greet them, track what their customers buy and make targeted customized offers using the collaborative filtering technology. If customers by more from a firm, that firm can refine their customer profile and market their products and services more effectively increasing customer satisfaction and loyalty. Customers are also given the opportunity to customize their products or services according to their preferences and choices.

Lower Cost, Openness, and Social Currency: Web technology allows firms to develop a properly planned and effectively targeted e-marketing campaign. These e-marketing campaigns can reach the right customers at a much lower cost than traditional marketing methods. In addition, the social media presence allows firms build customer loyalty and create a reputation for being an open company that is easy to engage with. E-marketing also makes it feasible to create campaigns using various types of rich media. These rich media campaigns can be passed from user to user and becoming viral and socially current.

Improved and Measurable Returns: Compared to traditional marketing analytics, Web analytics can provide a much more detailed and accurate online metrics and performance measures. The Web analytics can provide information regarding how effective a firm's campaign is, how customers use a firm's websites, and how customers are responding to online advertising and special promotions. By recognizing different stages of purchasing process, firms can improve conversion rates by offering e-marketing campaign that is seamless and immediate.

Clearly, e-marketing can offer some firms competitive advantage through cost reduction with automation and digitization, faster response, increased ability to performance management, personalization and customization, and increased interactivity. Most firms take advantage of this opportunity of e-marketing. With increased competition and adoption of e-marketing by many firms, it is important to develop e-marketing strategies that can make a firm more competitive in a global market space.

E-marketing brings new tools and technologies that can help firms develop and offer products and services more competitively. Traditional 4Ps are transformed and converted to an e-offering. The core of this transformation is digital products. Increasingly, more goods and services are digitized and delivered to customers through any digital medium. Another area of transformation is customer service and support. Web based customer service is replacing more costly human support and can increase customer retention with more responsive customer service. Web-based technology brings a new price mode called dynamic pricing that allows firms set the price according to the customer's desire to buy and their ability to pay. The most dramatic impact occurs in the area of product promotion and brand building. Web technology brings a new area of online advertising and search marketing. As customers are increasingly rely on websites for information and product search, firms are adopting search engine marketing techniques such as search engine optimization. Search engines list natural search results along with paid listings. Search engine optimization allows firms to improve a website's rankings. In addition to search marketing, the new web-based promotional tools include e-mail marketing, blogs, banner advertising, mobile marketing, and social media marketing. All these components need to be coordinated with and integrated into traditional marketing mix components. Marketing plan should also need to be realigned considering the introduction of web-based e-marketing components.

Website Marketing

It is important for the firm's website to meet the needs of the customers and enhance customer experience with the brand and firm. Elements that are on the website may have become dated or may be solely specific to the firm. For better web usage experience for customers, elements to change or enhance include removing complicated animations, avoiding industry-specific jargon, removing dated and overly detailed images, consolidating or dividing long pages of text, and removing the generic contact-us form. The firm may want to remove these elements from the website for a set period of time and determine how goal-oriented metrics like lead conversion and time-on-site were impacted.

By default, when the firm adds ideas and actions, websites become more complicated. Complication creates confusion and often translates to lower effectiveness. Various types of animations can inhibit search engine optimization as the search engine cannot determine what is included in the animation. Animation can also complicate the website experience for visitors by delaying presenting information the user has requested or by slowing the performance of the web page. The firm's website should be designed for and written at a level appropriate for the customers. Readability statistics can help determine if the website is created for the targeted persona. To assume that potential customers know, understand, or even care about industry terminology is a major mistake. The marketers should ask one of their customers if they are familiar with the terms before using them.

The firm does not want to have a website that is entirely text-based. It is important to recognize that placing images on the website is important. Images help communicate and convey information. However, many firm's websites have too many images and images that are too dense. This can dramatically slow down the load time for a web page. Since search engines take into account page load times, so complex and numerous images can negatively influence website ranking. Additionally, websites may have collected images that are no longer valuable.

To avoid having information ignored or missed, ensure that the web page the user lands on contains only the appropriate and necessary information. Having web pages full of text, charts, videos, comments, and images may take the customer many scrolls to reach the bottom. It is well accepted in the literature that internet users do not like to scroll. Therefore, firms should redesign product page that is full of text and graphs requiring several scrolls to reach the bottom. Focus on dividing the webpage into short pages such that each web page contains a single idea. This simplification will make it easier for visitors and search engines to understand the web site. "Having ... contact information as part of the website is critical. Landing pages provide a dedicated form that is linked to a lead generation offer. For example, if the firm has a form connected to a free assessment, the marketer clearly knows that submissions from that form are related to potential customers who want a free assessment. Response rates for dedicated landing pages are much higher."[19] In conducting website marketing, firms must ensure that the websites offer consistent and relevant interactions and digital experience for profitable customers.

Web Site Personalization

One method of creating customer value through touch point management is allowing customers the ability to customize the website they use to interact with the firm. While most of the sites that currently allow such capabilities are content providers, the possibilities are vast for better serving customer needs through personal sites. By allowing customers to choose the method they search for products on your website, they will be able to find what they want more easily, and keep them happier.

Beyond simply giving control to customers to build their own portal, the site can collect data based on customer clicks and buys. By keeping track of the habits of their customers, certain items and goods can be promoted. Using the simplest methodology, customers are recommended items similar to what they have purchased in the past. To yield more complex results, however, the web site can cross-reference the user's actions with users that have made similar purchases and make recommendations based on these similar customer's preferences. These dynamic promotion methods can increase customer loyalty and help form a relationship between buyer and seller that can be difficult without the face-to-face interaction afforded by traditional retailers. Website personalization helps firms to provide the perfect customer experience and strengthen customer relationships.

Various promotional methods and tools for online marketing can be used by the firm and added to the firm's website. Yet, the marketer must remember that currently the primary promotional tool for the firm to have in this digital era is an effective website. Several other promotional tools and methods can be added to the website including video, email, and advertising. Yet, adding these various promotional tools and incorporating various marketing ideas may have made the firm website overly complex and difficult for the customer to navigate. Marketing managers must assess the website from the vantage point of the preferred customer. If appropriate, the firm should then focus on reducing the complexity of the website by deleting various elements that have minimal value while adding elements to encourage interaction and collaboration for the target customer group. Customers can promote the firm's product and service through viral marketing. Viral marketing success comes from self-publishing web content that customers want to share. It is about harnessing word-of-mouth, the most empowering form of marketing that can benefit the firm and other current and potential customers.

Article Marketing

Article marketing can be considered as a type of advertising in which a firm writes short articles related to topics that they have expertise in their respective industry. These short articles are usually made available at no charge for distribution and publication in the marketplace. Each article can contain a byline that includes references and contact information for the author's firm. Well-written content articles released for free distribution have the potential of increasing the authoring firm's credibility within its market as well as attracting new customers.[20]

For a firm's websites, it is believed that increased traffic should translate into increased sales. One of the tools that can increase traffic to the website is effective article marketing. Article marketing has been shown to be useful and effective for internet marketing ventures. One strategy used during SEO is to obtain more authoritative backlinks to the firm's website. It is believed that the website's search engine ranking will rise as it obtains more authoritative backlinks. Therefore, writing and distributing articles that contain a link to the firm's website should result in more links back to the firm's website. The free distribution of articles has, however, led to a situation where there is a large amount of duplicate content appearing on blogs and websites across the internet. This distribution of content can be good as the firm is getting click-throughs from a variety of sources. However, the firm must remain vigilant as the quality of articles may suffer as some authors seek a large quantity of backlinks at the possible expense of content quality.[21]

Email Marketing

When a customer provides the information requested by the firm's website, it is important that the customer receive a compelling welcome message. The welcome message should be focused and perhaps can contain a discount offer or other similar type of incentive offering. The goal should be to encourage the customer to start engaging with the organization.[22]

Emails sent to customers typically contain the following types of information: 1) an informative subject line, 2) a clearly defined and recognizable from-line, 3) valuable and concise content in the message body of the email, and 4) a clear call-to-action with informational links and organizational contact information.

Consider integrating social media icons and links with the email message so that the user has at least one social sharing option. It is believed that email messages that contain social sharing options generate a much higher click-through rate (CTR) when compared with email messages that have not included social sharing options.[23] GetResponse, an email marketing organization, indicates that, from their research, promotional emails sent by small-to-mid-sized organizations that include at least one social sharing option have, on average, a 9.4% CTR. Also, they found that promotional emails that do not contain social sharing options have a 7.2% CTR. Hence, promotional emails including social network links generate an average CTR 30% higher than promotional emails without the links.[24] When organizations share their email marketing with online social networks, the average consumer they are reaching is 37 years old. According to a study conducted on email marketing trends, almost 89 percent of small and medium-sized (organization) customers said they intended to increase social sharing.[25]

There are some aspects of touchpoint integration that need to be better understood before they can be leveraged. The two most popular social marketing tactics were integrating (or publishing) links to current campaigns, newsletters, and contests on Twitter account pages and including one to five social media sharing icons in messages before sending.[26]

Previous research indicates that 1) emails that included at least one social sharing option generated a more than 30 percent higher CTR than emails with no social sharing options; 2) emails that included at least three social sharing icons generated a more than 55 percent higher CTR than messages without any sharing options; 3) 60 percent of all social emails included only one sharing icon and only 11.2 percent of social emails included three icons or more; 4) Twitter was the most popular social sharing option, included in 67.2 percent of all social emails and Facebook came in a close second at 62.7 percent; 5) emails shared on Twitter returned CTRs of 10.2 percent, more than 40 percent higher than messages not linked to any social media; and 6) almost 19 percent of small and medium-sized (organization) marketers used the Twitter integration feature (linked their campaigns to Twitter) at least once.[27] Email marketers were using Twitter and Facebook quite aggressively, but missed a huge opportunity in social sharing. The practice of hitting 'send' and waiting for a response has become too ingrained for email marketers. Instead, they need to present a more compelling reason for contacts in their emails.

Inbound Marketing for Lead Generation

Content marketing is increasingly becoming an effective lead generation discipline. The average cost per lead for inbound marketing is significantly lower than for outbound or traditional marketing. Given the growth in online social tools, inbound marketing will become the predominant type of marketing.[28]

Understanding the nuances of lead generation can be uncovered by examining the budget allocation for lead generation. Figure 9.1 shows the various components of the lead generation by organization size. The eight identified components of the lead generation budget include email marketing, blogs, social media, telemarketing, tradeshows, direct mail, paid search, and organic search.

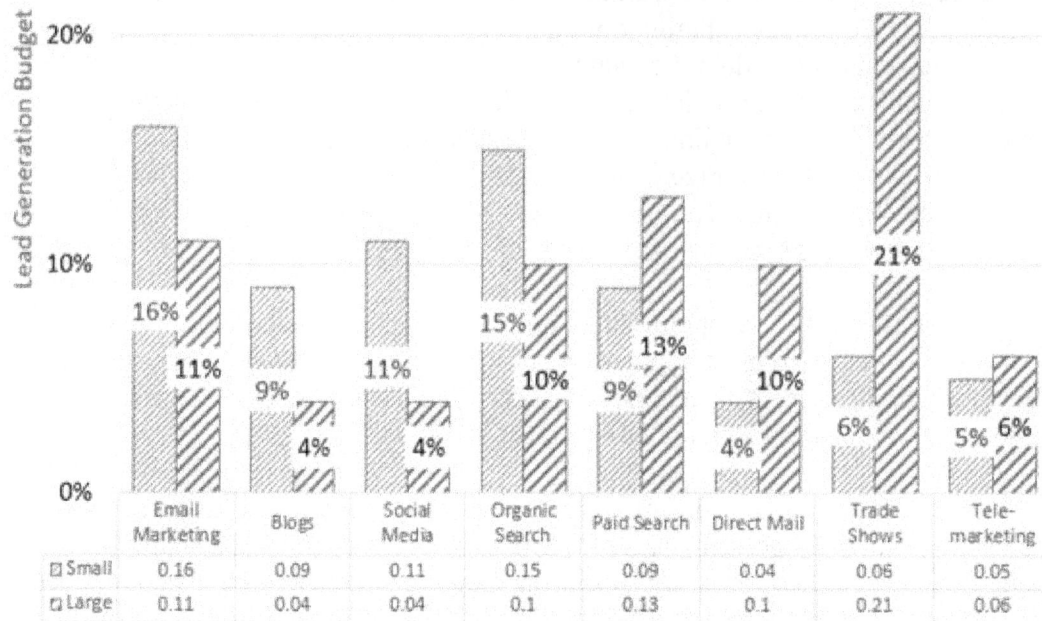

Figure 9.1: Lead Generation Budget by Organization Size

	Email Marketing	Blogs	Social Media	Organic Search	Paid Search	Direct Mail	Trade Shows	Tele-marketing
Small	0.16	0.09	0.11	0.15	0.09	0.04	0.06	0.05
Large	0.11	0.04	0.04	0.1	0.13	0.1	0.21	0.06

E-Retail Site Management

Firms utilize various touch points such as e-shopping sites, permission-based e-mail campaigns, and online social media sites to reach and manage their relationships with current and potential e-shoppers.[29] Research studies suggest that firms need to assess e-shoppers' reaction to the various touch points available to them.[30] Thus, effectively managing and coordinating multiple touch points is becoming extremely important for e-retail sites to succeed in this intensely competitive global internet marketplace. Satisfaction with the e-shopping site touch point is critical in understanding e-user behavior and purchase decisions.

Researchers report that satisfaction positively affects the individual's intention to shop online, to acquire products and/or services from the e-retail site, and to re-purchase products and/or services.[31] As customer satisfaction with touch points is found to be critical for customer retention and purchase for even experience products, e-retail sites must continually evaluate and improve their various customer touch points. Firms with e-retail sites should develop differential strategies of utilizing various customer touch points considering the type of products sold in their e-shopping sites. In addition, the relationship between loyalty intention and purchase is much weaker for experience products than for search products, e-retailers selling experience products should put an additional emphasis on customer retention and continued customer acquisition.[32] Firms can provide indirect experiences about dominant attributes, multi-media of user experience, consumer-generated reviews, and online community on their e-shopping site and social media sites for experience products.

Uncovering the various reasons given by the users for choosing the organization include 1) the previous experience that the user has with the organization; 2) the benefits and value the user derives from the organization's brands, products, and/or services; 3) the perceived trustworthiness and online reputation of the organization; and 4) the organization's commitment for making online transactions easy, safe, and secure. These four reasons focus on the user's perceived benefits, experiences, trust, value, and organizational commitment.[33]

Hence, based upon these four reasons, visitors and "prospects will judge the organization's worthiness based on how the organization makes them feel. This includes how well the organization communicates, the content depth, and the website's quality."[34] Ultimately, the organization must remember that they are marketing their brands, products, and services to people. So, the marketer must be focused on trying to create a connection with that particular website visitor. This interconnection can be accomplished in many different ways including remembering details about the user and most importantly by listening very carefully to the user's requests, expressed opinions, and comments. The organization must focus on the brand, product, or service's most compelling benefits as they communicate with the target audience as the benefits and value were key reasons the organization was chosen.

To ensure that the user's online transactions are easy, safe, and secure, "it is best for the organization to reassure potential customers with robust guarantees, a solid privacy policy, and secure payment procedures."[35] In the expanding digital marketing environment, superior online and offline marketing happens when marketers build genuine human connections. Digital marketing touchpoints can provide personal interactions, greater engagement and emotional connections, increased chance of quality referrals, experience enhancement, and customer loyalty.

Total CRM Based Relationship Marketing Template

Template 9.1: Website Ratings of Value Based Segments

Template 9.1 provides an overview of how well a firm's websites are contributing to the customer experience of each value based segments.

Type of Websites / Value Based Segments	Firm Level Site	Brand Level Site			Online Purchase Site	
	Firm Home Page	Brand 1 Site	Brand 2 Site	Brand 3 Site	B2B e-Purchase Site	B2C E-tailing Site
Gold						
Segment A						
Segment B						
Silver						
Segment C						
Segment D						
Bronze						
Segment E						
Segment F						

Real World Application Cases

Case 9-1: Cedar Fair Entertainment Company[36]

Cedar Fair is a publicly traded partnership headquartered in Sandusky, Ohio, and one of the largest regional amusement-resort operators in the world. The company owns and operates 11 amusement parks, six outdoor water parks, one indoor water park and five hotels. Its parks are located in Ohio, California, North Carolina, South Carolina, Virginia, Pennsylvania, Minnesota, Missouri, Michigan, and Toronto, Ontario. Cedar Fair also operates the Gilroy Gardens Family Theme Park in California under a management contract. Cedar Fair's flagship park, Cedar Point, has been consistently voted the "Best Amusement Park in the World" in a prestigious annual poll conducted by Amusement Today newspaper.

Cedar Fair is a leader in regional amusement parks, water parks and active entertainment. Recently, Cedar Fair announced that it has engaged accesso, a leading provider of commerce solutions to utilize their premier online commerce and mobile technology across its renowned portfolio of parks.

Along with redesigned websites for each park, Cedar Fair will replace its current in-house e-commerce solution with accesso's fully-hosted, dynamic online platform beginning in January 2012. Cedar Fair will also roll out accesso's integrated mobile platform with updated mobile websites along with iPhone and Android based apps including mobile ticketing.

"While 'Road Trip Cedar Point!' is a popular summer exclamation, the majority of our guests today reach for their keyboard before they reach for their car keys," said Matt Ouimet, Cedar Fair's president. "Our relationship with accesso helps ensure that all of the benefits of advance planning are readily available on our e-commerce platform. Whether it is a ticket for our guest, special food and beverage offerings or resort accommodations – they are easily purchased ahead of time, making their visit better before it even starts."

"Industry-leading organizations like Cedar Fair understand the increasing power of online commerce and mobile technology," said Steve Brown, accesso"s chief executive officer. "Our solutions are known for their easy-to-use designs with a focus on the user experience and sales results. We look forward to bringing our technology and unique service model to Cedar Fair and its customers in early 2012."

The key to a successful and profitable business not only requires a high-quality product or service, but a focused marketing strategy. Without the right marketing plan, organizations will not be able to attract customers.

Case Questions

1. How will Cedar Fair use mobile technology to reach customers?

2. What is Cedar Fair's marketing plan about?

3. Why did Cedar Fair change e-commerce providers?

Case 9-2: Clearscope[37]

Mushi Labs, the parent company of Clearscope, began as a search engine optimization (SEO) consulting firm. To help its customers create better-performing, highly relevant content with less effort, Clearscope wanted to create a product that could automate the previously manual content optimization process. The real work of SEO optimization is not only identifying what its customers need to do to make their content highly relevant for potential readers, but also to make it easy to take those actions effectively. Content that ranks high in online searches does more than make a reader want to share, click, or read it. High-ranking content provides more specific information based on the reader's search that engages the reader more than a competitor's content and keeps the reader engaged for longer periods of time. Mushi Labs wanted to create a product that could help automate the content optimization process.

Clearscope wants to remove the manual effort involved in analyzing its customers' web content to help them achieve higher search rankings with less effort. The Clearscope product helps customers analyze high-performing content and identify actionable recommendations on relevant terms, word count, readability and content type. Clearscope analyzes top content and advise customers how to improve their content by providing scores for each concept on salience, or how important each one is to improving search ranking.

Case Questions

1. How will Clearscope help marketing managers in reaching customers?
2. What is the advantage of using Clearscope service for effective eCRM?

Case 9-3: Autoglass®[38]

Autoglass® BodyRepair, a Belron brand, offers mobile repair of vehicles with accident damage such as dings, dents and scratches. Autoglass is manually assessing customers' vehicle damage to generate quotes, a process that was time consuming and also prevented the company from providing an online digital solution. On average, 260 people visit the Autoglass® BodyRepair website daily to request quotes. A team of three damage advisors examines photos that customers sent in through a portal or via email. They assess the vehicle damage and generate repair quotes from what they can see and by reading the damage notes on the system. The process can take an hour or up to a couple of days. The firm needs to make the process of quoting as efficient and hassle free for the customer as possible. Autoglass wants to use visual recognition capabilities to identify types of damage, such as scratches, dents, bumps and scuffs. Autoglass applies the IBM Watson Visual Recognition service to its website, eliminating the need to manually assess customers' vehicle damage and generate quotes. Autoglass spent six months training the Watson service, searching through nearly 50,000 images of different types of vehicle damage to select the best images to use. After training, the team spent just four months developing and deploying the solution.

Customers simply upload images of their vehicle damage on the website and enter some basic details about themselves and the vehicle. The service uses a library of roughly 2,000 images to analyze and organize customer photos based on four classifiers: type of vehicle, mobile repairable, product code and technician. From these findings it is then able to determine repair costs. The system categorizes the damage using one of 12 product codes related to the type of damage, such as a scratch, dent or a big dent. For each classifier, the system generates a score that reflects its confidence in its analyses of the images. The solution automatically scrutinizes and organizes customers' uploaded images based on custom classifiers and uses its findings to automatically recommend a repair price. If they meet the requirements, the service issues a quote. Customers can then book a service time and enter credit card details to facilitate payment after the business makes the repairs. When the service cannot calculate a quote, the company contacts the customer back and determines costs using the normal process. Autoglass is the first in its industry to use AI to provide customers with auto repair quotes.

Case Questions

1. How Autoglass is using visual recognition technology to reach customers?

2. What are the advantages of using visual recognition technology for Autoglass in customer relationship management?

Chapter 10. Managing Social CRM Touchpoints for Relationship Marketing

Section 1. Five-Stage Model of Social Media Relationship Marketing

> *"Social media isn't the end-all-be-all, but it offers marketers unparalleled opportunity to participate in relevant ways. It also provides a launchpad for other marketing tactics. Social media is not an island. It's a high-power engine on the larger marketing ship."*
> Matt Dickman

Utilizing social media can be an effective way for firms to reach significant numbers of customers. However, more than a mere presence on social media is required in order for firms to gain value using social media to reach customers.[1] Firms can enhance their presence on social media to gain value by specifically focusing on monitoring and managing specific social media activities for profitable customers. Firms need to understand what social media activities are required to remain competitive.[2] As part of the firm's social media strategy, customers are encouraged to share their experiences, opinions, preferences, and product reviews.[3] To implement this strategy, firms engage with online virtual communities, develop content creation processes, blog about educational information, and perform customer relationship management activities. In fact, engaging with online virtual communities positively impacts customer satisfaction.

In managing and coordinating various social media platforms, firms need to follow social medial relationship marketing models. The five-stage model of social media relationship marketing is introduced. Figure 10.1 shows the five-stage model of social media relationship marketing.[4] The first stage is to determine relevant social media goals, benefits, and roles. This stage also includes a diagnostic audit of the firm's digital presence. The second stage deals with understanding the target group's current social media behavior. The third stage is developing the right social media strategy to promote the firm's digital presence and enhance customer experience. The fourth stage is to implement the action plans for social media activities. The final stage is to develop a measurement or analytic strategy that includes monitoring and development of key performance indicators. Then, the firm should go back to the first stage and complete each of the stages again. It is a never-ending process. What should the firm's response be? The response should be to assess, determine goals, optimize, and get results. In the next sections, each of the five stages is discussed in detail.

Stage 1: Determine the Right Social Media Goals, Benefits, and Roles

In this first stage of the social media relationship marketing model, firms need to consider their relationship marketing goals and strategic directions. Depending on their relationship marketing goals, firms can set different social media goals. The set social media goals must be consistent with their relationship marketing goals and support the overall marketing strategic directions of the firm.

Stage 1

| Marketing Goals and Strategic Directions | User Interaction Context |

Social Media Goals, Benefits, and Roles for Relevance

Stage 2

Target Group Current Social Media Behavior

Level1: Primitive ⟶ Level 2: Intermediate ⟶ Level 3: Advanced

Stage 3

Social Media Strategy

| Development Strategy | Enhancement Strategy | Enrichment Strategy |

Stage 4

Action Plan for Desired Social Media Behavior and Enhanced Customer Experience

Stage 5

Measure Social Media Management Performance

| KPI Metrics for Development Strategy | KPI Metrics for Enhancement Strategy | KPI Metrics for Enrichment Strategy |

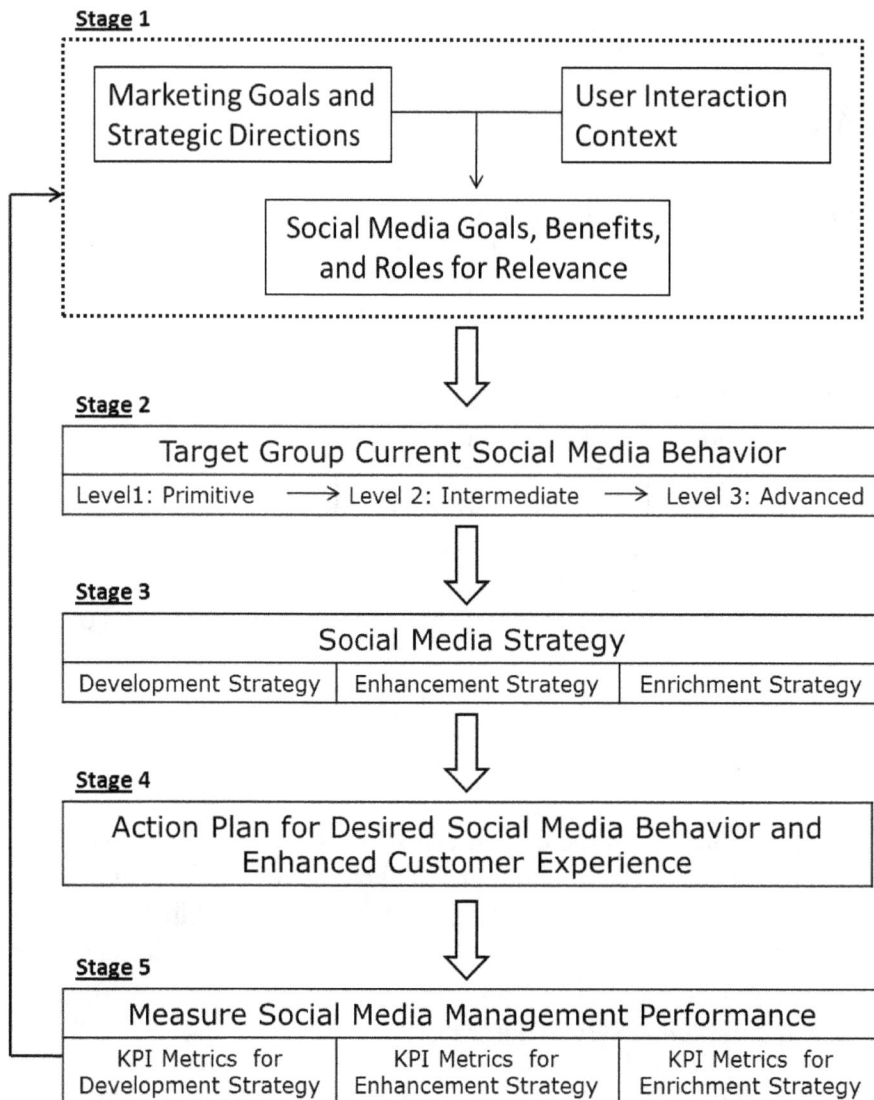

Figure 10.1: Five-Stage Model of Social Media Relationship Marketing

Marketing goals can focus on customer impact, market impact, financial impact, and impact on the organization value.[5] The goal of customer impact includes customer awareness, attitude, experience, and retention. The customer awareness of the firm focuses on the customer's recall and recognition of the firm's brand, products and services. The customer attitude considers the customer's overall evaluations of the firm and brand as well as the attachment and loyalty toward the firm and the brand. Finally, the customer experience investigates the customer's expected and delivered experience with the firm's products, brands, and various touchpoints of the firm. Social media can play an important role in improving customer awareness, influencing customer attitude, enhancing customer experience, and increasing customer retention through social network interactions and collaborations.

Market impact refers to the firm's market share, sales, and competitive position. Social media can be used as a tool for generating new sales leads or increasing sales and revenue through social commerce. Financial impact can be assessed by return of investment (ROI), net present value (NPV), and the economic value added. Impact on the firm's value requires linking marketing actions to customer value, and then, to changes in market value. Social media can play the role of the hub of information interchange and collaboration. Firms can benefit by monitoring social media networks. The insights and intelligence gained from social media can be used to develop new products and services, change the service delivery process, and identify potential problem areas or service issues.

In addition, firms should identify typical social media contexts of their primary target customers. It is important to understand when, where, and why customers are interested in interacting with various touchpoints and collaborating with other customers and firms. To accurately grasp the overall picture of social media contexts, firms need to perform a diagnostic audit. A diagnostic audit involves detailing the goals of the firm's website and social media pages. The audit includes various tasks such as looking at SEO, advertising (e.g. AdWords), and captured analytics (e.g. Google Analytics, HubSpot). The diagnostic audit assesses what's right and what's wrong with the firm's website and social media pages; determines how to fix the errors, insert missing elements, and/or enhance the website and social media pages; and details what the tradeoffs to accomplish those tasks may be.

Key goals for the diagnostic audit should include, at a minimum, to capture of the voice of the customer and understand what the customer is saying about the firm's digital presence. To perform a website and/or social media page analysis, the information professional can use the various free grader tools (e.g. marketing.grader.com from HubSpot). Managers can read and study the generated reports and determine how the firm's website and social media pages are graded and rated. Then, the marketing manager can determine if this grading result is valid and how to implement the suggestions provided by the grader tools. The diagnostics and performance analytics can be used to discover areas to make improvements.

The firm should also identify and understand the various competitors to the firm. A competitive analysis is a formal evaluation in which the marketer reviews the firms of one or more companies that compete, directly or indirectly, with them. Online competitors have access to each other's corporate information and marketing materials that they might not be able to have gathered as easily in the offline world. This allows for even greater opportunities to benefit from competitive data analysis. But how can firms improve by analyzing their competitors? And what is the best way to implement a thorough competitive analysis? The benefits of conducting a competitive analysis include identifying who the firm is competing against, identifying the firm's own weaknesses, identifying the firm's strengths, identifying the firm's unique value proposition (UVP), identifying the various factors that drive success in the firm's market space, and identifying the specific actions the firm needs to take. The firm will be able to assess the threat levels presented by other firms in their market space.

Firms "who do not pay attention to their competitors may not understand just what they are doing wrong because they have no frame of reference."[6] Focusing on competitors offers an opportunity for the marketer to find out how the firm can better serve their customers. Once the firm has identified their weaknesses, they will be able to improve the firm. "The order in which those identified improvements should be implemented will often be dictated by the analyses of the firm's competitors. For example, if all of the other firms sharing the target market space have a certain feature considered essential to that market, this will be one of the first things the firm will want to remedy."[7]

By comparing the firm's online presence to the online presence of the firm's direct competitors, the marketing manager will discover what sets the firm apart from their competitors. These qualities can then be emphasized in the firm's marketing efforts. The firm's unique experiential value proposition is the single most important element of the firm that can set it apart from its competitors in digital space. Performing competitive analysis can help the firm develop its unique value proposition and then to test the validity of the claims made about the firm. These unique value propositions may vary greatly from market to market, and may not be what was originally expected.

After considering the marketing goals and strategic directions as well as the target customers' social media interaction contexts, firms can determine the roles played by social media. This is done as a part of the determination of the roles played by various touchpoints. Social media goals can be classified into the following three major categories including communications, revenue, and knowledge management.

The firm's communication goal focuses on communicating and sharing information as well as user-generated content through social media sites to various target customers in support of the firm's relationship marketing with advertisements, brand management, customer service initiatives, and new product or service introductions. The revenue goal for the firm deals with increasing brick-and-mortar and online sales by generating sales leads through social media and then converting those leads into actual sales as well as providing purchase links within the social media sites. The knowledge management goal for the firm focuses on gathering information and then generating actionable insights from the social media sites to identify new product development ideas, detect customer problems, understand customer preference and trends, and change customer service processes. The primary cause of failure in social computing and social media initiatives is the lack of clearly defined goals and benefits for both the firm and the customer.

Firms need to develop an optimal combination of the above three social media goals with respect to their overall relationship marketing goals and the specific social media interaction context. The optimal social media goals within a firm would vary depending on the type of product category, brand, and customer groups. Therefore, specific goals can be developed for each of the brands and value based customer segments associated with the firm.

Stage 2: Understand the Current Social Media Behavior of Target Groups

The second stage of the social media interactive marketing model involves understanding the current target customers' social media behavior. To fully understand the social media user behavior, firms need to understand both individual and group behavioral aspects of social media usage. Firms need to assess the individual behavior of various value-based customer segments and their behavioral differences in using various types of social media applications and social network services. It is important to know and evaluate the frequency, length, and type of interactions and activities performed by individual customers in various social media network sites.

To prepare the firm's website and social media pages for the targeted value-based segments, marketing managers must first detail their intended targeted audience. This involves creating various personas. Then, to understand how the intended audience searches for the firm's brands, products, and services, a detailed keyword research project is required.

Persona Creation

Persona creation helps the firm identify major customer groups of their website and social media pages. Firms select the characteristics that are most representative of those groups and turn them into a persona.[8] A customer persona is a detailed profile of an example customer that represents the real audience – an archetype of the target customer. Firms can use customer personas to clarify the goals, concerns, preferences, and decision processes that are most relevant to their customers. Imagine how effective firms could be if (they) would all stop making stuff up and start aligning (their) messages and programs with the way real people think.[9] There are various activities involved in creating a persona that include detailed profile analysis, customer behavior, and decision context for the target customers.

Keyword Optimization

Keyword identification and analysis indicates what terms visitors and customers use to find the firm's website and social media pages. While the information professional does not know exactly which keywords will get the most relevant people to find the firm, there are ways to determine the popularity and competitiveness of certain keywords. Marketing managers can also test and analyze how effective different keywords are in drawing visitors to the firm's website.[10]

Focusing on keyword phrases is important. The phrase should be about three words long. The phrases to include should/could have about 500 hits per day. WordTracker keyword search tool is one of the various tools to help the marketer complete this task. Google AdWords is another keyword tool. Marketers can use this tool to find related keywords. The Google keyword tool allows the marketer to investigate keywords by looking at the firm's website and social media pages and also by searching on keywords.

The first step toward high ranking results for the most common terms that customers search on is to have the right keywords as part of the firm's digital presence. The firm's keyword goal is to get on the first or second page of search results. If the firm is not on first or second page of search results, it is almost like not being there at all. Shorter search phrases are searched more often. It is usually more difficult to be ranked on the first or second page for popular search. "Because users know that 'marketing' is searched more often than 'small business marketing', more marketers are trying to get onto the results for 'marketing' and it is usually more difficult to get highly ranked for the more frequently searched term."[11] The firm's website and social media pages should focus on relevance. If the firm's industry classification is manufacturing, the firm should provide information on the various products; if the firm's industry classification is e-retail then the firm should focus on website security and trust.

Stage 3: Develop the Right Online and Social Media Strategy

Social media strategy should be built around collaboration and customer engagement rather than traditional operational customer management. Social media strategy is about people and community. The basic premise of social media strategy is how firms intend to participate in the ongoing conversations taking place in social media sites and networks. It is important to build a reputation in the social media community that the firm is a valued member of the online communities and contributing to discussions. It is also important to develop a plan to embrace network leaders who are influential in various social media sites. These network leaders are popular industry bloggers, experts, or contributors that have many followers and friends.

Regardless of the nature and structure of the individual users and sub-networks in a firm's social media networks, firms need to develop strategies for managing their social media sites. Three basic strategies can be identified. These strategies are labeled development, enhancement, and enrichment strategies.

The development strategy involves cultivating the social media interactions of individual users and participants and initiating community building among friends, fans, and followers. Firms can influence formation of sub-networks and communities by providing information, posting videos, and social network service sites. They can also recruit potential network leaders and lead them to social media networks.

The enhancement strategy is related to helping the emerging network leaders to become more effective network leaders and facilitating formation of clearly defined sub-networks. This strategy also includes changing the composition of the existing communities by attracting more fans and advocates rather than those who are simply seeking access to exclusive specials and content.

The enrichment strategy deals with further developing the established networks by adding additional features, topics, and functions. This strategy goes beyond listening and learning about customers. Firms want to respond in more meaningful ways to customers by allowing input into which products they buy and the way they buy these products. This strategy allows firms to become true partners and collaborators with customers and share ownership of the brands and firm. The third stage of social media interactive marketing model is concerned with developing the right social media strategy.

Stage 4: Implement High Impact Online and Social Media Management Plan

The fourth stage of the social media interactive marketing model deals with developing an actionable social media management plan and implementing the detailed action plan to achieve the set goals. Social media strategy implementation concerns how firms manage their social relationships. While customers are using these social technologies and networks to share their voices, firms are having difficult times keeping up with this new development.[12]

These difficulties can come from many different sources and for many different reasons. First, real-time is not fast enough for firms. Firms cannot keep up with the social network information posted by customers and they cannot respond in real-time. Second, firms cannot scale to meet the needs of social media activities. Firms are not able to match the number of active customers in social media with their community managers. Third, firms would have solved the problems of the influencer of the social media better if they have known that the individual is the influencer.

A recently published report suggests that customers who are engaged with a brand on social media are in many cases advocates of that brand. Social media can breed advocacy of a brand when you consider the fact that customers can interact with each other as a result of brands and their communities. Brands can play the role of anchors for brand communities and social networks. Firms can create a social media site or network where customers can share information, common interest, and experience about their brands. For example, Novartis created a community of those individuals suffering from Cystic Fibrosis.

There are four basic guidelines for developing and implementing the right action steps in order to elicit the desired social media behavior. The first guideline is to monitor the right social conversations. The second guideline is to filter out the noise and identify all relevant conversations and user-generated content. The third guideline is to generate relevant insights and link them to existing customer information and formal processes. The fourth guideline is to participate in the right conversations with customers at the right time with the intelligence using the right approach.

An important issue is how to make social information actionable. Detailed steps in screening comments and complaints are required on social media sites such as Twitter and linking them into the process of marketing, sales, customer support, and other internal processes. Online tools and social media offer many opportunities for firms to build unique capabilities leading to effective relationship marketing. For example, firms can use social media feedback and support conversations to develop unique customer service strategies. This implies that firms need to integrate social media conversations and unstructured data with their marketing analytics system. The marketing analytics system then can disseminate the social media information to customer contact representatives and marketing personnel so that they can make an informed decision for the customers. In the past, it has been relatively easy in controlling the firm's brands. With the increase in online and social media conversations, the meaning of control has changed dramatically. Firms are required to develop true social media strategies for their brands. Dell and Comcast have recently integrated Twitter data to allow brand managers and support teams to actively track what is being said in tweets.[13]

The impact of social media is not limited to marketing and brand management. Social media tools are changing the way firms support their customers, generate sales leads, complete sales cycles, and develop new products. Firms need a comprehensive social media strategy and action plan to truly take advantage of social media tools and networks. Firms have to balance feedback and information from traditional touchpoints, online touchpoints, and social media touchpoints. Firms need to integrate valuable intelligence from social media with other qualitative and quantitative data from other sources to paint a holistic, unbiased, and accurate picture of their overall customer base.

Firms' social media strategy should embrace those social media sites that their customers use. Effective dialogues with customers can be created through those sites. Firms should provide relevant information and site support to help customers interact with other customers and with the firm. These sites can be mined regularly and continually to generate customer insights. Firms can use social media to create more robust service and support capabilities by providing social media tools and sites where customers can share their experience and find solutions to customer problems quickly and easily. For example, customer forums that are led by passionate customers or advocates can be used as the preferred sources of solutions to customer problems. Social media conversation can provide an early warning signal for possibly bigger product or service issues when left unaddressed.

There are many components in the firm's promotion strategy. Key promotional methods include email marketing, video marketing, RSS, and social bookmarking. The firm should consider creating a YouTube channel and creating ads to promote YouTube content. Social media marketing tools that the firm can use include Twitter, LinkedIn, Facebook, SlideShare, and Flickr as well as many thousands of other tools. Social media sites are becoming an integrated, customer-centric platform that help firms foster customer participation and improve customer experience. Social media action plans are the detailed action steps that can a) achieve superior customer engagement with the firm's brands, b) provide reasons to return to your firm's website and social media sites and to talk about the firm's brands, and c) provide all relevant information for the firm's customers to search, compare, evaluate, and make a purchase from the firm and not from the competitor.

The social media action plan requires a different game plan. Social media success requires firms to act human. In social media sites, customers are discovering their own things through referrals and recommendations. Rather than driven by click-through rates and lead conversion, social media is driven by relationships, interactions, and conversations. Firms need to develop the art of conversation. Beyond capturing leads and building databases, it is about talking to people with an authentic voice. Through this conversation, the firm can increase referrals, enhance customer experience, and build much stronger relationships.

Finding the right implementation approach is critical for the success of interactive social media marketing program. In a broad sense, there are three basic options for implementation.[14] The first option is adding social media features to existing e-commerce websites. This approach has been adopted by many firms and is gaining popularity. For example, the firm can add the Facebook Like buttons on their e-shopping websites to allow customers to share it with friends, to get opinions or just let them know what they found. The Digital IQ Index Specialty Retail report shows that retailers hosting the "like" button on their websites have 80 percent higher average three-month traffic growth. Other social features that can be added to the e-commerce sites include ratings, reviews, links to social sites such as Google Places, Facebook Connect or 'social sign on', social shopping cart, and services like Groupon.

The second option is to incorporate e-commerce functionality within social media websites. Many firms such as Brooks Brothers and Walmart adopt this approach. Brooks Brothers and 1-800-Flowers added e-commerce and transaction capabilities within the social media site. Walmart put a deals app on Facebook. Target put searchable product inventory on Facebook as part of their Club Wedd gift registry offering. Soap.com's Facebook store 'Shop My List' gives customers the option to log in to their customized list on Facebook. Customers can easily re-order their favorite items and access their friends' lists to find out new products. Twitter and YouTube also offers social commerce experience through Pay-With-a-Tweet and Plinking (Product Linking) respectively.[15] Similar feature by Facebook is called "Buy With Friends" to give users social incentives to increase purchases. In addition, Facebook is offering incentives, including promotion and premium ad targeting, to developers using Facebook Credits as their in-game currency.[16] What is important in this approach is finding the right way of adding e-commerce functionality such that social media sites still remain social and interactive not transactional.

The third option is to adopt both the first and second option. The firm can add social media features to existing e-commerce websites. At the same time, they can incorporate e-commerce functionality within social media websites. This combined approach requires coordination and cross-linking between e-commerce sites and social media sites. The coordination between the e-commerce site, brand sites, and social media sites can become a complicated and critical issue when the firm considers the limited functionality (for example, standardized Facebook design templates and framework) of many social media networks and the diverse platforms and features used for e-commerce.

Which action plan the firm adopts may depend on the firm's information technology infrastructure, brand strategy, and target customers' e-shopping and social media usage behavior. The social media action plan is implemented by various units of a firm. Regardless of the type of action plan firms adopt, they should carefully merge buying experience with the social experience for successful implementation of the social media action plan. Firms must go wherever the customers are at and engage in natural conversation by leveraging the available tools. If done correctly, this can be a win-win for both the firm and consumer and offers a new opportunity for firms to influence customers' entire purchase processes and customer experience. The fourth stage of the social media interactive marketing model focuses on how to implement the social media strategy and develop the right action steps.

Stage 5: Measure the Right Social Media Management Performance Indicators

The measurement strategy is to develop various key performance indicators and to analyze the information presented by the web, video, and mobile analytic tools. The firm should be looking for trends in the data. In addition to traditional metrics used for assessing marketing performance, online-related metrics for email and online chat has been developed and utilized by firms with advancement of e-commerce. With the emerging social commerce, firms are required to develop appropriate metrics for social media touchpoints. For example, in social media channels, customers are answering questions posted by fellow customers instead of firms. It is important to develop guidelines that are acceptable for firms in social media touchpoints and strategies to guide the discussions with the right and accurate information on social media. Firms need to ensure that consistent messages are communicated on social media touchpoints. Important metrics for social media touchpoints include the timing, frequency, and nature of participation by firms.

Firms can use relevant metrics to monitor various types of social media touchpoints.[17] These metrics can be organized by the social media objectives of brand awareness, brand engagement, and word of mouth. For blogs sites, metrics such as number of unique visits, return visits, number of times bookmarked as well as search ranking are useful for evaluating the brand awareness effect. Metrics such as number of members, RSS feed subscribers, comments, user generated content, responses to polls, contests, and surveys as well as average length of time on the site can be used for evaluating brand engagement impact. Metrics such as number of references to blog in other media, reblogs, badge displayed on other sites, and "likes" are useful to evaluate word of mouth activities. For microblogging sites such as Twitter, metrics such as number of tweets, valence of tweets, and followers are important for brand awareness evaluation; metrics such as number of followers and replies are important for brand engagement; metrics such as number of retweets are important for evaluating word of mouth activities. For social networking sites such as Facebook and LinkedIn, metrics such as number of membership/fans, installed applications, impressions, bookmarks, and reviews/ratings/valence need to be monitored to enhance brand awareness. Metrics such as number of comments, active users, "likes", user generated items, usage metrics, impressions-to-interactions ratio, and rate of activity are relevant for assessing brand engagement. Metrics such as number of posts on wall, reposts/shares, responses to friend referral invites are useful to evaluate word of mouth activities. For video and photo sharing sites such as YouTube and Flickr, metrics such as number of views and valance of video/photo ratings are useful for assessing brand awareness; metrics such as number of replies, page views, comments, and subscribers are important for brand engagement evaluation; and number of embeds, incoming links, references in mock-ups, times republished in other social media and offline, and "likes" are useful for evaluating word of mouth activities. These metrics can provide guidelines for managers regarding which metrics they should focus on in evaluating their social media activities and what tools or tactics need to be used to achieve the desired social media contribution.

The key performance indicators for firms implementing the development strategy include the increase of the regular participants and contributors, increased number of newly formed sub-networks, and increase in the number of recognized network leaders. The ultimate success is the conversion from the primitive level to the intermediate or advanced levels. The success of enhancement strategy can be assessed by such measures as the increase of network leaders, group coherence, strength of leadership of the network leaders, and increase in the number of sub-networks. This strategy should lead to transition to the advanced level. The enrichment strategy can result in the strengthened network structure and preferred individual user behavior. This strategy leads to greater contribution of social media to the attainment of communication, revenue, and knowledge management goals and results in revenue enhancement and enlightened customer experience. The final stage of the social media interactive marketing model deals with the measurement metrics for the effectiveness of the social media action plan.

Section 2. Managing Social Media Network

"In the beginning, all business was social. If someone sold you a bad chicken, you would badmouth the business and others would shun it until the merchant cleaned up his act. With social media, a massive platform of participation, the social infrastructure scaled to the point where the social made a difference once again."
Francois Gossieaux

In the new social network-enabled co-production communication form, the marketing messages and the perceived meaning associated with those messages are being exchanged among the participants in various virtual communities. The group influence and subgroup behavior factors are important for understanding group interaction behavior within social networks and social media sites.

For social media sites, it is important for marketing managers to know how effective their firm's social media sites are and what type of social groups are engaged in their digital sites generating the targeted and favorable posts and evaluative responses as well as uncontrolled favorable and unfavorable posts and responses. Marketing managers also need to understand how well the firm's social media network groups are organized and engaged with the firm's digital sites relative to competitors. The task is to understand the structure and nature of social media network groups as well as the interactive patterns of participants in the social media platforms. For social media sites, it is important to know who are network leaders and followers in their social media sites. Managers can make the right management decisions by understanding the network structure of their social media participants and visitors as well as their engagement patterns. Marketing managers have the analytic task of understanding and visualizing configurations of social ties within social groups formed within the firm's digital sites.

In addition to knowing individual user behavior, firms need to understand the nature and structure of group interaction and collaboration within the social media networks. Social network analysis can be performed to identify the characteristics of network leaders, the number of sub-networks, the relationship and interaction patterns between individual users, between individual user and sub-networks, and among various sub-networks. According to social network analysis (SNA), the social tie strength (social relations) determines whether users will assimilate or differentiate their opinions. In addition, if strong ties (connections) or a large number of ties exist, those ties impose greater demand for conformity on the users and those users are expected to heed the advice of their stronger ties. The affective content of these relationships further strengthens the role of their influencer or network leader as affective commitment manifests itself as belongingness or attachment to the community or group.

The social media behavior can evolve over time. Three levels of social media behavior can be identified. The first level is the primitive level, which is characterized by the lack of network or opinion leaders and organized sub-networks. In this first level, users visit or interact with a firm's social media sites on a random and occasional basis. In many cases, firms are simply setting up their social media sites and do not yet have clear direction or the intention of managing these sites. The second level of social media behavior involves the transition from the primitive level. This intermediate level exhibits the emergence of opinion leaders and the formation of sub-networks. In this level, either self-designated or firm-influenced opinion leaders will emerge and act as opinion leaders in certain topics or on certain issues. These leaders are not yet well established or clearly recognized as network leaders by the members or participants of the social network. In the final advanced stage of social media behavior, multiple network leaders are recognized by members or participants of the network. These leaders have established themselves as the leader through their expertise, popularity, or active participation. In addition, well-organized sub-networks are typically formed within the social media network. These sub-networks are led by one or more network leaders and create unique interaction patterns among themselves.

One of the key components of active, prosperous, and successful virtual communities within these social sites is the presence of active network leaders. These network leaders should have access to large social networks and be in the role of a key influencer.[18] The role of network leaders as advice provider, influencer, hub, and information search facilitator is not the same role as traditionally exhibited in marketing communications. These online virtual community leaders are providing global influence to potentially unlimited numbers of users who are seeking advice, information, and opinions regarding a firm's products, brands, and services.[19]

The role of network leader has become a co-influencing interactive role. Network leaders are participating in conversations, generating content, and occupying important positions in the virtual communities of many online social media sites. The influence of a user's social ties and how they affect the commitment of the user toward the use of the social media sites is important for understanding, explaining, and predicting social media site usage and acceptance behavior. In addition, the influence associated with social ties plays an important role in determining the acceptance and usage behavior of other participants in virtual communities.

Expanding the leader's influence requires access to the firm's website, social media sites, and the virtual community. Access to the social media site or virtual community is affected by the connectedness or structure of the social network as well as the position that the social media site or virtual community has within the social network. This makes it possible for the network leaders to still conform to the various expectations or norms of the various virtual communities they are associated with while sharing ideas. Also, participants in those virtual communities that have strong social ties tend to share group norms and beliefs so strongly that little effort is required by the network leader to share ideas and determine the intentions of participants in the group, since all of the participants in the virtual community are alike.

Network leaders are also information providers to users, online virtual communities, and various social groups. Network leadership is important as network leaders span the social boundaries among various virtual communities and social media site groups. Their influence comes from across the social context rather than solely from within a specific social group or virtual community. Thus, network leaders act as bridges or conduits between social groups gaining access to and providing valuable information from one social group and informing others in another social group. Because of their unique situation, the network leaders are often among the earliest adopters of brands, products, and services.

In an online, interactive environment, users can influence and be influenced by other participants in their social network. Network leaders are those users who can influence the attitudes, behaviors, beliefs, motivations, and opinions of other users in the online virtual community.[20] Thus, network leaders emerge as trusted users with access to a large social network and possess the ability to diffuse innovations and information.[21]

The network leader, in the role of a social hub, can exercise influence to affect the virtual community's information and innovation adoption. Based upon the group influences, users in the virtual community are willing to be influenced by network leaders as the network leaders are in a desirable social position and are viewed by the virtual community members as competent, unbiased sources of accurate and trustworthy information.

The identification of a network leader is focused on how often a user posts comments, information, pictures, videos, and opinions to a virtual community and thereby provides sought after information to other users. Therefore, network leaders are considered as influential members by other users and used as a primary source for information and advice. Members seeking advice usually follow the advice. By providing this advice, network leaders play a crucial role in forming the opinions of others in the group. They bring in new information and ideas and then disseminate that information via blogs, podcasts, videos, and wikis in their role as influential members of virtual communities. Network leaders are viewed as active co-producers of value and meaning.[22]

Thus, information access has become a function of searching whereas access to knowledge has become a function of the social network or virtual community.[23] Given the growing importance of this uncontrolled, indirect communication involving social media sites, it is critical for the firm to understand the various roles played by network leaders. Leaders are viewed as advice providers, influencers, and hubs in focusing the flow of comments, ideas, information, and opinions throughout the virtual community. Therefore, firms need to perform a detailed social network analysis to understand e-word of mouth (eWOM) behavior as well as the nature and structure of sub-networks and communities within their online and social media sites. Marketing managers can develop the right social media strategy and action plan with the understanding of the following issues that include which unique composition of social media platforms is required for the firm to deliver the right message to the right audience at the right time, how to build and maintain online community of brand advocates, and what are the drivers for a user to participate and interact with the community.

Section 3. Managing Social Media Touchpoints for Customer Relationship

> *"Quit counting fans, followers and blog subscribers like bottle caps. Think, instead, about what you're hoping to achieve with and through the community that actually cares about what you're doing."*
> Amber Naslund

Social media are connectivity-enabled platforms and applications that facilitate interaction, co-creation, collaboration, exchange, and publication of information among firms and their networked communities of users.[24] The expanding social media platforms require the firm to assess the allocation of resources to each platform. Firms are developing social media strategies to effectively utilize and coordinate various types of social media platforms and applications. Developing a social media strategy involves a systematic approach for making a series of choices and decisions.

Social Media Strategy

A social media strategy is defined as a firm's social media portfolio decision determined by three decision areas: the number of different social media platforms, the number of social media applications in a social media platform, and the level and nature of different firm activities sponsored, encouraged, or discouraged in a given social media application. First, firms have to determine how many different social media platforms a firm wants to utilize and support. To help firms understand with which social media platforms and applications to engage, social media applications can be categorized into six platforms based on the social media characteristics.[25] The six platforms are labeled collaborative projects, microblogs and blogs, content communities, social networking sites, virtual game worlds, and virtual social worlds. Firms need to determine the proper social media platforms that fit their strategic goals, business strategies, and marketing strategies.[26] Of these six social media platforms, the three main social media platforms that most firms engaged with are social networking sites, microblogs and blogs, and content communities with the most popular social media applications in each of the identified platforms being Facebook, Twitter, and YouTube, respectively.

Next, firms should review various applications in each platform and decide the number of applications a firm intends to support in a given platform. For example, a firm can support multiple applications such as Facebook and LinkedIn in the social networking sites platform. Finally, firms can decide how much resources to allocate to each of the applications selected and the degree and nature of activities intend to support and generate in a given social media application by a firm. Some firms concentrate on a specific social media application and generate significant traffic and e-word-of-mouth (e-WOM) while other firms spread their efforts on several social media applications to generate average activities on a wide variety of social media applications. It is also important to understand the nature of social media activities. Firms use social media applications to support different firm activities. Social media applications are used to support brand management, sales, new product development, customer service/support, and customer relationship management activities.

Firms also use various social media applications for customers who are at different phases of the buying cycle to focus on engagement, awareness, and word-of-mouth communication. Different strategic activity metrics are associated with each phase of the buying cycle. For example, metrics for awareness include number of followers, number of views of videos, and number of fans. Metrics for engagement include number of followers, number of active users, number of comments, number of replies, and number of page views. Word-of-mouth social media metrics focus on the number of likes, number of posts, number of retweets, and number of embeds. These metrics are reported by the various social media applications.

However, for firms just using the specific social media application does not generate value for the firm, but rather how the particular social media application is used and the information that is created and shared with that application is what ultimately creates value. Firms can employ social media applications as another channel or touch point for co-creating a wide array of informational objects.[27] One of the main reasons that makes those firms successful is that they make online users aware of the firm's activities and then the firm engages these users. Firms are increasingly hosting more diverse activities on social media that include entertainment, information sharing and promotion, customer service, crowd sourcing and marketing research.

Factors Influencing Social Media Strategy Decision

Previous research studies suggest that the optimal social media portfolio strategy varies by user characteristics, firm size, and industry classifications.[28] One of the primary differentiating factors of social media strategic activities employed by various firms is the brand origin of the firm. The brand origin refers to a country where the firm's brand originates and is associated. The usage of a firm's target users of social media applications varies widely among those target users in different countries. For firms operating in various locations around the world, it is important to understand the local culture and how each culture uses social media. The local social networking sites typically generate more traffic than the often cited social media application of Facebook.[29] For example, in China renren.com is the important social networking tool whereas in Russia it is vkontakte.ru, in South Korea it is kakao, and in Japan it is mixi. These social media applications in various countries may play differential role in brand and customer relationship marketing. Due to these country differences in social media usage, firms originated from various countries may take different social media focus and employ diverse social media portfolio strategies.[30]

Another differentiating factor involves the industry classification type of the firm. Industrial product firms are currently using social networking sites to achieve brand objectives such as attracting new customers. Consumer product firms report that individuals that are engaged with their social media applications are more likely to acquire the brand they engage with. Consumers are bringing their online experiences with these brands into their own virtual communities rather than solely engaging directly on the firm's various social media applications. Retail and service firms are also actively using social media applications and functionalities in their brand and customer management. For example, a location-based recommendation service combined with local knowledge and word-of-mouth offered by the social media application, Facebook, provides retailers with the ability to reach consumers and potentially attract them to a given retail store. Online retailers are using capabilities like this and are offering interactive features on their social networking sites to engage consumers with their brand. As shopping can be a popular social activity and easily combined with social networking experiences, retailers and service firms are adopting a social media strategy that combines their customers' shopping and social networking experience.[31]

Impact of Social Media Strategy

The social media activity outcome encompasses three distinct structural, relational, and cognitive dimensions of social capital that build and strengthen customer engagement, sharing, and trust with a firm's brands leading to firm performance. It is important that firms interact with individuals on social media platforms as these interactions influence an individual's ability to recall and recognize the brand. A firm's social networking platform activities such as exchanging ideas, providing product reviews, and sharing information can influence brand image and value. Activities in social networking platforms can promote engagement and help firms build relationships, promote brands, and ultimately improve products. Positive or negative impressions formed by videos or pictures posted on content communities platforms will promote peer-to-peer interactions that influence brand awareness and image. Exchanging ideas and feedback through social networking platforms and micro-blogs platforms allow the firm to engage with individuals more effectively creating trust and strong ties toward its brands.[32] In addition, interactions in social networking platforms and micro-blogs platforms trigger interpretations and discoveries that individuals thinking alone could not have generated. Social media activity outcomes in various types of platforms are found to have significant effects on brand reputation, attitudes, loyalty, experience, relationships, and equity.[33] The magnitude and direction of impacts depend on the posted contents, photos, or videos associated with the social media platform activity outcomes. The increased view of videos or number of likes can have a positive effect on brand equity if the posted associated contents, photos, or videos are perceived by users as favorable to the brand. On the other hand, if the posted contents, Flickr photos, or YouTube videos show significant defects or service problems related to the brand, the increased number of views or activity outcomes may lead to negative effects on the brand. As a result, the net significant effect of social media activity outcome variables can be either positive or negative depending on the nature and amount of the posted contents, photos, and videos

Social Media Marketing Program

Engagement with customers in the online and social network arena must be made with the relevant social media strategy. Selecting the right social media program is the key for social media marketing success. Social media program should be selected focusing on the desired digital interaction and customer engagement. Social media marketing is about building genuine connection with people and the community. In the social media marketing environment, superior online and offline marketing happens when firms build genuine human connections. Customers will evaluate the firm's worthiness of conversation based on how the firm makes customers feel. In the online and social media context, whether customers will engage with the firm would depend on how well it communicates and how well it offers the relevant content.

Social media marketing is not about quantity but rather it is about quality. It is not just about creating long lists of followers but rather it is about having a sincere desire to grow and nourish genuine relationships and doing whatever it takes to ensure those relationships happen. The social media strategy will determine how firms will conduct the ongoing conversations with customers in the social media sites and networks. Firms must develop effective strategies for managing their online and social media sites. As discussed earlier, three basic interactivity strategies and related programs can be adopted. Those strategies are development, enhancement, and enrichment. Each type of strategy can be composed of various social media interactive functions, features, and programs.

Social media marketing centers on efforts to create content that attracts attention, generates online conversations, and encourages readers to share the content in their virtual communities and with their social networks. The message spreads from user to user and presumably resonates because it is coming from a trusted source, as opposed to coming from the brand team or company itself.[34]

The three key concepts of social media marketing are content, conversations, and sharing. The first social media concept focuses on user-generated or firm-created content that is placed on the web. The content has to be of a quality that attracts the attention of potential users. The second social media concept is the online conversation. This online conversation is an important element as this dialog is the unique component. The third concept involves sharing. The content can be shared or distributed via blogs, newsletters, email, or other avenues. These three combined characteristics illuminate the importance of interaction and the evolution of the web. "If other people are heavily influencing our decisions, and in some cases making the decisions for us, how does this impact what we buy, what sites we visit, and how we spend our time? If we want people to use our products, to use our website, it is important that we design features that support our friends making decisions for us."[35]

There are a variety of reasons to focus on social media marketing. These reasons include that "social media marketing gives you unprecedented ability to listen to your customers, it can provide you with the chance to build or introduce a brand, it gives you a unique way to gather feedback, and it can give you the chance to demonstrate personality."[36] The logic behind why 'rate and review systems' increase the conversion is a debatable issue. It is well accepted in the literature that people are to some extent unsure about what they believe to be real or true. People tend to turn to groups to find reassurance on their decisions and choices.[37]

A firm's social media marketing describes how the firm will fulfill the needs and requirements of its customers' social interaction needs and collaboration requirements. It also includes activities associated with building and maintaining digital relationships with all stakeholders through online and social media sites. The social media marketing strategy entails a plan for how a firm will use its capabilities and resources to meet the social media interactive needs and requirements of the customers. The social media marketing consists of various online and social media programs. Each program must be designed to achieve specific goals of serving customers, maintaining mutually satisfying relationships, and creating value for both the customers and firm. In developing the interactivity strategy, marketing managers need to consider the gaps that exist between the desired future digital experience envisioned by the firm and the current state of the online and social media presence. These gaps can be filled by a firm's successful implementation of online and social media programs driven by the social media marketing strategy.

To create online and social media relevance, the firm must create and publish the right content. To create online and social media presence and interactivity, two basic decisions need to be made. The first decision the firm must decide upon is which type of social media interactive functions, features, and programs they want to use and get involved with for customer engagements. Social media interactive functions or features include blogging, podcasting, video-sharing, social bookmarking, to name a few. Firms can also adopt interactivity programs such as email marketing or lead generation. The second decision the firm must make is which type of social media applications that it wants to use and become affiliated. The social media firms are offering various types of services with diverse functionalities and limitations. The social media applications include Blipper, Facebook, FlickR, Groupon, Hulu, LinkedIn, OpenTable, SlideShare, StumbleUpon, Tencent, Twitter, Yelp, YouTube, and Zynga and many others. Firms can use various 'back link' components as a component in their social media marketing strategy. These functions and features are transformed into different social media marketing programs for various social media sites. When the right social media marketing functions, features, and programs driven by the social media marketing strategy are implemented, firms can reap the positive outcomes of marketing success such as enhanced customer experience, positive digital interaction and collaboration with customers, and increased revenue and market performance.

An important part of the social media marketing strategy is selecting the right social media functions and features as well as the type of services. This decision should be based on the customers' social media behavior patterns and preferences regarding the social media application and interactivity functions and features. This decision should be driven by the customers' needs and preferences not by the firm's competence or management decision.

With the increased use of social media, firms are establishing and customizing their social media applications and facilitating the creation of virtual communities to reach, interact, and collaborate with current and potential customers. The firms' social media sites are playing an increasingly critical role as a part of the new media and as critical touchpoints for interacting with customers.[38] For example, the e-shopping site of Teavana lists five social media site links where e-shoppers can visit those sites to join conversation with Facebook, follow the e-retailer with Twitter, pin with Pinterest, learn and explore with YouTube, and join the circle with Google plus.

Firms are pursuing specific impact on customers using social media programs. Social media programs are designed to use social media touchpoints as (1) media outlet for broadcasting to customers, (2) viral marketing platform promoting engagement and interaction such as word-of-mouth communication, (3) customer insight platform to capture information regarding customer preference, feedback, experience, and behavior, (4) brand management platform to increase brand awareness and improve brand image, and promote brand loyalty, and (5) customer engagement platform to build and enrich relationship.[39] Thus, it is important to assess the combined impacts of the various social media touchpoints of the firm.

Social Media Touchpoints as Media Outlet

Firms can use social media platforms as a media outlet to communicate their products, brands, services, firm, and interaction or collaboration opportunities. Several common social media programs serving as media outlets are introduced next.

Social Magazine

Flipboard is one of the world's first social magazines. Inspired by the beauty and ease of print media, Flipboard's mission is to fundamentally improve how people discover, view and share content across their social networks.[40] It creates different magazine sections from online news sources, Twitter, Facebook and curated content. Key benefits of social magazines include noise reduction, return to visuals, and social segmentation. Social magazines can help to filter and better display social streams. Even though firms are successful in getting social opt-ins on Twitter and Facebook from customers, much of it will be lost anyway because social streams of most people are filled with too much content. However, the content included in social magazines will be less likely to be lost to noise and companies will have better opportunities to connect.

As Twitter streams, "RSS readers and online news sources are dominated by catchy headlines and bullet points, social magazine prioritize the value of powerful images in online storytelling. Powerful images in the blog posts can illustrate the message of the post well. Pictures now have a greater impact on who reads the firm's content.

"Many large firms still publish magazines and distribute them to their B2B customers as a method of nurturing and educating potential buyers. Social magazines allow potential buyers to create their own magazine that is most relevant to them. This relevancy means that potential customers are more likely to read the magazines they create instead of the magazines that marketers print and mail to them. Marketers will need to shift focus and make it easy for content to be included in social magazines by providing RSS feeds and aggregating content through social media."[41]

Video Marketing

YouTube is a video sharing social networking tool in which users can upload and share videos. Since it is owned by Google, the analytics the marketer can access include keyword and traffic sources, hotspots (showing when viewers stop watching the clip), and insights about what other content users also watched. Google rewards multimedia content with a higher search rank. Uploading videos to the corporate channel, and linking or embedding those videos in news releases is helpful for search rank. YouTube clearly has the highest market share in the United States based upon visits. Figure 10.2 shows that the top three reasons respondents gave for using online video on their websites included increasing visitor engagement thereby increasing the time spent on the website (78%), strengthening their brand (61%), and increasing website visitors (58%).[42] So, firms believe that the use of video can be a major component in their marketing tactics to engage users. Video, if used correctly, can also increase the strength of the brand and as such is a key component in the brand management tactics.

Figure 10.3 shows that the majority of respondents indicated that they are using in-stream advertising as the dominant monetization strategy (50%) for video content, followed by in-page advertising (47%) and sponsorship (37%). Using in-stream advertising requires the firm to clearly know who is watching and how long they are watching the video content. Looking ahead, respondents were asked which monetization strategies they plan to add. Almost 50% of the respondents indicated that they would add "sponsorship" to their monetization strategy, followed by "in-stream advertising" and "in-page advertising." The dominant approaches for pricing and selling video advertising include cost per thousand impressions (CPM) (62%) and flat rate sponsorships (38%). Video presents an advertising format that is superior in its effectiveness to other mediums. According to Dynamic Logic, video advertising leads to purchase intent for 1.4% of all viewers that saw an advertisement, a number that's grown for three consecutive quarters and is more effective than other mediums.

Reasons for Using Video Sites

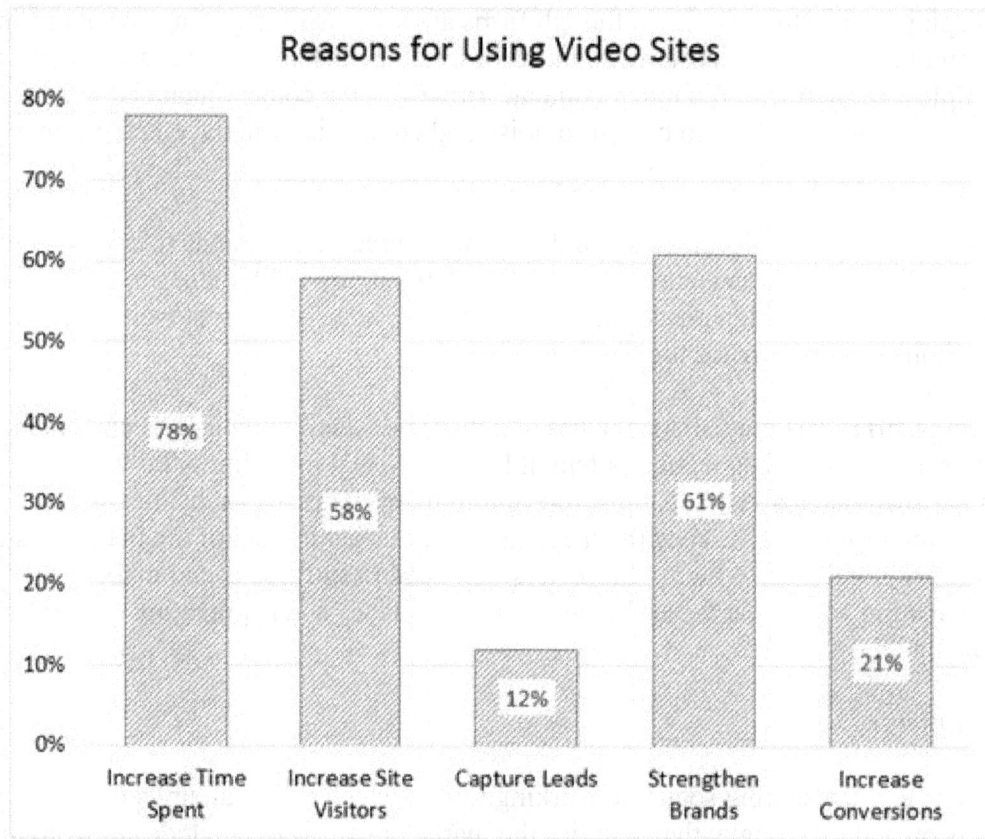

Figure 10.2: Why Are You Using Video On Your Site?

Video Content Monetization Strategies

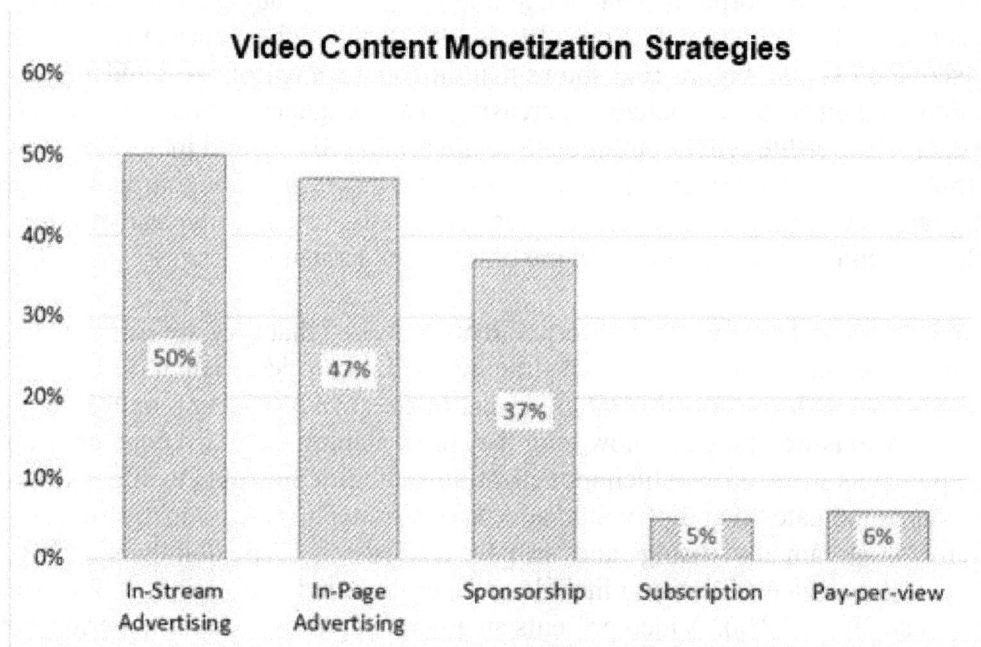

Figure 10.3: Monetization Strategies Used For Video Content

It should be noted that repurposed television advertisements more effectively influenced awareness, while made-for-web content affected persuasion more effectively. Videos of 60 seconds to 90 seconds in length typically shows the highest viewer completion rate. Firms should understand the value of integrating video and pictures into firms' digital strategy.[43] Firms need to manage contents, photos, and videos that are perceived negative to the brand in social media context in addition to contents perceived positive by target customers. Negative contents can directly influence customers' experience with the brand and firm leading to defection and negative word of mouth.

There is space on the search results page to show up to 11 different ads. So, if the average position of the firm's ad is greater than 11, it is not appearing on the first page of the search results. The goal should be to have the ad shown on the first page of the search results so that potential customers can more easily find the firm's advertisement. Each of the keywords the firm has chosen has a quality score calculated for it which can be found by clicking on the icon in the highlighted 'Status' column in the 'Keywords' tab of the Google AdWords reports. The keyword status report indicates if the ad is currently showing and the quality score for the keyword phrase. In addition, the quality-score report rates the keyword relevance, the landing page quality and the landing page load time.

The 'Average Position' column on the 'Campaigns' tab shown in Figure 10.4 shows where the ad is appearing on the search results page. This information shows the effectiveness of search engine optimization in terms of keyword search. Click-through rate is also important for marketing managers. A click-through rate (CTR) on Google under 1% indicates that the ads are not targeted to a relevant audience.[44]

Campaign	Budget	Status ?	Clicks	Impr.	CTR ?	Avg. CPC ?	Cost	Avg. Pos.	Conv. (1-per-click) ?	Cost / conv. (1-per-click) ?	Conv. rate (1-per-click) ?	View-through Conv. ?
Starter Campaign	$5.00/day	Eligible	46	32,734	0.14%	$0.75	$34.69	4.3	1	$34.69	2.17%	0
Total - all but deleted campaigns			46	32,734	0.14%	$0.75	$34.69	4.3	1	$34.69	2.17%	0
Total - Search ?			28	8,419	0.33%	$0.79	$21.99	3.4	1	$21.99	3.57%	0
Total - Display Network ?			18	24,315	0.07%	$0.71	$12.70	4.6	0	$0.00	0.00%	0
Total - all campaigns	$5.00/day		46	32,734	0.14%	$0.75	$34.69	4.3	1	$34.69	2.17%	0

Figure 10.4: AdWords Average Position Report

Social Bookmarks

Delicious is a social bookmarking web service for storing, sharing, and discovering web bookmarks. It can help the individual find highly relevant content from other users by seeing how they tagged it, if they gave it a description, and what other types of content they have saved.[45]

.

Photo Sharing

Flickr is an image and video hosting website, web services suite, and online community. In addition to being a popular website for users to share and embed personal photographs, the service is widely used by bloggers to host images that they embed in blogs and social media.

Social Media Touchpoints as Viral Marketing Platform

Customers will be more likely to engage in conversations with the firm when it allows customers to interact in ways they prefer. For example, some customers may better relate to a blog post while others are more engaged by video or audio content. The social media marketing strategy must be developed to focus on building the human connection by remembering personal details and listening carefully. It is also important to protect the firm's good name and ensure that customers view the firm as creating value. For this reason, firm should attempt to provide the feelings of credibility, plausibility, truthfulness, and value. In the social media world, value means great content, expert advice, and personal connections.

For example, Twitter is a "micro-blog" or "micro-communications" tool and platform. Twitter allows a user to send a text-based message, known as a "tweet", up to 140 characters in length, to other users. Twitter has become the new face of marketing. Twitter allows firms to listen in on and participate in public conversations customers are having, which could enable them to attract new customers and strengthen relationships with existing ones. Firms can test a new product or get feedback on an existing one for very little cost while creating a buzz at the same time.

Twitter is fast becoming a top referrer of traffic to blogs, news sites, and firm's websites. It accelerates and amplifies business, politics, and entertainment news and provides a new way to place stories with key players. People go to Twitter to find what others are talking about at that very moment. The user has the ability to examine the profile (name, biography, location), followers, and previous posts to Twitter of those doing the talking. Since Twitter profiles are mostly public, users can also have instant access to data contained in the network. Currently, the fastest growing demographic on Twitter is the 55–64 year age bracket. Thus, when composing tweets, it is important to clearly understand the targeted persona and the specific age demographic. Also, remember the ideal tweets consist of a balance with about 90% being about others, big ideas, and resources and just about 10% about the firm.[46]

Firms can provide social media platforms that encourage customers to create content targeted at other customers. There are many different community building features. Customer product reviews are product reviews and grades written by customers. Wish lists are where customers can list gifts they hope to receive from friends and relatives. Recommendation sharing refers to customers permit designated "friends" to view their recommendations and purchase history. Purchase circles are most popular items ordered by customers from a specific geography, school or employer.

Social Media Touchpoints as Customer Insight Platform

Firms can monitor conversations and locations of customers and their activities from social media.[47] Various social media metrics are captured from a firm's social media platforms to gain customer insight. Firms can use various social media platforms for marketing research and customer insight generation. Social media touchpoints can be used for marketing research by recognizing response pattern and gathering insights from social media consumer panels, social networks, online communities, listening platforms, and geo-tagging.[48] Firms can also use social media for competitor monitoring and information about the target audience.[49]

In addition to these metrics, firms can also use location based geo-tagging information using social media touchpoints. For example, Apple's privacy policy indicates that "to provide location-based services on Apple products, Apple and our partners and licensees may collect, use, and share precise location data, including the real-time geographic location of your Apple computer or device. This location data is collected anonymously in a form that does not personally identify you and is used by Apple and our partners and licensees to provide and improve location-based products and services. For example, we may share geographic location with application providers when you opt in to their location services. Some location-based services offered by Apple, such as the MobileMe 'Find My iPhone' feature, require your personal information for the feature to work."[50]

Geo-social networking is defined as social networking in which geographic services and capabilities such as geo-coding and geo-tagging are used to enable additional social dynamics. In addition, "geo-location on web-based social network services can be IP-based or use hotspot trilateration. For mobile social networks, texted location information or mobile phone tracking can enable location-based services to enrich social networking."[51]

"'Where are you?' and 'What are you doing there?' are the questions that popular location-based companies like Foursquare, Gowalla, Loopt and others are trying to determine. These location-based services let the user share the places they visit with their friends via check-ins. When a location-based user checks into a service, that user uses a cell phone with a GPS to share the location with their friends."[52] The market leader in location-based services, Foursquare, currently has over 50 million users worldwide with over 6 billion check-ins and over 1.7 million businesses using their Merchant Platform. Proponents of location-based services describe them as a way to bring together offline and online connections.

Firms like Starbucks have launched campaigns using these location-based services to offer special discounts to people who check-in at a location. Location-based services often function as a type of publicly facing customer loyalty program for firms. Instead of scanning or entering a customer's loyalty card at the cash register, users can check into a store and tell all of their friends they are there.

The firm can use the location-based service Foursquare to engage their increasingly mobile customer set with Foursquare 'specials'. These specials could be "discounts and prizes the firm could offer its loyal customers when they check in on Foursquare. Do not forget to show extra love to the venue's Mayor! Additionally, if the firm offers Foursquare specials to their customers, they will be able to track how their venue is performing over time."[53]

Social media and inbound marketing are increasingly important assets for firms to get found and engage with potential buyers on the web. People go to search engines like Google and various social networks for answers to their questions. The question for marketing managers to answer is, "Will the firm be there to answer it."[54]

Firms need to understand the drivers to social networking usage by various geographic areas. These social network usage drivers include receiving an email sent to the user's personal email address or to their work email address, signing in directly to the social media tool, receiving a text message, and receiving a direct mail request. It is important to understand the open rate, click-through rate, and conversion rate metrics for email newsletters. The email newsletters perform better when compared to general email messages as the newsletter emails generally contain more links to relevant information and contain additional promotional offers. It is interesting to note that the consumer and business metrics trend about the same for the three newsletter email metrics.

The ultimate performance indicator is how successful an organization is building meaningful and sticky relationships with its target customers. This relationship must be the right kind of relationship with the right type of customers. The metrics obtained from various social media touchpoints must be interpreted in consideration of the value and importance of those customers. The enhancement of customer experience through social media marketing should be consistent to a firm's customer portfolio management plan. The customer metrics would be used as a part of feedback mechanism and leads to continuous improvement of the social media marketing programs and activities.

Social Media Touchpoints as Brand Management Platform

 Firms need to understand the differences in the magnitude and direction of relationships between social media engagement and brand loyalty for each target customer group.[55] This understanding can help firms determine which type of social media engagements benefit their brands more and be used in managing social media more effectively.

"Ben and Jerry's Ice Cream of Vermont announced in an email to their subscribers … that they will be discontinuing their regular email marketing campaigns, in favor of social media. This was a major surprise. Usually, social media and email marketing (have) a close relationship and they are most effective when used together. However, Ben & Jerry's clearly feel otherwise. In their last email message, they invited their subscribers to connect with them via their Facebook or Twitter accounts."[56] Ben and Jerry's is a leader in utilizing social media platforms for managing its brand for customers.

Social media platforms are used by firms for brand engagement, brand communications, brand relationship quality, and brand advertising. It is important that firms interact with customers on social media platforms as these interactions influence an individual's ability to recall and recognize the brand. A firm's social networking platform activities such as exchanging ideas, providing product reviews, and sharing information can influence brand image and value. Activities in social networking platforms can promote engagement and help firms build relationships, promote brands, and ultimately improve products. Positive or negative impressions formed by videos or pictures posted on content communities platforms will promote peer-to-peer interactions that influence brand awareness and image. Exchanging ideas and feedback through social networking platforms and micro-blogs platforms allow the firm to engage with individuals more effectively creating trust and strong ties toward its brands.[57] Social media activity outcomes in various types of platforms can influence brand reputation, brand loyalty, and brand experience.

Social Media Touchpoints as Customer Engagement Platform

Given the proliferation of social media sites, it is important to understand the key attributes to better understand satisfaction and engagement patterns as these sites have collectively transformed into a specialized information-sharing communication channel.[58] Engagement is defined as an estimate of the depth of visitor interaction against a clearly defined set of goals with visitor interaction being measured by demonstrated interaction.[59] As part of the firm's social media strategy, customers are encouraged to share their experiences, opinions, preferences, and product reviews. To implement this strategy, firms engage with online virtual communities, develop content creation processes, blog about educational information, and perform customer relationship management activities.[60] In fact, engaging with online virtual communities positively impacts customer satisfaction by increasing the firm's credibility.[61] Firms are providing various social media platforms to customers for effective customer engagement.

Social Networking

Facebook is a tool for connecting people with those around them – friends, family, co-workers, or simply others with similar interests. The firm can establish goals for Facebook such as 1) get found by people who are searching for the brands, products, or services, 2) connect and engage with current and potential customers, 3) create a community around the firm, and 4) promote other content the firm creates, including webinars, blog articles, or other resources.[62]

On Facebook, profiles are meant for people and pages are meant for firms. There are a few key differences between pages and personal profiles. Pages are public and will start ranking in Facebook and public search results. Pages are split into different categories (local firms, brands, musicians) that help the firm get listed in more relevant search results. Personal profiles have friends, which require mutual acceptance, whereas anyone can become a fan of a firm's page.

"Because of Facebook's 'closed' platform, users may potentially feel more comfortable sharing personal information such as their political affiliation or their favorite movie than they would on other sites. These granular details about a user's preferences allow advertisers to create campaigns aimed at much smaller, more appropriate audiences than ever before, while maintaining user privacy."[63]

Business Networking

LinkedIn is a business-oriented social networking site that allows individuals to display their professional experience, academic accomplishments, connect with former and current colleagues, and perform prospect research. Using LinkedIn, individuals have the potential to rank well for their name in search results (depending on how many other people share the same name and their activity level online) with highly relevant content that the individual has control over, such as their resume. The LinkedIn platform is a tremendous source of information and conversation for professionals. LinkedIn can help business managers connect and network with others in their industry.

Social Media User Engagement

Social media has proliferated and transformed into specialized information sharing communication channels. In this evolving co-production communication channel, firms must focus on understanding how to engage with customers. Given the growing importance of this uncontrolled communication channel, it is critical for the firm to understand the customers' perception of social media sites and their impact on satisfaction and engagement. With the increased competition for a customers' attention, the firm must satisfy informational needs by offering the right kind and level of engagement instead of merely having a digital presence.

Marketing managers face this important task of understanding the level of customer engagement in various digital touchpoints. In order to accomplish this task, marketing managers need to ask the critical question of how well a firm's touchpoints such as a website or social media site are performing in engaging with customers. The understanding of the level of engagement in various touchpoints can help firms to change site content, improve click-through referrals, identify effective keywords, and recognize key prospects through triggered alerts signaling immediate purchase.

Marketing managers must understand what social media structures can nourish the online conversation and engagement of profitable customers, which social media platform is ideal for customer connection and experience sharing, how social media can be used for fostering relationships with customers, and what are the drivers that influence social media activity outcome such as the number of likes and the number of comments. Marketing managers can generate digital sites user engagement analytics and apply the understanding of digital touchpoint user engagement activities for relationship marketing.

Matching the Relevant Social Media Touchpoints with Customers

The selected social media marketing strategy and touchpoints must be relevant for the target customers and value based customer segments. Various target customer segments would offer different value to the firm. Some customer segments are more important for the firm in the perspective of customer portfolio management. For those important and high-valued customers, firms are willing to spend more time, money, and efforts to acquire, develop, and retain them. In developing the social media marketing strategy, the same principle can be applied. Firms should evaluate the time and efforts required to employ various social media functions, features, and programs.

Figure 10.5 shows the usage, effort required, and effectiveness of social media marketing functions, features, and programs. The three-dimensional view is presented in the figure. As you can see from the figure, blogger relations are the most effective tactic but it requires the most effort, so there is relatively low usage of this marketing tactic. Blogger relations can be used for high valued customer segments. You can compare that marketing tactic to social networks. Social networks are only half as effective as blogger relations but since there is a quarter of the effort required for this tactic there is a high level of usage. Advertising on Facebook and other social media platforms as well as social media news releases fall in a similar place on the effectiveness/effort matrix but are used much less, perhaps because of the increased cost involved.

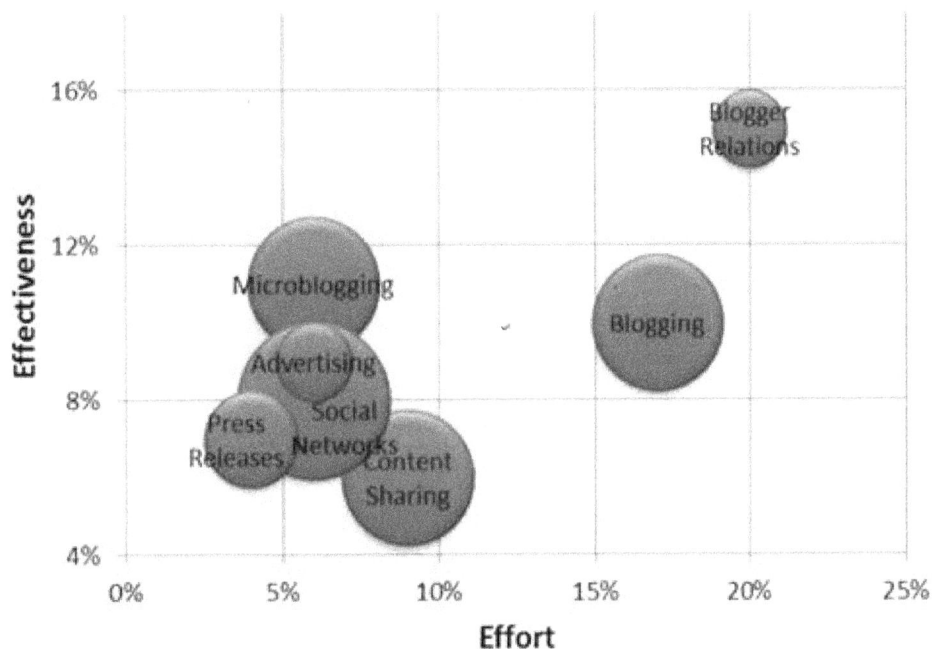

Figure 10.5: Social Media Effort, Effectiveness, Usage

This shows the importance of understanding the various methods that could be used to promote the firm's social media marketing programs. Link building, website marketing, user interaction, and video creation are components of the firm's social media marketing strategy that could be used. In addition, targeted advertisements and focused email marketing could be used as well. For complete understanding of the effectiveness of social media marketing, firms need to know why customers choose them and their firm.[64]

Uncovering the various reasons given by the customers for choosing the firm include 1) the previous experience that the customer has with the firm; 2) the benefits and value the customer derives from the firm's brands, products, and/or services; 3) the perceived trustworthiness and online reputation of the firm; and 4) the firm's commitment for making online transactions easy, safe, and secure. These four reasons focus on the customer's perceived benefits, experiences, trust, value, and formal commitment.[65]

Hence, based upon these four reasons, visitors and "prospects will judge the firm's worthiness based on how the firm makes them feel. This includes how well the firm communicates, the content depth, and the website's quality."[66] Ultimately, the firm must remember that they are marketing their brands, products, and services to people. Firms must focus on trying to create a connection with that particular customer. This interconnection can be accomplished in many different ways including remembering details about the customer and most importantly by listening very carefully to the customer's requests, expressed opinions, and comments. The firm must focus on the brand, product, or service's most compelling benefits and experience when the firm communicates with the target customers as the benefits, experience, and value were key reasons the firm was chosen.

In the expanding social media marketing environment, superior online and offline marketing happens when marketers build genuine human connections. Ultimately, social media marketing is not about the quantity of interactions, but rather, about the quality of those interactions.

Total CRM Based Relationship Marketing Template

Template 10.1: Social Media Ratings of Value Based Segments

Template 10.1 captures how well a firm's social media sites are contributing to the customer experience of each value based segments.

Type of Social Media / Value Based Segments	Social Networking Platform		Micro-Blogs Platform	Content Communities Platform			Other Platform	
	Facebook	LinkedIn	Twitter	YouTube	Instagram	Pinterest	Blogs	Game World
Gold								
Segment 1								
Segment 2								
Silver								
Segment 3								
Segment 4								
Bronze								
Segment 5								
Segment 6								

Real World Application Cases

Case 10-1: GoPro[67]

GoPro is a mountable camera company based in San Mateo, California. The company offers compact, lightweight, and durable cameras that can be mounted for extreme action video photography. Arising from the need for a durable camera that could capture in action sequences such as skydiving, surfing, and snowboarding the company was able to enter first and capture the market with their line of GoPro Hero cameras. As a mark of their success, GoPro founder Nick Woodman claims that GoPro holds as much as 90% of the wearable camera market. Frequently live action footage taken from these cameras has been featured on mainstream news. The company has established itself so well that any action footage taken on a camera is often referred to as GoPro footage or commented on by the common twitter trend of #GoPro and the company slogan *Be a Hero*.

While many companies create web pages exhibiting their product lines, GoPro markets experiences rather than products. GoPro's success can be partially attributed to its unique marketing approach accomplished through its cult following of customers in the extreme sporting market, dubbed the Go Pro Army. In addition, unlike many other approaches, GoPro markets itself through social media. In many ways this style of marketing has taken on a life of its own.

One method used by the company is its Facebook and Twitter pages. Instead of creating content about the product, the company displays what can be done with a GoPro camera by encouraging customers to post their videos onto GoPro pages through offerings and giveaways resulting in ever changing and unique marketing content. One of the most interesting ways GoPro has succeeded in marketing itself is through its use of YouTube. By creating tagged content and a page on YouTube, GoPro allows its fans to post and market the brand independently. An underlying value to this form of marketing is that the product does not need to rely on actors or gimmicks, the reactions in their videos are genuine. As a result, the brand has grown its fan base as well as drastically increase its sales. This approach is very unique because the company never actually shows the product and instead shows the real emotion and enjoyment that can come from their product.

Case Questions

1. What is the most important aspect of GoPro's marketing strategy?

2. How easily could another company copy GoPro's form of marketing? Would this even be possible?

3. What is the value of having customer created content as opposed to content created by the company?

Case 10-2: Influential[68]

Influential is in the business of helping brands, publishers and ad agencies create social media ad and sponsored posts that outperform organic content. The firm tries to achieve high level of engagement for clients as its chosen influencers help brands resonate with consumers. Although it's known that influencer marketing can help drive brand sales, there are concerns about fake likes and comments on social platforms. Influential's task is to overcome these objections and develop a system that matches brands with ideal influencers.

Influential develops Social Intelligence platforms ensuring that a particular influencer can support a brand's message and determine whether the demographics are cost effective. Influential chooses the right influencers by leveraging augmented intelligence and machine learning for effective influencer selection. Influential's platform works with 25,000 influencers reaching billions of followers. The firm applies AI to large blocks of unstructured data to help brands identify their audience, profile and personality as perceived on social media. To match brands with effective influencers, the system analyzes an influencer's last 22,000 words posted on Twitter, Instagram, Facebook, YouTube, and elsewhere. The psychographic analysis identifies 47 personality traits, from altruistic to adventurous, and pinpoints the sentiments within those words. The analyses help to predict the outcome of influencer campaigns before they happen, transforming influencer marketing into a credible media channel.

Case Questions

1. What is the most important aspect of Influential's influencer marketing strategy?

2. What are the advantages of having a large brands' share of voice over competitors across various social media platforms? Which social media platform(s) should firms focus on achieving large brands' share of voice?

3. What is the value of well matched brand and influencer in social CRM?

LIST OF FIGURES

LIST OF TABLES

ENDNOTES

Chapter 1

1. Babin, B. J., & Zikmund, W. G. *Exploring Marketing Research*. Cengage Learning, 2015

2. Antons, D., Brettel, M., Hopp, C., Salge, T. O., Piller, F., & Wentzel, D. "Stage-gate and agile development in the digital age: Promises, perils, and boundary conditions." *Journal of Business Research 110*, (2019): 495-501. John Naisbitt, *Megatrends* New York, NY: Warner Books, 1982.

3. Letsholo, R. G., & Pretorius, M. P. "Investigating managerial practices for data and information overload in decision making." *Journal of Contemporary Management,13*(1), (2016): 767-792.; Ron Sanchez, "Strategic Management at the Point of Inflection: Systems, Complexity and Competency Theory," *Long Range Planning* 30, Number 6, (1997): 939-946.

4. Vaill, Peter B., *Learning as a Way of Being,* San Francisco, CA: Jossey-Bass.Publishers, Inc., 1996.

5. Gardere, J., Sharir, D., & Maman, Y. "Consulting and Executive Coaching on Future Trends: The Need for a Long Term Vision with Apple and Samsung." *International Journal of Business and Social Science 9,* 3, (2018).

6. Naisbitt, John, *Global Paradox* , New York, NY: William Morow and Company, Inc., 1994 . Sadrudin, Ahmed, A., and Juan Rock."Exploring the Relationship Between Export Intensity and Exporter Characteristics, Resources, and Capabilities: Evidence From Chile." *Latin American Business Review* 13, (2012): 29-57.

7. Utterback, James M. and William J. Abernathy, "A Dynamic Model of Process and Product Innovation," *Omega*, Volume 3(6), (1975): 639-656.

8. Bengtsson, M., & Raza-Ullah, T. "A systematic review of research on coopetition: Toward a multilevel understanding." *Industrial Marketing Management 57*, (2016): 23-39.

9. Henry Mintzberg, James B. Quinn, and John Voyer, *The Strategy Process,* Englewood Cliffs, NJ: Prentice-Hall, Inc., 1995.

10. Kenneth Andrews, in Henry Mintzberg et al. *The Strategy Process,* Englewood Cliffs, NJ: Prentice-Hall, Inc., 1995.

11. Prajogo, D., & Olhager, J. "Supply chain integration and performance: The effects of long-term relationships, information technology and sharing, and logistics integration." *International Journal of Production Economics 135,* 1, (2012): 514-522.

12. Benjamin, Robert and Rolf Wigand, "Electronic Markets and Virtual Value Chains on the Information Superhighway." *Sloan Management Review*, (Winter, 1995): 62-72. Wigand, R. T. "20 years of research in electronic markets and networked business: An interview with Thomas Malone." *Electronic Markets 21,* 1, (2011): 5-17.

13. Bharadwaj, A., El Sawy, O. A., Pavlou, P. A., & Venkatraman, N. "Digital business strategy: toward a next generation of insights." *MIS quarterly*, (2013): 471-482. Glover T. Ferguson, "Strategy in the Digital Age." *Journal of Business Strategy, (*November/December, 1996): 28-31.

14. Lee, K. W., Tsai, M. T., & Lanting, M. C. L. "From marketplace to marketspace: Investigating the consumer switch to online banking." *Electronic Commerce Research and Applications 10,* 1, (2011): 115-125.

15. Nordin, F., Brozovic, D., & Holmlund, M. "Disintermediation in business-to-business service channels: Mechanisms and challenges." *Journal of Business-to-Business Marketing 20,* 4, (2013): 179-192.

16. Laudon, K. C., & Traver, C. G. *E-commerce 2017*, 2018.

17. Hult, G. Tomas M. "Toward a Theory of the Boundary-spanning Marketing Organization and Insights from 31 Organization Theories." *Journal of the Academy of Marketing Science,* 39, (2011): 509-36.

18. Regis McKenna, "Real-time Marketing", *Harvard Business Review* 73, Number 4, (July, 1995): 87-95. Scott, D. M. *Real-time marketing and PR: How to instantly engage your market, connect with customers, and create products that grow your business now,* John Wiley & Sons, 2011,.

19. Kirk W.M. Tyson, "Perpetual Strategy: A 21st Century Essential", *Strategy & Leadership",* (January/February, 1998). Cabrilo, S., & Dahms, S. "How strategic knowledge management drives intellectual capital to superior innovation and market performance." *Journal of knowledge management,* (2018).

20. George S. Day, "The Capabilities of Market-Driven Organizations." *Journal of Marketing* 58, 4, October, (1994): 37-52.

21. Kotler P. "Reinventing marketing to manage the environmental imperative." *Journal of marketing* 75, 4, (2011): 132-5.

22. Kumar V, Jones E, Venkatesan R, Leone RP. "Is market *orientation a source of sustainable competitive advantage or simply the cost of competing?." Journal* of marketing 75, 1, (2011): 16-30.

23. Slater, S. F. and J. C. Narver. "The positive effect of a market orientation on business profitability: A balanced replication." *Journal of Business Research,* 48, 1, (2000): 69-73.

24. Kaplan, R.S. and D.P. Norton. "Transforming the balanced scorecard from performance requirement to strategic management: Part II." *Accounting Horizons* 15, 2, (2001): 147-160.

25. Day GS. "Closing the marketing capabilities gap." *Journal of Marketing,* 75, 4, (Jul, 2011): 183-95.

26. Cravens, David. "Implementation Strategies in the Market-Driven Strategy Era." *Academy of Marketing Science Journal* 26, 3, (Summer, 1998): 237-241.

27. Kozlenkova IV, Samaha SA, Palmatier RW. "Resource-based theory in marketing." *Journal of the Academy of Marketing Science,* 42, 1, (2014):1-21.

28. Cravens, David." Implementation Strategies in the Market-Driven Strategy Era", *Journal of Academy of Marketing Science* 26, 3, (Summer, 1998): 237-241.

29. Magretta, Joan, "The Power of Virtual Integration: An Interview with Dell Computer's Michael Dell." *Harvard Business Review,* (March/April, 1998): 73-84.

30. Wolf C, Floyd SW. "Strategic planning research: Toward a theory-driven agenda." *Journal of Management* 43, 6, (2017): 1754-88.

31. Kotler P, Armstrong G. *Principles of Marketing,* Pearson education, 2010.

32. Michiels, Ian & Alex Jefferies, Web Analytics: Actionable Insights for Unlocking the Hidden Potential of Online Data, Aberdeen Group, 2009. – http://www.aberdeen.com

33. Sheth J. "Revitalizing relationship marketing." *Journal of Services Marketing,* (2017).

34. Kozenets, Robert V., Kristine De Valck, Andrea C. Wojnicki, and Sarah JS Wilner. "Networked Narratives: Understanding Word-of-Mouth Marketing in Online Communities." *Journal of Marketing,* 74, (March, 2010): 71-89.

35. Marta Kagan – http://www.slideshare.net/mzkagan/what-the-fk-social-media - Accessed on May 25, 2014

36. Kozenets, Robert V., Kristine De Valck, Andrea C. Wojnicki, and Sarah JS Wilner. "Networked Narratives: Understanding Word-of-Mouth Marketing in Online Communities." *Journal of Marketing,* 74, (March, 2010): 71-89.

37. The Russo Group, Branding with Social Media, (2009): 21.

38. Top 10 Brands on Facebook, David Nixon, March 2014, http://www.insidermonkey.com/blog/enter-your-zip-code-here-18-317028/

39. Joeri Van den Bergh and Mattias Behrer, How cool brands stay hot: Branding to Generation Y, 2011.

40. http://www.cmbinfo.com/news/press-center/social-media-release-3-10-10/ - Accessed on May 25, 2014.

41. Shaio, Dennis, Laura Aberle, Relationship Marketing, Blog Post, https://searchcustomerexperience.techtarget.com/definition/relationship-marketing, accessed October 27, 2020.

42. https://en.wikipedia.org/wiki/Relationship_marketing

43. Bean, Josh, The differences between customer relationship marketing and customer relationship management can be confusing. Here's what you need to know, Article Post, September 22, 2020.

44. Adapted from Rethinking Customer Relationship Management: Organizational Imperatives for Business Case Realization, Corporate Executive Board, 2002.

45. This case is based upon, "CASE STUDY: CBRE Sees 20-fold Return on CRM Investment Every Year." *B2B Marketing*. B2B Marketing, 9 Mar. 2010. Web. <www.b2bmarketing.net/knowledgebank/crm-marketing/case-studies/case-study-cbre-sees-20-fold-return-crm-investment-every-ye>.

46. This case is based upon Bernard Marr, Giovanni Schiuma, and Andy Neely, "The Dynamics of Value Creation: Mapping Your Intellectual Performance Drivers", *Journal of Intellectual Capital*, 5:2, (2004): 312-325.

Chapter 2

1. Payne Adrian, *Handbook of CRM: Achieving Excellence in Customer Management*, Elsevier, Burlington, MA, 2006. Kervok, E. and Vrechopoulos, A. "CRM Literature: Conceptual and functional insights by keyword analysis." *Marketing Intelligence and Planning* 27, (2009): 48-85.

2. Payne, Adrian and Pennie Frow. "Strategic Framework for Customer Relationship Management." *Journal of Marketing* 69, (October, 2005): 167-176.

3. Cambra-Fierro JJ, E Centeno, A Olavarria, and R. Vazquez-Carrasco "Success factors in a CRM strategy: technology is not all." *Journal of Strategic Marketing* 25, 4, (2017): 316-33.

4. Cambra-Fierro JJ, E Centeno, A Olavarria, and R. Vazquez-Carrasco (2017).

5. Peppers, Don, Martha Rogers, and Bob Dorf, *The One to One Fieldbook*, Dantam Doubleday Dell Publishing, New York, 1999.

6. Greenberg, Paul, *CRM at the speed of Light*, Fourth Edition, McGraw-Hill, 2009.

7. Richards, Keith A., and Eli Jones. "Customer Relationship Management: Finding Value Drivers." *Industrial Marketing Management* 37, (2008): 120-30.

8. Payne Adrian and Pennie, Frow, "Strategic Framework for Customer Relationship Management." *Journal of Marketing*, 69, (October, 2005): 167-176.

9. Reynolds, Janice, *A Practical Guide to CRM*, CMP Books, New York, 2002.

10. Janice Reynolds, *A Practical Guide to CRM: Building More Profitable Customer Relationships*, Berkeley, CA: CMP Books, (2002). Mishra, Alok, and Deepti Mishra. "Customer Relationship Management: Implementation Process Perspective." *Department of Computer Engineering* 6.4 , (2009): 83-99.

11. *Rethinking Customer Relationship Management: Organizational Imperatives for Business Case Realization*, Corporate Executive Board, 2002,

12. *Rethinking Customer Relationship Management: Organizational Imperatives for Business Case Realization*, Corporate Executive Board, 2002.

13. Dyche, Jill and Mary O'Brien, *The CRM handbook: A business guide to customer relationship management*, Addison-Wesley Professional, 2002. Meyliana, Z., Achmad Nizar Hidayanto, and EkoK. Budiardjo, "The critical success factors for customer relationship management implementation: a systematic literature review." *International Journal of Business Information Systems* 23, 2, (2016): 131-174.

14. Payne, Adrian and Pennie, Frow, "Strategic Framework for Customer Relationship Management," *Journal of Marketing*, 69, (October, 2005): 167-176.

15. Barak Libai, Das Narayandas, and Clive Humby, "Toward an Individuals Customer Profitability Model: A Segment-Based Approach." *Journal of Service Research*, 5, 1, (August, 2002): 69-76.

16. Payne A, Frow P, Eggert A. "The customer value proposition: evolution, development, and application in marketing." *Journal of the Academy of Marketing Science.* 45, 4, (2017): 467-89. Sunil Gupta, Donald Lehmann, and Jennifer Stuart. "Valuing Customers." *Journal of Marketing Research*, XLI, (February, 2004): 7-18.

17. Edmondson, Gail, "BMW's Dream Factory", *Business Week*, October 16, 2006.

18. Steinfield, Charles. "Understanding Click and Mortar E-Commerce Approaches: A Conceptual Framework and Research Agenda." *Journal of Interactive Marketing* 2, 2, (Spring, 2002): 1-13.

19. Paul Greenberg, *CRM at the Speed of Light,* Berkeley, CA: Osborne/McGraw Hill, 2001. Kamakura, Wagner, Carl F. Mela, Asim Ansari, Anand Bodapati, Pete Fader, Raghuram Iyengar, Prasad Naik, Scott Neslin, Baohong Sun, Peter C. Verhoef, Michel Wedel, and Ron Wilcox. "Choice Models and Customer Relationship Management." *Marketing Letters* 16, 3/4, (2005): 279-91. Thomas, J. S., Reinartz, W., & Kumar, V. "Getting the most out of all of your customers." *Harvard Business Review*, (July–August 2004): 116–123.

20. Mishra, A. and Mishra, D. "Customer Relationship Management: Implementation process perspective." *Acta Polytechnica Hungarica* 6, 4, (2009): 83-99.

21. Ghasemaghaei, M., Ebrahimi, S., & Hassaneinm K. "Data analytics competency for improving firm decision making performance." *Journal of Strategic Information Systems* 27, 1, (2018): 101-113.

22. Doumpos, M. & Zopounidis, C. "Editorial to the special issue Business Analytics." *Omega* 59, (2016): 1-3.

23. Davenport, T. H. & Harris, J. G., *Competing on Analytics: The New science of Winning*, Boston, MA: Harvard Business Press, 2007.

24. Watson, H. J. "Tutorial: business intelligence–past, present, and future. "*Communications of the Association for Information Systems* 25, 1, (2009): 487-510.

25. Wang, Y., Kung, L., & Byrd, T. A. "Big data analytics: Understanding its capabilities and potential benefits for healthcare organizations." *Technological Forecasting and Social Change* 126, (January 2018): 3-13.

26. Pape, T. "Prioritising data items for business analytics: Framework and application to human resources." *European Journal of Operational Research* 252, 2, (2016): 687-698.

27. Power, D. J., Heavin, C., McDermott, J., & Daly, M. "Defining business analytics: an empirical approach." *Journal of Business Analytics* 1, 1, (2018): 40-53.

28. Delen, D. & Ram, S. "Research challenges and opportunities in business analytics." *Journal of Business Analytics* 1, 1, (2018): 2-12.

29. Vidgen, R., Shaw, S., & Grant, D. B. "Management challenges in creating value from business analytics." *European Journal of Operational Research* 261, (2017): 626-639.

30. Doumpos, M. & Zopounidis, C. "Editorial to the special issue "Business Analytics." *Omega* 59, (2016): 1-3.

31. Schniederjans, M. J., Schniederjans, D. G. & Starkey, C. M., *Business Analytics: Principles, Concept, and Applications with SAS* , Upper Saddle River, NJ: Pearson, 2015.

32. Acito, F. & Khatri, V. "Business analytics: Why now and what next?" *Business Horizons* 57, 5, (2014): 565-570.

33. Marr, B., How Much Data Do We Create Every Day? The Mind-Blowing Stats Everyone Should Read. *Forbes*, 2018, Accessed on November 14, 2019 from https://www.forbes.com/sites/bernardmarr/2018/05/21/how-much-data-do-we-create-every-day-the-mind-blowing-stats-everyone-should-read/#7e7b1e1260ba.

34. Delen, D. & Ram, S. "Research challenges and opportunities in business analytics." *Journal of Business Analytics* 1, 1, (2018): 2-12.

35. Bayrak, T. "A review of business analytics: A business enabler or another passing fad." *Procedia-Social and Behavioral Sciences* 195, (2015): 230-239.

36. Holsapple, C., Lee-Post, A., & Pakath, R. "A unified foundation for business analytics." *Decision Support Systems* 64, (2014): 130-141.

37. Ducange, P., Pecori, R., & Mezzina, P. "A glimpse on big data analytics in the framework of marketing strategies." *Soft Computing* 22, 1, (2018): 325-342.

38. Bayrak, T. "A review of business analytics: A business enabler or another passing fad." *Procedia - Social and Behavioral Sciences* 195, (July, 2015): 230-239.

39. Heinrichs, J. H. & Lim J-S. *Business Intelligence Management: Competitive Business Analytics Approach,* 2016. Kindle.

40. Davenport, T. H. *What Do We Talk About When We Talk About Analytics*, in *Enterprise Analytics: Optimize Performance, Process, and Decisions Through Big Data*. Edited by Thomas H. Davenport, Upper Saddle River, NJ: Pearson, 2013.

41. Davenport, T. H., *What Do We Talk About When We Talk About Analytics*, in Enterprise Analytics: Optimize Performance, Process, and Decisions Through Big Data. Edited by Thomas H. Davenport, Upper Saddle River, NJ: Pearson, 2013.

42. Lim, Jeen-Su, Thomas W. Sharkey, and Ken I. Kim. "Determinants of International Marketing Strategy." *Management International Review* 33, 2, (1993): 103-120.

43. Peppers, D., and M. Rogers, *The One-to-One Future; Building Relationships One Customer at a Time*, New York, NY: Currency Doubleday, 1993. Arora, Neeraj, Xavier Dreze, Anindya Ghose, James D. Hess, Raghuram Iyengar, Bing Jing, Yogesh Joshi, V. Kumar, Nicholas Lurie, Scott Neslin, S. Sajeesh, Meng Su, Niladri Syam, Jacquelyn Thomas, and Z. John Zhang. "Putting One-to-one Marketing To Work: Personalization, Customization, And Choice." *Marketing Letters* 19, (2008): 305-21.

44. Lim, Jeen-Su, John Heinrichs, and Kee-Sook Lim, *AI and Big Data Driven Marketing Analytics*, 2020. Kindle.

45. Simon, A. R. & Shaffer, S. L. *Data Warehousing and Business Intelligence for e-Commerce,* San Francisco, CA: Morgan Kaufman Publishers, 2001.

46. Davenport, T. H. *What Do We Talk About When We Talk About Analytics*, in Enterprise Analytics: Optimize Performance, Process, and Decisions Through Big Data, Edited by Thomas H. Davenport, Upper Saddle River, NJ: Pearson, 2013.

47. Lim, Jeen-Su and John Heinrichs. *Handbook of Social Media Marketing: Five Principles of Online and Social Network Interactivity*, 2011. Kindle.

48. Adapted from *Rethinking Customer Relationship Management: Organizational Imperatives for Business Case Realization*, Corporate Executive Board, 2002.

49. This case is based on Field report, "In less than one year, this fabled wagering powerhouse developed advanced CRM and predictive analytics for deeper customer insight." Information Week, (2005).

50. Therkelsen-Terry, N. & Casey, S. I., How AI technology helps to boost the customer experience, 2018. Accessed on January 11, 2020 from https://www.ibm.com/blogs/client-voices/ai-helps-boost-customer-experience/.

Chapter 3

1. Day, George S., *Analysis for Strategic Market Decisions*, St. Paul, MN: West Publishing Co., 1986. Bryson, John M. *Strategic Planning for Public and Nonprofit Organizations: A Guide to Strengthening and Sustaining Organizational Achievement*, 4th ed. San Francisco: John Wiley & Sons, 2011. Dix, John F., and H. Lee Matthews. "The Process of Strategic Planning." Business Development Index Ltd., and The Ohio State University, August 2002. Web. Steiner, George Albert. *Strategic Planning: What Every Manager Must Know,* New York: Free, 2010.

2. Kotler P. *Marketing Management*. Pearson education; 2009.

3. Stull, Craig, Phil Myers, and David Meerman Scott. *The Secrets of Market-Driven Leaders: How Technology Company CEOs Create Success and Why Most Fail*. Pragmatic Marketing, 2007.

4. Shoham A, Rose GM, Kropp F. "Market orientation and performance: a meta-analysis." *Marketing Intelligence & Planning*. (2005).

5. Prahalad, C. K., and Gary Hamel. "The Core Competence of the Corporation." *Harvard Business Review*, (May/June, 1990): 79-91.

6. Boulding, William, Richard Staelin, Michael Ehret, and Wesley J. Johnson. "A Customer Relationship Roadmap: What Is Known, Potential Pitfalls, and Where To Go." *Journal of Marketing* 69, (October, 2005): 155-166.

7. Blattberg, Robert C. and John Deighton. "Manage Marketing by the Customer Equity Test." *Harvard Business Review* 74, (July-August, 1996): 136-44.

8. Rust, Roland T., Tim Ambler, Gregory S. Carpenter, V. Kumar, and Rajendra K. Srivastava. "Measuring Marketing Productivity: Current Knowledge and Future Directions." *Journal of Marketing* 68, (October, 2004): 76-89.

9. Rust, Roland T., Valarie A. Zeithaml and Katherine N. Lemon, *Driving Customer Equity: How Customer Life Time Value is Reshaping Corporate Strategy*, New York, NY: The Free Press, 2000.

10. Fournier, Susan. "Consumers and Their Brands: Developing a Relationship Theory in Consumer Research." *Journal of Consumer Research* 24, (March, 1998): 343-73.

11. David J. Teece, Gary Pisano, and Amy Shuen. "Dynamic Capabilities and Strategic Management." *Strategic Management Journal* 1, 7, (1997): 509-533.

12. Peppers, Don, Martha Rogers, and Bob Dorf, *The One to One Fieldbook*, Dantam Doubleday Dell Publishing, New York, 1999.

13. Arora N, Dreze X, Ghose A, Hess JD, Iyengar R, Jing B, Joshi Y, Kumar V, Lurie N, Neslin S, and S Sajeesh. "Putting one-to-one marketing to work: Personalization, customization, and choice." *Marketing Letters* 19, 3, (2008): 305-21.

14. Peppers, Don, Martha Rogers, and Bob Dorf, *The One to One Fieldbook*, Dantam Doubleday Dell Publishing, New York, 1999.

15. Adapted from Lim, J-S and J. Heinrichs, *Handbook of Social Media Interactive Marketing: Managing Traditional, Online and Social Media Touchpoints*, 2014. Kindle.

16. http://www.emarketer.com/Article.aspx?R=1007393 – Accessed on May 25, 2014.

17. Michiels, Ian and Alex Jefferies, Web Analytics: Actionable Insights for Unlocking the Hidden Potential of Online Data, Aberdeen Group, 2009. – http://www.aberdeen.com.

18. Greenberg, Paul, *Social CRM Comes of Age*, 2009.

19. Ente, Jeff, The Facebook Page Marketing Guide – 2010, 2010", p.24 – http://www.WhosBloggingWhat.com.

20. Choudhury MM and P. Harrigan "CRM to social CRM: the integration of new technologies into customer relationship management." *Journal of Strategic Marketing* 22, 2, (2014): 149-76. Morgan, Jacob, "Form Social Media to Social CRM, Does IBM know what Social CRM is?" March, 2011.

21. Owyang, Jeremiah, Social CRM: Not Your Father's CRM. April 2010.

22. Rust, Roland T.,Tim Ambler, Gregory S. Carpenter, V. Kumar, and Rajendra K. Srivastava. "Measuring Marketing Productivity: Current Knowledge and Future Directions," *Journal of Marketing* 68, (October, 2004): 76-89.

23. This case is adapted from Taylor, Natalie, Ocean Spray and Oppy extend partnership, Winsight Grocery Business, 2017.

24. This case is adapted from, Major, Meg, Giant Eagle launches AdvantagePay at GetGo gas pumps, Winsight Grocery Business, 2019.

Chapter 4

1. Aaker, David A. *Strategic Market Management*, 4th Ed. New York, NY: John Wiley & Sons, Inc., 1995. Reeves, Martin, Sandy Moose, and Thijs Venema. "BCG Classics Revisited: The Growth Share Matrix." *BCG. Perspectives by The Boston Consulting Group*. The Boston Consulting Group, 4 June 2014.

2. Buzzell, Robert D. and Bradley T. Gale, *The PIMS Principles, Linking Strategy to Performance*, New York, NY: The Free Press, 1987. *Advanced Diploma in Business Management: Strategic Marketing Management*. New Malden, Surrey: Association of Business Executives, 2008.

3. S. Q. Robinson, R. E. Hichens, and P. P. Wade, "The Directional Policy Matrix Tool for Strategic Planning." *Long-Range Planning, (*April, 1978): 8-15.

4. Biljana, Angelova, and Jusuf Zekiri. "Measuring Customer Satisfaction with Service Quality Using American Customer Satisfaction Model (ACSI Model)." *International Journal of Academic Research in Business and Social Sciences* 1. 3, (2011): 232-58.

5. Biljana Angelova et al., 2011. And Petersen, J. Andrew, Leigh Mcalister, David J. Reibstein, Russell S. Winer, V. Kumar, and Geoff Atkinson. "Choosing the Right Metrics to Maximize Profitability and Shareholder Value." *Journal of Retailing* 85,1, (2009): 95-111.

6. Source: Bradley T. Gale, *Managing Customer Value*, NY, NY: The Free Press.

7. Venkatesan, R. & Kumar, V., A Customer Lifetime Value Framework for Customer Selection and Resource Allocation Strategy, *Journal of Marketing* 68, 4, (October, 2004): 106-125.

8. Lynette Ryals, "Making Customer Relationship Management Work: The Measurement and Profitable Management of Customer Relationships," *Journal of Marketing* 69, (October, 2005): 252-261.

9. Werner J. Reinartz and V. Kumar. "The Mismanagement of Customer Loyalty." *Harvard Business Review* 80, (July, 2002): 86-94.

10. Simon Knox and David Walker. "Measuring and Managing Brand Loyalty." *Journal of Strategic Marketing* 9, 2, (2001): 111-128.

11. Cooper, Robin and Robert S. Kaplan. "Profit Priorities from ABC," *Harvard Business Review* 69, (May-June, 1991): 130-34. Dejnega, Oleg. "Method time driven activity based costing–literature review." *Journal of Applied Economic Sciences* 6, 15, (2011): 9-15.

12. Rust, Roland T., Katherine N. Lemon, Das, Naraandas, *Customer Equity Management*, Pearson Education, Upper Saddle River, New Jersey, 2005. Ho MH and HF Chung. "Customer engagement, customer equity and repurchase intention in mobile apps." *Journal of Business Researc,* 21, (2020): 13-21.

13. Kumar V and George M. "Measuring and maximizing customer equity: a critical analysis." *Journal of the Academy of Marketing Science* 35, 2, (2007): 157-71.

14. Tomás Bayón, Jens Gutsche, and Hans Bauer. "Customer Equity Marketing: Touching the Intangible." *European Management Journal* 20, 3, (June, 2002): 213-222.

15. Ryals, Lynette. "Making Customer Relationship Management Work: The Measurement and Profitable Management of Customer Relationship." *Journal of Marketing* 68, (October, 2005): 252-261.

16. Boulding, William, Richard Staelin, Michael Ehret, and Wesley J. Johnson. "A Customer Relationship Roadmap: What Is Known, Potential Pitfalls, and Where To Go." *Journal of Marketing* 69, (October, 2005): 155-166.

17. Michael D. Johnson and Fred Selnes. "Customer Portfolio Management: Toward a Dynamic Theory of Exchange Relationships." *Journal of Marketing* 69, (October, 2004): 1-17.

18. Holmlund M. "Analyzing business relationships and distinguishing different interaction levels." *Industrial Marketing Management* 33, 4, (2004): 279-87.

19. Johnson, Michael D. and Fred Selnes, 2004.

20. Palmatier, RW, Dant RP, Grewal D, Evans KR. "Factors influencing the effectiveness of relationship marketing: A meta-analysis." *Journal of marketing* 70, 4, (2006):136-53.

21. This case is adapted from Elberse, Anita, John T. Gourville, and Das Narayandas, Angels and Devils: Best Buy's New Customer Approach, Harvard Business School, 2005.

22. This case is based on Madhavan, RUser Engagement Company Improves Lead Quality Using Predictive Analytics, 2018. Accessed on January 14, 2020 from https://emerj.com/ai-case-studies/user-engagement-company-improves-lead-quality-using-predictive-analytics/.

Chapter 5

1. Schmitt, Bernd H., *Customer Experience Management*, John wiley & Sons, Hoboken, New Jersey, 2003.

2. Meyer, Christopher and Andre Schwager, Understanding customer Experience, *Harvard Business Review*, (February 2007).

3. Schmitt, Bernd H., *Customer Experience Management*, John wiley & Sons, Hoboken, New Jersey, 2003.

4. Bolton RN, McColl-Kennedy JR, Cheung L, Gallan A, Orsingher C, Witell L, and M. Zaki. "Customer experience challenges: bringing together digital, physical and social realms." *Journal of Service Management,* (2018).

5. Parise, S., P. J. Guinan, and R. Kafka. "Solving the Crisis of Immediacy: How Digital Technology can Transform the Customer Experience." *Business Horizons* 59, 4, (2016): 411-20.

6. Lemon, Katherine N., and Peter C. Verhoef. "Understanding customer experience throughout the customer journey." *Journal of marketing* 80, 6, (2016): 69-96.

7. Stein A, and Ramaseshan B. "Towards the identification of customer experience touch point elements." *Journal of Retailing and Consumer Services* 30, (May 1, 2016): 8-19.

8. Witell, Lars, Christian Kowalkowskia,h , Helen Perksc , Chris Raddatsd , Maria Schwabee , Ornella Benedettinif , and Jamie Burtong. "Characterizing customer experience management in business markets." *Journal of Business Research* 116, (2020): 420-30.

9. Rawson A, Duncan E, Jones C. "The truth about customer experience." *Harvard Business Review,* (Sep. 2013): 90-8.

10. Dyche J, and O'Brien M.*The CRM handbook: A business guide to customer relationship management.* Addison-Wesley Professional, 2002.

11. Richardson A. "Using customer journey maps to improve customer experience." *Harvard business review* 15, (Nov 15, 2010): 2-5.

12. Lemon, Katherine N., and Peter C. Verhoef "Understanding customer experience throughout the customer journey." *Journal of marketing* 80, 6, (2016): 69-96.

13. Witell Lars,, Christian Kowalkowskia,h , Helen Perksc , Chris Raddatsd , Maria Schwabee , Ornella Benedettinif , Jamie Burtong. "Characterizing customer experience management in business markets." *Journal of Business Research* 116, (2020): 420-30.

14. Witell Lars,, Christian Kowalkowskia,h , Helen Perksc , Chris Raddatsd , Maria Schwabee , Ornella Benedettinif , Jamie Burtong. "Characterizing customer experience management in business markets." *Journal of Business Research* 116, (2020): 420-30.

15. Rawson A, Duncan E, Jones C. "The truth about customer experience." *Harvard business review, (Sep, 2013): 90-8.*

16. Rawson A, Duncan E, Jones C. "The truth about customer experience." *Harvard business review, (Sep, 2013): 90-8.*

17. Witell Lars,, Christian Kowalkowskia,h , Helen Perksc , Chris Raddatsd , Maria Schwabee , Ornella Benedettinif , Jamie Burtong. "Characterizing customer experience management in business markets." *Journal of Business Research* 116, (2020): 420-30.

18. Schmitt, Bernd H., *Customer Experience Management*, John wiley & Sons, Hoboken, New Jersey, 2003.

19. Hughes, A. M., *Strategic Database Marketing: The Masterplan for Starting and Managing a Profitable Customer-based Marketing Program*. Fourth Edition, New York, NY: McGraw-Hill, 2012.

20. Rud, O. P., *Data Mining Cookbook: Modeling Data for Marketing, Risk and Customer Relationship Management*, New York, NY: John Wiley & Sons, Inc., 2001.

21. Kudyba, S. & Hoptroff, R., *Data Mining and Business Intelligence: A Guide to Productivity*, Hershey, PA: Idea Group Publishing, 2001.

22. Baird, L. & Henderson, J. C. *The Knowledge Engine: How to Create Fast Cycles of Knowledge-to-performance and Performance-to-knowledge*, First Edition, San Francisco, CA: Berrett-Koehler Publishers, Inc., 2001.

23. Bilal M, Gani A, Lali MI, Marjani M, Malik N. "Social profiling: A review, taxonomy, and challenges." *Cyberpsychology, Behavior, and Social Networking* 22, 7, (2019): 433-50.

24. Seybold, P. B., Marshak, R. T. and Lewis, J. M., *The Customer Revolution: How to Thrive When Customers Are In Control*, London, UK: Random House Business Books, 2002.

25. Kumar, S., *Chapter 5: Machine Learning (Unsupervised), in Essentials of Business Analytics: An Introduction to the Methodology and its Applications*, edited by Pochiraju, B. & Seshadri, S., Netherlands: Springer, 2019.

26. Karlson, K, 8 Ways Intelligent Marketers Use Artificial Intelligence. *Content Marketing Institute*, 2017. Accessed on January 14, 2020 from https://contentmarketinginstitute.com/2017/08/marketers-use-artificial-intelligence/.

27. Pahwa, A., 10 Brilliant Examples of AI in Marketing, 2019. Accessed on January 14, 2020 from https://www.feedough.com/examples-of-artificial-intelligence-in-marketing/.

28. Sentance, R., 15 Examples of Artificial Intelligence in Marketing, 2019. *Econsultancy*, Accessed on January 13, 2020 from https://econsultancy.com/15-examples-of-artificial-intelligence-in-marketing/.

29. Schmitt, Bernd H. *Customer Experience Management*, John wiley & Sons, Hoboken, New Jersey, 2003

30. Hill, J., How high-tech AI technology helps fulfill retail demand, 2019. Accessed on January 14, 2020 from https://www.ibm.com/blogs/client-voices/ai-helps-fulfill-retail-demand/.

31. This case is adapted from Lim, JS, J. Heinrichs, KS Lim, *Big data and AI driven Marketing Analytics*, 2020. Kindle.

32. Van Rijn, J., AI Finally Makes Micro Segmentation a Reality for Financial Marketers. *The Financial Brand*, 2019. Accessed on January 14, 2020 from https://thefinancialbrand.com/89462/ai-micro-segmentation-financial-institution-marketers/.

Chapter 6

1. Calantone R, Garcia R, Dröge C. "The effects of environmental turbulence on new product development strategy planning." *Journal of product innovation management* 20, 2, (2003): 90-103.

2. Crawford, C. Merle and C. Anthony Di Benedetto, *New Products Management*, 11th Ed. McGraw Hill, 2015.

3. Philip Kotler, *Marketing Management, Pearson Education,* 2009.

4. Schnaars, Steven P. *Marketing strategy: a customer-driven approach*, Free Press, 1991.

5. Shmueli, G., Bruce, P. C. & Patel, N. R., *Data Mining for Business Analytics: Concepts, Techniques, and Applications with XLMiner*. Third Edition, Hoboken, NJ: John Wiley & Sons, 2016.

6. Miller, T. W., *Marketing Data Science*, Old Tapan, NJ: Pearson, 2015.

7. Thomas D. Kuczmarski, *Managing New Products: The Power of Innovation*, 2nd Ed. Englewood Cliffs, NJ: Prentice Hall, 1992.

8. Thomas D. Kuczmarski, 1992. Bascle, Ivan, Sophie Ebeling, Hannes Pichler, Andreas Rainer, Elizabeth Rizza, and Miki Tsusaka. "Speed to Win: How Fast-Moving Consumer-Goods Companies. Use Speed as a Competitive Weapon." *The Boston Consulting Group*, 2012. The Boston Consulting Group. Web. <www.bcg.com/documents/file104158.pdf>.

9. Griffin, Abbie and Albert L. Page, "PDMA Success Measurement Project: Recommended Measures for Product Development Success and Failure." *The Journal of Product Innovation Management* 13, 6, (November 1996): 478-496.

10. Mas-Machuca, Marta, Marina Sainz, and Carme Martinez-Costa. "A Review of Forecasting Models for New Products." *Intangible Capital* 10, 1, (2014): 1-25.

11. Cheng, C. Using the Power of Artificial Intelligence (AI) to Reduce New Product Development Time, 2019. *Petuum.* from https://petuum.com/2019/05/30/using-the-power-of-artificial-intelligence-ai-to-reduce-new-product-development-time/.

12. Vandenberghe, A., 10 ways AI will completely change product management, *Time Hacker*, 2019. from https://gipsybot.com/ai-product-management/.

13. Piller, F. How to develop billion-dollar product opportunities, *The Leadership Network*, 2019. from https://theleadershipnetwork.com/article/how-to-develop-billion-dollar-product-opportunities.

14. Feyzioglu, O. & Büyüközkan, G. "Evaluation of new product development projects using artificial intelligence and fuzzy logic." *World Academy of Science, Engineering and Technology* 11, (2006):183-189.

15. Scholz, J. & Datta, A. How to succeed at AI Product Development, 2019. from https://rangle.io/blog/how-to-succeed-at-ai-product-development/.

16. Białek, B. Artificial Intelligence Disrupts UX and Product Design Like No Other Industry, 2019. from https://www.netguru.com/blog/artificial-intelligence-disrupts-ux-and-product-design-like-no-other-industry.

17. Brem A, Bilgram V, Gutstein A. "Involving lead users in innovation: A structured summary of research on the lead user method." *International Journal of Innovation and Technology Management* 15, 03, (2018):1850022.

18. Foreman, Susan, "Marketing," *Henley Manager Update*14, 3, (Spring, 2003): 14-23.

19. Roberts, Bill,."Hear Them Out." *Electronic Business* 26, 12, (November, 2000): 52-53.

20. Stremersch, Stefanl. "Bundling of Products and Prices: A New Synthesis for Marketing." *Journal of Marketing* 66, 1, (January, 2002): 55-72.

21. Olderog, Torsten and Bernd Skiera. "The Benefits of Bundling Strategies." *Business Review* 52, (April, 2000): 137-159.   Sharpe, Kathryn M, and Richard Staelin. "Consumption Effects of Bundling: Consumer Perceptions, Firm Actions, and Public Policy Implications." *Journal of Public Policy & Marketing* 29, 2, (2010): 170-88.

22. Stremersch, Stefanl. "Bundling of Products and Prices: A New Synthesis for Marketing." *Journal of Marketing* 66, 1, (January, 2002): 55-72.

23. Keller, Kevin Lane. *Strategic Brand Management: Building, Measuring, and Managing Brand Equity*, Upper Saddle River, NJ: Prentice Hall, 1998. Kuhn, Kerri-Ann L., Frank Alpert, and Nigel K. Ll. Pope, An Application Of Keller's Brand Equity Model In A B2b Context, 2008, 1-30. Griffith Business School, Department of Marketing, Griffith University. Web. <www98.griffith.edu.au/dspace/bitstream/handle/10072/22315/52703_1.pdf?sequence=1>.

24. Keller, Kevin Lane. *Strategic Brand Management: Building, Measuring, and Managing Brand Equity*, Upper Saddle River, NJ: Prentice Hall, 1998. Aaker, D. Aaker's Brand Equity Model, European Institute For Brand Management, 2009. Web. <www.eurib.org/fileadmin/user_upload/Documenten/PDF/Merkmeerwaarde_ENGELS/s_-_Brand_equity_model_by_Aaker_EN_.pdf>.

25. The Russo Group, "Branding with Social Media" 2009.

26. Joeri Van den Bergh and Mattias Behrer, How cool brands stay hot: Branding to Generation Y, 2011.

27. The Russo Group, Branding with Social Media, 2009, 22.

28. Marta Kagan – http://www.slideshare.net/mzkagan/what-the-fk-social-media - Accessed on May 25, 2014.

29. Lemon, Katherine N., and Peter C. Verhoef. "Understanding customer experience throughout the customer journey." *Journal of marketing* 80, 6, (2016): 69-96.

30. Roger J. Best, *Market Based Management: Strategies for Growing Customer Value and Profitability, 4th Ed.*, New Jersey, Pearson, 2005.

31. Komatsu, Y., Automotive design problems? AI helps find solutions, 2019. from https://www.ibm.com/blogs/client-voices/ai-solves-complex-design-problems/.

32. Vantomme, W., Gaining time-to-market edge with new 3D design technology, 2018. from https://www.ibm.com/blogs/client-voices/time-market-edge-3d-design-technology/.

Chapter 7

1. Bolton RN, McColl-Kennedy JR, Cheung L, Gallan A, Orsingher C, Witell L, Zaki M. "Customer experience challenges: bringing together digital, physical and social realms." *Journal of Service Management.* (2018).

2. Power D. "Supply chain management integration and implementation: a literature review." *Supply chain management: an International journal.* (2005).

3. Council of Logistics Management, 1994.

4. Day, George S., *Market Driven Strategies: Processes for Creating Value,* New York, NY: The Free Press, 1990.

5. Tracey, Michael, Jeen-Su Lim, and Mark Vonderembse, "The Impact of Supply-Chain Management Capabilities on Perceived Product Value and Market Performance." *AMA Conference Proceedings*, Boston, MA, (1998).

6. Baker P. "An exploratory framework of the role of inventory and warehousing in international supply chains." *The International Journal of Logistics Management.* (2007).

7. Cheng-Min F and Chien-Yun Y. "The impact of information and communication technologies on logistics management." *International Journal of Management* 23, 4, (2006): 909.

8. Manohar U. Kalwani and Narakesari Narayandas "Long-Term Manufacturer-Supplier Relationships: Do They Pay Off for Supplier Firms?" *Journal of Marketing* 59, (January, 1995): 1-16.

9. Sultan, Singh and Dixit Garg "Comparative Analysis of Japanese Just-in- Time Purchasing and Traditional Indian Purchasing System." *International Journal of Engineering Science and Technology (IJEST)* 3, 3, (2011):1816-834.

10. Milgate M. "Supply chain complexity and delivery performance: an international exploratory study." *Supply chain management: An international Journal.* (2001).

11. Stern, Louis and Adel I. El-Ansary, *Marketing Channels,* 4th Edition, Upper Saddle River, NJ: Prentice Hall, 1992. Szopa, Piotr, and Władysław Pękała "Distribution Channels And Their Roles In The Enterprise." *Polish Journal Of Management Studies* 6, (2012): 143-50. Częstochowa University of Technology, Department of Management.

12. Sophie Lapierre, Angel Ruiz, and Patrick Soriano. "Designing Distribution Networks: Formulations and Solution Heuristic." *Transportation Science* 38, 2, (March, 2004): 174-187.

13. Sudas, Roy. "Distribution Decisions and Consumer Behavior." *IIMB Management Review*, (September, 2003): 110-113.

14. Thomas, Jacquelyn S. and Ursula Y. Sullivan. "Managing Marketing Communications with Multichannel Customers." *Journal of Marketing* 69, (October, 2005): 239-251. Neslin, Scott, and Venkatesh Shankar. "Key Issues in Multichannel Customer Management: Current Knowledge and Future Directions." *Journal of Interactive Marketing* 23, (2009): 70-81.

15. Bland, Vikki. "One on One." *NZ Business*, (July, 2003): 35-38.

16. Thomas, Jacquelyn S. and Ursula Y. Sullivan. "Managing Marketing Communications with Multichannel Customers." *Journal of Marketing* 69, (October, 2005): 239-251. Ansari, Asim, Carl F Mela, and Scott A Neslin. "Customer Channel Migration." *Journal of Marketing Research* 45, (2008): 60-76.

17. Saghiri, S., Wilding R. and M. Bourlakis. "Toward a three-dimensional framework for omni-channel." *Journal of Business Research* 77, (2017): 53-67.

18. Ailawadi, K.L. and P.W. Farris "Managing multi- and omni-channel distribution: metrics and research directions." *Journal of Retailing* 93, 1, (2017): 120-135.

19. Payne, E.M., Peltier, J.W. and, V.A Barger. "Omni-channel marketing, integrated marketing communications and consumer engagement." *Journal of Research in Interactive Marketing,* (2017).

20. Carl Sewell and Paul B. Brown. *Customers for Life: How to Turn That One-Time Buyer into a Lifetime Customer*, New York, NY: Pocket Books, 1990.

21. Verma HV. "Customer outrage and delight." *Journal of Services Research* 3, 1, (2003): 119.

22. James M. Kouzes, and Barry Z. Posner, *The Leadership Challenge: How to Get Extraordinary Things Done in Organizations,* San Francisco, CA: Jossey-Bass Publishers, 1990.

23. Love Your Customer, *Newsweek,* June 27, 1988.

24. Presi C, Saridakis C and S. Hartmans. "User-generated content behavior of the dissatisfied service customer." *European Journal of Marketing*, (2014). Zeelenberg M and R. Pieters. "Beyond valence in customer dissatisfaction: A review and new findings on behavioral responses to regret and disappointment in failed services." *Journal of business Research* 57, 4, (2004): 445-55.

25. Zhao L, Lu Y, Zhang L, and PY. Chau, "Assessing the effects of service quality and justice on customer satisfaction and the continuance intention of mobile value-added services: An empirical test of a multidimensional model." *Decision Support Systems* 52, 3, (2012): 645-56.

26. Chauhan, Pragati, and Yogita Sharma. "Customer Dissatisfaction - A Valuable Source to Tap Entrepreneurial Opportunity." *Opinion* 1.1, (2011): 30-37.

27. Davenport, T. H. *Enterprise Analytics: Optimize Performance, Process, and Decisions through Big Data,* Upper Saddle River, NJ: Pearson, 2013.

28. Sem Borst, Avi Mandelbaum, and Martin Reiman. "Dimensioning Large Call Centers." *Operations Research* 52, 1, (January-February, 2004): 17-34.

29. Andrew Sergeant and Stephen Frenkel. "When Do Customer Contact Employees Satisfy Customers?" *Journal of Service Research* 3, 1, (August, 2000): 18-34.

30. This case is adapted from the *"The Dark Days of Dell,"* Business Week, by Byrnes, Burrows, and Lee.

31. Dollar Tea Club Inc., Using AI to cut email volumes 80%, improving user experience and revenue, 2018. from https://www.ibm.com/case-studies/dollar-tea-club.

32. Caffé Nero, 2017 from https://www.ibm.com/case-studies/caffe-nero.

Chapter 8

1. Maricris G. Briones, Outlook '99" *Marketing News* 32, 25, American Marketing Association, December 7, 1998.

2. Rawal, Priyanka. "AIDA Marketing Communication Model: Stimulating A Purchase Decision in the Minds of the Consumers Through a Linear Progression of Steps." *IRC'S International Journal Of Multidisciplinary Research In Social & Management Science S* 1.1, (2013): 37-44.

3. Little, John D. C. "Aggregate Advertising Models: The State of the Art." *Operations Research* 27, 4, (July/August, 1979): 629-667.

4. Blasko, Vincent J. and Charles H. Patti. "The Advertising Budgeting Practices of Industrial Marketers." *Journal of Marketing* 48, 4, (Fall,1984): 104-110.

5. Finne, A. and Gronroos, C. "Communication-in-use: customer-integrated-marketing communication." *European Journal of Marketing*, (2017).

6. Finne, Å., & Grönroos, C. "Communication-in-use: Customer-integrated marketing communication." *European Journal of Marketing* 51, 3, (2017): 445-463.

7. Batra, R., & Keller, K. L. "Integrating marketing communications: New findings, new lessons, and new ideas." *Journal of Marketing* 80, 6, (2016): 122-145.

8. Karlson, K., 8 Ways Intelligent Marketers Use Artificial Intelligence, *Content Marketing Institute*, 2017 from https://contentmarketinginstitute.com/2017/08/marketers-use-artificial-intelligence/.

9. Hall, J., How Artificial Intelligence is Transforming Digital Marketing, *Forbes*, 2019. from https://www.forbes.com/sites/forbesagencycouncil/2019/08/21/how-artificial-intelligence-is-transforming-digital-marketing/#a1b6c5e21e1b.

10. Brenner, M., Why AI is better than A/B Testing, *Concured*, 2018. From https://www.concured.com/blog/why-ai-is-better-than-a/b-testing.

11. Pahwa, A., *10 Brilliant Examples of AI in Marketing,* 2019. from https://www.feedough.com/examples-of-artificial-intelligence-in-marketing/.

12. Taylor, A., Artificial Intelligence in A/B testing: A Quick Look at What's Going Down Right Now *Convert*, 2019. from https://blog.convert.com/artificial-intelligence-in-testing.html.

13. Alford, E., How AI could make A/B testing a thing of the past, *ClickZ*, 2018. from https://www.clickz.com/how-ai-could-make-a-b-testing-a-thing-of-the-past/216302/.

14. Pilenwski, S., Machine Learning Based Optimization vs. A/B Testing, 2018. from https://www.experfy.com/blog/machine-learning-based-optimization-vs-ab-testing.

15. Boulding, William, Richard Staelin, Michael Ehret, and Wesley J. Johnson. "A Customer Relationship Roadmap: What Is Known, Potential Pitfalls, and Where To Go." *Journal of Marketing* 69, (October, 2005): 155-166.

16. Cao, Yong and Thomas S. Gruca. "Reducing Adverse Selection Through Customer Relationship Management." *Journal of Marketing* 69, (October, 2005): 219-29.

17. Jacquelyn S. Thomas and Ursula Y. Sullivan "Managing Marketing Communications with Multi-channel Customers." *Journal of Marketing* 69, (October, 2005): 239-251.

18. McWilliams. "Building Stronger Brands through Online Communities." *Sloan Management Review*, (Spring, 2000): 43-54.

19. Gianmario Verona and Emanuela Prandelli. "A Dynamic Model of Customer Loyalty to Sustain Competitive Advantage on the Web." *European Management Journal* 20, 3, (June, 2002): 299-309.

20. Robinson, Scott., THE 2013 MARITZ LOYALTY REPORT: US Edition: Summary Of Key Findings & Implications For Loyalty Marketers & Program Operators, Maritz Loyalty Marketing, 2013. <http://www.maritzmotivation.com/~/media/Files/MaritzMotivationSolutions/Product-Sheets/Maritz-Loyalty-Marketing_Loyalty-Report-US---Summary-of-Key-Insights.pdf>. MARKET EVALUATION SURVEYING DATA ANALYSIS BENCHMARKING ORGANIZATIONAL STRATEGY Consumer Loyalty Programs, *Hanover Research,* Hanover Research, 1 June 2011. <www.hanoverresearch.com/wp-content/uploads/2011/12/Consumer-Loyalty-Programs-Membership.pdf>.

21. Hellman, Karl and Ardis Burst. *The Customer Learning Curve*, South-Western Educational Publishing, Mason, Ohio, 2004.

22. David F. Ross. "E-CRM From a Supply Chain Management Perspective." *Information Systems Management*, (Winter, 2005): 37-44.

23. This case is adapted from Lim, JS and J Heinrichs, *Customer Relationship-driven Marketing*, Thompson, 2007.

24. Singeeham, T., AI insights from Behr help consumers pick their paint palette, 2019. from https://www.ibm.com/blogs/client-voices/ai-insights-help-behr-consumers-pick-paint/.

Chapter 9

1. de Vries, L., Gensler, S. and P. S. H. Leeflang. "Popularity of Brand Posts on Brand Fan Pages: An Investigation of the Effects of Social Media Marketing." *Journal of Interactive Marketing* 26, 2, (2012): 83-91.

2. Culnan, M. J., McHugh, P. J. and, J. I. Zubillaga. "How Large U.S. Companies Can Use Twitter and Other Social Media to Gain Business Value." *MIS Quarterly Executive* 9, 4, (2010): 243-259.

3. Lim, J.-S., Pham, P. and J. H. Heinrichs. "Impact of social media activity outcomes on brand equity." *Journal of Product & Brand Management* 29, 7, (2020): 927-937.

4. Kim, A. J. and E. Ko "Do Social Media Marketing Activities Enhance Customer Equity? An Empirical Study of Luxury Fashion Brand." *Journal of Business Research* 65, 10, (2012): 1480-1486.

5. Schweidel, D. A. & Moe, W. W. "Listening In On Social Media: A Joint Model of Sentiment and Venue Format Choice." *Journal of Marketing Research* 51, 4, (2014): 387-402.

6. Culnan, M. J., McHugh, P. J. & Zubillaga, J. I. "How Large U.S. Companies Can Use Twitter and Other Social Media to Gain Business Value." *MIS Quarterly Executive* 9, 4, (2010): 243-259.

7. Online video analytics, from http://en.wikipedia.org/wiki/Online_video_analytics.

8. Video Goals, from https://wistia.com/library/guide-to-video-metrics.

9. Image Analysis from https://en.wikipedia.org/wiki/Image_analysis.

10. Leidig, P., What is image analytics, 2018. from https://www.netbase.com/blog/what-is-image-analytics/

11. Komar, D., 7 Ideas for Image Analytics in Marketing, Blog post, 2019. from https://deepbrand.ai/blog/7-ideas-for-image-analytics-in-marketing/.

12. Meg, What is image analysis? 2019. from https://www.talkwalker.com/blog/what-is-image-analysis.

13. Sentance, R., 15 Examples of Artificial Intelligence in Marketing, *Econsultancy*, 2019. from https://econsultancy.com/15-examples-of-artificial-intelligence-in-marketing/.

14. Karlson, K., 8 Ways Intelligent Marketers Use Artificial Intelligence, *Content Marketing Institute*, 2017. from https://contentmarketinginstitute.com/2017/08/marketers-use-artificial-intelligence/.

15. Franks, B. *Analytics on Web Data: The Original Big Data*, in Enterprise Analytics: Optimize Performance, Process, and Decisions Through Big Data, Edited by Thomas H. Davenport, Upper Saddle River, NJ: Pearson, 2013.

16. Harrison, K., 4 Ways Artificial Intelligence Can Improve Your Marketing (Plus 10 Provider Suggestions), Forbes.com, 2019. from https://www.forbes.com/sites/kateharrison/2019/01/20/5-ways-artificial-intelligence-can-improve-your-marketing-plus-10-provider-suggestions/#102e72b56977.

17. Stoney deGeyter, Everything You Need to Know About Link Anatomy, 2010. from http://www.searchengineguide.com/stoney-degeyter/seo-101-part-14-everything-you-need-to-k.php.

18. http://www.searchengineguide.com/stoney-degeyter/seo-101-part-14-everything-you-need-to-k.php.

19. http://blog.hubspot.com/blog/tabid/6307/bid/6457/5-Items-to-Delete-From-Your-Website-Today.aspx/.

20. http://en.wikipedia.org/wiki/Article_marketing.

21. http://en.wikipedia.org/wiki/Article_marketing.

22. http://www.proimpact7.com/ecommerce-blog/5-great-welcome-html-e-mails-and-1-not-so-great/.

23. http://www.getresponse.com/.

24. http://www.marketingcharts.com/direct/email-drives-social-networking-13448/edialog-email-socnet-sharing-june-2010jpg/.

25. http://www.imediaconnection.com/content/27434.asp.

26. http://www.imediaconnection.com/content/27434.asp.

27. http://www.imediaconnection.com/content/27434.asp.

28. The State of Inbound Marketing 2010", http://hubspot.com .

29. Shankar VJ, Inman J, Mantrala M, Kelley E, Rizley R. "Innovations in shopper marketing: current insights and future research issues." *Journal of Retailing* 87, 1, (2011): 29-42.

30. Reinold T. and Tropp J. "Integrated marketing communications: how can we measure its effectiveness?" *Journal of Marketing Communications* 18, 2, (2012): 113-132.

31. Lim, K-S, Lim, J-S, Heinrichs, JH. "Testing an integrated model of e-shopping web site usage." *Journal of Internet Commerce* 7, 3, (2008): 291-312.

32. Girad T, Dion P. "Validating the search, experience, and credence product classification framework." *Journal of Business Research* 63, 9-10, (2010): 1079-1087.

33. Jarski, Veronica Maria, 6 Reasons Why People Will Buy From You-Not Your Competitors, 2010. From http://www.mpdailyfix.com/6-reasons-why-people-will-buy-from-you-not-your-competitors/.

34. Meyerson, Mitch, Success Secrets of the Social Media Marketing Superstars, Entrepreneur Media Inc., 2010.

35. http://www.masteringonlinemarketing.com/2010/05/6-reasons-why-people-will-choose-to-do-business-with- you/.

36. Cedar Fair Entertainment Company -- http://www.cedarfair.com/.

37. Clearscope, 2019. from https://www.ibm.com/case-studies/clearscope.

38. Autoglass® Repair from https://www.ibm.com/case-studies/autoglass-bodyrepair.

Chapter 10

1. Culnan, Mary J., Patrick J. McHugh, and Jesus I. Zubillaga. "How large U.S. companies can use Twitter and other social media to gain business value." *MIS Quarterly Executive* 9, 4, (2010): 243-259.

2. Schweidel, David A. and Wendy W. Moe. "Listening in on social media: A joint model of sentiment and venue format choice." *Journal of Marketing Research* 51, 4, (2014): 387-402.

3. Heinrichs, J., J-S Lim, K-S Lim. " Influence of social networking site and user access method on social media evaluation." *Journal of Consumer Behavior* 10, 6, (2011): 347-355.

4. Lim, J.-S. and J. Heinrichs, *Handbook of Social Media Interactivity Marketing: Managing Traditional, Online, and Social Media Touchpoints*, 2014. Kindle.

5. Lim, Jeen-Su and John H. Heinrichs. *Customer Relationship Driven Marketing*, Thomson, 2007.

6. http://www.marketingexperiments.com/improving-website-conversion/online-competitive-analysis.html.

7. http://www.marketingexperiments.com/improving-website-conversion/online-competitive-analysis.html.

8. http://www.usability.gov/methods/analyze_current/personas.html.

9. http://www.buyerpersona.com/2006/11/whats_a_buyer_p.html.

10. 2010 Online Marketing Blueprint: A Multimedia Guide to Growing Your Business Online; http://hubspot.com

11. http://www.hubspot.com/internet-marketing-tips/detailed-keyword-tips/?source=onlineblueprint_ebook#ixzz0vApEqEjk.

12. The Altimeter Report: 18 Use Cases of Social CRM, The New Rules of Relationship Management, March 2011.

13. Owyang, Jeremiah, "Social CRM: Not Your Father's CRM", April 2010.

14. Lee Odden, "Which Flavor of Social Commerce is Right For You"

15. Lauren Fisher, "Emerging trends in social commerce, March 2011.

16. Liz Gannes, "Facebook Testing Social Commerce Feature 'Buy With Friends'", January 2011.

17. Donna L. Hoffman & Fodor Marek "Can you measure the ROI of your social media marketing." *MIT Sloan Management Review* 52, 10, (Fall, 2010): 40-49.

18. Celen, B., Kariv, S., & Schotter, A. "An Experimental Test of Advice and Social Learning." *Management Science* 56 (October, 2010): 1687-1701.

19. Lyons, B. & Henderson, K. "Opinion Leadership in a Computer-Mediated Environment." *Journal of Consumer Behavior* 4, 5, (2005): 319-329.

20. Valente, T. W. & Pumpuang, P. "Identifying Opinion Leaders to Promote Behavior Change." *Health Education & Behavior* 34 (December, 2007): 881-896.

21. Lee, S. H., Cotte, J. & Noseworthy, T. J. "The Role of Network Centrality in the Flow of Consumer Influence." *Journal of Consumer Psychology* 20, (January, 2010): 66-77.

22. Kozinets, R. V., de Valck, K., Wojnicki, A. C., & Wilner, S. J. S. "Networked Narratives: Understanding Word-of-Mouth Marketing in Online Communities." *Journal of Marketing* 74 (March, 2010): 71-89.

23. Singh, J., Hansen, M. T., and Podolny, J. M. "The World Is Not Small for Everyone: Inequity in Searching for Knowledge in Organizations." *Management Science* 56, (September, 2010): 1415-1438.

24. Kim, A. J. and Ko, E. "Do social media marketing activities enhance customer equity? An empirical study of luxury fashion brand." *Journal of Business Research 65,* 10, (2012): 1480-1486.

25. Kaplan, A. M. and Haenlein, M. "Users of the world, unite! The challenges and opportunities of Social Media." *Business Horizons 53,* 1, (2010): 59-68.

26. Culnan, M. J., McHugh, M. J., & Zubillaga, J. I. "How large U.S. companies can use Twitter and other social media to gain business value." *MIS Quarterly Executive 9,* 4, (2010): 243-259.

27. Fournier, S. & Avery, J. "The uninvited brand." *Business Horizons 54,* 3, (2011): 193-207.

28. DiStaso, M. W. & McCorkindale, T. "A benchmark analysis of the strategic use of social media for Fortune's most admired U.S. companies on Facebook, Twitter and YouTube." *Public Relations Journal 7,* 1, (2013): 1-32.

29. Goodrich, K. and de Mooij, M. "How 'social' are social media? A cross-cultural comparison of online and offline purchase decision influences." *Journal of Marketing Communications 20,* 1-2, (2014): 103-116.

30. Berthon, P. R., Pitt, L. F., Plangger, K., & Shapiro, D. "Marketing meets Web 2.0, social media, and creative consumers: Implications for international marketing strategy." *Business Horizons 55,* 3, (2012): 261-271.

31. Harris, L. & Dennis, C. "Engaging customers on Facebook: Challenges for e-retailers." *Journal of Consumer Behavior 10,* 6, (2011): 338-346. VanMeter, Rebecca, Holly A. Syrdal, Susan Powell-Mantel, Douglas B. Grisaffe, and Erik T. Nesson. "Don't Just "Like" Me, Promote Me: How Attachment and Attitude Influence Brand Related Behaviors on Social Media." *Journal of Interactive Marketing 43,* (2018): 83-97.

32. Risius, Marten and Roman Beck. "Effectiveness of corporate social media activities in increasing relational outcomes." *Information & Management 52,* 7, (2015): 824-839.

33. Hsu, Liwu and Benjamin Lawrence. "The role of social media and brand equity during a product recall crisis: a shareholder value perspective." *International Journal of Research in Marketing 33,* 1, (2016): 59-77.

34. http://en.wikipedia.org/wiki/Social_media_marketing.

35. Adams, Paul, *Social Circles: How Offline Relationships Influence Online Behavior and What it Means for Design and Marketing,* Berkley, CA: New Riders, 2012.

36. http://www.searchengineguide.com/jennifer-laycock/four-ok-twelve-reasons-to-build-a-social.php

37. Jeff Ente, The Facebook Page Marketing Guide – 2010, 2010. from http://www.WhosBloggingWhat.com.

38. Edelman DC. "Branding in the digital age you're spending your money in all the wrong places." Harvard Business Review 88, 12, (2010): 62-69.

39. Desphandde, A. and A. Whiting "Towards greater understanding of social media marketing: A review." *Journal of Applied Business and Economics* 18, 4, (2016).; Felix, R., Rauschnabel PA., and C. Hinsch. "Elements of strategic social media marketing: A holistic framework." *Journal of Business Research* 70, (2017): 118-26.

40. http://www.ßlipboard.com/press/ßlipboard-launches-worlds-ßirst-social-magazine.

41. http://blog.hubspot.com/blog/tabid/6307/bid/6254/The-Next-Big-Thing-for-Marketers-Social-Magazines.aspx#ixzz0vpt231xb.

42. Online Video Best Practices: Data-Driven Strategies for Increasing Online Video Viewership, 2010. from http://tubemogul.com.

43. Lim, J.-S., P. Pham, and J. H. Heinrichs. "Impact of social media activity outcomes on brand equity." *Journal of Product and Brand Management*, (2020).

44. http://www.google.com/adwords/beginnersguide - Growing Your Business With AdWords.

45. Joe Chernov, Social Media Playbook: Everything Your Company Needs to Know to Succeed on the Social Web, Eloqua Corporation, 2009. from http://www.eloqua.com/ .

46. Joe Chernov, Social Media Playbook: Everything Your Company Needs to Know to Succeed on the Social Web, Eloqua Corporation, 2009. from http://www.eloqua.com/.

47. Schweidel, D.A. and Moe, W.W. "Listening in social media: A joint model of sentiment and venue format choice." *Journal of Marketing Research* 51, 4, (2014): 387-402.

48. Patino, A., Pitta, D.A. and Quinones, R. "Social media's emerging importance in market research." *Journal of Consumer Marketing*, (2012).

49. Rugova, B. and Prenaj, B. "Social media as marketing tool for SMEs: opportunities and challenges." *Academic Journal of Business 2,* 3, (2016): 85-97.

50. http://www.identityblog.com/?p=1137.

51. Joe Chernov, Social Media Playbook: Everything Your Company Needs to Know to Succeed on the Social Web, Eloqua Corporation, 2009. from http://www.eloqua.com/ .

52. http://blog.hubspot.com/blog/tabid/6307/bid/6329/The-4-Hottest-Social-Media-Marketing-Trends- Explained.aspx#ixzz0vpeA9m4v.

53. http://foursquare.com/businesses/.

54. "How to User Facebook for Business" http://hubspot.com.

55. Lim, Jeen-Su, Phuoc Pham, and John H. Heinrichs. "Impact of social media activity outcomes on brand equity." *Journal of Product & Brand Management. (*2020).

56. http://blog.hubspot.com/blog/tabid/6307/bid/6217/Ben-Jerry-s-Drops-Email-Marketing-In-Favor-of-Social- Media.aspx#ixzz0uKSJcK13.

57. Risius, Marten and Roman Beck. "Effectiveness of corporate social media activities in increasing relational outcomes." *Information & Management* 52, 7, (2015): 824-839.

58. Chau, M. & Xu, J. "Business intelligence in blogs: Understanding consumer interactions and communities." *MIS Quarterly* 36, 4, (2012): 1189-1216.

59. Peterson, E. T., The Analytics of Online Engagement. in *Enterprise Analytics: Optimize Performance, Process, and Decisions Through Big Data*, Edited by Thomas H. Davenport, Saddle River, NJ: Pearson, 2013.

60. Brodie, R.J., Ilic, A., B. Juric and L. Hollebeek. "Consumer engagement in a virtual brand community: An exploratory analysis." *Journal of Business Research,* 66, 1, (2013): 105-114.

61. Wilcox, K. and A. T. Stephen. "Are close friends the enemy? Online social networks, self-esteem, and self control." *Journal of Consumer Research* 40, 1, (2013): 90-103.

62. How to User Facebook for Business, http://hubspot.com.

63. Joe Chernov, Social Media Playbook: Everything Your Company Needs to Know to Succeed on the Social Web, Eloqua Corporation, 2009. from http://www.eloqua.com/

64. Lord Leverhulme, Founder of Unilever - http://www.slideshare.net/anilv13/conversion-tracking-with-google- analytics.

65. Veronica Maria Jarski, 6 Reasons Why People Will Buy From You-Not Your Competitors, 2010. from http://www.mpdailyfix.com/6-reasons-why-people-will-buy-from-you-not-your-competitors/.

66. Mitch Meyerson, Success Secrets of the Social Media Marketing Superstars, Entrepreneur Media Inc., 2010.

67. GoPro, inc.—http://www.gopro.com and Olson, John. "Online Marketing and GoPro, A Case Study." *Modern Marketing Review*. 25 Mar. 2013. Web. <modernmarketingreview.blogspot.com/2013/03/online-marketing-and-gopro-case-study.html>. and Loboda, Sandra. "GoPro's Analysis of the Internal Environment-Market Strategies and Financial Performance." *Marketing Talk*. 5 Dec. 2012. Web. <marketingtalkblog.wordpress.com/2012/12/05/gopros-analysis-of-the-internal-environment-market-strategies-and-financial-performance/>.

68. Detert, R., How to improve social influencer marketing with AI technology, Blog post, 2018. 0 from https://www.ibm.com/blogs/client-voices/how-to-improve-social-influencer-marketing-with-ai-technology/.

AUTHORS

Jeen Su Lim is a professor of Marketing and e-Commerce in the John B. and Lillian E. Neff College of Business and Innovation at the University of Toledo. He received his B.A. in business and M.B.A from Seoul National University and Ph.D. in marketing from Indiana University, Bloomington Indiana. His primary research interests include e-Commerce and social media strategy, marketing strategy, marketing analytics, business intelligence and data mining, research methods, innovation management, and AI application in marketing. He has published over 200 articles in referred journals or national and international conference proceedings, and five books. His work has appeared in many journals such as Journal of Marketing Research, Journal of Consumer Research, Journal of Academy of Marketing Science, Journal of Operations Management, Journal of Business Research, Industrial Marketing Management, Decision Support Systems, Supply Chain Management, International Marketing Review, Management International Review, Psychology and Marketing, Information Systems Research, and elsewhere. He has received several research awards, a teaching excellence award, outstanding paper awards, and many research grants. He was the Schmidt Research Professor of Marketing, Sales, and e-Commerce, a chairperson of the marketing department, a research director for the ISBM-affiliated Research Center, and a co-author of the Toledo Area Manufacturing Index. He was a BK 21 Distinguished Scholar of e-commerce and business intelligence, a finalist of the Instructional Innovation Award of the Decision Sciences Institute, and a thought leader/keynote speaker at the Microsoft International BI Conference. He has provided professional marketing research, consulting, and training services to companies.

John H. Heinrichs is an Associate Professor in the Information Systems Management department in the Mike Ilitch School of Business at Wayne State University. He focuses on how information technology can provide business and organizations with optimal placement in the marketplace. His research interests include competitive intelligence, eLearning, knowledge management, mobile application development, search engine optimization (SEO), and inbound marketing. His research has appeared in Decision Support Systems, Journal of Consumer Behavior, Journal of Strategic Marketing, and European Journal of Marketing. He incorporates these research interests with students in his Inbound Information Technologies course where students begin to understand how to position an organization in cyberspace.

INDEX

www.ingramcontent.com/pod-product-compliance
Lightning Source LLC
Chambersburg PA
CBHW061801210326
41599CB00034B/6836